The Oranges are Sweet

Major Don M. Beerbower and the 353rd Fighter Squadron

November 1942 to August 1944

By

Paul M. Sailer

*To Deane & Jill —
Best wishes,
Paul M. Sailer*

Loden Books

Loden Books, LLC
Wadena, Minnesota
56482

Major Don M. Beerbower

"Summer Fury" Ron Finger – RedPine Studio
The Ninth Air Force's leading ace, Don M. Beerbower, banks toward the hedgerows of Normandy on June 7, 1944

Copyright © 2011 by Paul M. Sailer. All rights reserved. This book may not be reproduced, transmitted or stored in any form without written permission of the publisher or author. Brief passages may be quoted for the purpose of a book review.

First Edition

Published by: Loden Books, LLC
www.lodenbooks.com

Publication management, maps, cover, and interior design by:
Chip Borkenhagen–RiverPlace Communication Arts,
www.riverplace-mn.com

Cover painting by Ron Finger. Prints are available from the artist at
www.redpine.net

Editing by Jonathan P. Eastman, M.A. English, M.F.S. Creative Writing,
www.21stcentury.weebly.com

Manufactured in the United States of America: Bang Printing
www.info@bangprinting.com

Library of Congress Control Number: 2011917459

ISBN: 978-0-9852705-0-6

To purchase additional copies of *The Oranges are Sweet,* please see the Loden Books website: www.lodenbooks.com. Thank you.

Dedication

To the wives and children
of those who served in the
353rd Fighter Squadron
in World War II.

"I didn't have my dad around to do things with me like others kids did. My grandpa Kutcher took his place . . . I have had many people that knew my dad say he was such a nice fellow. I have always been very proud of his accomplishments just like all that lost their dad in service to their country." Bonnie Beerbower Hansen, September 12, 2011

"I don't listen to the world news—it gets to me—all those folks not coming home!!" Elayne Kutcher Beerbower, April 22, 2005 (Reference to the war in Iraq)

Elayne & Bonnie Beerbower - May 25, 1952

Contents

Photographs, Images, and Illustrations/Drawings	x
List of Maps	xi
Foreword by Dr. Albert "Ben" Beerbower	xii
Introduction by Paul M. Sailer	xv
Part One	1
Chapter 1 A Sure Hit	2
Chapter 2 Now You Remember	9
Chapter 3 An Extremely Honest Kid	17
Chapter 4 Though the Mountains Shake	23
Chapter 5 For Thee They Died	35
Chapter 6 Wow!	40
Chapter 7 A Dark Day	49
Chapter 8 I'll Never Forget It	57
Chapter 9 We'll Like It	69
Chapter 10 No Horseplay	75
Chapter 11 Buzzbower	83
Chapter 12 We Talked Quietly	91
Chapter 13 Brave as Heck	96

Part Two		107
Chapter 14	Pulling Out Tonite!	108
Chapter 15	Really a Honey!	120
Chapter 16	First Loss	131
Chapter 17	A Gloomy Bunch Tonite	142
Chapter 18	It's Exciting Work	152
Chapter 19	Little Friends	161
Chapter 20	It's a Dangerous Game	176
Chapter 21	Damn!	191
Chapter 22	You Must Persevere	207
Chapter 23	On the Beam	221
Chapter 24	Flak Galore	239
Chapter 25	A Desperate Will	255
Chapter 26	Big Friends	273
Part Three		289
Chapter 27	Unbelievable!	290
Chapter 28	Over My Protest	302
Chapter 29	Gallantry in Action	316
Chapter 30	An Inefficient Use of Resources	333
Chapter 31	The Church of St. Anne	349

Chapter 32	OH, MY GOODNESS	367
Chapter 33	IN HUMBLE GRATITUDE	388
Afterword		399
Acknowledgements		401
Notes		404
Appendix I	Ninth Air Force Aces, Top Five American Fighter Groups and Squadrons	435
Appendix II	Group and Squadron Commanding Officers	436
Appendix III	Major Don M. Beerbower: Aerial and Ground Victories	436
Appendix IV	Letter to Clarence Beerbower	438
Appendix V	Distinguished Service Cross Citation	440
Appendix VI	Comparative American Officer Ranks of World War II	442
Abbreviations		442
Glossary		443
Bibliography		445
Index		451

Photographs, Images, and Illustrations/Drawings

Unless otherwise noted, all personal photographs and images are from the Don and Elayne Beerbower, Darrel and Arlene Beerbower, or Marshall and Lavaun Hankerson Family Collections.

The author's brother, Lieutenant Colonel Joseph J. Sailer (Ret.), kindly provided a photograph of his U.S. Air Force aviator wings. The wings are identical to those issued to Don Beerbower.

Any other photographs without a credit citation are from the 354th Pioneer Mustang Fighter Group Association's *History in the Sky*. The author, an honorary member of the association, thanks President Clayton Kelly Gross for permission to use these photographs.

Unless a credit is cited, all illustrations/drawings are by Staff Sergeant Nathan Glick, courtesy of Nathan Glick and the Air Force Historical Research Agency, which houses his collection.

The Northern Pacific monad, Northwest Airlines logo, and photograph of the *City of Bismarck* were graciously provided by the Northern Pacific Railway Historical Association and the Northwest Airlines History Centre, respectively.

The Ninth Air Force patch was made available through the Ninth Air Force Association Archives, Archival Services, University Libraries at the University of Akron, Akron, Ohio.

List of Maps

Map 1	Europe – 1932	Inside Front Cover
Map 2	Minnesota – 1940	7
Map 3	North Atlantic – Convoy UT-4	116
Map 4	British Isles – Convoy Dispersal	119
Map 5	The Low Countries – Winter 1943-1944	130
Map 6	London to Berlin – Strategic Bombing Campaign	136
Map 7	Northern France – Spring and Summer 1944	254
Map 8	Invasion	293
Map 9	Normandy Front – Stalemate	325
Map 10	Normandy Front – Breakout and Counterattack	365
Map 11	Mission to *Flugplatz A213*	377
Map 12	United States – 1944	Inside Back Cover

FOREWORD

Aside from being deeply honored and humbled, I was puzzled as to why Paul Sailer asked me to write this Foreword. Even though Don and I were cousins, our contact with each other was limited when we were growing up before he went into the service, and I didn't see him after that. People did not travel around in the 1930s as much as they do now. Paul must have sensed from our communications that the memory of Don and the events in his life had a great effect on me and influenced my life in a way that gave meaning to love of country and family. He must have also sensed my love of airplanes and aviation history. It gives me great pleasure that I was able to help Paul with this book, though in a small way, by furnishing family information and other things from memory and some research.

Don's father Clarence and my father Wayne were both born on a small farm near Des Moines, Iowa. Clarence was born before the turn of the twentieth century, and my father in 1900. When they each left home, they went different ways, and our families ended up in different states. Clarence took his family to Canada, where Don was born. They later came back to Hill City, Minnesota, where our family visited them in the 1930s. They would also come to Des Moines to visit us on occasion. Our grandmother lived in Norwalk, Iowa, and we all met there from time to time. Don had an older sister Lavaun and a brother Darrel, and I have a younger brother David.

I remember that Don was athletic, well-coordinated, and handled himself well. He always stood out and was good at whatever games we played. To me, the country was beautiful around Hill City, particularly the lakes. I can see why Don liked it so well. He and his brother had jobs at the family creamery, driving a truck on a route to pick up cream from the dairy farms in the region. They also delivered butter to Duluth and other cities. It seems that Don was only fourteen or fifteen years old, and since I was nine or ten, I really looked up to him and wanted to be just like him. Don and Darrel would take my brother and me out on their route in the creamery truck. It was a lot of fun to see the different farms and watch our cousins conduct their business with the farmers who seemed to like Don and Darrel. This was quite an adventure for city boys like my brother and me at our age. Don's mother Jo always had great meals for us, and we had plenty of butter from the creamery. Those pleasant days stand out in my memory.

When Don went in the service, we followed his career. When he started flying school, I was really interested, and I was influenced to the extent that I wanted to be an Army Air Corps pilot like him. He took his training in California and Arizona, and we didn't see him during that time. Later in the war, Don's brother Darrel was in the aviation cadet program. When he was stationed at an airfield in West Texas, he came to see our family in Dallas, where we lived at that time. He brought some letters from Don that we were able to read and get more information about him.

The war in Europe was winding down by the time I was old enough to go into the service, and the Army had quit training pilots. I didn't get to be a pilot in the service like Don, but I managed to get in the Army Air Corps and was trained as an aircraft mechanic, so at least I was able to be around airplanes. Before I went in, when I was seventeen years old, I soloed in a Piper J-3 Cub, so I did get to be a pilot in a small way. I was later stationed at airfields in Germany that Don may have flown over or attacked a year or so earlier. One of our jobs was to demolish aircraft from squadrons that had been de-activated. The charges were placed in the cockpit, at the engine mount, and in front of the tail. The only things salvaged were the radios, some instruments and the propellers. Along with our Republic P-47 Thunderbolts, I remember that we had to destroy a Messerschmitt Me-109 that was in flying condition.

When Don started flying the Bell P-39 Airacobra after he graduated from advanced flying school, I was really interested because I knew the P-39 was different in that it had the engine behind the pilot with a long prop shaft that went under the pilot's seat up to the nose. Some pilots did not care for it, and said that it was hard to handle, and if it got into a flat spin it could kill you, but Don liked it. He gained the reputation as a gifted pilot, and his squadron mates respected him. Later when he got to fly the North American P-51 Mustang, he thought it was the best fighter ever built.

When Don entered combat in Europe in December, 1943, our family was intensely interested in his exploits. He quickly became an ace and a flight leader, and we knew that he was going to stand out among the pilots in his squadron and group. We got news of his action in the 353rd Fighter Squadron fairly often, and his family sent us pictures once in a while. I remember a picture from his gun camera showing a Focke-Wulf FW-190 in its last dive. His experiences as a great fighter pilot are well covered in *The Oranges are Sweet*.

When word got to our family from Don's parents that he was missing in action, everyone of course was devastated and broken-hearted. We all thought that he had surely survived and was a prisoner of the Germans, or hopefully he was picked up by the French Underground and would be taken back to Allied territory, or maybe he could make his own way back to safety. Everyone was hoping and praying that he was okay, I even remember one opinion that "maybe the trees broke his fall." Sadly, after what seemed a long time, we received the awful words that he was killed in action. Don's death was personal to me, not only because he was the closest family member to be lost in the war, but also because I knew that I owed him something that could never be repaid.

I have always felt a deep sense of regret that his wife, daughter, and granddaughters have had to live their lives without a husband, father, and grandfather to help them through the trials and joys of life. I often wondered what Don would have done post war. I don't know, but I do know that he would have been outstanding and very successful, just as he was as a great fighter pilot and leader. One of the hardest things for me was to accept the fact that here was a young man who was denied the basic human opportunity to come home, pursue his hopes and dreams, and raise his family. He died too young and too soon.

The Beerbower family certainly owes a great debt of gratitude to Paul Sailer and his family for taking on this tremendous project. We will have information about Don's life that we would never have known, to pass on to our children and future generations, so that they will know that Major Don M. Beerbower helped make their world better and gave them a chance to pursue their hopes and dreams in a way that he was unable to do.

Dr. Albert "Ben" Beerbower

Introduction

Few people recognize the name of Major Don M. Beerbower or are aware of his contribution to victory in World War II. When he died strafing a German airdrome north of Reims, France, on August 9, 1944, he was the leading ace in the Ninth Air Force and the commanding officer of the 353rd Fighter Squadron. The Fighting Cobras, as the unit was known, ended the war with 290.5 aerial victories, more than any other squadron in the United States Army Air Forces. In *The Oranges are Sweet*, I tell the life story of Major Beerbower and the history of the 353rd Fighter Squadron between November 1942 and August 1944.

The war never strayed far from the thoughts of my father, Archie Sailer, an Eighth Air Force chemical warfare officer. I remember him discussing it with his friends, First Army infantrymen Frank Karsnia and Tom Haas, who both came ashore at Normandy on D-day; Ninth Air Force intelligence agent Elmer Bruhn, whose fluency in the German language earned him an assignment behind enemy lines; and my uncle, Chet Sailer, a Third Army radio operator wounded in action in 1945. At an early age, I witnessed how important it was for these veterans to honor those who had died in combat. On Memorial Day they marched in uniform to the cemetery or stood to the side, saluting, as the colors fluttered by.

I have a vivid memory from the 1950s of my father relaxing in an armchair in our living room, paging through his scrapbook. I sat beside him on the wide armrest while he showed me photographs, newspaper clippings, and other mementos from his past. Dad stopped when he came to a photograph of the basketball team that he played on in his hometown, Hill City, Minnesota, during the winter of 1932-1933. Standing beside him at the entrance to the high school was one of the team's mascots, Don Beerbower. Dad pointed to the eleven-year-old and said, "This boy was a real hero." He told me his friend had been killed during the war, shot down flying a P-51 Mustang. We talked about the other people in the photograph as well, but it was the youngster my age peering out at me from the past that caught my attention. Dad also treasured a letter he'd received from Don in the summer of 1944. In it, the combat-hardened pilot described his living conditions at a new airstrip in France, and an incident that occurred when he had to sleep on the ground his first night in Normandy. He wrote about reaching out in the dark and touching what he thought was a round rock; in the morning Don discovered beside him not a rock, but a human skull!

The experience of viewing the photograph and reading the letter from Don

1932-1933 Hill City Basketball Team
Front row: Left to right: Mascot Don Beerbower, Archie Sailer, Marshall Hankerson, Lee Mykkanen, Jim Sawdey, Bud Vashaw, Mascot Paul Boleman

left a lasting impression on me. As a teenager, I developed a serious interest in World War II fighter pilots and their airplanes. From this came a strong desire to someday fly in the military. During my senior year in college, I enlisted in the Army's aviation program. The day after my June 1969 graduation, I flew in an airplane for the first time, courtesy of Uncle Sam, to Fort Polk, Louisiana, where I commenced basic training. In September 1969 I began primary helicopter flight school at Fort Wolters, Texas, followed by advanced flight school at Fort Rucker, Alabama. After earning my wings and receiving the rank of warrant officer, I spent the month of June 1970 in transition school learning to fly the Army's new Bell OH-58A Kiowa. I piloted this aircraft and the Bell UH-1D Iroquois/Huey during a one-year tour of duty in Vietnam with the 20th Engineer Brigade and Engineer Command. I left the Army in August 1971.

My interest in Don Beerbower slipped to the back of my mind during the years I pursued a career in the human services field in Minnesota. Then, in 1995, the United States and many other countries commemorated the fiftieth anniversary of the end of World War II. I realized that the contribution of veterans I knew would soon be forgotten. Consequently, I asked my Uncle Chet if I could tape record an interview with him about his service in the 90th Infantry Division. He agreed. This was followed by recordings of other veterans in my extended family. The documenting of their experiences gradually renewed my desire to know more about the boy in the photograph of the Hill City basketball team.

On July 4, 1998, I had a chance encounter with Don's widow, Elayne Beerbower, in Hill City. During the parade, my aunt, Viola Dichtel Sailer, noticed Elayne standing nearby and introduced us. When I told Elayne about my interest in her husband, she said, confidently, "Well, I'm the person to talk to about Don." Within a few weeks Elayne provided me with several published articles. In addition she suggested I contact her brothers-in-law, Darrel Beerbower and Marshall Hankerson. I soon located records at the Air Force Historical Research Agency that documented Don's skill as a fighter pilot and his contribution to the success of the 353rd Fighter Squadron. I did not believe this information was well known by those interested in World War II aviation history. With the support of Elayne, Darrel, and Marshall, I decided to submit an application nominating Don for membership into the Minnesota Aviation Hall of Fame. This seemed like a good setting to recognize his achievements. In the process of preparing the application, I interviewed pilots who served overseas with Don. He was inducted into the hall of fame in April 2001.

Over the next several years, I interviewed additional members of the 353rd Fighter Squadron. I also assembled documents and photographs from the Air Force Historical Research Agency, American Fighter Aces Museum Foundation, Army Human Resources Command, Minnesota Historical Society, National

Archives and Records Administration, National Personnel Records Center, Navy Department Library, and Parks Library at Iowa State University. Many additional items were found through researching a variety of media sources. Most importantly, the Beerbower family allowed me access to Don's diary and correspondence. Much of what I compiled included unpublished material about important aspects of World War II aviation.

During my years of research, Elayne and I discussed my writing a book about Don as a way of remembering his significant contribution to the Allied air effort during the war. With her support, I began working on the manuscript in 2007.

With any historical figure, it is beneficial to understand what influenced the subject's character development during childhood and adolescence. In Don's case, family members and friends provided me with their personal observations. Through other sources, such as the *Hill City News*, I recognized the important role adults in the community played in shaping Don's life through the examples they set for him. In addition, I had the good fortune to interact with the people of the area, albeit a generation later. As a youngster, while visiting my extended family, I fished and swam in Hill Lake, participated in summer events such as Independence Day activities, and hunted the nearby woodland. By combining material from Don's contemporaries, the influence of the adults in his early life, and my understanding of Hill City, I believe I have created for the reader a realistic depiction of how Don developed into the young man who became a highly respected fighter pilot and combat leader.

Authentic history is elusive to say the least. To accurately portray the events that occur in this book, I used numerous primary source documents and provided the reader with endnotes and a complete bibliography. When possible, I cross-checked any statements I received from interviews or correspondence against information in the historical record. In a number of instances in the narrative, I inserted large portions of letters, diary entries, interviews, orders, and reports. I did this when I thought it important for the reader to examine firsthand what was said, how it was said, or how it was written by the subject of the incident or event. This created an occasional challenge. The application of a word or term in a primary source document did not always agree with the official, customary, or current usage or spelling. For example, the German Messerschmitt Me-109 and Me-110 aircraft are frequently identified today with a Bf- designation before the numerals. The Allied terminology used in World War II was Me-. It is the only way Don and his colleagues referred to these airplanes in their reports. Therefore, I used it as well. Another example is how he spelled the name of his two P-51s in his diary and letters. Don typically wrote *Bonnie "B"*, so I followed suit, even though he used several variations on his aircraft.

Don's Mustangs were named after his daughter, Bonita "Bonnie" Lea. As the reader will find, the war never totally superseded the home front in Don's thoughts. Bonnie and Elayne were the most significant people in his life. Because of his love for them and concern for their well-being, I have included in the narrative frequent references to family and community activities in and around Hill City.

Don Beerbower's tally of fifteen-and-a-half aerial victories and three ground victories between January and August 1944, places him among the top American fighter pilots of World War II. His exceptional leadership qualities and personal character were invaluable to the mission of one of the few units in the European theater to fly in both strategic and tactical combat operations. The pilots he fought with, and the officers and men who supported their effort, formed a unique nexus of determination that resulted in the 353rd Fighter Squadron's success in destroying a record number of enemy aircraft. As a member of the military family of pilots who followed in their wake, it is my privilege to tell the story of Don Beerbower and the men of the 353rd Fighter Squadron.

Paul M. Sailer

PART ONE

What did Churchill say . . . about leadership at Sandhurst? He said, "Now gentlemen, until it pleases the Almighty to make everybody equal, some of us will be obliged to be leaders," or something to that effect.

Kenneth H. Dahlberg, P-51 pilot
(interview with the author)

Cricqueville-en-Bessin, Normandy, 1103, August 9, 1944.[1]

    Twenty-two-year-old squadron commander Major Don M. Beerbower gave the pilots their last minute instructions at Advanced Landing Strip A-2 near Omaha Beach. With the briefing completed, the men went to the flight line, started the Packard-built Merlin engines in their P-51s, and taxied into position for takeoff. Down the runway rolled *Bonnie "B"*, the plane Major Beerbower had named after his daughter, Bonita Lea. To his left side and slightly back was wingman Second Lieutenant Frederick B. Deeds in *Joy*. Flight Officer Bruce W. Carr in *Angel's Playmate* and his wingman, Second Lieutenant Charles A. Olmsted in *Skibbereen,* followed the first pair off A-2. Others departed in *Beantown Banshee, Pretty Baby, Arson's Reward, and Rigor Mortis.* Finally, sixteen Mustangs climbed into the late morning sky over northern France. After gaining altitude, the pilots turned east and headed for an area beyond Paris where they would carry out an armed reconnaissance mission.[2] Below them the German Seventh Army counterattacked for the third day against the Allied breakout of the Normandy bridgehead. Beerbower and his men intended to attack any supporting elements of the Nazi war machine they found in their assigned sector.

1

A Sure Hit

Hill City, the hustling young place in northern Aitkin County, defies any place in the states of Wisconsin and Minnesota, and any man seeking occupation will make a sure hit if he turns his cap that way.

J. G. Lang, resident, Marathon City, Wisconsin
The Hill City Saga

It was a day in 1909 that appeared to be brimming with opportunity as twenty-seven-year-old Gay C. Huntley stepped off the train at the new depot in Hill City, Minnesota. He had traveled to the remote village to investigate the area's potential for a newspaper business. The small town's picturesque setting overlooking the largest lake in northern Aitkin County and the area's fine stand of hardwoods pleased Huntley. In addition, a freshly laid railroad spur connected the community to the outside world at Mississippi Junction, eighteen miles east of Hill City. To his way of thinking, a town with a railroad was likely to be a town with a future. He also found the merchants eager for a newspaper to promote what they referred to as the Hill Lake Country. Huntley had learned the printing trade while working for his brothers in Spring Valley and Duluth, Minnesota. Even though the budding entrepreneur wanted to operate his own business, he wondered if he could make a living in Hill City. After returning to his job in Duluth, he continued to think about his prospects in this relatively isolated region in northeastern Minnesota. A few weeks later, when Armour and Company of Chicago announced it planned to build a wood products factory on the edge of the village, Huntley decided to stake his future on Hill City. By spring the newspaperman had set up a hand press in the Sprout Land Office, the only business with space to rent.[1]

In the first issue of the *Hill City News*, May 5, 1910, Huntley announced to his readers: "It is our purpose to publish a live paper, irrevocably committed to the consistent boosting of Hill City, its industries and surrounding country.... We have a good, live town that is building up rapidly. Our people are progressive and up-to-date, everyone is ready and willing to boost for Hill City. This together with our natural resources, should, and will make a town of which we will all be justly proud."

Huntley, the son of a Civil War veteran, was patriotic, devout, civic-minded and conservative. In the coming years he would develop strong objections to sending American boys to fight in European wars. He and his bride, Duluth school teacher Emily Bartholdi, would raise three boys in the new town.[2]

The merchants built Hill City on the high ground along the west side of Hill Lake, a narrow, four-mile-long body of clear, spring-fed water that provided a source of fresh fish and recreation for the local residents. Rising above the lake's south shore stood 1,589-foot Quadna Mountain, the highest elevation in Aitkin County. Huntley praised the view of the countryside from this vantage point when he wrote: "Those who have never climbed to the summit of the mountain south of town (*Pequadna* the Indians named it) have missed a rare treat. After gaining the summit, you cast your eyes to the south and there stretched before you, extending for miles to the east and west, are the great Willow River Meadows in all their splendor. To the north is a panorama of undulating woodland extending as far as the eye can reach."[3]

Hill City is located seventy-five miles west of Lake Superior's largest harbor, Duluth, and twenty-five miles south of the Mesabi Iron Range. Its population in 1910 was two hundred twenty people. The area's great white pines had already been logged, but the remaining hardwood forest of aspen, basswood, birch, and oak was of interest to Armour and Company. It needed wooden pails and tubs for its packing business. In 1910 Armour dismantled its factory

Hill City depot with National Woodenware factory and Quadna Mountain in background

in Ithaca, Michigan, and transported it by rail to Hill City. The following year its subsidiary, National Woodenware Company, made its first outbound shipment on the Mississippi, Hill City, and Western Railway.[4]

The arrival of National Woodenware created a boom time in Hill City. The factory's payroll created a steady source of revenue for those in business. Two of the many merchants who benefited from this were George Hankerson and Joe Sailer. Both would contribute much to the village in the years to come.

The influx of workers provided many new customers at George Hankerson's general store, located on the corner of Main Street and Lake Avenue. Hankerson, who had come to Hill City several years before Huntley and Sailer, was a trustee of the recently dedicated Methodist Episcopal Church. He and his wife, Betty, lived next door to the Huntleys. Hankerson participated in community affairs and enjoyed baseball. His rich tenor voice could be heard in the church choir and at social events. He was also a noted amateur actor. The *Hill City News* carried a story once about a reading he presented at the Gem Theater on Lake Avenue. In the scene, Hankerson frantically implored his wife to dispose of a mouse that had run up his leg. "He wanted her to call the fire department, the chief of police, and the army," the *News* reported, "to drive one tiny mouse down his pants leg. Finally he collapsed from nervous exhaustion and the mouse fell to the floor dead. He had squeezed it to death."[5] Hankerson's frantic gyrations delighted the crowd.

Barber Joe Sailer was drawn to Hill City in 1909 by its energetic people, the area lakes, and the forest that stretched out in every direction. After setting up his shop in the office of a vacant livery, he went back to his hometown of Marathon City, Wisconsin, married Helen "Ella" Lang, and then returned with her to start a new life in Minnesota. An enterprising man, Sailer enhanced his barbering trade by adding a tavern which included, at one time or another, a dance hall, card room, bowling alley, pool hall, sporting goods shop, and a bait business. He was the son of German immigrants, an avid hunter and fisherman, drummer in the village orchestra, and a Spanish flu survivor. The powerfully built Sailer played baseball with passion;[6] as George Hankerson's son, Marshall, once observed, "[Joe] was a tremendous hitter. He could place the ball better than anybody I ever saw. He could hit balls down the third-base line, just barely foul, and the outfield would shift over and boom, off into right field the next one would go. And as far as his arm, well, he pitched a lot, too, and he had a heck of a throwing arm from shortstop to first base."[7]

By 1920 Hill City had made significant strides. Its population nearly quadrupled from two hundred twenty to nine hundred twenty-eight. Children attended school in a new two-story brick building. A water tower dominated the skyline. Electricity flowed from the power plant at the National Woodenware factory, a telephone exchange linked homes and shops together, and a new state trunk highway connected Hill City to Minneapolis and St. Paul, one hundred seventy-five miles away. Boarding houses and hotels enjoyed good business. Grocery, hardware, and dry goods stores had regular customers. Dr. Alex Stewart delivered many babies, and the 1918 flu epidemic had come and gone, leaving in its wake a path of death that affected Hill City as well as every other community in America.[8] World War I was over and those who had served in the military sought work and a place to raise a family. Two of these men were William Kucera and Clarence Beerbower.

After being drafted into the Army in 1918, Bill Kucera served seven months in the Carolinas and New York State.[9] In 1919 he changed the spelling of his name from Kucera to Kutcher so that it could be more accurately pronounced. Also that year he married Anna Benes at the Methodist Episcopal Church in

William and Anna Kutcher wedding party

Hill City. They moved into a log house on his property in Spang Township, five miles northwest of town. To help the young couple get started, Bill's parents gave them several cows, poultry, and a team of horses. Their immediate problem involved clearing land for fields and pasture. The white pines in this area had been logged off before the turn of the century, and now hardwoods dominated the landscape. These needed to be removed. Bill and Anna worked together sawing down trees, grubbing around roots with hand tools, and dynamiting hundreds of stumps. The Kutchers became parents at 4:30 a.m. on April 5, 1921, when their only child, Elayne, was born at home. Eventually the farm produced quality seed potatoes from the land and cream from its dairy.[10] The Kutchers sent their cream to the Hill City Creamery, where it was processed by a new buttermaker named Clarence Beerbower.

Beerbower's family had been in America since 1752 when his ancestor, Philip Bierbauer, settled in Pennsylvania. Philip hailed from a German region along the Rhine River known as the Palatinate. His offspring migrated with the great westward expansion of the 1800s to Ohio and finally to Iowa. Along the way the name Bierbauer was Americanized to Beerbower. Clarence was born in Linn County, Iowa, in 1895 to a farm couple, Albert and Lula Beerbower. On October 11, 1917, he married Josephine "Josie" Carson in Coggon, Iowa.[11] After stateside duty in the Army, Clarence returned to Iowa. Within a few months he moved with his wife and two children, Lavaun and Darrel, to a wheat farm near Kenaston, Saskatchewan, Canada. On August 26, 1921, Josie Beer-

Clarence and Josie Beerbower

bower delivered her second son, Don Merrill, at Union Hospital in nearby Davidson.[12]

Wheat does well on the high plains of North America, but it grew poorly during the extended drought that struck Saskatchewan in the early twenties. Beerbower's effort at farming failed, so he returned with his family to the United States where he found employment as a buttermaker with the Farmers Equity Creamery in Wadena, Minnesota. After a short period of employment, he accepted a similar position in 1923 with the Hill City Creamery.[13] It had been a hectic and difficult six years of marriage for the Beerbowers. Broke and with three children, they faced starting all over again. Clarence and Josie intended to succeed in the young, flourishing village of Hill City.

2

Now, You Remember

Fire demons held almost undisputed sway early Sunday morning, July 14, at the buildings of the former National Woodenware Co. factory. Blazing sparks as big as a man's arm were hurled in a steady shower over the south part of the village where every householder mounted guard over his own property. . . . Agents of the State Fire Marshall's Office have been working on the investigation of theories of incendiary origins of the fire.

Harold Walker, editor
Hill City News

Chet Sailer remembered the warm July night in 1929 well. He was at the Eastside Dance Hall near Hill Lake with his girlfriend, Virginia Berry. Her parents "were quite Methodist," as Sailer remembered. "They had to stop dancing at twelve o'clock. Having no car at that time, I walked her up the hill to her place, taking her home. I looked towards Hill City and it looked like the whole town was on fire. Here this factory had been torched. . . . I gave the alarm there at the dance. . . . Everybody took off for Hill City." When the out-of-breath teen arrived at home, he found his father, Joe, spraying water on the roof of their house, desperately trying to protect it from the burning inferno several blocks away.[1]

The National Woodenware Company had notified its employees several months earlier that it was ceasing operations in Hill City. With the hardwood timber in the area depleted, and lightweight corrugated fiber paper and veneer cut boxes replacing wood in packing containers, hundreds of factory and logging jobs disappeared.[2] Then, on October 29, 1929, the New York Stock Exchange crashed and soon the Great Depression came. By 1930 the population of the village had dropped to five hundred fifteen people. The national economy slowed to a sputter. During the first three years of the depression, five thousand banks closed.[3] The First State Bank of Hill City went out of business in 1931. Patrons received twenty-five cents on the dollar for their deposits.[4]

By 1932 one in four American workers was unemployed. President Herbert Hoover's attempts to pull the country out of the serious downward spiral had failed and, by year's end, his presidency would fail as well. For the businessmen of Hill City this was a trying time. The high quality hardwood stands had gone the way of the earlier white pine forests. This left agriculture as the mainstay of the community. But as hard times continued, prices for agricultural products fell. Between 1920 and 1932, total farm income in the United States declined from $15.5 billion to $5.5 billion.[5]

On May 19, 1932, the Hill City Creamery Association's board of directors announced the sale of their buildings and equipment to Clarence Beerbower.[6] The association had been buying cream from area farmers for years, turning it into butter and shipping it by rail to Duluth. Beerbower intended to continue this practice.[7] But ever since the loss of the National Woodenware Company, the situation with the railroad connecting Hill City to Mississippi Junction had been tenuous. George Hankerson was now the general manager of the Hill City Railway Company, a subsidiary of the Great Northern Railway.[8] After Hankerson went broke trying to operate his general store, he found work as an auditor, then agent, and finally as vice president and general manager of the Hill City Railway Company. The railroad could not afford to lose a regular freight customer. Beerbower's decision to purchase the struggling creamery was good news to Hankerson. It meant shipments of butter would continue over the spur line to Mississippi Junction and beyond to Duluth.[9]

The Hankersons and the Beerbowers lived several houses apart on Ione Avenue or "Silk Stocking Row," as the locals called it, not far from Hill Lake. In Hill City's prime, Ione Avenue had been home to the upper crust of the village.

Beerbower home - Hill City, Minnesota

This included the factory manager, bank president, and others. Now the Beerbowers lived in the house once occupied by the manager of the National Woodenware Company.[10]

The two families enjoyed frequent contact with each other through social events and church activities, such as the participation of their children, Marshall Hankerson and Lavaun Beerbower, in a Methodist Episcopal youth organization known as the Epworth League. Marshall's earliest memory of Lavaun's little brother, Don, involved a story which illustrated that the neighbor boy "could be naughty like little kids can."

> Don disappeared one day and a neighbor lady across the street, Mrs. Allen, saw him down by the lake. . . . She tore down there and told him, "Get away from that lake!" and he looked up at her and said, "You're not my sasser!" And, of course, that didn't set too well so she grabbed him by the arm and dragged him home and explained to Don's mother what happened. Don's mother looked at him and said, "Now, you remember, Mrs. Allen is your sasser, too." A little while later Don went across the street and stopped to see Mrs. Allen. He said, "I just want you to know that you're my sasser, too."[11]

Don had ventured outside his neighborhood; he had pushed past the limits set by his parents. There is no indication in the story that he was concerned about this, or, for that matter, afraid when he went exploring along the shoreline of Hill Lake. Although Don reacted angrily to being caught, he accepted his mother's statement about Mrs. Allen as fact and promptly (perhaps with motherly encouragement) went over and made things right with her. From an early age Don's basic nature was to be obedient to authority and respectful of others. But he also desired to push beyond what may have seemed normal or comfortable for many, to a place where danger loomed.

Bill and Anna Kutcher were also friends of the Beerbowers. They knew each other through the American Legion, attended the same church, and had a business relationship through the Hill City Creamery. Every month one of the families hosted the other for Sunday dinner. Kutcher's daughter, Elayne, was the same age as Don Beerbower.[12]

Don liked sports and enjoyed being around the older boys in town. In the summer of 1932 he and his friend Paul Boleman agreed to be the mascots, or batboys, for the Junior American Legion baseball team. Marshall Hankerson roamed centerfield that year. Gay Huntley's son, Philip, and Joe Sailer's boys,

Elayne Kutcher

Chet and Archie, played on the team as well.[13]

Joe Sailer's barbershop occupied a side room of the Rainbow Tavern, a business he owned on the corner of Main Street and Lake Avenue. At forty-five, he continued to enjoy playing town team baseball and umpiring games for the Junior American Legion. Sailer liked to help the boys improve their skills when they practiced at the ball park. If business slowed down in the summer, he often stepped-out on the gravel street to work with the kids hanging around his shop. Marshall Hankerson recalls, "He'd be showing us how to field the ball . . . coming in on the right foot and throwing on the right foot, doing the little things that probably we wouldn't have picked up. Maybe that's why we were a good ball team."[14]

High school teacher Floyd Kaslow coached the Junior American Legion club. He had accomplished much with the boys in 1931 when they fell one game short of going to the state tournament. They lost to St. Cloud in the district finals. Considering Minnesota had six hundred Junior American Legion teams, the boys had done very well for themselves.[15] The team expected a banner year in 1932.

In the June 30 issue of the *Hill City News*, Harold Walker complimented the baseball team for winning all but four of its games in the previous three seasons. He mentioned the upcoming Fourth of July contest was the last time for the public to see pitching ace Chet Sailer and second baseman Roland Vashaw in Junior American Legion uniforms, as they were aging-out of the program. Then Walker informed his readers about the upcoming match against Iron Range powerhouse Marble, a state tournament participant in 1929, 1930, and 1931. He reminded his readers that the teams had one win apiece in their

1931 Hill City Junior American Legion Baseball Team.
Front row: Left to right - Coach Floyd Kaslou, Phil Huntley, Ben Robak, Bob McGlade,
Back row: Roland Vashaw, Archie Sailer, Marvin Weller, Jim Sawdey, Chet Sailer, Lee Mykkanen, Marshall Hankerson, Joe Bela.

two contests in June. The last victory had gone to Marble in a thirteen-inning affair won on its home field. Walker concluded by saying, "This is the kind of competition the boys like and the kind that will provide the spectators far more than their money's worth at the big celebration here on July 4th."

Gay Huntley still owned the *News*, but since 1920 he had been the village postmaster. Walker published and edited the paper.[16] The *News* made a real effort to create interest in the Junior American Legion game and the upcoming festivities. Part of this had to do with Hill City being a baseball town. People loved the game and justifiably took pride in their boys. But Walker also remembered what happened in 1931 when the community did not promote an Independence Day event. By 1932 the national economy was about as bleak as it had been at any time in the country's history. Attracting people to town stimulated business and created an opportunity to energize the village as a whole. When the American Legion announced its intent to sponsor the traditional celebration, it proved to be a positive step forward for Hill City in this difficult depression year. The role of the *News* was critical to the success of the occasion. As the primary communications instrument within the Hill City trade area, the paper kept people abreast of state and local news and, to a limited extent, national news. It reached out to smaller rural communities like Shovel Lake, Spang, and Swatara, reporting weekly on the activities of neighbors and visiting relatives. As it had done since its inception in 1910, the *News* continued to boost Hill City.

July 4 began like most days for the Beerbower children. Lavaun, Darrel, and Don had their chores to do. Among other things, the family cow required milking and the hogs their father raised needed to be fed.[17] But beyond these jobs, it was a special day filled with excitement and anticipation, particularly for Don, who would be on the field for the afternoon baseball game. The festivities got under way with the newly reorganized Hill City-Swatara Band marching along the streets, stopping to play at each business corner, and finally ending up at the central square for a concert. Then former creamery manager F. W. Allin gave a speech in which he talked about Hill City's transition from an industrial base to a farming economy. In the afternoon sports program the youngsters participated in peanut scramble, pony and bicycle races, wrestling and boxing matches and, for the adults, a tug-of-war in which the village team surprisingly overpowered the country team. Finally it was time for the main event of the day. Harold Walker wrote about the game in the next issue of the *News*.

> One of the tightest baseball games witnessed here followed between the Marble and Hill City [teams]. . . . Three startling put-

outs by the visitor's base umpire at the most crucial points of the game wrecked the local boys' chances of winning the game with [the] Marble Juniors here Monday. Otherwise the game was fast, thrilling and replete with brilliant playing. It is not admitted that Marble won. The score stood 3 to 2 when the game broke up, for the home lads out-hit, out-played and out-gamed them in sportsmanship. . . .[18]

Although the loss frustrated the team, the boys did not let it get them down. They went on to win the district championship against St. Cloud, 8 to 1. The first game of the state tournament was played at 8:30 a.m. on August 8, at the University of Minnesota's historic Northrop Field in Minneapolis, when the Hill City Juniors "walloped" Benson 16 to 2. This caused so much excitement back home that "within ten minutes from the end of the game sirens in Hill City announced the victory upon receipt of telephone information through the *News*." Even though the boys lost in the next round to West Duluth, and the consolation game 6 to 4 in extra innings to Minneapolis Preston-Cricton, they had played exceptional baseball.[19] This was heady stuff for the young batboy. Don had traveled to Minnesota's largest city, walked on the well-manicured infield, and heard the excitement of the crowds. What an exhilarating feeling! Most importantly, he witnessed what can be accomplished through practice, discipline, sportsmanship, and teamwork.

Don spent much of his free time outdoors. Gazing east from the Beerbower home, Don could see the sun sparkling on the blue surface of Hill Lake, where he and Darrel always went for a quick swim on the last day of school. The dip into the frigid water gave them a breathtaking thrill. As Darrel recalled, "the lake also had about all the fish a person wanted to take the time to catch."[20] One day in June 1932, two fishermen caught a hundred pounds of fish, including a twenty-two-pound northern pike.[21] For all the beauty and pleasure the lake provided, it was also dangerous. The *News* carried a story on June 30 about a drowning that "snapped the thread of another young life when Durward Wilson sank beneath the waters of Hill Lake." Wilson had been demonstrating to a newcomer at the beach how far out it was safe to walk when he accidentally stepped over the drop-off. The nineteen-year-old inexperienced swimmer panicked, and then went under. Those present formed a human chain but "the lad could not be reached as he reappeared." Rescuers gathered as quickly as possible, but thirty minutes passed before divers found the body. George Hankerson's son, Bob, a physician home for a visit, pronounced Wilson dead.[22] Several days later the Methodist Episcopalian minister, Elsie Hartman, conducted the funeral.

In early winter the youngsters took their fathers' shovels out onto frozen Hill Lake and cleared an area for a skating rink. They had a lot of fun playing tin can and crack the whip. The kids played tin can like hockey except lengths of wood and an empty can replaced hockey sticks and a puck. If the snow got too deep, they moved to a hard-packed street.[23]

Not all of Don's activities took place outdoors. In the winter he played basketball. When the Hill City High School team started practice in November, Don and his friend Paul Boleman were named mascots. The squad members included many of the same fellows the two boys knew from summer baseball. The American Legion hosted the basketball games in its dance hall. Because of the poor economy, the community could not afford to build a school gymnasium.[24]

The Great Depression made life difficult for many Americans. In the general election of 1932, the people expressed their lack of confidence in Herbert Hoover by electing Franklin D. Roosevelt as their new president. His energy, ideas, and hope gave many in the nation assurance the economy would improve. In Hill City some businessmen continued to see opportunities. One of these individuals was Frank Dichtel, the new owner of the telephone company. When he arrived in town in 1932, the area phone "lines were in sagging shape, cable was wet, many lines were in brush and near the ground." Dichtel promptly put his crew to work on these time-consuming repairs.[25] He and others, like Clarence Beerbower, who was busy turning the creamery around, anticipated a bright future for their families in Hill City.

Deer hunting partners Joe Sailer and Frank Dichtel CHET SAILER PHOTO

3

An Extremely Honest Kid

When they came down to our farm Don and Darrel would take a couple of our draft horses out and ride. They also liked to split wood and my dad liked that.

Ronald L. Morton, cousin
(letter to the author)

In 1935 the Hill City Railway Company discontinued operations. General Manager George Hankerson never secured enough freight tonnage to replace the loss of business the railroad suffered with the closure of the National Woodenware Company. The end of railway service meant Clarence Beerbower no longer had a convenient way to ship butter to Duluth. His only alternative was to make the seventy-five-mile drive using one of his trucks. Because of the gravel roads, it took the better part of a day to travel there and back. This added to the cost of operating the Hill City Creamery. But Beerbower also saw an opportunity to improve his business. He negotiated a deal with Hankerson to

Josie, Don, and Darrel Beerbower, and driver in REO creamery truck

purchase the railroad roundhouse for a thousand dollars.[1] He then remodeled the four locomotive stalls and the workshop area so that he could expand cold storage space for the butter and provide inside parking for the trucks. He also purchased additional churn equipment and tanks.[2]

As these major changes were taking place in the operation of the creamery, the Beerbower children had grown old enough to help their parents with the family business. Lavaun assisted her mother with the bookkeeping and Darrel and Don learned to drive the REO Speedwagon trucks. Like many of the youngsters in Hill City, the Beerbower kids were taught a sound work ethic. Don, for example, had chores to do as a boy, helped on the cream routes when needed, delivered newspapers, and sold the *Saturday Evening Post*.[3]

As Don moved out of childhood, his personality and character had developed to the point that his future brother-in-law, Marshall Hankerson, considered him "an extremely honest kid." Thinking back over the years, Hankerson reflected, "I suppose his work selling papers and his work at the creamery helped him value money. He was very popular as a kid, everybody liked him. . . [Don had] a good disposition, was friendly towards everybody, and I expect his business dealings had a lot to do with that. He had to meet all kinds of people, talk with them and be friendly with them. . . . He was also active in church."[4]

Beerbower cousins: Front row: Left to right - David and Albert "Ben" Beerbower Back row: Don and Darrel Beerbower

During Don's formative years, he was privileged to have Reverend Elsie Hartman as his minister. She worked directly with him in Confirmation classes and the Epworth League.[5] Reverend Hartman served as the first female pastor in the Methodist Episcopal congregations in Hill City, Shovel Lake, and Swatara. This well-respected and well-liked single woman saw her strength in visiting homes and helping people during times of tragedy. She once observed, "So often I've had to give comfort after terrible accidents, children drowned, men killed on the job." Commenting on the favorite areas of her ministry, she said, "I get a lot of satisfaction out of working with children because I get to see results. Three boys from my church in Hill City, for instance, are now ministers themselves."[6] One year she refused a salary increase from the church board, asking that instead they use it to pay for a bus to bring children from Spang to Sunday school and Epworth League meetings.[7] This made it easier for farm kids like Elayne Kutcher to attend youth programs. The Epworth League meetings started at 7:30 p.m. on Sunday evenings. Here Don and others, like friends Morley Christensen and William J. "Billy J" Johnston, learned about their Wesleyan heritage from Reverend Hartman. When she left Hill City in 1942, Gay Huntley wrote admiringly, "Rev. Elsie Hartman has put in 12 years of earnest, faithful work. . . . Coming here when things were at their lowest ebb she has labored well and faithfully not only to keep the churches going, but to also build them up. In this she has been signally successful. . . . Her work among the young folks and in the home is especially commended."[8]

In addition to Don's family and church, he found much pleasure participating in Boy Scout Troop 53. Don and thirty-one other boys had joined the new organization in 1937, when it was organized by the American Legion. State forester Don Wilson served as the first scoutmaster. During their initial seventeen months the boys won all three of the competitions they entered against other troops. Beginning as a tenderfoot, Don advanced in the ranks, earning numerous merit badges. He and others received recognition for their achievements at special courts of honor. The boys gave back to their community at events such as Memorial Day services. During the program at the Hill City Cemetery in the spring of 1938, a scout placed a small flag on the grave of each veteran as the deceased's name was called out. By the troop's second anniversary in January 1939, however, fewer boys were participating.[9] Gay Huntley noticed this and on January 26 spoke out in an editorial:

> During the past few months interest seems to be lacking and we hear no more of the troop doing things and progressing. What's the matter? Does the fault lie with the scouts, scoutmaster and assistants, the scout committee or the sponsor? Perhaps it is the fault of all of them, a sort of slowing down and expecting a movement once nicely started to continue of its own momentum. . . . Here is a splendid thing, the best organization for boys in the world. A boy who grows up in scouting is certain to develop into a valuable citizen. It should not be allowed to go down.

The following week the *News* carried a front page article announcing that Boy Scout Council members F. J. Wallace, H. C. Eichorn, Leslie Carter, and Joe Sailer had accepted the resignation of Scoutmaster Roy Christensen. He was replaced by Clayton Sharp and two new assistants.[10]

The men guiding Troop 53 helped develop Don as a citizen. They expected him to memorize and live-out the Scout Oath:

> On my honor I will do my best:
> To do my duty to God and my country,
> and to obey the scout law;
> To help other people at all times;
> To keep myself physically strong,
> mentally awake and morally straight.[11]

Don's other interests centered on activities at the Hill City High School. An examination of his senior year (1938-1939) illustrates this. As a member of the declamation team, he won first place in the sub-district with his oration, "I Am Innocent of His Blood." And he was "very good" in the senior class production *Blackberry Winter*, a comedy/drama presented in front of two large audiences at

Don Beerbower, Elayne Kutcher, and Billy Johnston

the Gem Theater.¹² The Gem was the only place in town with a stage and adequate seating for plays. Here, in late March, Don very likely enjoyed watching the skill of renowned stunt pilot Paul Mantz in the movie *Flight of Fame*. The *News* described it as a "thrilling aviation drama . . . about a daredevil Army pilot."¹³

Don played guard and captained the basketball team. He also enjoyed Junior American Legion and high school baseball. Coach Floyd Kaslow described this young athlete as having "outstanding spirit."¹⁴ During the Junior-Senior spring banquet, Don was the admiral of the "good ship H.C.H.S," and as president of his class, closed the evening program with a "fine, well worded thank you."¹⁵ The small Class of 1939 included thirteen seniors, eleven of whom were girls. Reverend Elsie Hartman gave the graduation invocation on June 1. Herbert Sorenson, president of Duluth State Teachers College followed with the commencement address. During the ceremony, Don and classmate June Wilson each received the American Legion Citizenship Award.¹⁶

Don Beerbower and Elayne Kutcher wearing their 1939 Hill City and Grand Rapids High School graduation caps and gowns

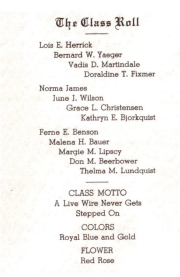

1939 Hill City graduating class

With high school behind him, Don started working full-time driving truck for his parents. His cream route included a stop at the Bill and Anna Kutcher farm. That summer, their daughter, Elayne, entered the Lake District Fair and Festival queen contest in Hill City. The selection of the queen was based on popularity, with different businesses promoting their own candidate. The public could vote at participating stores. The Hill City Creamery sponsored Elayne. The *News* printed the voting results each week. By August 17 Elayne had moved from sixth place to first place. However, when the final tally was taken a few days later, she had been edged out by Eastside's Selma Weller. In September Elayne enrolled at Itasca Junior College in Coleraine, about twenty-five miles from her parents' farm.[17] Darrel Beerbower was working in Iowa in the summer of 1939. Earlier in the year, he had gotten into a "big fight" with his father and left home. He hitchhiked to Waterloo, where someone he knew helped him find a job in a meat-packing plant. The father and son later patched things up, and in August Darrel married his hometown sweetheart, Arlene Ziegenhagen, in Iowa. Later that fall, they moved back to Hill City.[18]

Darrel and Arlene wedding photograph - 1939

Don Beerbower turned eighteen on August 26, 1939. Six days later German Stuka dive-bombers were screaming earthward toward military and civilian targets in Poland.

4

Though the Mountains Shake

War is the ultimate of human brutality and is resorted to when selfishness and greed for power cannot gain their ends otherwise. . . . Young men and boys are "called to the colors" and put through a course of intensive training in the art of wholesale murder of other young men who are unknown to them and against whom they have no quarrel.

Gay C. Huntley, editor/publisher
Hill City News

  The world had been changing while Don Beerbower was growing up in Hill City, Minnesota. During the 1930s, Japan, Italy, and Germany initiated hostile actions that would culminate in war. In 1931 the Japanese occupied the Chinese province of Manchuria to gain control of its coal, iron, and fertile farmland. Italy invaded Ethiopia in 1935, thereby strengthening its position in East Africa. That same year, in violation of the Treaty of Versailles, Germany began conscription and universal military training. In 1936 Chancellor Adolf Hitler sent troops into the Rhineland, the demilitarized zone along Germany's western border. Two of the victors of World War I, Great Britain and France, responded to the German breach of the treaty with only words. The League of Nations also failed to block Italian and Japanese aggression. Thus, a series of events followed that ended in the greatest cataclysm of the twentieth century.
  By 1937 full-scale war had broken out between Japan and China. In 1938 Germany annexed Austria and then seized the western portion of Czechoslovakia known as the Sudetenland. Nazi armies marched into Bohemia and Moravia in the spring of 1939. When Hitler ordered his troops to invade Poland on September 1 of that year, Great Britain and France declared war on Germany.
  These far-off events did not go unnoticed in northeastern Minnesota. By 1936 Gay Huntley was again the publisher and editor of the *Hill City News*. Late in the decade, as the clouds of war formed across the Atlantic, he began to write about his concern that American involvement in another European

conflict would seriously affect the lives of the people of Hill City. Others in the village understood his apprehension. They discussed the possibility of a major world conflict at family gatherings, in local business establishments, in school classrooms, and at the American Legion Post, where men remembered the trench warfare of 1917-1918. An examination of Huntley's editorial comments in 1939, 1940, and 1941 illustrates the level of discourse in the community during the years preceding American participation in the war.

On the eve of the German invasion of Poland, August 31, 1939, Huntley commented in his newspaper, "Again the militarists in Europe and at home are making the most of a critical situation trying to get the people in a mood for war." After hostilities broke out and it became evident the United States was building up its sorely neglected military forces, Huntley stated, "The *News* is opposed to war on the grounds that it is an unnecessary evil, that it does not settle anything and that only evil results from it. We boast of being a Christian nation, but there is nothing Christ-like about war, or even about the training of men for war."[1]

Later that fall when Minnesota's famous aviator Charles Lindbergh was being criticized in the national press for a speech on neutrality, Huntley quipped, "Perhaps we need a few more outspoken citizens to wake us up to minding our own business and staying out of Europe's wars."[2] He did not trust the motives of those who wanted the United States to fight the Axis forces. On April 25, 1940, Huntley, the father of three boys, warned his readers, "The same propaganda is being spread abroad in our land that we heard back in 1916, '17 and '18. Every day via radio and daily newspapers subversive elements are at work trying to break down the resistance of our people and to make them war minded so that they would once more become maddened with the blood lust, willing to sacrifice their sons for some high sounding slogans."

In the spring of 1940, Franklin D. Roosevelt was running for his third term as president. Huntley questioned the Democrat's forthrightness about wanting to keep the country out of the European war when he wrote, "If our president has followed Mr. Wilson's footsteps and already committed the United States to this war, he owes it to the American people to tell them so frankly [and] without any delay." That summer the Huntley family vacationed in Washington, D.C. The editor later told his readers he thought a trip to the nation's capital helped "round out one's education." He went on to say he had a question for his subscribers to ponder. While at Arlington National Cemetery he had watched a lone sentry guarding the Tomb of the Unknown Soldier. To his many friends and acquaintances he now asked, "Are we going to allow the war makers to again compel us to build another such tomb?" He then answered his own question by saying the people should respond with "a NO so thunderous that no government official would dare to even suggest it." Yet Huntley was a person who respected the law and the democratic process. When Congress passed conscription legislation that he opposed, he informed the young men of the area, "We advise all those affected by it to cheerfully comply with the law." He hoped that draftees would be used only for the defense of the country. The *News* supported Republican Wendell Willkie in the general election of 1940, but when Roosevelt won, Huntley conceded positively by writing, "The election is over so let's forget the differences and all unite in an effort to make our country an even better place in which to live."³

Post-War Huntley family photograph
Front row: Left to right - Billy Huntley, Emily and Gay Castle Huntley
Back row: Robert Huntley and wife Ruth, Marjorie and husband Phil Huntley

By the early spring of 1941, the Nazis controlled most of Europe. Only Great Britain stood between the United States and German aggression. In a March 27 editorial, Huntley's tone seemed to concede the inevitable when he said, "President Roosevelt says we must make sacrifices to help defeat the dictators. That's understood and he will find that the people generally will be willing to tighten their belts and dig deeper in their pocketbooks to help pay the costs. There will be some grumbling but they will not only go on short rations but will offer the pick of the country's manhood if necessary." When Hitler boasted about the strength of the Axis powers compared to the weakness of any combination of democracies, the *News* reminded the community that Germans, like most Europeans, didn't understand the "spiritual might of a free people.... Although we scrap among ourselves," Huntley wrote, "yet there is a unity when danger threatens that dictators cannot understand."[4]

The might and unity Huntley referenced was coming together. Soon this powerful force would sweep before it people like Don Beerbower.

The outbreak of war in September 1939 did not materially affect Don's life. He continued his full-time employment at the creamery. When Don had time off, he enjoyed a variety of activities. That fall he and his brother, Darrel, hunted with Ed Skinner, a family friend who happened to be part-American Indian. Ed and his wife lived across Hill Lake in an area known as Eastside. The Skinners had once been neighbors of the Beerbowers. After Ed lost his job at the National Woodenware Company, he had decided to try farming. The older man and the boys enjoyed hunting ducks, geese, ruffed grouse, and white tail deer.[5] Perhaps Don's most successful hunt happened when he shot an eight-point buck in the Willow River meadows near Hay Point, south of Hill City.[6]

During the Christmas holidays of 1939, Don and others his age gathered at the Kutcher farm in Spang Township. Anna Kutcher liked to open her home to young people. She had been a 4-H leader for many years and enjoyed hosting her daughter Elayne's friends. Bill Kutcher built a new home in 1939. The construction boards came from pine trees he cut on their land.[7]

Kutcher farm house - Spang Township, Itasca County, Minnesota

The third anniversary of Boy Scout Troop 53 occurred in January 1940. As an eighteen-year-old, Don was no longer eligible to be a scout. Leadership changes in the group had continued, however, and that winter he accepted the assistant scoutmaster position under Leslie Carter, a local attorney. The troop now included twenty-five boys. The guidance the organization received from these two men pleased Gay Huntley. In the spring, he reported the scouts were busy with "lots of activities."[8]

In the years Don participated in scouting, the *News* never reported a Hill City youngster achieving the honor of becoming an Eagle Scout. Yet, Darrel Beerbower, Marshall Hankerson, and friend Clark Rice all state Don achieved this distinction.[9]

With summer came baseball. Don played first base for Hill City in 1940. He batted a respectable .270 on a town team made up of some of the fellows from the successful 1932 Junior American Legion ball club. The players included Lee Mykkanen, Marvin Weller, and Sailer brothers Chet and Archie. His friend Billy Johnston played beside him at second base and his old mascot pal Paul Boleman filled in as a utility player. With a record of 17-4, the team gained a league championship and second place in the regional tournament.[10] In addition to baseball, Don liked playing golf with his father and brother at the Pokegama Golf Course between Grand Rapids and Hill City.[11] Don's participation in sports, including hunting, helped in the development of his hand-eye coordination, a skill he would find useful in the future.

Hill City town team baseball - Archie, Joe, and Chet Sailer

For a number of months there had been a new interest in Don's life. His friendship with Elayne Kutcher, which went back to childhood visits between their families and participation together in church activities and social gatherings with other young people, was developing into a serious romance. They enjoyed going to the movies at the Gem Theater and the Rialto in Grand Rapids, dances at the American Legion Club, baseball games, and summer events like the Independence Day celebration in Hill City. Work didn't keep them apart either. Every few days Don hauled a load of hundred-pound tubs of butter to Duluth in one of his father's enclosed, single/tandem trucks. Elayne often rode along with Don. She loved going with him on these day trips to the big port city.[12]

Elayne Kutcher

It wasn't always easy for Elayne to get away. The Kutcher farm had grown to four hundred eighty acres of fields, pasture, and timber. Everyone helped with the chores. Elayne drove her father's Series B John Deere tractor when needed, milked cows, helped process five hundred chickens each year, and assisted with planting and harvesting the potato seed crop, which was sold to the Farmers' Seed and Nursery at Faribault, Minnesota. In thinking back about the chores, Elayne said, "If I never see another rock or hay rack to fill, I'll not miss it! We picked rocks forever it seemed." Electricity did not reach the farm until after the war.[13]

In the fall of 1940, Don began a two-year creamery operator course at Iowa State College in Ames, thirty miles north of Des Moines. This program qualified students for positions as "butter, cheese, and ice cream makers, milk plant operators, or managers of dairy plants."[14] Because Clarence and Josie Beerbower expected their son to help run the family business, Don planned to return to

Hill City after completion of his studies. It came as no surprise that Don's parents supported his attending college in Ames. They had been raised in that part of Iowa and had regular contacts with family there. During Don's childhood, his aunt and uncle, Elizabeth and Wayne Beerbower, and cousins, Ben and David, resided in Des Moines. Also, his grandmother, Lula Beerbower, and aunt, Marie Snyder, lived nearby at Norwalk and Cumming.[15]

Dairy Building - Iowa State College 1941

The decision for Don to attend Iowa State had one major drawback: he and Elayne would be separated from each other for months at a time. Sending Don off to college also meant one less helper at the creamery. Clarence and Josie resolved this problem by hiring Darrel and Arlene for twenty dollars per week, Monday through Saturday. Darrel earned fourteen dollars and Arlene six. In addition, the parents agreed to send Darrel to Iowa State in 1941.[16]

In September Congress passed the Burke-Wadsworth Act. It was the first peacetime conscription law in American history. With the German Luftwaffe and the British Royal Air Force (RAF) locked in deadly aerial combat over the skies of England, the United States rushed to train its men for war. All males between the ages of twenty-one and thirty-five were required to register for the draft. Of these, eight hundred thousand would be inducted for military training.[17] The population of Hill City had bounced back a little to six hundred forty-one people. On October 16, one hundred of its sons registered at the fire hall.[18] Conscription created a conundrum for those eligible for military training. Was it better for a man to wait out the draft—gambling his number would not be drawn in the national lottery—or enlist? If he enlisted, he had some assurance of his job assignment in the service. It was a difficult choice. This decision did not require the immediate attention of nineteen-year-old Don Beerbower.

At Ames, Don found a place to stay in a rooming house located at 2717 West Street. He was fortunate to be living by another creamery operator major, Glenn J. McKean from Dolliver, Iowa.[19] They soon became fast friends. Don concentrated on his studies—English, physical education and three dairy industry classes. He ended his first quarter with a grade point average of 2.87, with 4.0 being "straight A" work. This compared favorably with his high school GPA of 2.83.[20]

I.S.C. Creamery Operator students Don M. Beerbower and Glenn J. McKean

When Don returned to Hill City for the Christmas holidays, he and Elayne became engaged. They did not set a wedding date. Don would continue at Iowa State and Elayne at Itasca Junior College, where she was taking a business course.[21]

After completing the winter quarter, Don returned home again in late March for a short break.[22] During the spring quarter he worked off campus to gain practical experience in the creamery business. This he did in Cedar Rapids, Iowa. That summer Don gained additional knowledge of the dairy industry through employment at the Wapsie Valley Creamery in Independence, Iowa.[23]

American sympathy for the resilient British and their few remaining allies became more evident in the spring of 1941 when Congress passed the Lend-Lease Act. The new law gave Great Britain and other countries access to billions of dollars worth of military equipment and other needed supplies to use against the Axis powers. In June Congress expanded conscription to include draft registration for all males between eighteen and twenty-one. As more and more young men from the area went into the military, Gay Huntley made an offer to the families and friends of these individuals. He wrote, "The editor will meet you half way on any subscription for the boys at camp. . . . The boys who are in training may be called on to go to war so let's do all we can for them." A subscription to the *News* was a buck fifty per year, down a half-dollar from the 1910 price. Several weeks later Huntley announced: "The American Legion voted to take advantage of the offer of the *News* for subscriptions at half price. . . . The 'boys' . . . having been through the experience of training and war know the value of messages from the home town so they decided to do a fine thing. . . ." But Huntley stubbornly refused to accept the inevitability of war. He closed his editorial with these words: "We are in favor of letting the British have munitions, etc. but we have ever been opposed to participation in this war and we see no reason for changing that opinion."[24]

In late August Don returned home from Iowa. His job at the Wapsie Valley Creamery had ended. One of the things on his mind during the brief interlude before starting his second year of college was his interest in becoming a U.S. Army Aviation Cadet. Aerial flight fascinated many youngsters in the twenties and thirties, including Don.[25] He had grown-up during an era when American pilots like Jimmy Doolittle, Amelia Earhart, Charles Lindbergh, Wiley Post, and Eddie Rickenbacker had become household names. The war in Europe brought military aviation to the forefront as well. During Don's first year at Iowa State, the RAF had won a convincing victory over the Luftwaffe in the Battle of Britain. Americans followed this struggle with keen interest. The public also learned through newspaper stories about the exploits of American volunteer pilots serving in special RAF Eagle Squadrons. In addition, Hill City already sported several military pilots. Two of these men were Don's friends and Itasca Junior College graduates, Morley Christensen and Billy Johnston. In the fall of 1941 they received their pilot's rating. Second Lieutenant Christensen and Ensign Johnston were assigned respectively to Army and Navy air units in the Pacific.[26]

Don did not discuss with Elayne his desire to enlist.[27] She and his parents expected him to finish his two-year creamery operator course and then return to Hill City to help in the family business. Don, Darrel, and Arlene left for Iowa State in September 1941. The three found an apartment to share at 241 North Hyland. Arlene soon secured employment at the college.[28]

Back in school, Don was reunited with his friend Glenn McKean. Glenn, two years older than Don, had grown up on a farm in Emmet County, Iowa, a few miles south of the Minnesota state line. Like Don, he was a Methodist. In the four quarters Don and Glenn spent on campus, they took exactly the same classes.[29] Even though their living arrangements had changed, the friends were together throughout the day. This gave them ample opportunity to discuss their mutual interest in becoming military pilots.

Darrel and Don Beerbower at 241 North Hyland, Ames, Iowa, Fall 1941

Within weeks of his return to Ames, Don decided to submit an application for entrance into the aviation cadet program. The application required a flight physical. This was completed on October 21 by Captain William Moore, Medical Corps. The doctor's examination notes stated Don had contracted measles and mumps during childhood and had fractured his nose. He had received the injury during a scuffle with his brother three years earlier. Other than this, he was in excellent health. Captain Moore qualified Don for flying duty.[30]

On November 6 Gay Huntley reported that the American Legion had organized a women's auxiliary. Josie Beerbower, long active in civic affairs such as the school board, was elected first vice president. Huntley noted, "The new auxiliary has the honor of having a Gold Star Mother, Mrs. W. Carter, as a member." Her son had been killed in World War I. Mrs. Carter would not be the last Gold Star Mother in the new auxiliary.

Also in this issue of the *News*, Huntley printed letters from three servicemen who expressed to him how much they appreciated receiving their hometown paper. In one letter, former American Legion baseball player James Sawday wrote from California, "Just a few lines to thank you and the American Legion Post for sending me the [paper]. . . . I have been here six months now and consider myself very fortunate getting in such a nice camp. . . . Had a card from Roland [Vashaw] a few days ago and he is only about fifty miles from here receiving his primary training for cadets."

Thus began a new feature in the *News* that continued throughout the war. Servicemen and women would write directly to Huntley telling him about their assignments. He in turn published excerpts of the letters on the front page of the paper. Because all military personnel were mailed the News, this became a convenient way for them to stay in touch with each other during the war.

In November, Huntley's mind was also on his annual Thanksgiving editorial column. A profoundly religious man, he did not let Thanksgiving, Christmas, or Easter pass without reflecting on the spiritual significance of the day. On the eve of the United States entry into the Second World War, he quoted Psalm 46, verses 1-3, 7:

> God is our refuge and strength,
> a very present help in trouble.
> Therefore we will not fear . . .
> though the mountains shake . . .
> The Lord of hosts is with us . . .

And then he added, "In these days when the world is torn with strife and trouble as a result of mankind forgetting to conscientiously ask for Divine guidance, it is time that there be a spiritual awakening among the people, for only by such an awakening can order be restored to a world of chaos."[31]

Huntley did not realize the American people were on the cusp of a great stirring. This awakening would be much different than what he had in mind. When aircraft from the Japanese Imperial Fleet struck Pearl Harbor on December 7, 1941, a shocked nation responded first with outrage and then a united desire to crush its enemy. The *News* ran the story of the "unprovoked attack" on December 11, the same day Germany and Italy declared war on the United States. Huntley reported that recruiting stations were being mobbed by men wanting to enlist: "In all branches enlistments have been from 10 to 100 times greater than normal. . . . The *Hill City News* is enlisted in this war and we pledge unqualified support of President Roosevelt and Congress in every way possible." Congress extended the period of service for all military personnel through the duration of the war, plus six months. Within a few weeks, Huntley, Clarence Beerbower, Frank Dichtel, Joe Sailer, and all the other men in town between the ages of forty-four and sixty-five were required by law to register their names with the government. This solemn event took place at the fire hall.[32]

Don Beerbower finished the fall term in December with a GPA of 3.38, his best in four quarters at Iowa State.[33] He and Glenn McKean parted for the Christmas break, both heading for their homes. Don had many things on his mind when he returned to Hill City. He was two quarters shy of completing his coursework and only a few months away from a job in the family business that would qualify him for a military deferment. Don had a fiancée waiting for him as well. In the end, his desire to join the Army Air Corps outweighed everything else. Many months later Don referred to this in a letter he wrote to his brother. At the time, Darrel was trying to decide whether to apply for the aviation cadets or continue working until he was drafted. Don wrote, "I know you don't want to get in as bad as I did or you'd be in too." And then he added, "Elayne and her folks were all against it too but they've swung over to my way of thinking instead of me swinging to theirs."[34] Clarence and Josie Beerbower also had hopes and dreams for their youngest son's future, but for now these were placed on hold. Don left Hill City for Ames on Saturday, January 3, 1942. His intention was to enlist in the Army.[35]

5

For Thee They Died

War is a question of who screws up the least. . . . It seems to me the thing that the enemy did badly was strategic thinking. Like Hitler, for example, taking on the Russians before he had things settled on the Western Front. Like Japan, before Pearl Harbor. There was only one nation in the whole world that could challenge Japan. . . . No other power but us could do it, and yet they chose to pick a fight with us. And then they make an alliance with a virulent racist who wouldn't have given them the time of day once things were straightened up.

William C. Healy, B-17 pilot
(interview with the author)

Gloom hung over much of humanity in 1942. Most of Europe and parts of North Africa were in the grip of German and Italian forces. In the Far East the Rising Sun cast a shadow from Kiska in the Aleutians to Nanking, China, from Tarawa in the Gilberts to Guadalcanal in the Solomons, across New Guinea, Java, Sumatra, and beyond to Rangoon, Burma. In the first six months of the year, German submarines sank three hundred eighty-two ships in Canadian, American, and Caribbean waters.[1] Packs of these U-boats prowled the North Atlantic, attacking convoys bound for Allied ports in the British Isles and northern Russia. Yet, in this most dismal year of America's involvement in the war, there were positive accomplishments. The aircraft carrier *Hornet* delivered Colonel Jimmy Doolittle, the commanding officer of sixteen B-25 Mitchell bombers and crews, to within striking distance of Tokyo. In addition, the Allies blocked Axis expansion in the Coral Sea, at Midway, El Alamein, and Stalingrad.

In 1942 American factories produced 47,859 military and special-purpose aircraft.[2] These airplanes needed pilots.

After returning to Ames, Iowa, Don Beerbower and Glenn McKean talked with college staff about their decision to enlist in the Army Air Corps. Their transcripts note that an "order to settle" was completed on January 16, 1942.[3]

North American B-25 Mitchell bomber departing Hornet *for Tokyo April 18, 1942*

Leaving the campus for the last time, they passed near Memorial Union. When undergraduates and faculty used the busy north entrance of this student center, they passed through the solemn confines of Gold Star Hall. Beside them, stone columns stood like sentinels between stained glass windows through which light emanated a spectrum of colors that surrounded the chamber. People customarily removed their hats in respectful tribute to those whose names were engraved beside a gold star in the limestone walls. These were the Iowa State students who had died in World War I. A quotation from poet John Drinkwater graced the space over the entrance to the north door:

> For Thee they died
> Master and Maker, God of Right
> The Soldier dead are at Thy gate
> Who kept the spears of honor bright
> And Freedom's house inviolate.[4]

In the coming years the small constellation of gold stars would burst forth into a galaxy of fallen alumni.

Don reported for his physical at Fort Des Moines on January 22. His height, 5 foot 7½ inches, and his weight, 152 pounds, placed him slightly below the average for an airman in 1942, 5 foot 9 inches and 154.3 pounds.[5] Records describe him as having a medium complexion with dark brown hair and gray eyes. Upon completion of his examination, Major Robert A. Culbritson, Medical Corps, found Don "mentally and physically qualified for service in the Army of the United States."[6]

Don returned to Fort Des Moines on January 23. He met with First Lieutenant Alfred J. Ludwig, Infantry, to complete an application for enlistment. The information Don provided the recruiting officer gave his age as twenty years four months, and Davidson, Saskatchewan, as his place of birth. He acknowledged his American citizenship, white race, fourteen years of schooling, and that he had no dependents. He declared he had never been charged with a felony or been imprisoned and had never used illegal drugs, suffered from venereal disease, wet the bed during adolescence, spat up blood, or suffered any illness or injury requiring hospitalization. Then Don signed a Declaration of Applicant form acknowledging that he could later be subject of a court-martial if any of his statements proved false. Private Jerome T. Walsh witnessed Don's signature. Enlistment was scheduled for the following day.[7]

Joining the military in wartime is a life-changing event. Did Don question his decision? Certainly his affection for Elayne was strong. To draw away from the power of love is very difficult. Even though Don wanted to do his share in the national crisis, he would have had some anxiety about what lay ahead. Moving from the civilian world to that of the Army meant coming under the control of an organization where failure or disobedience led to serious consequences; where courage was challenged; where lives were lost. But Don understood the growing danger America faced from her enemies. Devastating German U-boat attacks against coastal shipping began off the East Coast on January 12, and the Japanese continued their rapid expansion southward toward Australia and westward to the Indian Ocean. In the Philippines, enemy forces had cut off thousands of American and Filipino soldiers at Bataan and Corregidor. With the nation's security in the balance, Don and many of his countrymen chose military service.

On January 24, Don completed his final enlistment document at Fort Des Moines. It stated he agreed to serve in the Army of the United States for the duration of the war plus six months. He gave the following oath:

> I do solemnly swear that I will bear true faith and allegiance to the United States of America; that I will serve them honestly and faithfully against all their enemies whomsoever; and that I will obey the orders of the President of the United States, and the orders of the officers appointed over me, according to the rules and articles of war.

Don's first act as an enlisted man involved naming his father as his beneficiary and as the person he wanted notified in case of an emergency. He then received a fifteen-day furlough.[8] Don wasted little time in traveling to Hill City to see Elayne and his parents. He arrived there on January 26. Home never looked better, even in the dead of winter. His grandmother, Lula Beerbower, was staying with his parents, so he was able to see her during his leave. He also spent time at the Kutcher farm. On Sunday February 1, Don and Elayne and his parents and grandmother drove to Grasston, Minnesota, one hundred five miles distant, to visit his sister Lavaun, her husband Marshall Hankerson, and their daughter, JoNett. Lavaun and JoNett then returned with them to Hill City for a few days. Don left many sad and anxious loved ones behind when he returned to Iowa on February 5.[9]

On February 9, Private Beerbower and Private McKean received orders to report to a replacement training center at Higley Field, Arizona, for service in the Army Air Corps.[10] During their time at Higley Field, the base received a new name, Williams Field. The one-year-old facility was located thirty miles southeast of Phoenix, near Chandler.[11] Don and Glenn were housed together with others in large tents.[12] At Williams Field, their orientation to military life began in earnest with the issuing of clothing, learning basic Army protocol, and a flight physical. Any recruit failing to pass this examination found himself screened out of the aviation cadet program or delayed at Williams Field until his health-related problem improved. Don completed his flight physical on February 11. The examiner noted the stocky twenty-year-old had had whooping cough, chicken pox, measles, and tonsillitis as a child, and that his tonsils were removed in 1939. Don denied any history of air, sea, swing, or train sickness. The dental exam revealed his wisdom teeth and his eyetooth on the right side were missing. Major Steven V. Guzak, Medical Corps, stated Don met the physical requirements for pilot training. He happily accepted an upgrade from Private Beerbower to Aviation Cadet Beerbower and assignment to Class 42-H. On February 24, he and Glenn departed Williams Field for Santa Ana Army Air Base at Costa Mesa, California, a few miles southeast of Los Angeles.[13]

Santa Ana Army Air Base had been activated on February 23, 1942, as the Army's third classification and preflight training center. Maxwell Field, Alabama, and Randolph Field, Texas, hosted the other centers. Santa Ana ranked as the largest of the three bases, with eight hundred buildings spread over 1,300 acres. Here cadets received their classification as navigators, bombardiers, or pilots. Barracks replaced tents for housing.[14] Don and Glenn roomed together again. When Don had some free time, he enjoyed spending it with Stanley F. "Ace" Olson and with Glenn, whom he called Mac. Don said they were like the three musketeers.[15] Their classes at Santa Ana included mathematics, signals, plane identification, semaphore code, and the manual of arms. They also had athletics and many hours of drill.[16] The training officers pushed the cadets hard during preflight. The Army wanted loyalty to the group, not to the individual; attention to detail, not carelessness; and instant obedience to commands, not hesitation.

The pressure inherent in preflight eliminated a few cadets. As with each phase of pilot training, some washed out. For both Don and Glenn, it had gone well. On March 28, after successfully completing the four-week course at Santa Ana, the two pilot candidates received orders to report to the Air Force Training Detachment at Glendale, Arizona, for primary flying school.[17]

6

Wow!

Great pilots are made not born. . . . A man may possess good eyesight, sensitive hands, and perfect coordination, but the end product is only fashioned by steady coaching, much practice, and experience.

John E. Johnson, Group Captain, RAF
Full Circle–The Tactics of Air Fighting

As the aircraft moved forward with a roar, the instructor pilot gave the engine increasing amounts of throttle until the tail wheel finally lifted off the ground. Simultaneously, the Stearman's nose dropped forward allowing the student pilot in the front seat of the primary trainer to see down the runway. The air swirled around their faces as the ship gained speed. As the instructor applied gentle back pressure on the stick, the nose came up and the pilots felt a slight bump. The PT-17 had transitioned into flight. They were airborne. What a feeling! It was one thing to desire to fly. It was another to actually experience it. After one of his first training flights, Don Beerbower expressed it this way in a letter written on April 7, 1942, to his brother Darrel and sister-in-law Arlene, "Johnson showed me how to do stalls and spins today–Wow!"

America was unprepared for war when it began in Europe in 1939. Fortunately, before the attack on Pearl Harbor, the United States had two years to begin building up its military forces. Aviation received much attention during this period as military leaders realized the need for a strong, flexible Army Air Corps. They had been impressed by the innovative way the Germans used the Luftwaffe to support ground forces in a new form of warfare known as *blitzkrieg*. The American leadership also learned much by monitoring how the German and British combatants utilized their fighter and bomber forces during the Battle of Britain. One of the conclusions reached during the lead-up to the American entrance into the war was the need to replace the name "air corps" with "air forces." In Army jargon a corps was a title for a much smaller unit than the military envisioned for the future needs of the expanded air service. Even though the change to Army Air Forces occurred on June 20, 1941,

Cadet Don Beerbower beside a PT-17 Stearman

throughout the war most pilots stuck with the old name, Army Air Corps.

Global war required many aircraft and a huge pool of pilots. There simply were not enough training facilities and military instructors available to meet the demand. Consequently, the military brokered deals to use community airports and signed contracts with private companies to teach aviation cadets the basics of flying. This was the case with the new training center located at Glendale, Arizona, a few miles northwest of Phoenix.

The Army established flying schools mainly in the southern and western parts of the United States, where mild weather allowed for year-round use. The airport at Glendale had been designed by artist Millar Sheets. It resembled the mythic American Indian bird of thunder; thus the name, Thunderbird Field.[1] The contract to provide primary training was with Southwest Airways. Each of their instructors started with six students. Discipline remained with the Army.[2]

Don soloed in less than average time in the Boeing PT-17 Stearman, a sturdy biplane equipped with a two-hundred-twenty-horsepower Continental radial engine.[3] The aircraft cruised at just over a hundred miles per hour. Nicknamed Kaydet by the Canadians, the Stearman entered Army service in 1936. Cloth covered the PT-17's metal tubular fuselage and wooden wings. The stu-

Postcard photograph of Boeing PT-17 Stearman trainers at Thunderbird Field

Dear Kids,
 This is what I'm flying. I've had a sorethroat & cold in my chest yesterday & today and couldn't go up. Tomorrow I'm going to solo though! I'm pretty sure of it unless I get "off the ball". I'll write too. Love Don

Mr & Mrs. D. W. Beerbower
129 Franklin
Danville,
Illinois

Postcard message from Don to Darrel and Arlene

dent pilot sat in tandem in front of the instructor in this open cockpit airplane. Because of the Stearman's tail dragging characteristic, the pilots couldn't see directly down the runway until enough airspeed accrued to lift the rear wheel off the ground. The instructor and the student communicated through a flexible tube known as a gosport.[4]

The cadets needed to solo in twelve hours or they failed the program. Beginning with takeoffs, landings, and straight and level flight, student pilots quickly advanced to emergency procedures, aerobatics, and cross-country flying. Each cadet also spent many hours in ground school, athletics, and drill.[5]

Ten days after arriving at Thunderbird Field, Don explained to Darrel and Arlene some of the things expected of him in primary flying school.

> 4/7/42
> Dear Kids
> I just got your address, so I guess I'd better get busy while I have a chance. I'm out on the flight line and have already done my flying for today. I had classes this morning and athletics. . . .
> After being here this long, I can see why it's so much harder to fly Army style than just free style. Every maneuver has just one set way to be done. Any variation is wrong and you catch h___. For instance, the landing on our field. You come into the pattern at 500 ft. and at a direction so a 45 degree turn brings you in the opposite direction you want to land. Then you drop to 200 ft. in two gliding 90 degree turns and come in and land, finally. Fun eh?
> I'm sure that it would really be fun to just play around with a plane out in a pasture though! This way, it's work, and mighty exhausting. I love it though.
> We have two tests tomorrow! In engine and in Theory of Flight. They are really going to be duezzies! We had one in Math last Friday and I got 79! 70 was passing. I was really off the ball on a couple of catch problems. . . .
> I must sign off now and get busy. Write soon.
> Love Don

The Army had originally designated Don as a member of Class 42-H, but during preflight at Santa Ana Army Air Base he was reassigned to Class 42-I. The number of the class represented the year, and the letter symbolized the month in the year when the class was scheduled to graduate from flying school.

Since "I" is the ninth letter of the alphabet, Class 42-I expected to graduate in September 1942. Every thirty days a new group of cadets began primary. The students were known as dodos until they flew solo. Each phase of flying school—primary, basic, and advanced—lasted approximately sixty days.

As Don's training continued, he faced challenges to his judgment and his ability to react to an unanticipated situation. Since Don had already soloed, he was spending time alone in the Stearman. With this came an increased-but-necessary risk to him and other student pilots. Don felt comfortable writing to Darrel and Arlene about his close calls. He was careful about telling others about them. He did not want to worry his parents and Elayne.

> 4/26/42
> Dear Sis and Brother
> This won't be much, but enough to let you know I'm thinkin' of ya! I liked Arlene's letter last week. What's the matter with you Darrel? Sore arm I suppose. . . .
> Our upper class left Friday and the dodos came in yesterday so now I'm an upperclassman! I'm a platoon sergeant and pretty proud but it's going to be a headache in a lot of ways. Good experience though.
> I flew one hour of dual and 2 hours of solo Friday. That gets to be work after the first 2 hours in a wind like we had. It was gusty and made maneuvers hard and rough. Fun though. My first spin solo was quite a thrill. It takes a little nerve to pull it up into a stall and then kick it over and head straight down in a fast spiral when the instructor isn't there to help you get it out if you have trouble. After the first one, it's fun.
> It's easier to land when the instructor isn't watching too. I've been dropping it in about 5 feet when he's along. It's okay as long as you make it 3 points, but if you don't get the stick way back before you hit, he really gives (you) me h___! I don't guess I've written to you about my ground loop. The folks don't know. On my second solo, I had a strong cross wind and didn't drop my wing into it. When I hit bottom (That's the way I described my landings then!) the wind got under the wing and the first thing I knew, I was going along the ground 40 miles an hour with one wing dragging on the ground. Me in there all alone fighting the controls trying to get the wing back up. My instructor really gave me heck at first but after he had me scared enough, he admitted that I did

pretty good, considering the wind I had to contend with. They cut out solos 15 minutes later because of it. There were 9 ground loops that morning. More fun!

From now on, we'll fly about 3 hours a day besides ground school etc. etc. Today we marched 2½ hours! Yesterday, 8 miles around the field; last Tuesday, from 7:30 to 9:30 [p.m.] Final test in Engines next day. Nice eh?

I gotta close now kids. Write lots. Please!!!
Don

At Thunderbird Field, Don and Glenn McKean were separated into different companies within Class 42-I. This happened because the Army assigned cadets alphabetically by company. Since Beerbower was at the beginning of the alphabet, Don was placed with student pilots whose names began with A and B. He became good friends with some of these men. Two of them, Harvey J. "Frenchy" Bevier from Westbrook, Minnesota, and Harry E. "Bish" Bisher, went all the way through flying school with him. He served with others like William Y. "Willie Y." Anderson throughout his time in the military. Although Don and Glenn did not see quite as much of each other, they still occasionally found opportunities to do things together.[6] As Don gained experience and confidence, he was developing a passion for flying; it was as much fun as it was work. To no small degree, his instructor deserved credit for much of this.

5/19/42
Dear Kids
. . . I'm just about finished here! I've taken and passed my final, 60 hour check ride. Last Friday. I took my cross-country flight today. Only 64 miles but at least I got to see some of the country 'fore I leave. I have less than two hours left to fly now. I'll probably finish tomorrow. Then I'll have sometime to spare. I hope. . .

We have to have a minimum of 23 hours of dual time out of our 60 hours here and I needed 31 minutes today to make it so Johnson told me we'd finish it after I got back from C.C. He got in and said to go up and do what ever I wanted to. He was just going along to get my dual in. So–I had fun. I tried everything I'd ever heard of. I pulled an inverted split S on him–first one I ever tried and I came out much better than I expected to. I had quite a time convincing him that I hadn't been practicing it. We aren't supposed to try anything our instructor hasn't shown us how to do.

I did two snap rolls and a slow roll and came out in a plain split

S. But I lost so much altitude, I had to quit cause I hadn't enough time to climb back up. It was really fun.

The snap rolls are fun but the slow rolls are a honey cause the engine won't keep running long enough to go clear over [on] these old buggies. Then the nose starts to drop and you have to shove the stick way forward and try to keep the thing rolling straight with the rudders while your feet are doing their damnedest to come up around your neck. All this happens while you're hanging by the safety belt. Quite a busy moment. It's quite easy to do a slow roll, but the idea is to hold the nose on a point on the horizon–That's where the trouble comes!

Now that I'm about done here and know for sure that I'll go to Basic, I can hardly wait to get going. About 4 months more of this and I'll be done. It's going to be an awful long time! I'd give anything to see you guys. . . .

We had open post last weekend. I played a round of golf with Glenn Sunday morning, 18 holes–84. Believe it or not! It's an easy course but I was hot for some reason. I got one drive of over 250 yds. I had to rent the clubs but we got there at 6:30 in the morning and I got a swell set. We play for half price, being in uniform. Nice eh?

I don't think there's much more to write now. So I'll close. It's about time for lights out anyway. In fact, I'm going to have to hurry. Write lots.

Love Don

Aerobatics

Separation from those Don cherished made him homesick. He had been away from family members and Elayne for several months at a stretch while in college, but then he always knew a date when he was returning to Hill City. In the Army it was different; a furlough for him drifted far beyond the horizon. Don had to accept this. The daily routine of mail call and letter writing provided a critical emotional link with those he loved.

5/25/42
Dear Arlene and Darrel

Well, I finally got a note from Darrel. Don't mind me, brother, I'm just so darn lonesome lately that I never get enough word from home. I just finished reading it and just to show you I can, I'm answering right now!

I just finished getting my clearance papers all checked on and I'm ready to go anytime. We'll leave Wed. to Minter Field, Cal. I guess. I'll drop you all a card as soon as I have my new address for sure. Okay? Okay! . . .

I was into Phoenix yesterday noon with Glenn. Played 18 holes of golf, 91. Wait till I get you and Dad on a course again. I'm getting good! Not bragging, of course!

. . . It's been around 105 degrees here almost every day for the last two weeks. Last Friday, I believe. Over 110 degrees once. . . . It cools off about 1:00 [a.m.]. till about 5:00 [a.m.]. It's been 96 degrees at 9:00 P.M. though. We have a cooling system in the barracks so it isn't too bad!

I hate to think of coming back here to Luke Field later for Advanced training though. It'll be up around 120 degrees then. I can't imagine the old sun getting any hotter, but I guess it does. . . .

I gotta go eat dinner now. Be back in a flash.

Just for the fun of it–here's our dinner, Liver-n-onions, hot rolls, lettuce salad, iced tea, strawberry short cake–potatoes and butter! Pretty good eh? Yes!!. . .

I don't know much more to write about. I'm sure anxious to get into a B.T. (basic trainer) and see what it feels like. We'll have 450 H.P. there instead of 220 as in our P.T.'s. And only one wing. My instructor was telling me some of the things we'd have to watch when taking one of them off. Propeller pitch, wing flap setting, mixture control and throttle, tachometer, air speed indicator, oil pressure and temperature and fuel pressure! There are probably a few more but I guess those are the important ones.

Ought to be exciting eh?!! We'll have a lot of cross-country flying there. Very few acrobatics unless we decide to do it off the record. They're pretty dangerous in a B.T. though.

I better close. Write lots.

Your brother Don

Forty-two percent of Class 42-I did not complete primary flying school. The weeding-out process had begun in earnest. Friends separated, never to see each other again. Don believed he was leaving the "country club" of primary flying schools. To him the civilian instructors at Thunderbird Field had been great. Now he and Glenn headed for Minter Field near Bakersfield, California, for basic flying school. Here things would be different. "It was," Don later wrote, "like going back in the Army."[7]

7

A Dark Day

Minter was an Army base. Here, the instructors were Army officers and there was more discipline . . . There were roughly 230 of us, flying formation, doing acrobatics and night flying, learning instrument flying in the aft cockpit under a hood . . . I remember the food being super, the hours being long, and being confined to quarters for half of the two-month stay because of an outbreak of mumps.

Clarence E. Anderson, student pilot
To Fly and Fight

Bakersfield is in the horseshoe-shaped, southern end of the San Joaquin Valley. It is a semi-arid region in California immediately west of the Mojave Desert. Minter Field, thirteen miles northwest of town, experienced many cloud-free days per year. By 1942 the Army had developed this base into the largest training facility of its type on the West Coast. It was home to seven thousand personnel. Nine auxiliary landing strips were needed to accommodate the many student pilots practicing in the Vultee BT-13 Valiant, an all-metal, fixed-gear monoplane with an enclosed cockpit.[1] Gone was the gosport. The instructor and the student communicated by intercom. Unlike the Stearman, the BT-13 had a radio. Its 450-horsepower Pratt and Whitney Wasp Junior nine-cylinder radial engine produced a maximum speed of one hundred eighty miles per hour.[2]

Vultee BT-13 Valient

On May 28, Aviation Cadets Don Beerbower and Glenn McKean reported to the Air Force Basic Flying School at Minter Field. Here the two friends were again split up by alphabet. This kept Don with Willie Y. Anderson, Frenchy Bevier, Bish Bisher and others, but also added a new friend, Clarence E. "Andy" [later Bud] Anderson from California. Their squadron commander was First Lieutenant "Grump" Grumbles. The cadets quickly processed and then hurried out to the flight line where Don met his new instructor, Second Lieutenant W. C. Stewart.[3]

With the war going badly in 1942, there was little time to waste. Army officers pushed the men hard. The fast pace would tire students and instructors, add stress, and in some situations produce serious consequences. Don described the increased pace of activity in a brief letter to Darrel and Arlene written a few days after his arrival at Minter Field.

> 6-8-42
> Dear Kids
>   I think you owe me a letter but I have a spare minute so I'll start one. It's 5:50 [a.m.] I've had breakfast and have my room cleaned up. Waiting for drill call. We'll drill for an hour, then athletics for an hour, link trainer for an hour and then ground school till noon. From 1 to 7 this afternoon we'll be on the flight line. That's our daily schedule. Sundays and all, so far.
>   Both my roommates are in the hospital so I have to clean up the room all alone. One has appendicitis and the other one has mumps. . . .
>   I've got about 12 or 14 hours in the B.T. now. Soloed it in 3½ hours. Some of the guys still haven't soloed. Glenn is getting along

okay. I saw him for the second time since we got here. He was at the mess hall this morning. We just don't have a spare minute to look up anyone. It's time for drill now!

[Later] Another morning is gone. I'd give $5 if I could curl up in the nest for about 48 hours.

I don't know much to write about and I have to get ready for the flight line so I'll mail this. Write soon & lots.

Your loving brother Don

The next morning was a great day for flying. The ceiling and visibility were unlimited. Second Lieutenant Ralph A. Robedeau had been in the air since 7:30 a.m. with three of his four students, Aviation Cadets Mills, MacGregor, and McKinney. Each had flown an hour. At 10:30 a.m. it was Glenn McKean's turn. After Glenn checked the fuel and found it sufficient for the hour of dual training, he and Lieutenant Robedeau took off. A light wind blew from the northwest, and the temperature lingered at a mild seventy-six degrees as they began practicing in the vicinity of the Famosa air strip. At 10:55 a.m. student pilot Paul H. Kilpatrick made the following observation: "Shortly after takeoff from Famosa field and while at about 400 feet altitude I noticed an airplane descending quite rapidly. It was at an altitude of approximately 400 feet and about one and one-half miles away. Its path of descent was at an angle of about forty-five degrees. The nose did not seem to be sufficiently down for a steep glide and the wings seemed to flutter from side to side. This condition continued until the airplane struck the ground. The airplane did not go into a spin."

Ralph Robedeau and Glenn McKean were killed instantly as their BT-13A, #41-10931, slammed into the ground belly first.

On June 12 an Aircraft Accident Classification Committee concluded: "It is the opinion of the committee that the accident was the result of an error of judgment and carelessness or negligence on the part of the pilot. While instructing his student in simulated forced landings, the instructor apparently failed to use the degree of care which the circumstances justly demanded in permitting the airplane to become involved in a stall at an altitude too low to regain flying speed."[4]

When Don learned of Glenn's sudden death, it shook him to his core. He confided to Elayne that he was considering dropping out of pilot training. However, Don did not want her to tell his parents that he was thinking about quitting.[5] Several weeks later he wrote in his new diary: "My best friend and Buddy; who I had gone to school with, joined up with and had been with from the start was killed after only 2 weeks at Basic. Glenn McKean. –He was a good flyer and a great guy. It was a dark day when he and his instructor crashed."[6]

Large, congested training bases like Minter Field experienced numerous individual accidents and mid-air collisions. Many BT-13s shared the airspace around Minter's nine auxiliary landing strips. An instructor pilot had a difficult job. He was tasked with teaching students a variety of different procedures while at the same time monitoring the traffic in the area. Accidents were relatively common. During the war nearly fifteen thousand air crew members died in flying mishaps.[7]

Within a few days after Glenn's death, Don wrote to Darrel and Arlene. He had gotten over his initial shock of losing his friend.

6-18-42

Dear Sis and Bro

Well—seeing I finally got a letter out of that sweet little brother of mine, I'll keep my word and squeeze one in. I'm missing supper to do this so you'd both better answer—pronto. I have some fruit that will run me till breakfast—I hope.

About Glenn, the instructor and he were both killed. Two more got it today. These planes are [the] hardest and trickiest planes there are to fly safely. They are so darned heavy, 4500# and are underpowered for the weight, 450 H.P. They can stall out or spin without hardly any warning and lose 2000 feet just like that. If you get into a spin, the centrifugal force holds you down so you can't hardly get out. There—you asked for it—you've got it. No one knows how it happened and probably never will. If one is careful, it won't be very apt to happen. And I will be! So don't worry about me. I don't—so why should anyone else!!?? . . .

Monday we have a 250 mile cross-country with 4 stops. More fun. We also start formation flying and nite flying next week. I guess we'll fly in the afternoons and then about 3 or 4 hours at nite. Something tells me we're going to have a worse schedule next week than this. We go steady from [reveille] at 5 a.m. to Link trainer from 8 to 9 at night right now. We get a few minutes at noon and before supper. That's when I have to study and write letters—By the way—are you busier than that Darrel? I doubt it so you'd better get busy on some letters. Just write any old thing—you'd be surprised how much I'll enjoy it. . . .

I've got about 35 hours here now. Passed my 20 hour check ride O.K. last week. These ships are a cinch for me. 2 guys just soloed last week! Not bragging . . . gotta get busy. Write.

Love Don

Basic began to demand more of Don in terms of concentration and poise. In addition to long cross-country flights, Class 42-I was practicing formation flying and night landings. When Don flew in formation, he had to fix his attention on the BT-13 a few feet away from his trainer. Don's position was slightly above and slightly back from the lead aircraft. As he looked down and across the other Valiant, he kept the star insignia on the lead ship's opposite wing between the canopy and tail section so he could see it just above the fuselage. This gave the trailing plane about a three-foot radius of action to stay in position. Formation flying required Don to focus his eye alignment on the adjacent leading BT-13 while constantly making minor adjustments with his controls to hold position. An hour of formation flying was a very tiring exercise.[8]

Don wrote Darrel and Arlene about his night landings. Bringing an aircraft in after dark can be dangerous, especially for a novice pilot. It is easy to tighten up on the ship's controls instead of staying relaxed. This didn't seem to be a problem for Don.

6-27-42

Dear Darrel and Arlene

It's Saturday evening and here I sit! Our barracks is quarantined for mumps, so no open post for us. I'll get caught up on letter writing anyway. I think it was Wed. we were put under quarantine. Our only formations are for flying and eating. We aren't allowed out otherwise. I don't know how long it will last.

I've been flying 2 and 3 hours in the afternoons this week and then again at nite from 1½ to 3½ hours. Last nite I flew from 8:30 to 12:00, coming in for a landing about every 20 minutes. After 10 o'clock, the stage commander who calls us in for landings from our zones, had me making black out landings. More fun! He left a few of the runway markers on to show me where to go but I couldn't use my landing lights. The landing lights are about the size and strength of auto headlights and are built into the wing. It's fairly simple with them. On the black out landings though one just puts the plane into a 90 mph. glide and flies it till the front wheels hit and then hold it that way till one slows down so you can let the tail down. Then hop on the brakes before you run into the fence. I like them. The moon was bright last nite so it wasn't so bad but it's hard to judge distance in that light. . . .

Arlene, I couldn't think of anything nicer than living near you and Darrel. When a guy gets off at a place like this, with absolutely no old friends, he realizes how much that sort of thing really means . . .

Are you going to be able to get a vacation in Sept. so you can be home for a while when I go home? I sure hope so.

Elayne and I are kinda planning on being together a little during Advanced. I surely hope it works out! So–we may be married when we come home. I don't know for sure about it yet though. The more I see of the crashes and stuff around here, the more I figure–one only lives once–and maybe not for long. So why not enjoy one's self a little. Don't you guys agree?

I have to go to supper now. I'll mail this on the way. Keep those letters coming and I'll sure try to keep them answered.

Love Don

Don's decision to enlist in January had interrupted any plans he and Elayne had for marriage after his graduation from Iowa State. Now, Don was looking ahead to completion of advanced flying school in the fall as a possible time for a wedding in Hill City. He was also beginning to consider his post-flight-training options. On July 6 he mentions one possibility to Darrel and Arlene.

Dear Sis and Brother

I got your swell letter today and I really enjoyed it. All the rest of the flight are out finishing up their nite flying tonite . . . I'm all done nite flying–except for 2 hours of nite formation we'll all get toward the end of this week. . . .

I had a great Fourth of July! Still confined, of course. They let us out to march in the parade in Bakersfield and then we had to come right back–just our barracks. We flew [Link] trainer all our spare time Sat. and all day Sun. Trying to catch up on the time we miss during the week. Then, they let the trainers' air out over nite and the rest of the guys can use them for another week. . . .

So my big brother would like to give me a left jab. He'd better watch his step! I'm in pretty good shape these days! Weigh about 160 though I don't know how I hold my weight with all my perspiring. It runs up well over 100 degrees about every day here. One nice thing–an order came out today that we no longer have to wear our ties while on post. Quite a relief!

We go to advanced school on about the 26th of this month, but I don't know for [sure] where. If I go to pursuit, it'll probably be Luke Field back at Phoenix. If I'm to be an instructor, I'll probably go to Stockton, up the valley here a ways . . .

I changed instructors today. I'm flying with the assistant flight commander now. He's been kinda feeling me out, so to speak, as to how I'd like to be an instructor for 6 mo. or a year–or more if I get into it and like it. I'd like it for maybe a year to pile up some hours and really learn everything about flying but then I'm afraid I want to go across for some action.

Write lots!!! I really must close now,

Love Don

Don's training continued at a fast pace, and with it the mumps epidemic. Fortunately for him, he had had mumps as an adolescent. While others risked falling back to another class, he stayed on schedule with Class 42-I.

The flying skill Don developed in basic was beginning to show itself in the aerobatic maneuvers he was learning. A time arrives in flying when a pilot does something complicated, like a snap roll, and realizes he has done it without giving it any thought. When the pilot flies without thinking about what his hands and feet are doing with the controls, the airplane becomes an extension of the pilot. Man and machine merge. It is a joyous feeling. Don hadn't quite reached this apex, but he was getting close. He touched on this and other things in his last letter from Minter Field to Darrel and Arlene. It was written on Sunday evening, July 18.

Dear Kids

. . . I haven't much time so this won't be much. Half our barracks, me included, are confined again for being 30 seconds late for reveille. Our bell didn't ring and we'd been up till 11:00 the nite before at Link. Speed was waiting for us. Damn him anyway. We just got out of quarantine Wed. too. I got my Link time all finished up though. Rode it four hours today.

I'll finish my flying tomorrow. One hour of radio beam and 50 minutes of formation left. Had my instrument check yesterday. Passed okay. The Lt. told me before we went up what he wanted me to do. He took off and I went under the hood and did climbing turns up to 4000 then I did stalls, timed turns and steep turns; picked up a compass heading and held it for a while; then I did a spin. He didn't say a word all the time! We still had quite a bit of time before the period was over so he said we would have a little fun. I knew that he was pleased. He did a slow roll and shook the stick; I took over and did a honey–almost as good as his. So–I shakes the stick and he did a snap roll and shook the stick and I did one. We really had fun. Neither of us said a word. We did loops and immelmans and split s's and came on in and landed then. He said the ride was satisfactory–that was all–he took it for granted that I wouldn't tell anyone here, what we had done. Made me feel good.

The instructors are like that. If you give them a good ride, they let you have a little fun. But Burris, my new instructor, doesn't play around much. But last week I really gave him a good ride on the beam and finished early. On the way in to the field from the radio station over by Bakersfield, he did a couple of slow rolls. They weren't at all good! He turned around and held his nose–showing he realized they stunk. He asked me if I thought I could do one!!– I guess he thought I hadn't done any here–which would have been proper! But my old instructor, Stewart, had let me do a few before. I told him I'd like to. As luck would have it, I did a honey–He said that was what he had tried to do. I kinda wished I hadn't done such a good one. He had kind of a suspicious look and a little sheepish too, I think.

I think he must have brushed up on them a little cause the next day, he did a couple on the way in and they were sweet! He's really smooth! I can do most aerobatics but I'm never sure how they'll be and not too smoothly.

It's lights out now so I better close. . . . We leave next Sat. . . .

Your loving brother. . . Don

About ten percent of Class 42-I did not complete the course at Minter Field. Those who graduated moved on to advanced flying school at Luke Field, Arizona, where the Army separated the students into two groups. Those slated for single-engine aircraft remained at Luke Field, while others traveled to nearby Williams Field to train in twin-engine aircraft.[9] Weight determined most student assignments. Cadets less than one hundred and sixty pounds were given a shot at pursuit planes.[10] Size mattered. The cockpit in a single-engine plane accommodated a smaller man better than a larger man.

8

I'll Never Forget It

The first week they went from 4:45 [a.m.] to 8:30 [p.m.]. In one letter [Don] he said, "War may be hell but it can't be worse than Luke, but I guess we'll live through it."

Josie F. Beerbower, mother
(letter to Wayne P. and Elizabeth Beerbower)

When Aviation Cadet Don Beerbower reported to Luke Field, Arizona, on July 27, 1942, for advanced flying school, he was introduced to the well regarded North American AT-6 Texan. This excellent all-metal, low-wing trainer boasted a 600-horsepower Pratt and Whitney air-cooled radial engine. Although it weighed 5,300 pounds, it did not feel underpowered. Unlike the primary and basic flying school trainers, the Texan had retractable landing gear allowing it to cruise comfortably at one hundred fifty miles per hour. The AT-6 was a tail dragger like the PT-17 and the BT-13, so the pilot had to make "S" turns while taxiing to see around the front of the airplane. It was a smooth aircraft to fly, and in the hands of a competent pilot, performed precision maneuvers with ease.[1] After an initial period of adjustment, Don really liked the Texan. He would later describe it as a "swell" airplane.[2]

Luke Field was named after the "Arizona Balloon Buster," Second Lieutenant Frank Luke, Jr., a World War I fighter pilot and first Army aviator to receive the Congressional Medal of Honor. The base was located in the desert west of Phoenix on 1,440 acres of land the city had leased to the federal government. Construction began in March 1941, and by June the first class of student pilots arrived for advanced flying school. Luke Field eventually became

A formation of North American AT-6 Texans

the Army Air Forces' largest fighter training base, graduating twelve thousand pilots by war's end.[3]

Lieutenant Colonel George Bosch commanded the four sections of student pilots in Class 42-I. Section 1 was under the leadership of Major W. E. Hubbard. Don and his friends from Minter Field joined this group. He and a new friend, Edgar "Ed" Bennett, were assigned to "F" Flight, one of twenty-one flights of approximately five students in Section 1.[4] Don's flight commander and instructor was Lieutenant D. R. "Red" Bridges.[5]

*Cadet
Don Beerbower
Class 42-I*

The task of Bosch, Hubbard, and Bridges was to graduate their charges as Army officers and aviators; and to find and weed out anyone who wasn't ready for these responsibilities. The officers' modus operandi soon became clear to Don—to put maximum pressure, in a variety of ways, on the student pilots during their first few weeks at Luke Field. Don's future colleague and a member of Class 42-H, Jim Cannon (an upper classman during Don's first thirty days at advanced flying school), recalled their treatment at Luke Field:

> As lower classmen, we absolutely got no respect at all. Upon arrival with baggage in hand wearing class A uniforms, we were ordered to do pushups to begin with and lectured too, that set the tone for our lower class treatment. We had heard it was going to be bad before we got there. The only good thing was that most graduates would become fighter pilots. I was confined to the post for the duration of my training for a minor infraction that was not my fault. The martinet responsible for my punishment that included 20 tours [hours of walking/marching], showed up at one of our combat mission briefings at Boxted [England]. I was a Captain and he was still a 1st Lt., so I took the opportunity to remind him of his past chicken shit administration and hoped he had changed his attitude since then. He had nothing to say, but I felt better.[6]

Don's classmate Bud Anderson remembered being ordered to stand at attention for up to two hours in the midsummer heat. It made him so angry he hoped the officer responsible would "spend all eternity at attention in a place just as hot."[7] A week after Don arrived at Luke Field, he expressed his irritation about advanced flying school in a letter to Darrel and Arlene. He also gave them his initial impressions about the handling characteristics of the AT-6.

Cadet James Cannon
Class 42-H

Cadet C. E. "Bud"
Anderson Class 42-I

8-2-42

Dear Bro and Sis

Sun. afternoon on the post–as last nite. We're beginning to find out that a guy is mostly lucky if he gets off this post more than once in his whole stay here! The bums! We drilled from 8 to 10 this morn, then a meeting till almost noon. An open locker standby inspection at one and finally we're free–If they don't figure out something else–So I try to catch up on letters.

I had my physical exam yesterday morn so I didn't fly. I was supposed to solo. I should tomorrow though–so I guess it's all right.

These AT's are quite the gig to fly. The retractable wheels and flaps are hydraulic and in operating the flaps one has to be really careful. . . .

These planes are the very dickens to keep straight after landing till you slow down. You can't use the rudders cause it throws the tail wheel out of lock and then around you go. Ya have to just use the brakes–hydraulic, also very touchy! They have that type of landing gear so that we can handle anything after we get on to these. I should hope so! . . .

Our barracks don't have rooms . . . 28 of us in the upstairs here. Yesterday the inspecting officer found a piece of paper under my bed and now I have 2 tours to walk. I'm sure it wasn't there when I left. It probably blew under there from some where else. But!–the fact remains I have 2 hours of walking in the sun this afternoon. I'll have to get busy pretty soon too. I don't want to let them stack up as we have little time during the week.

We have every kind of plane operating out of here. Chinese flying P-40's, a couple of P-38's, a P-39; some A-20's, B-25's & B-26's come in here all the time. Also DC-3's & others. It's fun to watch them.

I better go get those tours walked off now. Wish I could think of more to write. Please write lots.

Love Don

Don had been away from home over six months, and he was anxious to return to Hill City after graduation from flying school. On his third Sunday at Luke Field, he alerted his brother and sister-in-law that a leave was no longer assured. Don wanted time at home with Elayne and his family. The threat of going directly from flying school to his next assignment would eventually cause him to develop a backup plan. For now, he continued to deal with the daily harassment, while at the same time gaining confidence in the AT-6. In fact, Don got so comfortable with the Texan, he regularly put himself in danger while flying it.

8-9-42

Dear Arlene and Darrel

. . . We were all confined again this weekend. Also, we had a ten mile hike out in the desert with no water. Just on general principals I guess. That was this morning. Nice eh? I wished I could have had my camera along to take pictures of the cactus–and the cadets.

What's getting me down now is wondering whether we'll get any furlough after graduation. I've been looking forward to it for so long now that the thought of not getting any, really hurts. And we may not get one. Some do & some don't. I guess it depends on where we're to be sent.

I'm really getting to like the AT-6. It's a sleek plane when you get the wheels up and it's fast when you get up about 10,000 feet with the mixture control adjusted and the prop pitch back about 1750 rpm. Thursday I did that and put on 30 inches of manifold pressure and was cruising around at 190 mph. Then I dived it to almost 300 mph. It's red-lined at 250 mph so I tell no one around here about it, of course. I was really coming down though. I almost blacked out on the pull out.

This week we start instrument flying and instruments and formation. Also start skeet shooting. We get at least 300 rounds of skeet apiece. That comes with ground school–which reminds me– have a navigation test tomorrow & I'd better brush up a little. So– I'll close. Write lots.

Your Brother Don

With Class 42-H scheduled to graduate from advanced flying school in late August, Don's Class 42-I would gain upper class status. As Don and the other student pilots moved to within a few days of this happening, training officers cut them some slack—time off to relax and go into Phoenix for most of the cadets. Don looked forward to graduation a month away. He had invited Elayne and their two fathers to come to Arizona for the ceremony. He still hoped to return home with them for a few days, but events beyond his control would determine his whereabouts in October. Across the country pilot training continued at an urgent pace.

Don also hoped his brother could arrange a vacation in Hill City during his leave. Darrel now managed a creamery in Illinois. In a letter Don wrote to Darrel and Arlene on August 25, he updated them on his leave, kidded with his brother about his new job, and poked some fun at sparring with Darrel, a former Golden Gloves boxer.

8/25/42

Dear Sis and Brother

    Just got your letter before dinner Darrel, so I'll answer pronto! Our section flew and had ground school Sun. so this is our day off. Open post last nite and all. Not much doing in town though. I went in and had a few drinks and came back out.

    We get off this afternoon till 8:30 today too. I'm going in to get a couple sun tan shirts and get my new watch band put on. I told you I had bought a Chronograph wrist watch, didn't I? I got it from a kid who washed out here. It's a regular pilot's watch with everything. They just can't be bought new anymore. It's about a $65 Swiss watch and I got it for $25. Elayne gave me a new band for it . . . I broke one of the little pins when I took the old band off so I have to get a new one.

    They sure pulled a neat trick on our upper class today. They are to graduate day after tomorrow. Of course, they planned on some nice exercises and an air show etc. This morning the order came out; they would pass thru the theatre to receive their wings and bars and be sworn in. No ceremony at all. Nice for those who planned on something and invited their folks out eh? I don't imagine we'll have any either. At least we have an idea in advance as to what will come off and can plan accordingly. I wonder if Dad and Bill will want to come out now. I hardly know what to think. . . .

    I'm smoking a big cigar. Can you smell it? I suppose that by the time I get back there, Darrel, you'll be sitting behind a big desk with a box of them to offer me one! Not?

I sure wish I could go thru the plant with you. But don't be too sure about that beating you're looking forward to handing out. I'm in tip top shape!! . . .

We had all our cross-country hops last week. One up over the Grand Canyon. It was beautiful! One over into Calif. And up a ways and back. There–you can trace another trip Arlene. To Blythe and up to Needles (both in Calif.) and back.

Sat. we took an oxygen hop. Went up to 20,000 ft. with oxygen masks. I was sure a tough looking customer with that on. We're flying mostly formation (but close too!) and instruments now. We'll start nite flying next week I guess.

I must close now. Write lots.

Love Don

Several days before Don's birthday, he received a gift from Elayne and her parents: a diary published by the Remington-Morse Company entitled *My Life In The Service*. It included sections such as *My Buddies In The Service, Officers I Have Met*, and *Army and Navy Insignia*. At the bottom of each page, the publishers placed a quotation intended to inspire the owner of the diary. A fitting verse that accompanied one of Don's first entries in August was by the poet Robert W. Service:

> Just draw on your grit: it's so easy to quit–
> It's the keeping your chin up that's hard.[8]

Like many Americans his age, Don had been doing a man's duty, but legally speaking he was still considered a minor. This changed on August 26 when he turned twenty-one. Don admitted feeling a little morose that evening when he opened his diary to comment about his first birthday away from home: "My 21st birthday but the Army must have forgotten. It was just another day. Wound up our regular ground school with 3 tests. Flew 3 hours and one hour of link this morning. My nose runs and my feet smell today. Don't know where I caught it. Just finished a letter to Elayne. I surely do miss her. Must drop a note to the folks and tell Dad there probably won't be any graduation exercises or air review. Hope he still wants to come out."

On August 28, members of Class 42-I officially became upper classmen. Don now shared a double room with his friend, Ed Bennett, who was the barracks captain. Don's bed became the model for the new students to use when making their own beds. He proudly noted in his diary, "It's tight as a drum!"

During Don's first week as an upperclassman, 42-I had the delicate task of learning how to fly formation at night. One evening Don flew a mission with Section Commander Hubbard. On the two ensuing nights, he flew cross-country, with the longest trip a tiring five-hour-and-twenty-minute, three-leg flight due west to Blythe, California, then southeast to Tucson, Arizona, and finally northwest back to Luke Field. This ended night flying. The upper classmen now moved on to aerobatics, or acrobatics, as it was often referred to by pilots. Don commented that his first flight with Lieutenant Bridges "proved exciting, with loops, rolls and simulated forced landings which led to a little buzzing. It was the first 'legal' acrobatics I'd done in this ship."9

Elayne, who planned to quit her job and come with their fathers for the graduation ceremony, crossed Don's mind a lot. He wrote in his diary that she "surely sounds enthusiastic about going home and getting ready for the trip. I don't know what we'd do now if something came up to put the trip off!–We've looked forward to it so much."10

Don's plan to return to Hill City after graduation didn't have a chance. The Army's need for pilots turned desperate. American forces were engaging the Japanese in a new offensive in the Solomon Islands north of Australia; and Operation Torch, the invasion of German-and-Italian-occupied North Africa, was scheduled for November 1942. The weapons available for these actions were adequate at best. New and improved killing equipment flew along assembly lines, and millions of farm boys and city kids flowed through the personnel pipeline, learning the art of war. A sense of urgency galvanized the military. Lieutenant Colonel Bosch and his staff rushed the cadets through flying school. Unfortunately for Don and the rest of Class 42-I, formal graduation exercises and post-graduation furloughs became dispensable frills.

To generate additional pilot experience in pursuit planes, the brass gave Don and others in his class the opportunity to fly the Curtiss P-36 Hawk. This aircraft looked like an early version of the Republic P-47 Thunderbolt, a fighter destined to become a workhorse in the war against Germany. The P-36, no longer competitive in its class, still outperformed the AT-6. Don enjoyed flying the Hawk. He took one up on September 11 for forty-five minutes. He later described the flight as "a thrill." And then he enthusiastically added, "That 1200 hp really pulls it thru things. I was first in our section to fly it. I rolled it and put it up to 300. I wish the rest of my training here were in them. . . ."11

With graduation approaching, Don was preparing for the arrival of Elayne, Bill, and Clarence. He made "reservations for the gang" at a motel and then went to the courthouse in Phoenix to gather information about getting a marriage license in Arizona. He worried that a recent change in the availability of gasoline might prevent Elayne from making the trip. He said in his diary, "I

Curtis P-36 Hawk NAT'L MUSEUM OF THE AIR FORCE

hope and pray that the new gas rationing doesn't throw our plans out of kilter." Don also felt pressured to finish making arrangements by mid-September because later in the month his schedule called for a week at a gunnery range near Ajo, Arizona.[12]

On September 18 Don passed his instrument check ride and then as he noted in his diary, spent an hour practicing "solo acrobatics in some 6000' clouds–some real fun for a change." Flying like this is one of the ultimate experiences in aviation. Royal Air Force pilot John Gillespie Magee, Jr., who wrote *High Flight* in the fall of 1941, described best what Don meant when he referred to flying acrobatics in the clouds as "real fun."

> Oh, I have slipped the surly bonds of Earth,
>   And danced the skies on laughter silvered wings,
> Sunward I've climbed and joined the tumbling mirth
>   Of sun-split clouds–and done a hundred things
> You have not dreamed of–wheeled and soared and swung
>   High in the sunlit silence hovering there,
> I've chased the shouting wind along and flung
>   My eager craft through footless halls of air. . . .[13]

Ajo Army Airfield, in the southern part of Arizona, struck Don as a miniature Luke Field. He and his classmates stayed in three rebuilt Civilian Conservation Corps barracks. The cadets were doubled-timed to and from the flight line where they remained all day in the heat, even if they were not flying. Major Hubbard had promised the soon-to-be officers they could go off post at night, but this did not turn out to be the case. On Don's second day at gunnery school, he wrote in his diary, "No one will get off the post while here!"[14]

His irritation with being confined countered his enjoyment of firing at ground targets. The student pilots learned how to fire the AT-6's single thirty-caliber machine gun at ground and aerial targets.[15] The thirty-caliber round compared favorably with the standard rifle cartridge Don used when deer hunting near Hill City. The newest American fighters, like the P-38 Lightning and P-47 Thunderbolt, were fitted with much larger and harder hitting fifty-caliber machine guns. On September 25 Don mentioned in his diary the "fun" he was having with gunnery: "This low flying down at the target and the steep chandelle up is really okay with me. I love it. When one is flying almost 200 [mph] at 20 feet from the ground things really go by."

Top: .303 Cal. Savage   Bottom: .50 Cal. Browning (both actual size)

Foremost on Don's mind on September 25 were his wedding plans. He commented in his diary, "Can hardly wait for them to get here. I made arrangements last Tues. to be married at 4:00 [p.m.] at the chapel at Luke. Hope we can get all set in the short time we'll have Tuesday."

Bill, Clarence, and Elayne left Hill City in Kutcher's brand new 1942 Chevrolet during Don's week at Ajo. Their trip took them west to North Dakota and then south to the Black Hills, where unfortunately they were unable to view Mount Rushmore because it was cloaked in fog and rain. They continued along the eastern side of the Rocky Mountains through Wyoming and Colorado, then crossed New Mexico into Arizona where they were pleasantly surprised to find areas of irrigated farm land in the desert around Phoenix.[16] The trip was a new experience for Elayne—her first opportunity to travel outside Minnesota except for family visits with relatives living in Canada. She and Don had not seen each other since February. Elayne didn't realize he intended to ask her to get married while there for his graduation.[17] Don expected Elayne and their fathers to arrive in Phoenix on Sunday, September 27.

With graduation on Tuesday, he held out hope that gunnery school would end early so he could get back before September 29 to finalize his plans with Elayne.

Before any of this could transpire, the student pilots at Ajo needed to complete aerial gunnery, which involved shooting at a target being towed by another aircraft. The use of color-coded ammunition made it possible for ground personnel to determine how many hits a particular pilot made on the drag target.[18] On September 27 Don commented in his diary, "Fired all 800 rounds of aerial today and really worked on it." After Don completed the exercise, he returned to the Ajo. He was surprised with what he found there: "I no more than parked the ship on my last flight when Bennett came running out saying we were flying back to Luke right away. He had my stuff all packed and we took off in a few minutes." Back at Luke, Don immediately arranged for a ride into Phoenix; he "[f]ound the gang at about 5:30. They had a room out at the La Fiesta Motor Court with an extra bedroom for Elayne. It was sure good to see them all again. Elayne hasn't changed a bit in the 8 months we've been apart. I had to come back to the field at 2:00 a.m. so they all brought me out. It was a full day and one I'll never forget. Elayne agreed to get married on the 29th at the Post Chapel and everything in the world was rosy with me." The many months of separation finally over, Don summed it all up with a simple sentence, "What a day!"

On Monday Don and Elayne purchased their rings and a marriage license and picked up Don's uniform. Graduation was on Tuesday morning at eight o'clock. Clarence later described to his brother, Wayne, his impressions of Don's physical stature at the brief ceremony, "He sure is hard as nails. I don't believe I would want to try to handle him. [He] is sure a swell looking soldier."[19] About four hundred men in Class 42-I each received a second lieutenant's gold bar and the silver wings of a U.S. Army aviator during the ceremony. Custom called for a mother to pin the government-issued wings on her son, but since Josie was not present, Don sent his home with Clarence. He then purchased a pair to wear on his uniform.[20]

In the afternoon, Don and Elayne and Clarence and Bill, all a long way from home, gathered at the base chapel for the wedding. A few days later, Gay Huntley announced their marriage in the *Hill City News*: "The ceremony took place in the camp chapel and was performed by an army chaplain. Only the bride's and groom's fathers William Kutcher and C. W. Beerbower were present at the ceremony. So the 29th was a red letter day for Don, as he not only won his wings as one of Uncle Sam's fliers that day, but a lovely bride as well. Both of these young folks are so well known to people here that any introduction seems superfluous . . . The *News* joins with their many friends in wishing them every happiness."[21]

Elayne Kutcher and Don Beerbower, La Fiesta Motor Court

Clarence Beerbower and Bill Kutcher, La Fiesta Motor Court

Don thought it was, "Quite the day in this forlorn life of Don M. Beerbower–Lt.!! 'Got my wings this morning and got them clipped this afternoon,' as Dad said. The wedding was at 4:00 sharp and I'll never forget it. . . . Words can't tell my feelings." As an officer, he was now able to sleep off post. Don and Elayne stayed at the La Fiesta for a couple of days until he was ordered to his next assignment.[22]

9

We'll Like It

I certainly hope the war is over before he gets into combat because the life of a flyer in combat is an average of one and a half minutes. . . .

Clarence W. Beerbower, father
(letter to Wayne P. Beerbower)

Josie Beerbower knew Don had been asked while at Minter Field about his interest in becoming an instructor pilot. Like her husband, she worried about the consequences for their son if he ended up in combat.[1] The chance of Don becoming an instructor was now slim. His recently completed training at Luke Field and his new assignment to Hamilton Field, California, defined him as a future fighter pilot.

Clarence and Bill transported Don and Elayne's heavy luggage to the railway station on Thursday afternoon, October 1, 1942. After saying their goodbyes, the two fathers left for Minnesota. Later that evening Don and Elayne departed Phoenix by passenger train on the first leg of their trip to San Francisco. The young couple's accommodation for the overnight run to Southern California was in a sleeper car. They were scheduled to arrive at eight o'clock the next morning.[2]

Don and Elayne had an all-day layover ahead of them when they stepped off the train in Los Angeles on October 2. While in the city they planned to visit friends Del and Ardis Rabey. The Rabeys, like many others from Hill City, left their hometown because of military service or the attractive wages offered in defense plants, such as those in the burgeoning aviation industry in Southern California. Shortly after the newlyweds arrived, Del took them out to tour the plant where he worked. Later, after a few phone calls, others from Hill City arrived at the Rabeys: "Myrtle, Norma and Jimmy James, Lee and Johnny Mykkannen, Chuck Strom and a couple of other Hill City folks." After the conclusion of a very enjoyable day, Don and Elayne boarded the night train for San Francisco.[3]

In the morning, they took a bus across the towering Golden Gate Bridge to San Rafael and then traveled another twelve miles north to Hamilton Field on

San Pablo Bay. While there, they made inquiries about housing and looked over the base. Later in the day, they went to San Anselmo, two miles from San Rafael, where they found a room to rent at the Norman Smith residence on Idalia Road. The short, one-car-width lane wound its way to the top of a steep rise above the quaint old village. Don noted in his diary, "It isn't much but so little is to be had, we grabbed it and felt lucky to get it."[4] After a lazy Sunday of well needed rest, Don felt a little better about the lovely setting of their first home together. He wrote, "This old house is beautiful up on the side hill looking over the tree tops and the town. I think we'll like it though it's not so handy."[5]

Don and Elayne had to adjust to a significant amount of change in a very short period of time. Used to being independent and on their own, they now were dependent on each other; and they were living in an unfamiliar part of the country. Elayne would need to learn how to be a military wife and homemaker while Don, as an officer and pilot, took on new duties that carried much greater responsibility than he had experienced as an aviation cadet. In addition, Don and Elayne had to cope with the uncertainty of the future. They didn't know how long they would be together or where Don would be sent next. Their situ-

Elayne and Don Beerbower - wedding photograph

ation was not unusual for couples in wartime America. Like everyone else, the newlyweds would need to build their new life while under ever-increasing levels of stress.

On Monday, October 5, Don reported for duty at Hamilton Field, a nine-year-old air base with runways laid out adjacent to attractive Spanish-style administrative buildings that fit in well with California history and architecture.[6] His new assignment was with the 326th Fighter Squadron, one of three squadrons of the 328th Fighter Group, Fourth Air Force. The 328th Fighter Group, under the command of Captain E. W. Hewlitt, was responsible for air defense in the San Francisco Bay area.[7] It also served as an operational training unit. Once the pilots completed training, they rotated to new units or became replacements for existing units.[8]

The 328th Fighter Group flew the uniquely designed Bell P-39 Airacobra. In an effort to improve the fighter plane's maneuverability in flight, the manufacturer had located the 1,325-horsepower Allison liquid-cooled V-12 engine behind the cockpit instead of in front of it. In addition, access to the cockpit was unusual because the pilot entered it through an automobile-style door. Each door had a roll down window. The P-39's design included a tricycle landing gear which allowed the pilot to see well when he taxied the aircraft. Armament included two thirty-caliber machine guns in each wing, two fifty-caliber machine guns in the front of the fuselage (fired through the propeller arc), and one thirty-seven-millimeter cannon mounted in the propeller hub. Lacking a supercharger for high altitude flight and with a maximum speed of only three hundred eighty miles per hour, the P-39 saw limited combat duty in the Army Air Forces. The U.S. shipped nearly half of the 9,585 P-39s produced to the Soviets, who used them with some success against German ground targets.[9]

Bell P-39 Airacobras

DON BEERBOWER PHOTO

Don, Bud Anderson, Ed Bennett, and others from Class 42-I spent their first few days at Hamilton Field learning the basics about the Airacobra. Early in the week, Don commented in his diary about ground school and his satisfaction over finalizing his living arrangements.

> 10-6-42
>
> We have to read and memorize tech. orders and engineering data for about a week before we can check out. Have to pass a blindfold test on cockpit procedure also.
>
> I'm spending the nites in town so far. We're supposed to stay on the post for 90 days so I have to have a room in the B.O.Q. [Bachelor Officers Quarters] anyway. I'll use that when I can't get to town and back. Lt. Bill Beck, an engineering officer, stays at the same house and drives back and forth. I ride out with him. He's swell. Bennett and I have a room together in the B.O.Q.

It was more costly for married officers to live off post than for single officers to live on base. Fortunately for Don, his pay had risen significantly since his promotion to second lieutenant; he now earned two hundred and fifty dollars a month instead of seventy-five.[10] The extra money helped Don and Elayne meet transportation, housing, and meal expenses.

After a week of concentrating on the Airacobra's flying characteristics and technical data, Don could finally take one of the ships up for a flight around the local area. He recorded the experience in his diary on October 13 with these words: "My first hop in a P-39! I like it swell. It's like a baby carriage to land, which suits me fine!"

Don couldn't wait to build up his flying time, but his squadron contained sixty-two pilots, twice the norm. In addition, there would be a shortage of P-39s until new aircraft could arrive from the Bell factory in New York.[11]

An assignment with the 328th Fighter Group meant training, and to this end Don spent the next few weeks flying formation, learning fighter tactics, and practicing his shooting skills at the skeet range. With the seasonal change in temperature, marine fog affected northern California more than usual. At Hamilton Field, it restricted flying time. Don's October 24 diary entry cited a typical situation when he reflected on the weather and a high-altitude observation: "Not much doing at the field today. Fogged in most of the day. I was up to 25,000 feet yesterday afternoon and saw the fog roll in off the ocean and thru the Golden Gate into the Bay. It was really beautiful!" The dense fog that placed a shroud over the red twin towers of the world's longest suspension bridge complicated air defense in the Bay area. The fog could be used to advantage by an enemy approaching the coast in surface craft. During one alert, Bud Anderson waited up all night for an attack that did not come. An inbound convoy had been misidentified as Japanese when in reality they were American vessels.[12]

Anderson was in a different squadron than Don. The two classmates separated in November when Anderson's unit transferred to Oakland. They would not see each other again until 1944. Don mentioned this in his diary on November 2 when he wrote: "My time is building up in the P-39 but it's pretty slow with our lack of planes. Tomorrow is my day off and I'm glad to have a chance to rest up. Though we don't fly a lot, we have something to do all the time. Shot skeet today for almost 2 hours and boy is my arm sore! Should start gunnery in a few days. The 329th moved to Oakland today so quite a few of the guys from Luke will be leaving us. They patrol their part of the alerts from there. Elayne's about ready for bed so I'd better hit the hay too."

As Don grew more and more proficient as an aviator, a new unit was being formed at Hamilton Field—the 354th Fighter Group, a single-engine outfit consisting of the 353rd, 355th, and 356th Fighter Squadrons. Officially activated on November 15, its mission was to provide tactical training in the P-39 while defending against aggressive action by the Japanese along the West Coast. On November 26, Major Kenneth R. Martin took command of the new unit.[13] Prior to being assigned to Hamilton Field, Martin had been in command of the San Diego Air Defense Wing. A few months earlier, he had test-flown the new single-engine P-51 Mustang, an aircraft destined to play an important role in the 354th Fighter Group's future.[14]

Martin moved quickly to establish a cadre of officers to help bring the group up to its full strength of a thousand men. A new executive officer, Major Wallace Mace, transferred in from Salt Lake City. Operations officer appointee Captain Al Dutton would join the group once he recovered from injuries received at Guadalcanal. Dutton had downed several enemy aircraft during his tour in the Southwest Pacific.[15] Major Owen M. Seaman, fresh from two years of service with the 78th Fighter Squadron in Hawaii, stepped in to command the 353rd Fighter Squadron.[16] Captain George R. Bickell, a P-40 pilot with experience gained during the Battle of Midway, received the 355th Fighter Squadron. Captain Charles C. Johnson, on the mend from wounds received while flying near Port Moresby, New Guinea, got the 356th.[17]

Dutton, Seaman, Bickell, and Johnson all came to the 354th Fighter Group as veteran pilots. This mattered because the new flight leaders for each of their squadrons would be selected from the junior officers of the 328th Fighter Group—four flight leaders for each squadron.[18] During December, Seaman, Bickell, and Johnson gathered background information on potential pilots to fill these positions. Seaman, for example, visited all three squadrons "scouting around" for those he might want as flight leaders.[19]

Don may have heard about the formation of a new fighter group; if so, he did not mention it in his diary. He was preoccupied in December with Elayne not feeling well and with a visit from his mother, whom he had not seen for a nearly a year. In his first diary entry since early October he wrote:

> 12-22-42
>
> Quite a skip but I'll try to be more attentive to this little book after this. Mom arrived today to visit, spend Christmas and take Elayne home. She, Elayne, has been sick for a month–going to have an addition to our family!! We feel it's best that she go home to her mother's care till she's built up anyway. Then we'll see if we can arrange for her to come out again. Sure is swell to see Mom. She's an angel and is making our last week here seem a lot like being home. More than it ever could have before. There's something about having "Mom" around once in a while even.

Don and Elayne had enjoyed a wonderful three months together in California. Being apart would be difficult for them, but the best place for Elayne to be was with her parents. The evening Elayne left for home (December 28), Don expressed his anguish in his diary with these words: "She's gone! Left Oakland at 8:20 p.m. God–how can anyone feel so all alone with so many people around. I never missed anyone so much before. It wasn't like this when I was away from her before. Maybe it's worrying about how she's getting along. I wonder how it'll be after I start hearing from her. I hope I don't get any more lonesome for her than now or I'm apt to go A.W.O.L. and head for Minn!"

The last goodbyes in Oakland had left Elayne and Josie with deep down, wrenching feelings as well. The women had no idea whether they would ever see Don again.

On New Year's evening, 1942, Don's friends likely encouraged him to join them in revelry, but the person he loved was gone and he felt despondent. He confided in his diary, "What a dreary New Year's Eve. All alone in my barracks. Just wrote to Elayne and now if I'm not careful I'll be crying myself to sleep.–Maybe it would help."

Much had changed for Don. A year earlier, while home from college for Christmas vacation, he had announced plans to leave Iowa State with his friend, Glenn McKean, to join the Army Air Corps. No one could talk him out of doing this. Now, a married Army officer stationed halfway across the country without his wife—and a pilot training to fly fighter planes in combat—he would forge ahead alone. It had been a year of heady personal accomplishment for Don. What 1943 would bring he did not know. That it would lead him further along the path to war—of that he must have been certain.

10

No Horseplay

The P-39 was a tricky airplane. . . . I had a healthy respect for it. It was very easy to get into a spin [but] difficult to get out of it a lot of the times. It had very short wings and was a small airplane. In fact, it was the only airplane that had a reputation of being able to tumble when it stalled.

John D. Mattie, P-39 pilot
(interview with the author)

    Don Beerbower had been influenced by many people in his first twenty-one years of life: his family and his wife, the people of Hill City, friends, teachers and coaches, and military officers all helped him become the person he now was. They were with him in his tender years as a child, when playing ball, while scouting and hunting, during church and school activities, at work in the creamery, while attending college, and when learning to become a fighter pilot. These people all contributed to the development of his character and his ability to lead others. He was well prepared for a new assignment, and it came in January 1943 when Major Kenneth Martin and his squadron commanders selected their officer cadre. Don wrote in his diary on January 8 of his transfer to the 354th Fighter Group: "I'll be a flight leader in it. Not a bad deal if it all comes thru." Six days went by without any further word about the transfer. Don noted, "It's still up in the air." He did know the group was headed for Tonopah, Nevada, "Up in the mountains. We're still 'sweating out' our orders and it's a dreary job. I'm going to write 'my wife' now. Guess she's really getting along swell!"

    Don finally received his orders on January 16, with departure scheduled for noon the next day. Suddenly, he had much to do "getting things cleared up and things packed." That evening Don concluded his brief diary entry with a comment about his weariness: "I'm dead tired now and have to get up at 6:00 tomorrow." Don and the other initial members of the group left California on January 17 for Nevada. Fortunately for the men, the slow-moving troop train was outfitted with sleeper cars. They arrived at Tonopah Army Airfield on January 18. After Don got settled into his new quarters, he and several friends drove to Tonopah, the county seat of Nye County, seven miles west of the base. He wasn't impressed with the mining town: "What a joint! Once is enough for me if we stay a year!"[1]

At an elevation of six thousand feet, the airfield made up part of the Tonopah Bombing and Gunnery Range, an area encompassing thousands of acres of rugged, semi-arid public land. The location was ideal for military use. For anyone stationed there, however, it felt remote and isolated. Tonopah was the only town of any size between Reno and Las Vegas, each over two hundred miles away. The only entertainment in Tonopah catered to the vices of men: gambling, drinking, and prostitution.[2]

On January 19 Don, Jack T. Bradley, James "Jim" Cannon, and John G. Montijo were assigned to the 353rd Fighter Squadron as flight leaders. Don took charge of "D" Flight. He had much work to do before the squadron's remaining pilots arrived. Don mentioned in his diary how busy the four of them were "setting up an operations system where there's never been one before. Nothing to work with and it's a headache. Good experience!"

Squadron Commander Owen Seaman appointed Jack Bradley as the operations officer. This additional responsibility would have him overseeing the training and scheduling of the four flights. Bradley and Don had not become well acquainted at Hamilton Field. This changed with their assignment to the 353rd Fighter Squadron. Bradley described Don at this time as "very quiet and very confident."[3]

Of the four flight leaders, only Don was from Class 42-I. Bradley, Cannon, and Montijo had graduated from Luke Field one month ahead of him in Class 42-H.[4] The flight leaders were dependent on Major Seaman for direction on how to develop a viable operations office. Seaman had most recently served at Wheeler Field, Hawaii. A recipient of the Southwest Pacific Theater ribbon with one star, he hailed from Greenville, Illinois, where he was born on May 23, 1916. Prior to joining the Army Air Corps, Seaman had attended college for three years at the University of California and had worked a year in Personnel at Standard Oil of California. He earned his wings at Kelly Field, Texas, on March 24, 1940.[5] Tall, good-looking, and quiet, the commanding officer was well liked by the men of the squadron. Flight Leader Jim Cannon considered him "a very fair man [who] wasn't really a strict disciplinarian. He flew with us a lot."[6]

Seaman delegated to the flight leaders the responsibility of preparing for the arrival of the new pilots who were expected within days. A tent became the pilots' assembly room, and a small shack, operations. The place was so crowded with desks and filing cabinets that turning around became difficult. The weather didn't help matters; it remained cold and wet. But discomfort didn't dampen Don's enthusiasm. He felt sure everything was going to work out fine.[7]

When the 354th Fighter Group had been organized in November, the Fourth

Don Beerbower at Tonopah Army Airfield, Nevada

Air Force designated Hamilton Field as its permanent headquarters.[8] The movement of the group to Nevada was a temporary change of station. The men would leave Tonopah as soon as bombing and gunnery training ended. Before this could happen, the three squadrons needed pilots and airplanes. Soon new men began arriving. On January 24 Don recorded in his diary, "Most of the new pilots are here–my old classmates who went up to [Paine] Field, Wash. Quite a surprise for both them and me to be their flight leader. . . . Have the operations all set up & ready."

Excitement exploded at the airfield on January 26 when the first P-39 Airacobras arrived. When they "roared overhead in formation everyone was out to watch them come in," wrote one of the officers, "and [we] experienced a thrill at seeing the first squadron planes assigned."[9] Don made a brief notation in his diary about the event: "Planes came in today. 4 per squadron. Not much but at least they're planes. Have some flying tomorrow. We each have 7 fellows in our flight. Combat strength." In addition to Don, "D" Flight included John Anderson, Ridley E. Donnell, Wallace N. "Wally" Emmer, Norman C. Gross, Paul A. Leydens, John D. Mattie, and Donald M. Schultz. They were all from Class 42-I.[10]

By January 27, a total of twenty-six pilots had joined Seaman and his officer cadre at Tonopah. Of these, a core of leaders evolved that greatly influenced the squadron's future: Donnell, Glenn T. Eagleston, Buford M. Eaves, Emmer, Carl M. Frantz, James W. Kerley, Charles W. Koenig, Mattie, Arthur W. Owen, and James J. Parsons. All were second lieutenants.[11]

The pilots' uncertainty grew about where they would be sent after their training was completed. The three major combat theaters for the Army Air Forces in early 1943 were in the southwest Pacific, China, and North Africa. Army pilots had helped defeat the Japanese at Guadalcanal, but now they slowly advanced with American ground forces along the northeast coast of New Guinea. They also fought in China and Burma as the main force blocking the Japanese push toward India. But in North Africa the situation had soured. The Americans suffered a major defeat at Kasserine Pass in February. A fourth effort underway in early 1943 was the gradual build up of forces in England for the strategic bombing of Germany. Many fighter units would eventually be needed to support this endeavor.

The 354th Fighter Group's immediate problem was to train pilots. As a flight leader, Don was the primary flight instructor for the officers under his command. On February 2 he referenced this in his diary: "Finding out how little the fellows know. All they've had is formation. Around 30 hours average all around. Have wrong ideas on formation too as far as combat goes. All my boys are good flyers tho and will catch on fast."

Don quickly adjusted to his new role as a flight leader, comfortable with the responsibility of preparing "D" Flight for combat duty. On February 4 he added in his diary, "Started dry runs on ground gunnery today. Took one or two over at a time and showed them what I wanted for a pattern and dive angle, etc. Haven't had a day off since we've been here."

If Don was flying day after day, other flight leaders were working long hours as well. On February 5, Jack Bradley, on his last mission of the day, was returning in clear weather to Tonopah from ground gunnery practice with two pilots from "A" Flight, Gordon W. Chapman and Stanley E. Chatfield. The three ships cruised in formation about four thousand feet above the Revielle Valley. Twenty minutes from home, Bradley signaled the other pilots to spread out in trail as they began a slight descent toward the airfield. As he looked back to check on how they had executed the maneuver, he could only see one of the planes in the formation. Bradley started to bank to the right as he looked over his left shoulder and inadvertently began a diving turn. He later wrote, "After completing a 180 [degree] turn I looked back and not seeing the second ship, I started scanning the area and saw gray smoke over the spot where Lt. Chapman's plane had hit the ground." Nine days later the aircraft Accident Classification Committee issued its report:

> No member of the formation saw Lt. Chapman's plane at the time of the crash; therefore, there is no information as to what actually happened. It is possible that Lt. Chapman was not alert and was surprised by Lt. Bradley's turn. In his attempt to stay in formation he over controlled and rolled his plane over on its back. He did not have quite enough altitude to recover by diving out of the inverted position.
>
> The plane probably mushed into the ground at about a 30 degree angle while going at a very high speed. The pilot and seat were evidently thrown clear of the plane at this contact. The body was found about 150 yards from the first impact signs. The top of the head was missing, but otherwise the body was in good condition. The plane bounced about 50 yards and began disintegrating upon the second contact with the ground.
>
> The flight leader is supposed to be free to make turns or other maneuvers at his desire; therefore, if Lt. Chapman was surprised by the turn the flight leader should not be held responsible. It is felt that the major factor contributing to this accident was the pilot's inexperience with flying this type of aircraft.[12]

Don mentioned the death of Gordon Chapman in his diary on February 5. He and Chapman had served together in the same section of Class 42-I at Luke Field so they were well acquainted. Don seemed to take the death in stride, something he hadn't been able to do with the loss of Glenn McKean. Chapman's demise received about as much attention in Don's diary as his tiring day of flying: "Flew again today. 'B' and 'C' flights were off for the day. Over 5 hours of dry runs and ground gunnery. I'm pooped out. Gets tiresome trying to force the fellows into the position I want in the pattern. Bradley lost one of his boys today. Chapman. –Section 1 boy back at Luke. Good boy too. Didn't get out of a split S. Last flight of the day too. Fellows are feeling pretty bad about it tonite but they'll get over it soon. Got a very sweet valentine from Elayne today."

To squadron pilot Richard M. Coffey fell the duty of escorting Gordon Chapman's remains to Spokane, Washington. He represented Majors Martin and Seaman at the funeral service. Coffey extended the "sympathy of the entire organization to the bereaved parents. . . ."[13]

Gordon W. Chapman

On February 6, tragedy struck again when the commanding officer of the 356th Fighter Squadron, Captain Charles Johnson, died in another crash. Johnson lost control of his aircraft while experimenting with a procedure to use in combating the dangerous spin tendencies of the P-39. Because the accident took the life of one of the group's most experienced pilots, Major Martin decided to personally take over the task of finding a solution to this serious problem. Soon, pilots had a standard operating procedure to use when they found themselves spiraling earthward in an out-of-control Airacobra.[14] One way to end up in a spin was to stall the aircraft. Flight Leader Jim Cannon described what had to be done to stabilize a ship when it went into a violent spin at full power: "When in a spin," he said, "the power must be reduced to idle before a recovery is possible."[15]

A pleasant surprise for Don on February 6 was the arrival of his friend Willie Y. Anderson. Another future leader in the squadron, Willie Y. was lucky to be in Tonopah at all considering a recent flying accident in California. Years later he explained what happened: "I crashed at March Field, bellied in, in a girls' campus.... I hit the gun sight glass with my hand to break it off because normally if we went forward the gun sight's glass would catch you right under the nose and remove it. So, I cut my hand pretty bad there and after I got out of the hospital they sent me home on leave. When I came back I had been transferred to Tonopah, Nevada."[16]

Training intensified, with the flight leaders spending many hours in the air. On February 8 Don jotted down a quick couple of lines in his diary, saying, "Flew 4 flights of ground gunnery today. Makes a full day! Guys are coming along pretty good. Got a box of cookies and a valentine box of candy from my honey too. She surely is sweet."

While Don taught the pilots in "D" Flight, he was also receiving instruction on ways to improve his own flying proficiency. This two-way-street education speeded his development as a leader and as a skilled flyer. Don touched on this in a brief diary entry on February 11: "Four more flights of gunnery today.

One with Major Martin on my wing. Had fun with him but trouble in the pattern. Learned several points from him on flying though."

At Tonopah, the twenty-five-year-old Martin was promoted to lieutenant colonel. He had risen in rank rapidly during his six years in the service. Martin was born in Lees Summit, Missouri, on July 17, 1917. After completing high school, he attended the University of Kansas City for two years. During this time he served in the Marine Air Reserve. An apprentice mechanic in civilian life, he also managed to own and operate a service station before joining the Army Air Corps. He graduated from flying school at Kelly Field, Texas, in February 1938.[17] Jim Cannon considered Martin a fine officer. Years later he recalled, "[Martin] didn't drink, smoke or cuss. His worst words were, 'Dad gum it!' He was really strict from a military view point in the way we all dressed. He was just a good officer all the way around. . . . He'd listen real carefully to what was being said. But you had a lot of respect for him and therefore there was no horseplay when he was around."[18]

Commanding Officer Kenneth R. Martin

Martin set the tone for the whole organization. Operations Officer Jack Bradley had the highest respect for the group commander. He believed Martin had tremendous influence on the future development of the pilots under his command.

> We were all very impressed by him. . . . He was a great leader and he instilled some decorum that we otherwise wouldn't [have] known about. . . . One thing he did, he made us all wear our Class A jackets and uniforms to the mess hall. Well, there was quite a lot of dissension. These guys with their flying suits on, they'd have to go change clothes to get in the mess hall. Well, after we had done that awhile these guys would go to other fields where other

fighter groups were and see them living in a mess, so to speak, and they were all proud they belonged to the 354th. . . . [He was] just a super guy."[19]

The constant training began to wear on Don. When given a day of rest on February 12, he slept until noon. Although things had been hectic for the past month, he often drifted into thoughts of Elayne. He wrote in his diary, do miss her when I have a day off and nothing to do. I miss her enough when I'm busy. Sure hope I get to see her soon." Others missed their wives, as well. John Mattie wrote to his wife asking her to join him at Tonopah, "[The] wives came up at the same time on this bus from Santa Ana. Tonopah was a wild-west town, a gold mining town, and it had quite a reputation. But the one hotel there said they did not take women. They wouldn't be responsible for any women living there. So the girls had to get back on the bus and [return to California.]"[20]

Though absent female companionship, the 353rd was finally getting more ships. On one trip Don and several others traveled to Hamilton Field in a twin-engine B-34 Lexington to pick up five P-39s. Don led the flight back through Reno, where they spent the night because of inclement weather. After "looking over the town," they arrived back at Tonopah on February 15.[21]

Word came late in the month that the squadron was being sent to Santa Rosa, California, for another temporary change of station. Don had no regrets about leaving Tonopah: "I for one, won't be too sorry to leave this place and the planes." On March 1 they left by train for an overnight trip to their new base. With bombing and gunnery training behind him, Don did not expect to see Nevada again. He was looking forward to his return to California, where improved N- and O-model P-39s awaited the pilots.[22]

11

Buzzbower

It's against the regulations. . . . He [Don Beerbower] should have known better, basically. I make no excuses for a guy that will do that. We used that AT-6 for instrument flying . . . . There was no reason for a guy being down there tooling around among the wires. I don't think it was his usual habit. I think a man can learn from that.

James Cannon, P-39 pilot
(interview with the author)

    The train ride across the Sierra Nevada Range was stunning and, moving from the desolate, barren conditions around Tonopah to the wine-growing country of Sonoma County, California, proved a pleasant change for Second Lieutenant Don Beerbower. Located only seven miles northwest of Santa Rosa, a one-hour drive from San Francisco to the south, and a few minutes away from Hamilton Field by air, Santa Rosa Army Air Base was anything but isolated. The 354th Fighter Group had returned to its original mission of providing coastal defense against the Japanese while continuing the tactical training of its pilots.

    The 353rd Fighter Squadron quickly built up its strength of new P-39s. Major Seaman and Don flew two planes back from Hamilton Field on March 4. "[They are] Ns and Os and they're swell," Don wrote. Three days later, the squadron boasted ten aircraft, although one ended up in the sub-depot because Flight Leader Jim Cannon accidentally touched down short while landing.[1] Cannon's P-39 had a belly tank, the consequences of which Cannon failed to anticipate in his final approach to the airfield.

> It was business as usual on my part, then reality set in on final as I leveled off and surprisingly had sunk a little faster than normal . . . causing the two main wheels to dig into the dirt bank a little short of the runway. . . . The extended nose wheel gear was not damaged because of the plane's nose high landing attitude. The

plane came to a smooth stop on the runway, riding on the nose wheel, main gear stubs and the belly tank that became detached in the process. Later, I told Major Seaman that I had no excuse for the mishap and heard no more about it until later after WWII [when] Arthur W. Owen reminded me of it. He thought the camouflaged runway didn't help matters."[2]

Santa Rosa Army Air Base had been camouflaged earlier in the war to make it more difficult for Japanese to spot from the air. The runways were painted to look like the adjacent pastureland.[3] On this day Cannon was a lucky man.

With the influx of new P-39s, the flight leaders could concentrate on tactical flying. It was also time to identify the pilots most qualified to be element leaders. Each flight of four planes made two elements of two aircraft. Logically, the flight leader flew in the lead element, followed by the other pair, called the second element. Each element leader had a wingman whose job in combat was to protect the leader from attack. On March 14 Don mentioned in his diary the two pilots he thought capable of serving as element leaders in "D" Flight: "A full day! 4 flights. All 4 ship tactical. I'm trying to pick out a couple of the guys to lead 2nd element. Emmer and Donnel work out about best, I guess. I'll try them all then work on the two that work out best. Just wrote to Elayne and now I'm 'out'–like my light is going to be in a minute."

Six days later disaster struck "D" Flight. John Anderson and Paul Leydens went on a two-ship mission which left Santa Rosa at 1345, with visibility unlimited. The two pilots were cruising at ten thousand five hundred feet north of the airfield when the element leader, Anderson, signaled Leydens to move off his wing and into string formation. Anderson peeled off to his left and, at nine thousand seven hundred feet, lifted the nose of his aircraft thirty degrees above the horizon. His airspeed was two hundred fifty miles per hour. He then completed a slow roll to his left. After flying straight and level for a few seconds, he completed a slow roll to his right. When he looked for his wingman, Leydens was nowhere in sight. An Aircraft Accident Classification Committee Report filed several days later said, in part: "It is believed that Lt. Leydens fell into a spin, from which he could not recover, while trying to do a slow roll. The possibilities were that the pilot may have tried to recover with throttle on, as witnesses heard the roar of the engine, or from investigation made at the scene of the crash there is a possibility that the right elevator was disconnected or sheared off before the crash which would hinder recovery."[4]

Leydens was married. His wife had moved to Santa Rosa to be near him while he completed this phase of his training. Don had responsibility as flight leader to tell the young woman about her husband's death. No one had trained him in the proper procedure for this difficult task. In his diary that evening (March 20) he lamented, "Lost my first pilot today. Hope it's the last. Paul Leydens. Spun out of a slow roll at 10,000 feet—how—I don't know. I sent him up with J. Anderson. I was leading a 4 ship flight in tactical work at the time. It was tough going to take his car out and tell his wife about it. She took it like a trooper though. Poor Kid."

Squadron Historical Officer William Moneta later wrote, "Lt. Leydens was a quiet, modest young man whose death was keenly felt by all." Lieutenant Howell accompanied the remains to New Sharon, Iowa.[5]

Paul A. Leydens

Being a flight leader merited promotion to a higher rank. On March 25 Don commented in his diary that he was now First Lieutenant Beerbower. Pleased to be exchanging his gold bar for a silver one, he wrote, "It seems pretty good [to] get that silver bar. . . . It feels the same tho!!" Bradley, Cannon, and Montijo were promoted as well. For several days the "hangar, barracks and Orderly Room were shrouded in cigar smoke."[6]

On March 26 Don heard from his old friend, Navy Lieutenant Bill Johnston, who was in California for a couple of weeks and wanted to get together. Johnston had just arrived in San Francisco after a few days in Los Angeles, where he'd visited their mutual Hill City friends, Bud Vashaw and Lee Mykkanen and their families. During his short stay in San Francisco, he decided to contact Don. Johnston flew the Consolidated PBY-5A Catalina, a twin-engine patrol plane capable of landing on the sea or an airstrip. Johnston mentioned his visit in a letter he later sent to Gay Huntley at the *Hill City News*: "While in 'Frisco I contacted Don Beerbower. We still haven't decided which is the better plane—the P-39 or the PBY. He sure looks neat in his uniform. He must be a swell pilot, too."[7] Johnston was about to leave the West Coast for Pearl Harbor when, by chance, he connected with his friend. As Don mentioned in his diary on March 27: "Bill Johnston called from S.F. yesterday noon just as

I was leaving operations for my day off so I went down and spent the evening with him. Sure was swell to see him again. He hasn't changed a penny in two years. A little broader maybe. Flying's been going along swell. I'll have over 50 hours this month, which suits me fine." And then he added, "Elayne seems to be getting along swell. I'd sure like to see her again. I wonder at times if she tells me all the trouble she has or if she really is getting along ok. Sure hope so. Wish so much she could be out here."

Consolidated PBY-5 Catalina "Black Cats" in the southwest Pacific

Although Don thought of Elayne often, his flying duties demanded much of his attention, and he had recently been selected for a new responsibility. He wrote about his latest assignment in a letter to Darrel and Arlene.

4-15-43

> Dear Kids
> . . . I'm so far behind on this letter writing that it isn't a bit humorous. We have an AT-6–like we flew at Luke . . . and whenever I'm not flying in the P-39's I'm the squadron checker-outer on spin recovery technique [in the AT-6]. Major Seaman flew with each flight leader and then said I should be the one to do it. It's fun to spin it but it whips into it like a top and they aren't supposed to always come out. They wouldn't even let the instructors spin them at Luke. I had one guy up day before yesterday and he got into the first one and couldn't get out. I sat there in the backseat, telling him what to do and he wouldn't do it right. After 8 or nine turns, I took over and forced the controls way in with the spin and then snapped them opposite with all I had and the ship just snapped

and shuddered out of it. We came out of the dive at 2500 feet from 10,000. Nice feeling. So we climbs back up and got those ironed out. He just wasn't snapping his controls hard enough. . . . He won't be the only one like that either.

I also check their technique on acrobatics. Yesterday one of them was trying to do an Immelmann [turn] like we would in a P-39—not good, but it would work in a 39. But in the AT—we wound up on our back with the nose way up in the air and all our flying speed gone. Can you imagine the feeling? There we hung till I kicked rudder and we whipped down and tried to spin. More damned fun! A flight like that wears a guy out. I have to keep the AT going when I'm not flying 39's so I'm on the jump! . . .

You asked about my pay now Darrel. It's $166.66 base pay, $83.33 flying pay, $75 rental allowance, $42 subsistence. Comes to around $365 per month. Not too bad eh? Plus the $10,000 insurance policy.

Sure wish they'd decide what they're going to do with us pretty soon. I have almost 200 hours in the P-39 and I'm rarin' to go—soon's I get to go home! Write lots.

Your Brother Don

Lieutenant Don Beerbower

Because of Don's training responsibility in the squadron, it was imperative that he maintain his own skill in spin recovery and acrobatics. He had authorization to practice by himself in the AT-6. Flying alone, however, changed the weight and balance-point of the aircraft. To counter this, Don liked having someone in the ship's empty seat.

On April 16 he decided to go up in the AT-6 to work on the Immelmann turn. This is a maneuver in which a pilot completes a half-loop and then half-rolls the airplane back to normal, upright flight. The Immelmann turn allows the pilot to gain altitude while reversing direction. Don's passenger on April 16 was a fellow Minnesotan, Private First Class Richard Springer. At 1645 they departed Santa Rosa on a southerly heading. Don did not have a lot of time to practice because they both needed to be back by 1830 to stand for Friday evening inspection. He climbed to an altitude of ten thousand feet and, within twenty minutes, completed the aerobatics. At 1710 Don was still south of the field and descending through four thousand feet when he decided against entering the downwind leg of the traffic pattern in the standard manner for a landing from the north. Instead, as he later reported to the Aircraft Accident Classification Committee, ". . . I decided to duck down around the hill to the east of the field and come up and enter traffic to land. I crossed the highway and railroad tracks with over 2,000 feet of altitude and after passing over all signs of habitation, headed east and down. I came around the hill, gradually increasing the bank." And then suddenly, "At about half way round the hill and in about a 60 degree bank the plane struck the high lines. I never saw the lines before we struck them. They must have been stretched across the little ravine between the hills about 40 feet from the ground. The jolt slowed the plane some but I managed to pull it up to find that a long piece of wire was hanging from the left wing. I couldn't see the end of it. . . ." Springer stated in the report how Don responded to the collision with the power line: "He gained altitude and at 5,000 feet asked if I wanted to bail out. In reply I said, 'No sir.' We then tried to lose the wire which we found was impossible. After finding that useless we headed in to the field and landed with no further damage."[8]

Springer later divulged his actual statement to Don when asked about bailing: "No Sir, I came up with you and I am going down with you!"[9]

Richard R. Springer overseas 1944

Jim Cannon was working on his instrument procedures in a Link trainer when Don hit the wires. The resulting power outage knocked out the lights in the building and caused the trainer to topple over at an odd angle. A few minutes later, Cannon saw the AT-6 approaching the runway under full power with a length of twisted electrical wire wrapped around one of the wings. Realizing the pilot was his fellow flight leader, he thought, "What the hell, you're in deep trouble here."[10]

When Don sat down to write in his diary later that evening, he wasn't sure what his fate would be. From his comments, it is clear this was not the first time he had violated flying regulations. He may also have misstated the length of wire attached to the left wing. Eyewitnesses indicated it was approximately two hundred feet in length. Don wrote: "Well–it finally happened. Had it coming, I guess. My accident! Flew the AT-6 into some power lines east of the field. Took out 2 main lines carrying 60,000 volts each; 6-3 strand cables and pulled over a large metal tower. And came out with over 2,000 feet of wire on the left wing. Had to land with it. Got it in okay. Illegal buzzing with the AT of course. What now–I don't know?! Major Seaman and Col. Martin are with me but General Maurice [Morris, E. M.] of the 4th Fighter [Command] is up in the air. Have to sweat it out."

Military personnel at the air base put some spin on the incident to feed to the public. The following day the Santa Rosa newspaper editor reminded his readers, "Our boys are going overseas and they have to learn this type of low level flying."[11] Don had every reason to be concerned about the consequences for his action. Area utility services had been severed, wires and a tower were down, the aircraft was damaged, and he had endangered the lives of himself and his passenger. In addition, his colleagues had given him a new handle. No longer "Beerbower," he was now nicknamed "Buzzbower," or "Buzz" for short.[12] Although some obviously saw humor in the matter, the accident was serious business and Don knew it. He had much to lose by his careless stunt, including his recent promotion, flight leader position, AT-6 training duties, and possibly his pilot rating.

On April 25 Martin acted. Don's diary entry was brief. "Half base pay–it cost. Cheap if that's all. Lucky to be here to pay it!!" Now he had to wait for the decision of the Aircraft Accident Classification Committee. The officer in charge of the investigation, Captain William M. Casey, issued his report on April 30. After summarizing the written statements of the pilot and his passenger, Casey concluded the responsibility for the accident "is that of the pilot." He made no recommendation for disciplinary action.[13] It was over, the matter closed.

During April, six of the squadron's pilots—J. Anderson, Bullock, Chatfield, Coffey, Gross, and LaBarge—were sent as replacements to American units in

North Africa, where they would be flying the RAF's well-regarded Supermarine Spitfire, a single-engine fighter plane that came into its own during the Battle of Britain. Other changes included the transfers of Campbell to the 4th Air Defense Wing at Hamilton Field, and Flight Leader Montijo to the 356th Fighter Squadron.[14]

On April 30 Don noted in his diary that plans were underway for the 353rd Fighter Squadron to relocate to Oregon, where they would serve under the Portland Air Defense Wing—another temporary change of station. The squadron's pilots departed Santa Rosa in early May for the seven-hundred-forty-mile trip north to Portland. Bad weather en route held them up at Medford Army Airfield in Oregon for two days. They finally arrived at their destination, Portland Army Air Base, on May 7. Don was impressed by the bomber force stationed at the facility. Adjacent to Portland Airport, the large complex was located six miles northeast of the city along the south bank of the Columbia River. It was now home for the 353rd Fighter Squadron's pilots, support staff, and planes—eleven P-39s and one AT-6.[15]

The move to Oregon delayed the overseas assignment Don desired, but his longing to return to his wife and family in Minnesota would soon be satisfied.

12

WE TALKED QUIETLY

I was exempt from being drafted because of essential work, driving the school bus. Anyway, as soon as school let out, by gosh, why here I come–got my draft call. Clarence Beerbower run the creamery down there at that time, and, of course, creamery work was essential, so he told me, "Chet," he says, "if you don't want to go, I'll give you a job down at the creamery." Well, he had [one] of his boys in the service and I thought, "Boy, how would I look to go to work and take that job at the creamery." And Archie, my brother, he was already in the service. I told him, "No, Clarence, no. I'll do my duty with the rest of the fellows."

Chester T. Sailer, 90th Infantry Division, radio operator
(interview with the author)

First Lieutenant Don Beerbower was not expecting to become a father until midsummer. When the telegram arrived from home on Monday, May 20, 1943, he was stunned; his wife had delivered premature twin girls. His diary notation said, "I hardly knew what to think–I hardly could! Elayne was in serious condition as I knew she must [be]. The babies were only a little over seven months and I knew they couldn't be too strong. Couldn't get an airliner out till 11 that nite so called Dad in the meantime. He said everything was okay now with all three. I was somewhat relieved. . . ."[1]

Don wanted to return home as soon as possible. Major Seaman promptly responded by authorizing a leave and by making arrangements so that Don would qualify for priority air travel. Don's trip back to Minnesota turned "hectic" when he had problems with his connecting flight, and he couldn't stop worrying about his wife and daughters.[2] When Don landed at Wold-Cham-

berlain Field near Minneapolis on Tuesday evening, brother-in-law Marshall Hankerson, sister Lavaun, and niece JoNett met him. Crowding into Marshall's 1930 Chevrolet coupe, they headed north to Hill City. Passing through the McGregor area, they paused for a moment to watch eight deer standing in the beam of the car's headlights. The whitetails were a welcome sight for someone who'd been away for fifteen months.[3]

Shortly after midnight on Wednesday, May 22, they arrived at his parents' home. There Don learned one of his daughters, Dawn Marie, had died. Borrowing a car, he hurried north along eighteen miles of dark, forest-lined U.S. Highway 169 to the hospital in Grand Rapids to see Elayne.[4] Because of the difficulty of the delivery, Dr. McCloud could not be certain whether she and the surviving twin, Bonita Lea, would live. When Don entered Elayne's room, he found her asleep. Gently pulling up a chair beside the bed, he waited an hour until she awoke.[5] Don later wrote in his diary, "It sure was a lift to see how nicely she was doing in spite of everything. She wouldn't go back to sleep so we talked quietly till almost daylight."[6] By morning Don could barely stay awake. He had not slept in a bed for three nights. Leaving the hospital, he very likely went directly to his parents' house to rest. That same day, Darrel and Arlene arrived from Danville, Illinois. Everyone was now home.[7] On Thursday Don and the grandfathers made internment plans for Dawn Marie. Don described the sad occasion in his diary after he returned to Oregon, "I made arrangements and Dad and Bill helped like a million and we buried Dawn Marie. Rev. Hoenoff gave a short talk which was very befitting and I appreciated it very much."[8]

The Beerbower Family: Clarence, Josie, Darrel, Lavaun, and Don

Thankfully, Elayne's condition improved. On Sunday, May 30, she returned to her parents' home, and Don breathed a happy sigh of relief. But premature Bonita, or Bonnie Lea as they were now calling her, needed ongoing care at the hospital. Most importantly, she was alive and making incremental progress. Don concluded, "I'm sure I never saw anything so cute and tiny in my life."[9]

In most respects Hill City had not changed in the time Don had been in training. As usual, the community honored its war dead on Memorial Day except this year also saw a local boy, Glenn Foust, remembered as Hill City's first soldier to die in World War II. And there was a wedding. Don's friend Archie Sailer married Jean Nelson of Butterfield, Minnesota, at St. John's Catholic Church, a couple of blocks from the Beerbower home. But Sailer, a brand new second lieutenant in the Army, would be leaving shortly for Edgewood Arsenal, Maryland. People seemed to have the basic things they needed, yet the *Hill City News* carried front-page stories about rationing coffee, sugar, meat, butter, cheese, cooking oil, gasoline, tires, and shoes. In addition, regular notices asked people to put ten percent of their income into U.S. War Bonds and Stamps. During the first week Don spent at home, two movies played at a Civil Defense rally in the new high school auditorium: *How to Act in a Gas Attack* and *The Air Raid Warden*.[10] The national authorities were concerned about the perceived threat of enemy bombers based in the Aleutian Islands and Norway attacking cities like Duluth, the vital iron ore port on nearby Lake Superior.[11] For nearly a year, a large contingent of local volunteers, including Clarence and Josie Beerbower, had been monitoring air traffic for Japanese and German aircraft. The spotters stationed themselves at an observation post in town.[12]

Perhaps the most noticeable difference about Hill City was the shortage of young men. Gay Huntley's boy, Philip, was an Army officer. Joe Sailer had one son in the service and another, twenty-eight-year-old Chet, had just received his draft notice. George Hankerson, who still returned to Hill City for visits from his home in Grand Forks, North Dakota, had a son, Bob, serving as a flight surgeon in the Army Air Forces in Burma. Many households had empty chairs around the table because of the war.[13]

During Don's emergency leave, a major change took place in the 354th Fighter Group; tall, lean Captain James H. Howard arrived in Oregon to take command of the 356th Fighter Squadron. Born in Canton, China, on April 8, 1913, Howard at age thirty was one of the oldest pilots in the group. He had graduated from Pomona College in Claremont, California, and the Navy's flight school at Pensacola, Florida. After three years of flying, including a stint with Squadron VF-6 on board the aircraft carrier *Enterprise*, Howard resigned his commission. In 1941 he returned to China with the American Volunteer Group (AVG). The "Flying Tigers," as they were better known, flew the Curtiss P-40 Tomahawk and Kittyhawk fighters. These men were military pilots who had resigned their commissions to serve in the AVG under former Army officer Claire Chennault. The Flying Tigers protected the flow of war supplies between Rangoon, Burma, and southwestern China, from bombing attacks by the Japanese Imperial Air Force. Howard served as Chennault's operations officer until July 1942, when the AVG was absorbed into the Tenth Air Force headquartered in India. He returned to the United States with several aerial and ground victories to his credit. Howard eventually decided to accept a commission as a captain in the Army Air Forces.[14] He joined the 354th Fighter Group at Santa Rosa on May 24, 1943, and immediately took over his new responsibilities. Howard brought valuable combat experience to the group. By June 1, he and the rest of the 356th Fighter Squadron's pilots were at their new base, Salem Army Airfield, near Salem, Oregon.[15]

James H. Howard

On Saturday, June 5, Don said goodbye to Elayne at Wold-Chamberlain Field and then boarded an airliner for the return trip to Portland. Their daughter was gradually getting better, but she remained in the hospital because of her small size.[16] Elayne had "improved quite rapidly" during Don's emergency leave at home. Even though she was still weak from her difficult delivery and ten-day stay in the hospital, Don said, "We enjoyed ourselves a lot." He returned to duty on June 7.[17]

During Don's absence, the squadron's four flights had been reorganized. Jack Bradley had been bumped up to full-time operations officer. Jim Cannon now led "A" Flight, Don, "B" Flight, Buford Eaves, "C" Flight, and Don's former assistant, Wally Emmer, held responsibility for "D" Flight. Three pilots—Barris, Duncan, and Lamb—had been transferred to the 356th Fighter Squadron, and Don Schultz was gone. He had bailed out of an aircraft on May 30, landing on the roof of a local hospital. The injuries he sustained during this incident kept him from ever returning to flying status. Replacements for these four officers and others lost during the squadron's time at Tonopah and Santa Rosa arrived on June 8. The seventeen new second lieutenants were dispersed among the different flights. Don received five of these junior pilots: W. Frank Alford, Wah Kau Kong, Carl Lind, Don McDowell, and Felix M. Rogers. He appointed Ridley Donnell as his assistant. Donnell was Don's only remaining experienced pilot. John Mattie had been transferred to "C" Flight.[18] Don summarized his thoughts about the new pilots in his diary entry for June 25: "The five are Kong, Chinese-Amer. and pretty darn good. Lind, not too hot but fair; Rogers and McDowell–both good. And Alford–who I'm afraid for. I've been spending a lot of extra time with him and he's improving some– but slowly. Just can't pull it in on a turn at all. A few more days and I'll pretty well know whether he can make it or not. We've had no accidents with them yet which is a record in itself!"

Of the remaining pilots who joined the squadron in June, several would play important roles in the coming months: Carl G. Bickel, Edward E. Hunt, Richard M. Klein, N. Grant Logan, David B. O'Hara, Edward R. Regis, Robert G. Silva, and Thomas S. Varney.[19]

The reports Don was receiving from Elayne concerning Bonnie Lea's progress continued to be good, although the doctor had stated it would be weeks before her weight gain would be sufficient to allow her to leave the hospital. Don proudly wrote about her in his diary in late June.

> 6-25-43
> Bonnie Lea is still in the hospital but is coming along swell. Every time Elayne sees her and writes, she's gaining weight and looking stronger and nicer. . . . I'm always waiting from one day to the next for word about her from Elayne. She's going to be a wonderful little girl and I know she'll make us very happy when we finally get settled down in a little home of our own. . . . Elayne wants to come out very badly and I want her like everything. I hate to ask her tho cause it would be quite a strain with all her time alone to worry about Bonnie. Am leaving it all up to her. Sure hope she comes soon.

Don did not have long to wait for Elayne's decision.

13

BRAVE AS HECK

I bounced a P-38 one day and we were rating around the skies trying to get on each others tail and . . . I rolled over on my back and then I split-s'd, completed a loop, and pulled out over the ground at a couple of hundred feet, but the '38 didn't make it and he went right into the hill. And when I got back to the base I told Major Seaman about it and he said, "Okay, thanks for telling me." "Okay, [I said]." And that was it, never heard anything else. So we used to generally carry on quite a bit.

Willie Y. Anderson, P-39 pilot
(interview with the author)

As the sleek, twin-engine Northwest Airlines DC-3 carrying Elayne Beerbower touched down in Portland, Oregon, on July 1, 1943, she did not know how long it would be before overseas duty called her husband away.[1] She did know her daughter needed to remain in the hospital in Grand Rapids, Min-

Northwest Airlines DC-3 City of Bismarck *– One of seven DC-3s flown by NWA during World War II*

nesota, for a number of weeks. Elayne realized her visit would end when the call came from Dr. McCloud that Bonnie Lea was ready to come home, or when Don received orders for a war zone.[2]

Three days later, the members of the 353rd Fighter Squadron once again experienced the fragile nature of life. The pilots had a BT-13 Valiant available for training purposes. On July 4, First Lieutenant John H. Tennant decided to clock some cross-country time with Operations Clerk Max Hall. With visibility unlimited, they lifted off the airfield in the BT-13 at 1608 for a late-afternoon flight to Salem. The trip took less than half an hour. After a few minutes on the ground, they departed at 1715 for the return flight to Portland Army Air Base. As Tennant flew north, he followed the general course of the Willamette River, which empties into the Columbia at Portland. Because of air turbulence, he decided to fly at five hundred feet above ground level. Three miles south of Oregon City, Tennant rounded a sharp turn in the Willamette River and ran smack into a down draft, temporarily losing control of the airplane. At about one hundred forty feet above the water, the right wing of the Valiant struck two power transmission lines that carried electricity from the Bonneville Dam to Oregon City. The collision with the wires severed half of the wing. The aircraft careened out of control, landing upside down at the base of Pete's Mountain on the west bank of the river. Although Tennant had serious first-degree burns, he was able to release himself from the cockpit and drop to the ground. Several times Tennant struggled to climb back toward the ship to help his passenger, but with each attempt he stumbled further down the steep slope. Nearby witnesses could not reach Sergeant Hall who was engulfed by the flames. On July 8, the Aircraft Accident Investigation Board announced its findings: "Lieutenant John H. Tennant did operate army aircraft BT-13A, #42-42933 at low altitude thereby violating Army Air Force Regulation 60-16. While operating his aircraft in this hazardous manner, said aircraft struck a power line went out of control and crashed into a mountain with subsequent loss of life and property." The board concluded the accident was caused by pilot negligence and recommended "Such action as higher authority may deem justified and necessary."[3]

Tennant's injuries were so serious that he was hospitalized for months. He never returned to the 353rd Fighter Squadron. Staff Sergeant Pomeroy escorted the body of twenty-four-year-old Max Hall to Northfield, Vermont, for burial.[4] Although the incident bore striking similarities to Don's accident earlier in the spring, Don did not record his reaction to Hall's death in his diary.

In July, First Lieutenant John Mattie transferred back to "B" Flight in exchange for Second Lieutenant Don McDowell, who moved over to "C" Flight. This swap gave Don another senior pilot to serve as an element leader with the new junior pilots. Through John Mattie, Don and Elayne found a motel apartment at 9200 N.E. Prescott.[5] The apartment had adjoining rooms with Mattie and his wife. Six years older than Don, Mattie was a business college graduate from Beaverdale, Pennsylvania, a small coal mining town in the Alleghany Mountains. Drafted prior to the United States entrance into World War II, he worked on the flight line at Ellington Field, Texas, after completing training. When Mattie realized how much he enjoyed being around airplanes, he decided to apply for the aviation cadet program. He eventually graduated with Class 42-I. Mattie did not associate much with Don at Luke Field, as they were in different sections. But at Tonopah and Santa Rosa, they spent many hours together. Not until they lived next to each other in Portland did Mattie get to know Don in a more personal way. He admired Don's "relationship with his wife" and knew how proud Don was of his daughter. Mattie had a lot of confidence in his flight leader. Many years later he said, "I trusted him in anything he told me. I took his word for it. He was very fair to all the pilots. No pilot received any special attention. We all got the training we were supposed to get and he, of course, was in charge of that as flight leader in coordination with Jack Bradley who was operations officer." Mattie enjoyed his work. He never turned down an opportunity to fly. Some pilots did not like to get up for early morning patrols along the Pacific coastline, but he happily volunteered for these sunrise flights.[6]

Elayne and Don Beerbower at 9200 N.E. Prescott, Portland, Oregon

On July 19 the squadron returned to Tonopah for bombing and gunnery training. This served as a refresher course for the senior pilots.[7] The desert weather, however, was anything but refreshing. Midsummer temperatures soared. The high heat and dry, dusty air tormented pilots and airplanes alike, especially when taxiing the long distance between the hardstands and the end of the runway. Engines often overheated, causing delays in departures. No one complained when training came to an end at Tonopah.[8]

During Don's ten days in Nevada, Elayne went to visit friends Frank and Lizzie Betzer at Lebanon, Oregon, south of Salem.[9]

One of the pleasures for Elayne while in Portland was meeting some of Don's fellow squadron members. Jack Bradley paid frequent visits to their apartment. In addition to Bradley and John Mattie, Elayne enjoyed getting to know Glenn Eagleston, Wally Emmer, Wah Kau Kong, and Felix Rogers.

The time passed swiftly after Don returned from Tonopah, and soon Dr. McCloud called to say Bonnie Lea was ready to leave the hospital.[10] On August 15 Don took Elayne to the railroad station to catch the evening train back to Minnesota. Later that night he reflected in his diary about their special six weeks together in Portland: "We've had a great time while she was here. . . . Elayne was brave as heck going to the train." She sent him a letter when she passed through Butte, Montana, and a telegram when she arrived at the depot in Aitkin, Minnesota.[11] Her parents met her there on August 17, then drove thirty miles north to their farm near Hill City.[12]

Training for Don and his fellow pilots began to focus on coalescence. The three squadrons were frequently brought together now to practice working as one unit. This provided an excellent opportunity for Group Commander Kenneth Martin to develop his skill in managing a large formation of forty-eight planes. Likewise, Squadron Commanders George Bickell, James Howard, and Owen Seaman, through observation, could sharpen the performance of the sixteen fighters under their control. Within each squadron, four flight leaders learned to monitor radio traffic emanating from the levels of command over them, and to control their two element flights while maintaining position in the group formation.[13]

Flight leaders encouraged mock aerial combat with other fighters in the area. These engagements helped pilots hone the quick-decision-making skills they would need in dogfights. Although mishaps could occur, these exercises gave the men an opportunity to learn from their mistakes. On one occasion, Emmer's flight tangled with Don's flight in what Ed Regis described as a "pretty wild affair." As Regis remembered it, "I got on [Felix] Rogers' tail and he started going straight up and so forth and I said, 'No way. He's never going to get away

353rd Fighter Squadron - Tonopah Bombing and Gunnery Range, July 29, 1943
Front Row: Left to right - Major Owen Seaman, First Lieutenant Jack Bradley.
Second row: "A" Flight - James Cannon, Willie Y. Anderson, J. J. Baird, N. Grant Logan, Carl Carlson, Robert Silva, and David O'Hara. "B" Flight - Don Beerbower, Wah Kau Kong, Felix M. Rogers, W. Frank Alford, John Mattie, Ridley Donnell, and Carl Lind.

from me like that.' All at once I looked and I had zero air speed, and so did he. Both of us just flip flopped out of the thing. I ended up with a spin and just got out of it."[14]

A natural rivalry existed between the different branches of the service. The Navy had planes stationed at Tillamook and Astoria, a short hop from Portland along the Oregon coast. It was not unusual for the Army's P-39 pilots to bounce, or attack, their foes' stubby Grumman F4F Wildcats. Squadron member Carl Bickel considered the Airacobra the better aircraft in any action against the Wildcat.[15] The Navy had just brought on line a vastly improved fighter, the Grumman F6F Hellcat. In any serious engagement with this aircraft, the P-39 would not have fared well. On August 20, however, Don scattered four

Third row: "C" Flight - Buford Eaves, Carl Frantz, Richard Klein, Thomas Varney, Carl Bickel, Don McDowell, and James Parsons. "D" Flight - Wally Emmer, Glenn Eagleston, Donald Stretz, Edward Regis, Charles Uhlenberg, and Edward Hunt.
Not pictured: James Kerley, Charles Koenig, and Arthur Owen.

Hellcat flights and several Avenger torpedo bombers when he attacked them with an eight-ship formation. He described what happened in his diary: "Big battle with 25 navy ships this afternoon, 16-F6F's and 9-TBF's. I had 8 ships and we gave them quite a time. But it was overcast at 5000' so we couldn't mix it much when they went into the hills. Fun while it lasted." The superior Hellcats may have lacked the room to maneuver against the pesky Airacobra pilots. Regardless of this possibility, Don's aggressive leadership style began to blossom.

On August 26 Don celebrated his 22nd birthday; "[I] had a nice birthday for having to spend it out here alone." It was his second in a row away from home. He received a carton of Camels from Ridley Donnell and Wally Emmer,

and Elayne sent him a cigarette case from Bonnie Lea.[16]

Wally Emmer and Don had developed a close friendship through their association in the same flight at Tonopah and Santa Rosa, and now as flight leaders at Portland. Emmer, four years older than Don, hailed from St. Louis, Missouri.[17] He'd earned a solid reputation in the squadron. Flight member Ed Regis described him as a "fairly quiet individual [who] was a good leader, explained things in detail and was a really good pilot."[18] Willie Y. Anderson found Emmer's humor different from his own: "You had to know Wally to know when he was really kidding. I enjoyed him. Don was about the same as me, your humor [was] right out in the open. . . ."[19]

Emmer enjoyed drawing. At Luke Field his cartoons graced the Class 42-I class book.[20] Later, after joining the 353rd Fighter Squadron, Emmer again put his artistic skill to good use by helping design a squadron emblem that depicted a winged snake. It represented the unit's moniker, Fighting Cobras, a takeoff on the P-39's nickname. Jim Cannon recalled Emmer as "the mainspring in the development of our first squadron cobra patch. [It was made] using heavy paper stencils for each color. Several helpers used brushes to spread the paint colors onto the light canvas material that was trimmed into the cir-

Original Fighting Cobras patch

COURTESY JAMES CANNON

cular patch. They were crude compared to the later improved methods, but . . . we wore them on our jackets."[21]

Word filtered out that the 354th Fighter Group was being sent overseas. On September 10 Don mentioned in his diary that the squadron had completed about everything necessary for leaving Portland, including a final two-day "inspection by a colonel and his whole party." Don yearned to return to Minnesota for five days, but he felt his "chances [were] getting slimmer each day." With time running out, Don decided to act. In his diary entry for September 15, he mentioned spending the afternoon flying on instruments and practicing gunnery, and that the previous evening they "went to the Pagoda and Kong ordered [them] a family Chinese dinner that was really tops, then a show and home." Then he added, "I just called the orderly room to have them type a request for a leave dated the 17th. I've finally decided to take things into hand and try to sneak one in fast before it's too late."

Major Seaman approved the request. Don departed Portland by airliner early in the morning on September 17. The trip proceeded uneventfully until his stop in Billings, Montana. Here, someone with "higher priority" bumped Don off the flight. The best way home now was by bus. Frustrated as only a man who is racing a ticking clock can be, Don called his father in Hill City and made arrangements to be picked up the following day in Fargo, North Dakota, six hundred miles away. The twenty-four-hour stop-and-go trip on U.S. Highway 10 took Don along the Yellowstone River to Miles City, Montana, across the Badlands of western North Dakota, over the Missouri River at Bismarck, and finally into the pancake-flat Red River Valley. When he arrived in Fargo on Saturday morning, September 18, Elayne and Clarence were waiting for him in the family pickup. They still had one hundred seventy miles of asphalt and gravel roads to travel before arriving in Hill City, but at least now Don had his arm around his wife. Don later wrote Darrel and Arlene that the bus ride took "a day off my leave but it was still more than worth the trip."[22]

Everyone knew this was Don's last visit home before he went overseas. In the short time they had together, the Kutcher and Beerbower families, friends for many years, strived to accommodate each other's desire to be with Don. On Sunday, his parents and Marshall, Lavaun, and JoNett were dinner guests at the Kutcher farm.[23] Marshall remembered "having a great feast. . . . It was a happy day to have him home."[24] Darrel and Arlene did not come from Illinois as Darrel was not well; however, Don did talk to them by telephone. He also worked in a round of golf with his father, whom he "couldn't quite beat." Mostly Don enjoyed being with Elayne and Bonnie: "Gosh it was swell to be with Elayne even for only a few days. Bonnie is growing like everything and she should with the care she gets. She sure is cute. We had a big time with

Elayne and Don Beerbower, Marshall and Lavaun Hankerson, and Josie Beerbower at the Kutcher farm

her."²⁵ Don later wrote Darrel and Arlene, boasting, "she smiles and plays so much. Likes her Daddy too! And what a kicker! Just can't keep covers on her when she's awake without pinning them down or holding her."²⁶

All too soon the furlough came to an end. A final photograph was taken of Don in his uniform—a rich, dark-olive "loden" green jacket with accompanying light taupe shirt and slacks, or "pinks" as they were called—and Elayne in

Don, Bonnie, and Elayne Beerbower

Don & Elayne Beerbower by 1942 Chevrolet at the Kutcher farm

a stylish Chesterfield overcoat and dress, holding hands beside her father's 1942 Chevrolet Special Delux.[27] They left the Kutcher farm and drove into town. Don's parents, very concerned about his flying in combat, said their last goodbyes as the young couple boarded the bus that would take them to Minneapolis.[28] It left Hill City on U.S. Highway 169, skirted Quadna Mountain south of town, and crossed Willow River meadows, where Don had hunted deer several years earlier. As they rode over the familiar peat bogs of Aitkin County, Elayne sensed that Don would not be returning home for a long time. All across the country, husbands and wives were making similar last trips together. The war was pulling people toward it as a vortex draws fragments to its center. The feelings of love, worry, and fear that bound these couples to one another resisted the heartbreaking inevitability of separation caused by this powerful, swirling force. Like all the others, Don and Elayne had to overcome the emotional torment stirred by these intense moments in history. As they tearfully parted at Wold-Chamberlain Field, Don's true destination remained secret. How long he would be away, or whether they would ever be together again, were questions no person could answer.

Elayne spent the night with her aunt, Adeline Kutcher. She returned the following day, alone, to Hill City.[29]

During Don's return to Portland, he again was bumped off his flight; this time at Spokane, Washington. When Don called Major Seaman to explain the delay, Seaman sent the squadron's AT-6 to pick him up. Don was needed to run operations because Jack Bradley had left that morning for a brief furlough in Texas.[30]

Misfortune and mishap had again visited the group in Don's absence. Felix Rogers broke the squadron's accident record when he inadvertently "pulled his wheels up on a hard spot," and Ben Bedehop from the 355th Fighter Squadron was killed during an aerial gunnery mission when his ship hit the tow cable of the target aircraft. Cecil Duncan, now a member of the headquarters squadron, put one of the planes in the Columbia River "on a sneak approach."[31] John Mattie, flying beside Duncan when the mishap occurred, pulled up from the water's surface to enter the traffic pattern at Portland Army Air Base, but not Duncan—his "propeller drug him under." Fighting panic, Duncan held his breath as the sinking P-39 came to rest on the bottom of the river. When the water pressure on the outside and the inside of the cockpit equalized, Duncan forced open one of the Airacobra's doors and escaped. To Mattie's amazement, "they recovered the airplane and put it back into use again."[32]

By the end of September the unit's departure for overseas service was imminent. On September 30, Don wrote in his diary, "Things are getting hot–I mean No Flying last 3 days. Getting planes ready to turn over to Base." After a year and a half of training, Don had developed into a skilled army aviator and a trusted, competent officer. His nation had prepared him well to face the ultimate test of a fighter pilot.

Part Two

After thirty seven years of service and three wars and having arisen to four star rank, I attribute a large measure of my success to my initial service under Major Beerbower.

Felix Michael Rogers, General
(letter to the Minnesota Aviation Hall of Fame)

    The sixteen Mustangs of the 353rd Fighter Squadron climbed to nine thousand feet before clearing the thick haze that draped over northern France on August 9, 1944. They were twenty-three minutes behind the twelve P-51s of the 356th Fighter Squadron, which had left A-2 at 1040. The assigned targets for both squadrons lay in the Epernay area of the old French province of Champagne, one hundred fifty miles east of the Normandy bridgehead. Flying in a line-abreast formation and on a heading of approximately ninety-seven degrees, the 353rd's squadron commander, Major Don M. Beerbower, guided the P-51s north of Paris and then slightly south of Château-Thierry on the most direct route to Epernay. The haze persisted, with visibility at lower altitudes ranging from three to six miles. Just before noon, the squadron descended to six thousand feet and began circling an area north of the city searching for a railroad spur that led to a German ammunition dump hidden in the woods.[1] Captain Felix M. Rogers later recalled, "We couldn't find what we were looking for [from] the air."[2] After orbiting the vicinity for fifteen minutes and finding nothing, Major Beerbower directed Flight Leaders Rogers, Bickel, and Montijo to follow his lead as he pointed *Bonnie "B"* north toward the city of Reims, a few miles away.[3]

    At 1200 the 356th Fighter Squadron attacked fifty oil and freight cars southeast of Epernay, severely damaging forty percent of the rolling stock. The three flights then continued along the railroad tracks toward Chalons-sur-Marne. Here, they came across thirty flak cars. After making an initial pass and receiving intense twenty-millimeter-cannon fire, the 356th returned to A-2 where the pilots reported, "There are plenty of targets left in this general area."[4]

14

Pulling Out Tonite!

It was a boring train ride, although as we went through various parts of the country, the leaves were all turning into a gorgeous profusion of yellows, reds, and browns . . . [Camp] Kilmer seemed to be a staging area for shipment overseas. Everyone wondered just where we would end up. It seemed like it could be Africa, England, or any number of places.

Carl G. Bickel, P-39 pilot
Before the Contrails Fade Away

The 354th Fighter Group members arrived at the Spokane, Portland and Seattle Railway station in Portland, Oregon, on Tuesday evening, October 5, 1943, and promptly began boarding a troop train bound for Camp Kilmer, New Jersey. It took several hours to load the thousand men and their baggage. Finally, at 1:30 a.m. the big steam-powered locomotive began to whistle and puff and soon was underway.[1] The train headed east following the Columbia River and then wended its way across the southeast corner of Washington to Spokane.[2] From there it climbed through the Bitterroot Range of Idaho and western Montana on the tracks of the Northern Pacific Railway. As the 354th left the Rocky Mountains, the scenery changed to rangeland, buttes, and prairie. Don Beerbower expected the trip to be "dull and long." It didn't take him and others much time to get a poker game going. Progress across Montana and North Dakota was excruciatingly slow. On the morning of October 8, they came through Fargo, where Don's father and Elayne had met him three weeks earlier. As the group left the Red River Valley, the many lakes and ponds of Minnesota popped up everywhere. The countryside began to look like home. The train passed through Detroit Lakes, where in September Clarence had turned his pickup east to deliver Don and Elayne to Hill City. Further along the line was Wadena, the town in which the elder Beerbower had been a buttermaker when Don was a toddler. In the afternoon the train arrived in Min-

Northern Pacific troop train stopping at Missoula, Montana, in 1945

Lorenz P. Shrenk Collection/Ronald V. Nixon photo

neapolis and stopped for three unexpected, potentially precious hours. Later in the day Don reflected in his diary, "Wish I could have been with Elayne for that time. It would have meant an awful lot. But I guess I was plenty lucky to be home just a week before leaving."[3]

The long troop train rolled on across Wisconsin and the rich farmland of the Midwest before entering Pennsylvania, where on October 10 Don sent a letter to Darrel and Arlene.

> Dear Kids
>
> We passed pretty close to you yesterday! Thru Chicago. Minneapolis, also. Sure would have liked to have seen you, if only for a few moments–but it was impossible of course.
>
> We've been on the train since Tuesday nite and now it's Sunday morning. We've been able to get off a couple times a day to stretch but it's getting awfully tiresome! These seats are no longer comfortable. I have a lower berth and I've been having the porter leave it down all day so I can lie down when I want to. Helps a lot.
>
> We've had a dandy poker game going for 15 of every 24 hours so far and little Donnie is doing all right–to the tune of $212.00 smackers. . . . I'm going to send some of it home as soon as we get to the port–which will be this evening. . . .
>
> I don't think this will be cut down any [censored] so I'll finish on the back. Hard to write with the train going. –And hard to read, I imagine.
>
> I'll write again soon as we get somewhere.
>
> > Love Don

Camp Kilmer was one of the main staging areas for soldiers and airmen heading to Europe. The big processing center, located thirty miles southwest of New York City, was spread over 1573 acres of New Jersey countryside. Construction of its twelve hundred thirty buildings had begun in January 1942.[4] Don's Hill City friend Archie Sailer had moved through Camp Kilmer the week before Don's arrival, and was now at sea aboard the Army transport *Edmund B. Alexander*, part of a troop convoy sailing for the British Isles.[5]

While the 354th Fighter Group waited for its convoy to assemble, the men took advantage of the pleasant fall weather to play softball. On October 11, Don pitched the 353rd Fighter Squadron's senior pilots to victory in a four-to-three squeaker over the junior pilots. Two days later, with his arm rested, they pounded the 355th Fighter Squadron's best team nine-to-six. On October 14, they defeated the group headquarters team seven-to-two. After their third victory in four days, Don wrote in his diary, "More Fun. We're getting a darned sharp team organized now."[6]

Perhaps it was fitting for the men to relax and enjoy the group's championship game. Soon enough, many of them would be in combat. On the day Don and others were having "fun," pilots and airmen in the Eighth Air Force over Schweinfurt, Germany, were in serious trouble. What happened on their mission has been forever known as Black Thursday.

American military leaders believed that precision daylight bombing was necessary to defeat Germany. The British had tried it and failed. Consequently, the RAF now limited its attacks to nighttime raids.

The Boeing B-17 Flying Fortress was the principle heavy bomber used by the Eighth Air Force in 1943. The well-armed B-17 proved to be a formidable opponent when protected by America's best fighter planes, the P-38 Lightning and P-47 Thunderbolt. But at this stage of the air war, fighters couldn't carry enough fuel to stay with the bombers all the way to the target. On October 14, the Luftwaffe held off its attacks on the Flying Fortresses until the Lightnings and Thunderbolts had turned for home. Twenty percent of the heavies sent to Schweinfurt went down in flames. The loss of sixty aircraft and their 10-man crews made precision daylight bombing unsustainable. If the brass wanted to continue it, fighters would need to have the range to protect bombers all the way to their targets and back.[7]

After the softball game, Don and some friends procured passes to go into the city. Based on his diary entry for October 15, the fellows had a good time: "Did New York City up last nite. From 6:30 [p.m.] till 4 [a.m.]. We were going strong! Got back just in time for reveille at 6:15. Really hit all the high spots we could think of."

A massive buildup was underway to open a second front in France. The Soviet Union had been demanding the Allies do this as a way of forcing the Germans to shift some of their resources in Russia to ward off a threat from the west. Although the Allies already had a second front in Italy, progress had been slow in the well-defended mountains south of Rome. The fighting in Italy did not significantly affect the war in Eastern Europe. During the Trident Conference at Washington, D.C., in May 1943, President Roosevelt, Prime Minister Winston Churchill, and the Combined Chiefs of Staff had agreed on the tentative date of May 1, 1944, for the invasion of northern France.[8] Don, speculating about his group's role in supporting a second front, closed his diary notation on October 15 with this comment: "We're part of a large task force they're sending over. Looks like we won't be stopping for long in England."

The convoy forming in and around New York harbor had been given the designation UT-4. It was the fourth in a series of special United States troop convoys being sent to the United Kingdom to support the invasion. The first, UT-1, had left on August 21. Ten more of these UT convoys would sail to the British Isles over the next few months. The convoys with their escorts averaged thirty-three vessels, transported at least fifty-three thousand troops per trip, and didn't have any ships sunk or damaged by the Germans in their eleven crossings of the Atlantic. One rule was strictly adhered to: only ships that could maintain a minimum speed of fifteen knots were allowed in these convoys.[9]

In some respects it was understandable that all of the UT convoys arrived safely in Britain. In the month of May, German U-boats sent forty-one ships to the bottom on the North Atlantic and Arctic runs. But by October, the number had dropped to eleven. Over the summer, the Americans, British, and Canadians had expanded aerial surveillance from land bases in New England, Newfoundland, Greenland, Iceland, and the United Kingdom. In addition, the introduction of small, escort aircraft carriers allowed the Allies to pursue U-boats in areas where land-based coverage was unavailable. Also, sailors and airmen were using improved radar and direction-finding devices to locate enemy submarines running on the surface.[10] With all of these advantages, a disaster could still happen. The worst in 1943 occurred with the torpedoing of the Army transport *Dorchester* bound for Greenland in February. Its sinking ended the lives of six hundred seventy-seven men.[11] Even though fewer ships were being lost, the untested troops making their first crossing in the UT convoys felt uneasy. They had been hearing about U-boat attacks for several years. The thought of spending time in the dark, frigid waters of the North Atlantic appealed to no one.

After ten days in New Jersey, departure time finally arrived. The group

British converted passenger/merchant vessel Athlone Castle preparing to leave the west coast of Scotland for Bombay, India, May 1942

boarded a train at Camp Kilmer for the short ride to New York City.[12] At the Hudson River, the men ferried over to Manhattan where they were loaded onto the British merchant vessel, *Athlone Castle*, a 25,564-ton troopship built in Northern Ireland in 1935 for the Union-Castle Line. Prior to the war, the *Athlone Castle* regularly transported passengers and mail between South Hampton, England, and Cape Town, South Africa. This merchant ship had an overall length of six hundred ninety-six feet, a width of eighty-two-and-a-half feet, and a service speed of twenty knots. After war broke out in 1939, the *Athlone Castle* underwent retrofitting to carry troops. To this end, on October 20 she found herself at dockside in New York City taking on the men from the 354th Fighter Group and other units.[13]

As part of the group's officer cadre, Don Beerbower was given a less-than-exciting responsibility on the ship; he was named the sanitation officer for the top deck. Nevertheless, this duty did not limit his enthusiasm about sailing for the first time. He wrote in his diary, "Pulling out tonite! It's a British ship, 'Athlone Castle,' It's a good fast ship, 6500 men and officers on board! Good show!"[14]

Thirteen transports, three tankers, and British escort carriers *Trumpeter* and *Slinger*, which were ferrying aircraft to Northern Ireland, departed New York at 2230Z (1730 Eastern Standard Time) on October 21. The convoy commodore, Rear Admiral H. D. Cooke, USN, had orders to rendezvous with four transports from the Boston section of Convoy UT-4 south of Halifax, Nova Scotia, at latitude 42-20 north, longitude 64-05 west, at 1100Z (0700 Atlantic Standard Time) on October 23. Ten of the twenty-two ships in the convoy were troop transports.[15] To protect it from U-boats and the German battleship *Scharnhorst* and heavy cruiser *Lutzow* (stationed at the northern tip of Norway), the British Admiralty and the United States Atlantic Fleet assigned surface craft to accompany the convoy.[16] Task Force 69, under the command of Captain Roy Pfaff, USN, consisted of the American battleship *Texas* and thirteen warships, primarily destroyers and destroyer escorts.[17] Pfaff was on board *Texas*, a 34,000-ton New York Class battleship commissioned in 1914. This veteran dreadnought of World War I measured five hundred seventy-three feet long and one hundred six feet wide. Her main battery boasted ten fourteen-inch guns placed in five turrets. Each gun was capable of firing a fifteen-hundred-pound armor-piercing projectile twelve miles.[18]

Once the New York and Boston sections of UT-4 joined forces, Rear Admiral Cooke directed the convoy to depart the area on a heading of ninety degrees, and to remain on this course until they were due south of Cape Race, Newfoundland. En route to this location, Cooke ordered the master of the American transport *Golden Eagle*, T. Angell, into Halifax as his ship could not maintain the requisite fifteen knots and was smoking excessively. *Golden Eagle* left the convoy, but instead of retiring to port as ordered, she sailed for the British Isles alone. Angell's insubordination later resulted in a six-month suspension of his license.[19]

Lieutenant Colonel Kenneth Martin had been placed in charge of all troops on the *Athlone Castle*. He used the group's officers to assist him in managing the needs of the soldiers and airmen. Unlike the officers, who shared three-or four-man cabins, the enlisted men found themselves crammed into the hold, where conditions were less than ideal. They waited in long lines to use the latrines and for twice-a-day servings of chow.[20] Weather permitting, the men spent as much time as possible on deck getting some exercise, sunshine, and fresh air. Poker games were perpetual and alcohol available to those who'd smuggled it aboard. Other entertainment arose spontaneously. Carl Bickel, for instance, purchased a full case of one-pound almond Hershey bars from the ship's store, depleting most of its supply; and he soon discovered Wah Kau Kong was ridiculously passionate about chocolate. Kong would knock on Bickel's cabin door, crawl in on his belly with an outstretched hand, and plead for a Hershey bar. Bickel couldn't resist his friend's comical way of requesting the delicious candy.[21]

Members of the 353rd Fighter Squadron held Wah Kau Kong in high regard. Born on January 17, 1919, Kong, like many of the pilots, was older than Don. His hometown was Honolulu, Hawaii.[22] Kong had received his commission as a second lieutenant through the Reserve Officers' Training Corps (ROTC) program at the University of Hawaii, where he'd studied to be an engineer. As an officer, Kong avoided the harassment dished out to the aviation cadets in flying school. He joined Don's squadron at Portland in June. Flight member Felix Rogers considered Kong "a really outstanding guy."[23]

Wah Kau Kong

By October 26, Convoy UT-4 had turned slightly to a heading of eighty-four degrees as it plowed steadily along in an east-northeasterly direction nearly equidistant between the Flemish Cap, off Newfoundland, and the Azores. North of these Portuguese controlled islands at latitude 44-30 north, longitude 29-25 west, it turned abruptly to a course of thirty-eight degrees and stayed on this bearing until off the coast of Ireland.[24]

Because of the threat from U-boats and surface craft or a collision within the convoy in bad weather or at night, the men practiced abandoning ship. Richard Turner from the 356th Fighter Squadron woke abruptly one night about ten o'clock when the ship's alarm sounded. As the men scurried to their assigned lifeboats, he saw in the distance a skyward eruption of yellow and red flame, followed by the sound of ships' whistles and the blinking of signal lights. After the fireworks quieted down, Turner and the others went back to their bunks where many of them spent a restless night.[25] Ed Regis remembered being told that destroyers were practicing dropping depth charges, but many years later he said, "[I] never believed that and I don't to this day."[26] Whatever caused the explosion that Turner, Regis, and others saw, it did not come from a submarine. Only two U-boats were sunk by American forces in the North Atlantic during UT-4's crossing. The closest sinking happened hundreds of miles away. *U-220* had been seeking out its supply ship after laying mines in the harbor at St. John's, Newfoundland, when bombed northeast of the Flemish Cap on October 28 by aircraft from American escort carrier *Block Island*.[27]

As the *Athlone Castle* moved farther away from America, Don and the others moved closer to something ominous that most of them had never experienced. Richard Turner described it as "an awakening awareness of the nearing reality of combat."[28] This awareness raised questions that lacked answers. How dangerous will my duty be? Will I have the skill and concentration it takes to stay alive in aerial combat? Do I have the courage to risk my life for others if called upon to do so? Can I kill another man? Will I ever see my home and my family again?

At latitude 55-20 north, longitude 15-50 west, UT-4 swung east, slowly crossed above Ireland, and then passed through the North Channel into the Irish Sea. Two of the tankers had already split off to deliver fuel to Iceland. On November 1, several more ships diverged, these heading up the Firth of Clyde to ports in Scotland; then *Texas*, *Trumpeter*, *Slinger*, tanker *Enoree*, transport *Fair Isle*, and four destroyers slipped away into Belfast Lough. The remaining ships continued on to Liverpool and its sub-ports, and to ports along the Bristol Channel. On *Texas*, Captain Pfaff was angry that UT-4 had been denied access to safe waters in the United Kingdom until November 1. He believed they could have arrived twenty-four hours earlier. In a letter he sent to the British

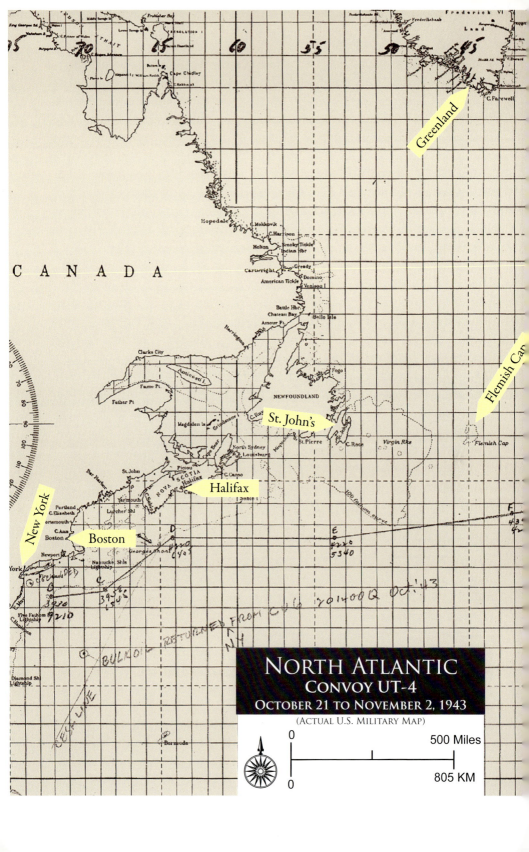

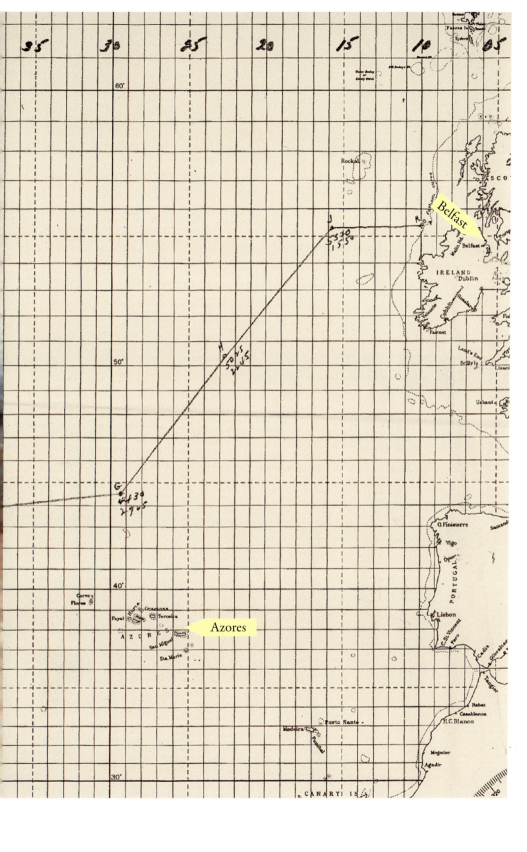

Admiralty and the United States Atlantic Fleet, he wrote, "It is considered very undesirable to keep a convoy, especially a troop convoy, on the high seas an unnecessary day." He felt "ships could anchor in the Belfast Lough or even cruise up and down the Irish Sea while waiting for ports of destination to clear for them."[29]

When Don and the other members of the 354th Fighter Group reached Liverpool on England's northwestern shore, the harbor was hidden by a fog bank so thick "you could barely see the deck of the ship, let alone the docks."[30] All hands breathed a collective sigh of relief to be in a protected anchorage. The atmosphere on board relaxed, and the spirits of the men returned as they prepared to disembark from the ship.[31] As with any convoy, however, it took time to rotate each vessel from the roadstead to the pier for unloading. The *Athlone Castle*, her sister ship *Capetown Castle*, and *Empress of Australia*, *Monarch of Bermuda*, and *Surprise* had arrived on November 2.[32] But not until the evening of November 4 did the men actually walk down the gangplank, "tired but thankful to be on dry land once again."[33] The pilots boarded a train which took them through the night to their first overseas base, Greenham Common Airdrome, near Newbury, in Berkshire.[34] Off the *Athlone Castle* after two weeks at sea, Don wrote in his diary on November 5, "We're in England finally."

The group's transfer to an overseas base had begun on October 6 at the train station in Portland; now a month later it was ending at another station in Newbury, sixty miles west of London. After a short truck ride through the countryside, the men arrived at the airdrome. Ed Regis marveled at his new surroundings: "I thought it was absolutely beautiful. It was maybe like I'd pictured England in my mind. They had buildings with thatched roofs and everything else around the place."[35] As Regis and the other pilots headed off to their assigned quarters, they had another reason to be pleased; a rumor that had been circulating among them was true; they were going to be the first fighter group to fly the new P-51B Mustang.[36]

15

Really a Honey!

[The P-51B] was so stable you could stall it and it would just fall out. It wouldn't spin. To get in a spin in that airplane, you had to physically do it. The flying characteristics on the thing were just absolutely fantastic.

Edward R. Regis, P-51 pilot
(letter to the author)

The United Kingdom of Great Britain and Northern Ireland had been at war with Germany since 1939. Sixty thousand civilians lay dead from the bombings of her cities. The country was in a complete blackout. All highway sign posts had been removed. Her citizens accepted the strict rationing of clothing and food, and the short supply of personal items such as soap. In these trying times, the morale of the people remained high. They were holding their own against the enemy.

When First Lieutenant Don Beerbower and the other members of the 354th Fighter Group arrived in England in early November 1943, they came with a basic understanding of the geography, government, language, money, weights and measures, and the customs and manners of the British people. While on board the *Athlone Castle*, the men had been briefed about Britain and the British way of doing things. The orientation countered German propaganda intended to create mistrust among the military forces of the United States and the United Kingdom, and between the British civilians and the increasing number of Americans moving into their cities, villages, and rural areas in preparation for the invasion. Officers and enlisted men alike received the same direct instruction about the importance of getting along in their new surroundings: "You are coming to Britain from a country where your home is still safe, food is still plentiful, and the lights are still burning. So it is doubly important for you to remember that the British soldiers and civilians have been living under a tremendous strain. It is always impolite to criticize your hosts. It is militarily stupid to insult your allies. So stop and think before you sound off about lukewarm beer, or cold boiled potatoes, or the way the English cigarettes taste."[1]

It was a common practice for British civilians to invite Americans to their homes. Many Yanks responded with gratitude for this courtesy. On one occasion, Willie Y. Anderson and several friends were luncheon guests of an English family. Anderson took a cab over to the home where he discovered the family didn't have much to offer them, but "we appreciated it and we thanked 'em. We went back later with . . . a ham and some eggs or something to make up for what they had to feed us because they had less than we did."[2]

The invasion was seven months away when the 354th Fighter Group arrived at Greenham Common Airdrome as the first of many such units assigned to the Ninth Air Force. The Ninth itself was new to England, having only recently been transferred from the Mediterranean theater. Its commanding officer, Major General Lewis H. Brereton, brought with him experience from serving in the Far East, India, and North Africa. The mission of the Ninth Air Force was to provide tactical air support for Allied land forces during the upcoming assault on Western Europe. As soon as its new air crews were trained, they would begin strikes against short-range targets across the English Channel. Brereton oversaw six commands: Air Defense, Bomber, Engineer, Fighter, Service, and Troop Carrier. The 354th Fighter Group fell under the watchful eye of Brigadier General Elwood R. "Pete" Quesada. His IX Fighter Command included all fighters, fighter-bombers, and reconnaissance planes within the Ninth Air Force.[3]

Lewis H. Brereton

Elwood R. "Pete" Quesada

Ninth AF unit patch

A problem arose when the Ninth Air Force's new fighter group received the first P-51B Mustangs. Because of the airplane's long-range capability, the Eighth Air Force wanted to use it to escort heavy bombers in the strategic bombing campaign against Hitler's war production capability deep inside Germany. Therefore, since D-day was not scheduled until spring, Army Air Forces officials decided to temporarily loan the 354th to the Eighth Air Force. This did not change the command structure. The Mustang pilots, as part of the Ninth Air Force, would answer administratively to Brereton and Quesada; their day-to-day operational control, however, resided with the Eighth Air Force.[4]

Lieutenant Colonel Kenneth Martin and his men had been sent to Greenham Common to familiarize themselves with the older P-51As of the 67th Tactical Reconnaissance Group while they awaited delivery of their new fighters. The P-51A, though similar to the P-51B in appearance, differed greatly in handling characteristics. The earlier model had come into existence as a result of a contract signed in early 1940 between the British Direct Purchasing Commission and North American Aviation of Los Angeles, California. North American, whose reputation hinged on its success with the single-engine AT-6 Texan trainer and the twin-engine B-25 Mitchell bomber, had limited production experience with fighters. The British wanted them to manufacture the existing Curtiss P-40 Flying Tiger. The company, on the other hand, felt they had a viable idea on the drawing board for a new type of pursuit plane. When the British agreed to the development of a prototype, the firm quickly produced the NA 73X. Its maiden flight was on October 26, 1940. The 73X was an all-metal aircraft with an advanced laminar-flow wing and a liquid-cooled Allison engine. The engine's radiator was located in the lower rear area of the fuselage. These features, along with its superb aerodynamic design, reduced drag, which in turn increased speed and fuel efficiency. Impressed with the aircraft, the British agreed to purchase it for their air force. The RAF named it the Mustang Mark I. British pilots soon discovered the Mustang could outperform their well-regarded Rolls-Royce Merlin-powered Supermarine Spitfire below thirteen thousand feet, and with its fuel capacity, could fly three times farther than the British fighter. However, at mid-altitudes and above, the eleven-hundred-fifty-horsepower Allison engine did not perform well.[5] In 1942 Rolls-Royce proposed installing the more powerful Merlin engine in the Mustang. The U.S. Army supported this recommendation. It had a contract with North American for one thousand two hundred P-51A fighters and five hundred A-36 dive-bombers. By the fall of 1942, the converted Mustang achieved a speed of four hundred twenty-two miles per hour at twenty-two thousand feet. It later reached four hundred fifty miles per hour at thirty thousand feet. This was a significant improvement over the three hundred eighty-two miles per hour the

Allison-powered Mustang produced at fourteen thousand feet a year earlier. The increase in speed did not come entirely from the Merlin engine, which had nearly a four hundred-horsepower advantage over the Allison. The new design also included a four-blade propeller and an advanced supercharger, which replaced the three-blade propeller and single-stage, one-speed supercharger on the P-51A and A-36. Testing in England and California proved so successful that by January 1943, the air chiefs at the Pentagon ordered two thousand P-51Bs.[6]

North American P-51A Mustang

U.S.A.F PHOTO

The pilots had to complete several days of orientation at Greenham Common before they could check out in the P-51A. On November 9 Don Beerbower and the other flight leaders went to Membury Airdrome at Hungerford to learn how to fly these aircraft. Three days later, ten pilots were sent to Warton, near Liverpool, to pick up the group's first P-51Bs. Don was placed in charge of this detail.[7] At Warton he encountered support personnel in no hurry to give the budding fighter pilots their new airplanes. Don described the confrontation in his diary entry on November 16:

> Back at the Squadron again! Only it's all moved over onto the east coast! Operations for sure now. Got the ten ships after a real battle! Everybody was mixed up on this deal! It was a real headache for yours truly. Ferry Command was all p-d off at us for busting into their little party, and wasn't going to let me have the planes. I couldn't do a thing but I found the ones who could and a direct

order from General Quesada finally got it straightened out. I had the Ferry boy's eating out of my hand before I left! We all got a bang out of their change of tune!

The P-51B is really a honey! I believe it when they say it's the best fighter ship in the world! I'm afraid that Elayne and Bonnie have competition for just a little of my love tonight. –It's my ship! I had the one I flew out of assembly at Warton assigned to me so I'll be the only one to ever fly it! Have my crew Back at the Squadron again! Only it's all moved over onto the east coast! Operations for sure now. Got the ten ships after a real battle! Everybody was mixed up on this deal! It was a real headache for yours truly. Ferry Command was all p-d off at us for busting into their little party, and wasn't going to let me have the planes. I couldn't do a thing but I found the ones who could and a direct order from General Quesada finally got it straightened out. I had the chief assigned too. He's a good boy! Lot's of work to do for the next week or two!

Once Don had clearance to leave Warton with the ten Mustangs, his emotions, which had been all astir, were stirred again when he walked out on the tarmac to inspect the brand-new P-51B he was going to fly home, #43-12457. The clean lines, fresh interior, and subdued color of the fighter filled him with deep proprietary pleasure as he anticipated the power and grace of the aircraft in flight. A few minutes later, as Don built speed heading down the runway, he could feel in the throttle-control the latent energy of the smooth-running Merlin engine. Flying back to group headquarters was unlike anything he had experienced before, and so it is understandable that he wanted '457 as his personal airplane. When his wish came true, Don tucked away the aircraft authorization form given to him by the 27th Air Transport Group at Warton, and saved it as a memento of his first Mustang.[8]

The ship's new crew chief, Sergeant Leon H. Panter, also thought of '457 as his airplane. Panter, born in 1909, was twelve years older than Don.[9] The younger enlisted men fondly called the native of Sand Springs, Oklahoma, "Pappy."[10] Now that Panter had his own ship, he received a code letter for it. The letter designated for '457 was E. Each American fighter squadron also went by a two-letter designation. The 353rd Fighter Squadron's code letters were FT. The unit's letters and Panter's letter were placed on both sides of the fuselage between the wing and the tail. The American star symbol sat between the FT and the E. If the crew chief's aircraft became unserviceable for any reason, the letters followed him to his next P-51.[11] Don decided to name the plane *Bonnie*

"B", in honor of his daughter.¹² He asked Panter to arrange to have the lettering placed on the nose of the fuselage. In reality, the new fighter was the shared responsibility of both the pilot and the crew chief, and she was known by two names: *Bonnie "B"* and FT-E.

Crew Chief Leon H. Panter

Bonnie "B" had been manufactured at the North American Aviation plant in Inglewood, California, at a cost of $38,893. The Army Air Forces accepted her on August 25, 1943, and promptly shipped the airplane overseas through Newark, New Jersey. On September 12, the Ninth Air Force took possession of the ship in England.¹³ A Packard-manufactured twelve-cylinder Merlin V-1650-3 engine powered *Bonnie "B"*. With a rating of one thousand five hundred twenty horsepower, a two-speed, two-stage supercharger, and a Hamilton Standard Hydromatic four-blade propeller, she possessed excellent speed and climbing ability. Armament included two Browning fifty-caliber machine guns in each wing. The canopy had a "bird cage" or "greenhouse" cockpit cover with metal reinforcements built into the glass that restricted visibility. Because of the difficulty in seeing well through the back of the canopy, a small rearview mirror was installed to compensate.¹⁴ Jack Bradley didn't mince any words when it came to the cockpit area: "[It] had a terrible canopy on it. . . . You couldn't move your head three inches to either side. . . ."¹⁵ Eventually, engineers would solve the problem.

The Mustang's pluses far outweighed its minuses. Veteran 356th Fighter Squadron commander James Howard loved the static-free, four-channel very-high-frequency (VHF) radio and the high-altitude demand-type oxygen system. After many hours of flight time in the F4F, P-39, and P-40, he considered the P-51B a "pilot's dream."¹⁶

By mid-November the group had moved to East Anglia in eastern England to prepare for operations against the Luftwaffe. The new base at Boxted Airdrome in Essex was about sixty miles northeast of London, near the city of Colchester, and a short distance from the North Sea. The one-year-old airdrome had two six-thousand-foot runways with adjoining taxiways and hardstands for parking aircraft. The living quarters were long Nissen huts heated by small, coke-fueled stoves. Each squadron had its own mess, administrative offices, and maintenance facilities. Along with the group's arrival in East Anglia came the cold, damp rain of early winter. Boxted became a sea of mud. This slowed the unit's training in the P-51B.[17]

When the 353rd Fighter Squadron relocated to Boxted, it did not have a full compliment of pilots. This changed on November 20 with the arrival of Bernard F. Durham, Jerry D. Leach, and Robert L. Meserve, followed a few days later by Edward F. Fox, Glenn H. Pipes, and Albert J. Ricci.[18] Meserve transferred from the 67th Tactical Reconnaissance Group. Flight Leader Jim Cannon thought Jack Bradley had arranged for the transfer because of the impressive way Meserve "conducted the transition training sessions" at Membury.[19]

In late November Don led a group of pilots to Warton again, this time bringing a sixteen-ship formation back to Boxted. By the end of the month, the pilots proved ready for combat operations. On November 29 the three squadrons participated in a group assembly formation in preparation for their first mission the following day. Don had accumulated eight hours of flying time by now, and perhaps because of this, he found himself penciled in as Major Seaman's wingman. Brigadier General Quesada and Lieutenant Colonel

Don Beerbower wearing a "Mae West" life jacket

Martin were scheduled to fly in the squadron as well. Don went to bed early that evening because, as he wrote in his diary, "it's sharp that I'll [want] to be tomorrow." Regrettably, the weather on the November 30 was "no good" over Belgium and France. Instead, the disappointed squadron pilots flew along the English coastline and test-fired their guns.[20]

In addition to the Ninth Air Force having Quesada present at Boxted, the Eighth Air Force brought in twenty-six-year-old Ohio-born Lieutenant Colonel Donald Blakeslee to guide the 354th Fighter Group on its first few missions. Blakeslee had resigned from the Army Air Corps in 1940 to join the Royal Canadian Air Force. By 1941 he was flying Spitfires against the Luftwaffe. When the British placed American volunteers into newly formed Eagle Squadrons, Blakeslee was named the commanding officer of one of these units, 133 Squadron. In the fall of 1942, he transferred to the Eighth Air Force to fly P-47 Thunderbolts and to provide leadership to the 335th Fighter Squadron, 4th Fighter Group. When he arrived at Boxted he was already an ace. His last two victories were against Focke-Wulfs he shot down near Knocke, Belgium.[21]

Blakeslee came to Boxted with the experience of a veteran and a reputation that commanded respect. A serious man, he made it quite clear to the new pilots that their job was to kill Germans. Prior to mission departure on December 1, Blakeslee briefed the men on the tactics that worked best against the Luftwaffe. One of these left a distinct impression on those present. He told the attentive new pilots to "never break" when attacking a German head-on. If unable to shoot down the aircraft, they were to remain on a collision course forcing the enemy to break first. Failure to do this, Blakeslee warned, would give the Hun a psychological advantage. With this thought on their minds, the pilots picked up their gear and motored to the hardstand area.[22]

Donald Blakeslee

The group's first mission was specifically chosen so the leadership of each squadron could experience what it took to manage a formation under combat conditions. Don mentioned in his diary that the earliest operations were designed "for us flight leaders to get a good look at the country over there so we can lead our own flights over and back, more competently."[23]

Blakeslee decided to fly with the 353rd Fighter Squadron on the mission, a fighter sweep to the area around Knocke, Belgium. He flew in a three-ship flight with Jack Bradley and Don Beerbower. Major Seaman led the other flight with Wally Emmer on his wing. Buford Eaves took the second element with James Kerley on his wing.[24] Kerley replaced Flight Leader Jim Cannon, who was away at gunnery school.[25]

By early afternoon, the clear sky that had welcomed everyone in the morning no longer existed. Heavy clouds obscured the end of the runway, one mile distant. On a typical mission, aircraft formed below the overcast before moving up through it in tight formation. On December 1 the ceiling was too low to allow this, so Blakeslee directed each element leader to take off with his wingman as usual, but then to turn left to a fixed heading while climbing. Once the pair broke out of the overcast, they were to close with the rest of the group. Although inexperienced, the pilots had trained on instruments, so Blakeslee's decision to fly through the clouds in this manner was tenable. Each element soon departed as directed, disappearing into the moist fogbank. As the lead pilot's eyes shifted to his instruments, he banked the plane to the correct heading while holding the nose in a climbing attitude. The seconds slowly ticked by and became minutes, ample time for the normal uneasiness of flying blind to become numbing fear. There is something about the sound and feel of an airplane that is different when the pilot does not have an outside visual reference. Any hint that the engine is not running well can play on the pilot's mind. Worry over a mid-air collision with other nearby aircraft can create panic. So it was a great relief when the elements finally emerged intact from the thick, gray blanket into pure sunlight and unlimited visibility. The novice group had climbed through nearly twelve thousand feet of solid cloud cover.[26]

With the 353rd Fighter Squadron in the lead, Blakeslee began a gentle climb to seventeen thousand feet as the group headed southeast across the North Sea toward the Dutch-Belgian border, one hundred ten miles away. His orders said to "use utmost discretion regarding [the] weather, route and timing" so as to arrive five miles east-northeast of Knocke at 1500. When the group entered Nazi-controlled Belgium at zero hour, Blakeslee continued inland for several miles then turned southwest, keeping the coastline to his right. His orders dictated he patrol across Flanders to Bruges and Ypres, and then continue northwest to Gravelines, France. From Gravelines he was to cross the North Sea near

Pas de Calais before returning to Boxted, eighty-five miles away.[27] Blakeslee's actual course took him about twenty miles further inland, as he used the discretion allowed in his orders to fly over Ghent, Belgium, then on to Lille, France, before swinging northwest to St. Omer and home.[28] German radar tracked the Mustangs, but no enemy aircraft came up to challenge them. Some antiaircraft fire greeted the formation from three miles below. Although the exploding shells caused only minor damage, they did get everyone's attention.[29]

As Blakeslee led the three squadrons back out over the North Sea, he used his VHF radio transmitter to request a heading and weather conditions for landing at Boxted. Navigational aids for pilots were limited to the VHF direction finder (D/F) at each airdrome. Captain Edward P. Elliot manned the D/F equipment in the Boxted tower for the 354th Fighter Group. Jim Cannon considered him the "best operator in the business." When Blakeslee contacted Elliot, he used the group operator's code name, Goodall, and the 353rd Fighter Squadron code name, Jackknife, along with his call sign (30, 31, etc.) to ask for a compass heading and landing conditions. Goodall replied by acknowledging the call and asking for a ten-count from the pilot. Once he had a good signal, Goodall gave Blakeslee a vector to Boxted and advised, "the 'Oranges are sweet,' meaning good visibility and adequate ceiling for a safe letdown."[30] These comforting code words cheered Blakeslee and his new veterans as they continued inbound over the North Sea.

The first use of the P-51B Mustang in the European theater by the United States Army Air Forces was a success. The twenty-three pilots with Lieutenant Colonel Blakeslee had done well when they encountered adverse weather conditions upon departure from Boxted.[31] Although the mission had been relatively short, the group's leaders garnered a sense of what it was like to fly over German-occupied territory. Don, or Jackknife 39 as he was known in the air, clocked an hour and twenty-five minutes in a borrowed P-51, FT-J. Don could hardly contain himself when he made his diary entry on December 1: "First Mission!! Over Belgium & France. We got indoctrinated to Flak too. And it was damned accurate stuff! One of the boys–(Lane)–Got a hole in his rudder! It was really an experience! We'll keep things moving now whenever the weather permits."[32]

Unfortunately for the 354th, the weather was not going to be very accommodating.

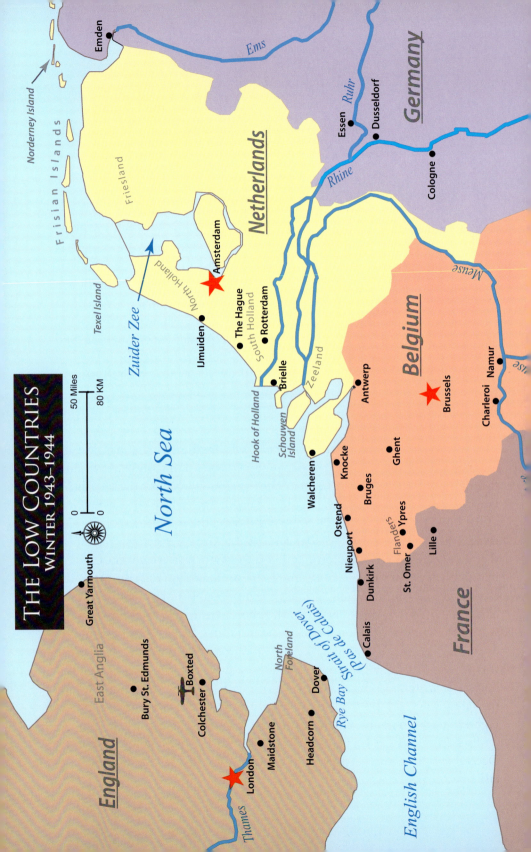

16

First Loss

After escorting our second force of bombers over the target at Kiel on Dec. 13, 1943, our flight, led by the group leader [Donald Blakeslee] whose wing I was flying, engaged a Ju-88 at about 1315. This was in the vicinity of Hamdorf, Germany. We were above the e/a [enemy aircraft] and to the left. The group leader made a pass at the e/a from dead astern as it went into a steep dive. I followed in trail and took a three second burst from about 200 yards range. I observed no strikes. I broke right and pulled up, rejoining flight in front. This engagement took place between 22,000 feet and 20,000 feet.

James W. Kerley, P-51 pilot
(Encounter Report)

  The American commitment to the daylight bombing of German war industries and military facilities in the winter of 1943-1944 was hampered by the location of its base of operations. The airfields occupied by the Eighth Air Force's heavy bombers, primarily in East Anglia, received less than nine hours of light a day in December. Although this limited flying time, a more serious concern was the weather. Colchester lies three hundred fifty miles farther north than Don Beerbower's hometown of Hill City, Minnesota, where temperatures in the center of the continent can drop to minus forty degrees Fahrenheit. The climate in East Anglia is mild by comparison. It is affected by the warm waters of the Gulf Stream and proximity to the North Sea. In the winter the combination of cool, moist air and moderate temperatures creates overcast skies that often produce a bone-chilling, damp mist or occasional, snow. Even on days when the bombers could fly, cloud cover would still obscure the target. If the heavies were grounded because of conditions in England or over German-controlled territory, the fighters stayed home as well. For these reasons, the 353rd Fighter Squadron got off to a slow start in December 1943.

  Inclement weather kept the squadron from flying its second mission until December 5, when it contributed twelve aircraft to the 354th Fighter Group's task of escorting bombers to the Paris area. It was the first time over France for

Carl Bickel, Glenn Eagleston, John Mattie, Arthur Owen, James Parsons, Ed Regis, and *Bonnie "B"*. Felix Rogers failed to get off the ground because of engine trouble.[1] The mission was designed to ease the pilots into combat by penetrating as far as the French capital. No enemy air activity interrupted this raid, but as Don noted in his diary, flak downed seven B-17s "over & near" the two airfields they had attacked that morning.[2]

For the next several days, fog interfered with operations. Don used the time to wire Elayne flowers for Christmas through a florist in Grand Rapids, Minnesota. This was his response to a "very sweet" Christmas card he received from her in late November. Elayne had sent her greeting early because civilian mail did not have as high a priority as military shipments between the United States and the United Kingdom.[3]

On December 11 the weather improved enough for the squadron to escort the bombers across the Dutch border to Emden, Germany. For the second time, Lieutenant Colonel Donald Blakeslee flew with the Fighting Cobras. Don and the other flight leaders continued to rotate pilots to give everyone the opportunity to gain combat experience, so this third run was the first mission for Willie Y. Anderson, Edward Hunt, Carl Lind, Don McDowell, and Robert Meserve. Ridley Donnell had to abort because of engine trouble.[4] The squadron's course took them over the Zuider Zee, (Southern Sea) a large body of water along the primary route for bombers striking targets on the North German Plain. The Dutch had separated the Zuider Zee from the North Sea before the war by constructing a dike overlaid with a roadway between Friesland and North Holland. That evening Don described the mission in his diary: "16 ships from each squadron escorted B-17's this noon. Took off at 11:30, flew over the Zuider Zee and picked up two large boxes of forts and brought them back. No enemy aircraft sighted. Over clouds all the time. Weather was stinko. Landed my flight 20 miles from home for lack of gas. Used no belly tanks. Up 2 hours and 50 minutes which is too close to figure on with no extra gas."

A box of bombers in 1943 was a combat wing consisting of three groups of eighteen aircraft each, for a total of fifty-four B-17s or B-24s. The three squadrons within each group were staggered in such a manner as to provide maximum defensive fire against attacking fighters. The boxes followed each other in trail, six miles apart. In January 1944, the Eighth Air Force would adjust the formations to create more flexibility and greater protection from the Luftwaffe. In the new model, the number of bombers per box decreased to one group of thirty-six aircraft. Each group continued to include three squadrons, but the number of heavies in each squadron increased to twelve. The new formation still had the groups follow in trail with each box staggered slightly left or right of the line of flight. Separation between boxes shrank from six miles to four miles.⁵ Groups aligned left and right of the line of flight to avoid turbulence and, in some instances, condensation trails or contrails created at high altitude by one hundred and forty-four radial engines churning the air in the box ahead of them.

Contrails at high altitude U.S.A.F. PHOTO

The two types of four-engine bombers used by the Americans in the European theater were the Boeing B-17 Flying Fortress and the Consolidated B-24 Liberator. In a combat situation, a fully loaded bomber carried heavy armament and bristled with gun turrets that reduced the aircraft's efficiency. Outbound airspeed was less than two hundred miles per hour. The B-17, the older of the two ships, was slower, had less range, and couldn't carry as much payload as the B-24, but its flying characteristics, design, and endurance made it one of the most memorable airplanes ever built. William C. "Bill" Healy, a 94th Bomb Group pilot familiar with both aircraft, described them this way: "[The B-17G] was a very forgiving airplane, easy to fly, rugged. . . . It could come back on two engines, really shot practically to pieces, and hold together in the air, so it was durable. Those of us who flew it got very proficient. We could handle it like a fighter . . . . B-24s were from my point of view, flying coffins. . . . It had the armament. It didn't have the durability. It took fewer shots to shoot it down and it was harder to fly. I flew them a little bit, I just didn't like them."⁶ Those who loved their Liberators would have been quick to challenge Healy's summation of the big ship's characteristics.

Boeing B-17 Flying Fortress

Consolidated B-24 Liberator

One of the Army Air Forces' objectives was to strike Berlin. The British had already started this but they attacked at night without fighter escort. In December, external tanks for the Mustangs arrived at Boxted. With the additional fuel capacity, the P-51s could accompany the bombers to more distant targets in Germany. This also meant that Don and his colleagues were about to be assigned the most dangerous duty on a strategic bombing mission—fighter protection over the strike area. But with the added risk came opportunity for an aggressive pilot to mix it up with the Luftwaffe. Don wrote in his diary on December 12 that he expected to see more action soon: "Fogged in today. Tomorrow we'll have our belly tanks ready for use and if the weather is ok, we'll be going out well toward Berlin. We'll really have the range with the extra tanks. And we'll be the ones to use it. We'll be going way farther with the bombers than the P-47's can."

The 354th Fighter Group's fourth mission, on December 13, involved participation in an attack on targets at Kiel, a major German port on the Baltic Sea. Each time the group flew escort for heavy bombers, it deployed with all three of its squadrons, the 353rd, 355th, and 356th. On this operation, Jim Cannon was back from gunnery school and flying with the 353rd for the first time. His flight included James Kerley and Lieutenant Colonels Blakeslee and Martin. It was also the first mission for Carl Frantz, who was wingman for Major Seaman in a flight that included Buford Eaves and Carl Bickel. Felix Rogers' turn had come up again, and this time his aircraft worked fine. He flew off John Mattie's wing in the tail-end Charlie position or rear position, in Beerbower's flight. The Fighting Cobras could contribute only fourteen Mustangs to the group's effort, as Ed Regis and Carl Bickel aborted because of engine trouble.[7]

The pilots enjoyed good weather until they encountered a solid ten-tenths overcast a hundred miles west of Kiel. Rendezvous with the bombers took place near Eutin, southeast of the target. With the port city concealed, the bombers circled the area twice before releasing their ordnance. The P-51s bounced along in heavy, accurate flak outbound from the target until relieved by friendly fighters. For the first time, several pilots engaged enemy aircraft.[8] Don noted in his December 13 diary entry how this memorable mission was the last one for Buford Eaves:

> This was the day. Went clear over Denmark to Kiel with B-17's and B-24's. 4 hours 10 min in the damn thing and my butt is really sore tonite. Lots of flak and I saw one Ju 88 and an Me 110 but couldn't get a shot at them from my position. Eagleston got a hit on the 110. I was about the only one who brought his whole flight home intact. All the way across Denmark, the Zuider Zee & Holland with no maps–3 other ships tacked onto my flight & we came on in okay. The Ju 88 put a hole in Roger's wing. Eaves is missing. Last seen going straight down after a Ju 88. First loss!

Several incidents distinguished this raid. Rogers avoided death or imprisonment when a Jerry's aim fortunately missed the vulnerable wing root/cockpit area of his P-51. Eaves failed to return after Seaman's flight pursued a Ju-88.

Frantz was the last to see Eaves as he disappeared into the overcast while pursuing the twin-engine aircraft.[9] Glenn Eagleston recorded the first hit on an enemy aircraft while he and Wally Emmer provided mutual support for each other near Frederickstach. When Eagleston spotted an Me-110 three thousand feet below them, he "peeled off" from eighteen thousand feet, slid under Emmer, and dove to his right in pursuit of the Messerschmitt. He made three passes at the German aircraft, knocking out the rear gunner and setting the right engine on fire, but he couldn't quite finish off the '110 because his guns jammed. Emmer, whose electrical system failed, couldn't assist Eagleston. In the course of the encounter, the two pilots lost sight of each other and flew home alone.[10]

Glenn Eagleston proved to be an aggressive pilot. Born in Utah in 1921, he joined the Army Air Corps in 1940 and eventually became an aviation cadet, graduating with Class 42-I.[11] He later served with Wally Emmer and Willie Y. Anderson at Paine Field, Washington, before being transferred to the 353rd Fighter Squadron at Tonopah, Nevada. Eagleston, Buford Eaves, James Parsons, and several others were assigned to Jim Cannon's "C" Flight. Cannon considered Eagleston to be one of the "wildest . . . gung ho" pilots in the squadron, right up there with his close friend Snapper Parsons. Cannon recalled that Eagleston liked to play cards, as did a number of the pilots. "Every time we sat around," Cannon explained, "particularly at Tonopah . . . we gambled. John Mattie was the biggest gambler we had of the whole bunch. They played blackjack a lot and he won everybody's money. Eagleston was also one who'd play all day pretty much. Generally old Mattie would wind up with all of Eagle's money. . . . He'd borrow from me all the time. He was always broke."[12]

Glenn T. Eagleston

A bit of Eagleston's character is illustrated in the closing two paragraphs of the encounter report he wrote after returning to Boxted on December 13.

> E/a took no evasive action following rear gunner's retirement from active duty and when last observed was still in shallow glide, right engine dead and aflame, heading through the overcast which was estimated at about 6,000 feet. All breaks from engagement were made with a skidding roll to right and down, then up above E/A for position for next attack.
>
> Following final engagement with e/a, I scanned the sky for sight of friendly aircraft and upon perceiving not even the most remote indication of any such pleasant sight, I immediately hauled ass for home.[13]

A ranking officer "asked" Eagleston to rework these last two paragraphs. The more concise, professionally written second-encounter report that follows suggests the standard Lieutenant Colonel Martin and Major Seaman expected of the pilots.

> E/A took no evasive action after second pass and when last observed was still in shallow glide, right engine dead and aflame heading through the overcast which was estimated at about 6,000 feet. All breaks from engagement were made with a skidding roll to right and down, then up above E/A for position for next attack. I returned home alone.[14]

In Cannon's opinion "Eagle . . . really turned out to be a fine pilot. . . . He was a great fella. He gave Eaves the nickname Hard Rock. That seemed to fit his character pretty well."[15] And now Hard Rock was missing.

The twin-engine aircraft encountered by the squadron on December 13 had little in common with each other. The Messerschmitt Me-110 had been developed as a fighter but lacked the speed and maneuverability to last long against a P-51. However, armed with twenty-millimeter cannon and two-hundred-ten-millimeter rocket tubes, it was a lethal *zerstorer* or destroyer of unescorted bombers. The Junkers Ju-88 fighter-bomber was twice as heavy as an Me-110, included upper and lower rear gunners, and could fly at speeds in excess of four hundred miles per hour. It was one of the most versatile aircraft developed during World War II. The Ju-88 night fighter variant, armed with radar, struck fear in the British crews that flew the four-engine Lancaster heavy bombers in the dark skies over Germany.[16]

Captured Messerschmitt Me-110 with RAF markings

Captured Junkers Ju-88 with RAF markings

In mid-December the squadron received another injection of fresh pilots, enough to finally get up to combat strength. The new men would spend time training before going out on their first mission. Harry R. Baer, Omer W. Culbertson, Thomas L. Donohoo, Ralph M. Hanson, James P. Keane, Donald J. Munger, John B. Nall, Charles F. Read, John Rody, and Leo F. Skenyon brought the squadron's compliment up to fifty-two officers and two hundred fifty-one enlisted men.[17]

The weather cleared enough on December 16 for Blakeslee to lead the group on its fifth mission, this time to Bremen on the Weser River, fifty miles southeast of Emden, Germany. Blakeslee directed the group from one of the flights in the 353rd Fighter Squadron. Beerbower, Cannon, and Emmer were in charge of the other flights. It was the first mission for Ridley Donnell, Charles Koenig, Wah Kau Kong, Grant Logan, and Thomas Varney.[18]

Shortly after departing Boxted, Blakeslee received a radio message informing him that the bombers would be thirty minutes late in reaching the rendezvous point. The fighters reduced their speed but still had to wait for the heavies, which eventually joined them west of Bremen. The flak over the target grew intense, and both Seaman and Frantz, flying in Blakeslee's flight, took hits. The Bremen mission was noteworthy because First Lieutenant Charles F. Gumm, Jr., of the 355th Fighter Squadron recorded the first victory for the group when he shot down a single-engine Me-109.[19] The operation held further importance for Don, as he explained in his diary on December 16:

> Been fogged in since last mission but today we did something that I'm sure has never been done before. Took off at 10:30 this morning with a solid overcast at 450 feet and poor visibility below that. Climbed up thru to the top in flights and assembled the squadrons up there and flew to Bremen on top of an 8 to 10 tenths coverage and escorted the largest bunch of bombers to ever be sent over one target at one time, 800 +. They flattened the place out. Smoke billowed up to 22,000 ft. We were the only fighters out in this weather so we had the whole area over the target to protect. Had to all split up into our flights again and just cover sectors. The Germans had no fighters up at all tho and the raid went off like clockwork. Saw one Ju 88 but he beat it off into the clouds.
>
> The amazing thing is that 48 single engine fighters flew over a solid overcast for 4 hours +, did swell work on the escort and came back, let down thru the clouds to a 500 foot ceiling and landed without losing a one. They must believe in the training our group has cause in spite of our lack of combat experience over here, we were the only group of fighters ordered up through the weather. We're making a hell of a good name for ourselves. . . .

Only Don, Wally Emmer, and Owen Seaman had been on all five of the squadron's missions. Operations Officer Jack Bradley flew on four of them, and Jim Cannon now had two missions to his credit. The leadership of the squadron was intact except for the loss of Buford Eaves. All had gained confidence and valuable combat experience as they dealt with the longer missions, poor weather, larger bomber formations, antiaircraft fire, and increasing enemy activity.

17

A Gloomy Bunch Tonight

Before we left the ship I was giving him [Gordon E. Smith, tail gunner] medical aid. . . . Most of his fingers were shot off . . . and his arms were badly shot so it made him unable to use his arms to be able to swim ashore. Germans from [the] look out tower claim they saw him drown.

Joseph J. McDonald, waist gunner
(Missing Air Crew Report)

The Allied meteorologists expected the skies over northern Germany to be unusually clear by 1200 on Monday, December 20, 1943, one of the shortest days of the year. By the end of the week, not everyone at Boxted Airdrome would be alive to celebrate Christmas. Lieutenant Colonel Donald Blakeslee's temporary assignment to break in the new Mustang group was about to end. On the upcoming mission, he would turn the lead over to Lieutenant Colonel Kenneth Martin. He had done this once before when he observed Martin direct the three squadrons on the Emden raid; he would do so permanently two days later, on his sixth and final indoctrination of the 354th Fighter Group to air warfare.

Kenneth Martin and his crew chief, James G. Morrison

The group was scheduled to return to the Bremen area, site of its most recent engagement. Major Owen Seaman, with John Mattie on his wing, headed the 353rd Fighter Squadron. Don Beerbower filled the second element leader in Seaman's flight. Wah Kau Kong protected Don's wing. Jack Bradley, Jim Cannon, and Wally Emmer commanded the other flights. Finally getting a crack at combat, Richard Klein and Robert Silva would be flying their first mission. Frantz and O'Hara in Bradley's and Cannon's flights, never got off the ground.[1]

Bomber crews received a briefing in the early morning darkness, and now, shortly after sunrise, the heavies—loaded down with fuel, ammunition, bombs, and men—began to lift off runways all across East Anglia and several neighboring counties. The 96th Bomb Group at Snetterton Heath, thirty miles north of Boxted, put up thirty-one B-17s in two groups of three squadrons, each between 0815 and 0851. The 96th was the first double-strength bomb group in the Eighth Air Force.[2] Their target was the Focke-Wulf aircraft components factory at Bremen. Thirteen of the Flying Fortresses returned to base after they lost the formation in heavy clouds and condensation trails, or as a result of mechanical problems.[3]

One of the fighter units escorting the first wave of bombers to hit Bremen was the 338th Fighter Squadron based at Nuthampstead, north of London. This squadron sent up eight twin-engine P-38 Lightnings at 0955, two of which later returned to base. Their capability of providing top cover in the frigid, sub-zero temperatures at twenty-nine thousand feet gave the bombing run excellent potential for success. They rendezvoused with the bombers at 1127 and proceeded on to Bremen. As the formation approached the city, the Luftwaffe attempted several coordinated attacks, but the enemy fighters dove away as soon as the P-38s made feints toward them.[4]

The 353rd Fighter Squadron and her sister squadrons had departed Boxted at 1036. As the forty-four Mustangs crossed the North Sea, they gradually climbed to an altitude of twenty-five thousand feet. At 1155 they rendezvoused with the bombers from the 2nd Air Task Force. Providing penetration and general support for the heavies, they would escort the B-17s and B-24s into and over the target.[5]

Already near Bremen, the 45th Combat Wing, which included the 96th Bomb Group "B," encountered intense and very accurate antiaircraft fire. At noon, seven minutes before the group released its ordnance, one of its ships, B-17 #42-3288, took a flak hit, lost power, and turned northwest toward the sea and home. Another damaged bomber dropped out of formation. The two ships were not together,[6] and neither B-17 was observed going down by the 338th Fighter Squadron or any other friendly fighters in the area. The P-38s turned west after the bomb run and soon met the 2nd Air Task Force and its fighter escort proceeding to Bremen. The six Lightnings skirted south of the Zuider Zee and Amsterdam and then headed across the North Sea for home.[7]

Haze but no clouds hung over Bremen as the second wave of bombers approached the city; the Germans were using smoke generators in an attempt to make it more difficult for the bombardiers high overhead to locate their target. Numerous enemy aircraft patrolled the vicinity.[8] The 353rd Fighter Squadron

B-17 overflies smoke generators

was providing area coverage for two boxes of bombers when Flight Leader Jack Bradley and flight members Thomas Varney and James Parsons spotted several single-engine fighters ten miles south of Bremen. Bradley described their response to the sighting:

> At approximately 1235, while the squadron was making a wide sweeping turn to port over the bombers I saw seven Me-109s pass under my left wing going almost due east. My flight was on the outside of the formation at about 25,000 feet altitude. I called these in to the squadron leader and broke to the right, dropping my belly tanks. . . . I approached the nearest e/a from [a]stern at about 20 degree deflection and closed to 150 yards. I fired about

a one second burst which I believe must have killed the pilot, due to the later action of the aircraft. I broke to the right and up at the same time observing my second and third man passing under my left wing. At this time the e/a was flying slightly sideways but taking no evasive action. I recovered and came in again in line astern. I gave a five second burst from 100 yards line astern at 0 deflection. I observed strikes on the engine and saw pieces flying off the cockpit. There was white smoke coming out of the engine and cockpit and black smoke pouring out of the belly. I saw the other two planes of my flight on my right and rejoined them without observing the final result of the encounter.

Varney and Parsons had each fired a short burst at the '109 before breaking off the attack and rejoining Bradley. Following this encounter, the squadron's four flights continued their circling maneuver around Bremen.[9]

By now B-17 #42-3288 was approaching the East Frisian Islands many miles northwest of Bremen. The bomber was under the command of First Lieutenant Stanley P. Budleski, on his first mission with the crew of the Flying Fortress named *Green Fury II*. The navigator and bombardier from his own crew had recently been killed. Budleski skippered a "battered," older B-17F that had seen hard service with the 96th Bomb Group.[10] It lacked the firepower of the chin turret found on the newer B-17G (the extra machine guns provided additional protection against frontal attacks).

The Army had accepted delivery of *Green Fury* from Douglas Aircraft in Long Beach, California, on May 8, 1943. The ship's construction cost $330,297. She had been in service with the Eighth Air Force for six months.[11]

Although his B-17F had seen its better days, Budleski had a solid, experienced crew. His co-pilot was Second Lieutenant Bernard C. "Bernie" Jackson, who had flown nine missions, his last six at the controls of *Green Fury*. Most of the rest of the crew had thirteen or fourteen missions to their credit. Second Lieutenant John P. Coyle handled the navigation responsibilities. The other officer was the bombardier, Second Lieutenant Donald G. Spanier. Technical Sergeant Marco J. Coolum manned the radios; his position was near Technical Sergeant James M. Thompson, the engineer and top turret gunner. The remaining crew members included Staff Sergeants Donald F. Totz and Joseph J. McDonald at the waist gunner positions, and Melvin M. Brunner and Gordon E. Smith at the ball turret gunner and tail gunner positions. When Budleski left the formation near Bremen, his most direct route back to England would have been over Holland and the Zuider Zee. By choosing to fly northwest to the Frisian Islands and then across the North Sea, he was adding about an hour of flight time to the trip home, but by doing so, he was following the route assigned the bombers for their return to England. Flying alone, *Green Fury* risked almost-certain destruction if detected by enemy fighters, but by staying in the path of the returning bomber formation, Budleski increased his chances of being sighted by the friendly fighters responsible for covering the last leg of the mission.[12]

As the 353rd Fighter Squadron circled Bremen, the two boxes of bombers they were protecting completed their bomb run. Thomas Varney described what happened at 1245 when Bradley's flight again encountered enemy aircraft:

> [About] 15 miles north of Bremen on a course almost due north I saw another Me-109 about 300 yards above and 500 yards ahead cruising in the same direction. As our flight moved in to attack, I cut my throttle so as not to over run the flight leader who was firing at the e/a from astern. I slid in behind e/a and as the flight leader broke off fired a long burst from 75 yards to 20 yards from 5 to 0 degrees deflection, closing slowly I made a violent break away down and to the right in order to avoid collision with the No. three man [Parsons] who was coming up from below and apparently didn't see me."[13]

Parsons only had eyes for the enemy aircraft. He described his encounter this way:

> I attacked from below and dead astern firing a long burst as I raised on level with e/a passing only about 25 feet above him. I opened fire at about 40 yards and continued until line astern about 10 yards from e/a. I observed strikes along fuselage from tail to engine cowling and e/a was smoking. Pilot was slumped over in cockpit and appeared "Out." After breaking away I noticed my oxygen hose had become disconnected and I was feeling a bit woozy by this time. I pulled out of the immediate area and after correcting my oxygen trouble rejoined my formation.[14]

In their aggressive approach to eliminating the Messerschmitt, Varney and Parsons narrowly avoided a mid-air collision by luck, a factor that played a significant role in the careers of all fighter pilots who survived combat.

While the 353rd Fighter Squadron finished patrolling near Bremen, *Green Fury* came under attack off the coast of Germany near Norderney Island in the East Frisians. Hit by twenty-millimeter cannon fire from an enemy aircraft, top turret gunner James Thompson was dead, and tail gunner Gordon Smith was seriously injured and struggling forward from the rear of the plane. Fire burned furiously around Marco Coolum's work area, making it impossible to use the radios. Bombardier Donald Spanier heard co-pilot Bernie Jackson yell out, "Get that Jerry bastard!" Spanier and navigator John Coyle were at their stations in the nose of the bomber when suddenly the number-two engine was hit. The explosion blew the two men out of the aircraft. As the aerial combat intensified, ball turret gunner Melvin Brunner was blown out as well, but without his parachute. When waist gunner Joseph McDonald heard Stan Budleski give the order to bail out, he and the other waist gunner, Donald Totz, along with Coolum and Smith, jumped for their lives. Struggling with the crippled ship, Budleski and Jackson decided their best chance for survival was to crash-land the aircraft. At 1250 the pilots brought *Green Fury* down on the east end of Norderney Island, skidded along the surface of the beach, and struck a sand dune. Budleski and Jackson died at the controls near Thompson's lifeless body. Brunner's mangled remains lay on a hilltop not far away. By 1300, Spanier, Coyle, McDonald, and Totz were prisoners. The North Sea claimed Coolum and Smith. In the distance, a lone German plane was seen circling the island.[15]

At 1307 the six P-38 Lightnings from the 338th Fighter Squadron landed at Nuthampstead without having fired a shot. Their trip to Bremen and back had taken three hours and twelve minutes.[16]

As the 353rd Fighter Squadron's relief arrived to escort the 2nd Air Task Force home, Major Seaman gathered his individual flights together and proceeded northwest toward the East Frisian Islands where they planned to turn west and cross the sea to England. Near the German coastline, Flight Leader Jim Cannon noticed James Kerley falling behind the squadron. Cannon later reported what happened:

> We were line-abreast with the squadron and had just gotten into squadron formation, when I noticed Lt. Kerley, who was slow in forming with the flight, make a 180 degree turn. The turn was coordinated and rather tight; he then started a slight dive of about 30 degrees and disappeared from view. I informed the Squadron Commander of this and the formation made a large circle hoping to sight Lt. Kerley. The approximate time was 1330 and we were about 10 miles from the coast of Northwest Germany. It is my belief that he developed engine trouble and he turned inland rather than to take a chance on crossing the Channel.[17]

Kerley, unable to communicate by radio with his flight leader, began his descent near Aurich, Germany. He turned northwest toward the coastline and proceeded in the general direction taken by the squadron. Near Norderney Island, Kerley went down, breaking his collarbone in the process. Whether this happened in an attempt to bail out of his Mustang or upon impact from ditching in the sea is unknown. The injury would have made it very difficult for him to climb out of the cold water into his dinghy. That afternoon a civilian named Harms Cassen was walking along the beach on the east end of the island when he discovered Kerley's body.[18] He also found the remains of Marco Coolum and Gordon Smith. Cassen alerted German naval authorities who concluded all three were crew members of the downed B-17, *Green Fury*.[19]

James W. Kerley

After the 353rd Fighter Squadron crossed the German coastline, Major Seaman swung the remaining thirteen Mustangs to the west and began the final leg of their mission back to Boxted. Northwest of the Zuider Zee, Seaman alerted his wingman, John Mattie, that he was having problems with his P-51's engine. Consequently, Seaman couldn't maintain his position in the formation. Mattie believed the plane had been hit by flak earlier in the mission.[20] With flight members Don Beerbower and Wah Kau Kong nearby, Seaman began a gradual descent. When he returned to Boxted, Mattie filed this report:

> We were approximately 10 miles N.W. of Texel [Island] when I had the first indication that the Major was in trouble. I throttled back completely to stay at at 9,000 feet on a heading of 270. He maintained this course but kept losing altitude slowly until after approximately 20 minutes of flying we were down to an altitude of 1000 feet. I saw his canopy come off at this time and as I pulled up on his wing he began a slight climb and maintained it for a

few seconds after which he assumed a shallow glide, hitting the water in this position. The plane made a large splash on hitting, bounced once, went up on its nose with the tail in a vertical position, and settled into the water rapidly.[21]

Instead of turning south toward enemy-controlled Holland and certain capture, Seaman had gambled on nursing his fighter across the North Sea to England, one hundred twenty-five miles away. When the gamble failed, his choices came down to parachuting into the sea or attempting a wheels-up landing. Seaman knew because of his training that trying to inflate, retrieve, and crawl into a dinghy was hard to do before being disabled by the cold temperature of the water.[22] By landing on the sea, a pilot gave himself a few seconds to stand on the wing and maneuver the floatation device before the aircraft went under. Regrettably for Seaman, when his P-51 struck the water, he hooked the air-intake scoop on the surface, upending the aircraft. The location of the scoop under the mid-section of the Mustang made it very difficult to safely land the airplane on water. Mattie continued:

> Lt. Beerbower and Lt. Kong, who had been following us closely, began circling the spot the plane had gone down in while I climbed for altitude and began calling for a fix on the B channel. I called intermittently from 3000 feet to 8000 feet, and after receiving assurance that a launch was on its way, dropped down to a low altitude and began circling and searching the area. Lt. Kong and I circled for 20 minutes. As our gas was getting low and we did not see anything, we set course for home at 1402 and made landfall north of Yarmouth at 1425. I saw no parachute leave the plane before it hit the water nor did I see a dinghy or any sign of life after the plane went in.[23]

Mattie and Wally Emmer each clocked four hours and thirty minutes of flight time on the mission to Bremen, the most of any fighter pilots in the squadron. Mattie landed at Boxted shortly after 1500.[24] The eight remaining bombers of 96th Bomb Group "B" arrived at Snetterton Heath between 1504 and 1509. All but one of these aircraft had sustained light to severe flak damage. The bomber crews had been in the air for nearly seven hours.[25]

The 354th Fighter Group as a whole could count itself successful for the day. In addition to Bradley's flight, Bickell, Blakeslee, James B. Dalglish, and Howard all had kills. Five other pilots submitted claims for damaging enemy aircraft.[26] Don Beerbower expressed his view on the mission in his diary on December 20:

Another fair do! 180 each of B-24's and B-17's. To Bremen and Wilhelmshaven. Good weather this time though. The mission all went off okay. Lots of Jerries around tho I couldn't get a shot at one. I think my flight looks too good cause when ever I start for one with the other three after me, the Jerry just rolls over and hits for the deck and I have to come back up with the bombers. I'll get some yet.

The important thing about this raid is that on the way back over the Channel, the Major had engine trouble and went from 9,000 feet down into the water trying to get the thing going again. He knew better than to ride his ship into the water but he must have just kept trying to get it going till it was too late to bail. It was sure something to see the plane skip once and nose up and disappear, wondering if Seaman would get out. I was second flight and circled low and thought I saw him pop up & thresh around but I lost it in the waves right away & wasn't sure. I had two guys climb up & call in Mayday to Air Sea Rescue & get a fix over the position to send out a boat. Had to leave soon then because of gas. We'd been out nearly 4 hours. We haven't heard anything from the Rescue outfit and I'm afraid we've seen the last of him. It was almost 90 miles out, I figured. It's hard to think, as much as I hope he did, that he could get out after he hit. We're a pretty gloomy bunch tonite.

With Seaman missing, Lieutenant Colonel Martin decided to fly with the squadron on December 22 when the group went to Munster, Germany. David O'Hara and John Nall finally got their turn at a mission.[27] Nall was an experienced Eagle Squadron pilot, having recently transferred to the 353rd from the RAF.[28] Don's notation in his diary that evening was brief and to the point: "Nothing doing 21st but today we took the 'Big Friends' to Munster on a good 'show.' About 450 of them. Very little Enemy Aircraft up for that area. Still haven't fired my guns on a mission! If I ever get on the tail of a Jerry after all this waiting, he'd better say his prayers! Still no word on Major Seaman, so we're left with only the facts and no hope for our wishes to come true. The [RAF] is going out in force tonite."

Earlier in the day at a military cemetery near a rest home for German sailors, James Kerley and six members of the *Green Fury* crew were buried in wooden caskets provided by Norderney Islander Johann Janssen. Under the supervision of cemetery caretaker Johann Visser, Lieutenant Spanier and Sergeant Totz carried each American to his grave site.[29]

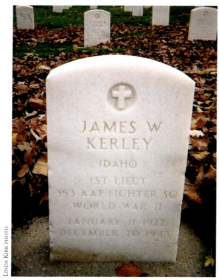

Morris Hill Cemetery, Boise, Idaho

Shortly after Christmas, Owen Seaman's wife Elizabeth learned that her husband was missing in action. She was pregnant and would deliver their son on March 13, 1944. Four days after the birth, the War Department notified the family by telegram that Owen Seaman had been killed in action.[30]

Squadron Commanders James H. Howard, George R. Bickell, and Owen M. Seaman

18

It's Exciting Work

[After the loss of Buford, Kerley, and Seaman] we had more aborts than we did normally. . . . Some of the [pilots] just went back to the group if they had a high rate of something wrong, oxygen wasn't working, airplane wasn't flying right. . . . I used to do flight tests for the engineering officer. . . some of the airplanes I flight tested I couldn't find anything wrong. But that is just a natural tendency. It happens in war.

John D. Mattie, P-51 pilot
(interview with the author)

    An unpleasant fact was becoming apparent. Every time the 353rd Fighter Squadron departed Boxted on a combat mission, pilots couldn't help thinking how recent history reflected that someone would not return. Three pilots were missing. Others had been hit by flak, enemy aircraft fire, and friendly fire. On December 24, Lieutenant James Lane from the 356th Fighter Squadron had crashed-landed at Earls Colne Airdrome after being shot up by a flight of four P-47 Thunderbolts.[1] Who was next? It could work on a man's mind. Each pilot came to terms with this in his own way. Stoic Jim Cannon wasn't concerned about it. His attitude was, "It can't happen to me."[2]

    The 353rd Fighter Squadron's mission on December 24 was to protect bombers attacking Hitler's secret rocket installation sites in the Pas de Calais area across the English Channel from London. British Intelligence had been monitoring the construction of approximately a hundred thick-walled concrete emplacements that looked like giant skis from the air. From these "ski" sites, it was estimated that two thousand tons of explosives could be launched over a twenty-four-hour period on London and adjacent areas. The Allies code named the destruction of the German rocket sites, Operation Crossbow.[3]

    Lieutenant Colonel Kenneth Martin led the Fighting Cobras on Christmas Eve day. Jim Cannon flew in the second-element-leader position in this flight, and Jerry Leach, on his first mission, took Cannon's wing. The other flights were led by Don Beerbower, with Felix Rogers on his wing, Jack Bradley, and

Lockheed P-38 Lightning

Republic P-47 Thunderbolt

Wally Emmer. The squadron picked up its bombers off the coast of France and, with them, flew in the crowded skies to the target area east of Pas de Calais.[4] This mission proceeded without enemy interference except that both the 355th and 356th Fighter Squadrons were harassed by P-38s and P-47s.[5] Rogers had a close call when he crashed-landed at Boxted after spray from a leaking oil line partially obscured his view through his ship's windshield. On final approach for landing, Rogers' airspeed was excessive and he overshot the runway. He ended up in a field with a slightly damaged aircraft.[6] That evening Don described the day's events in his diary: "Had an air umbrella over all of N. France today. Fighters all over up high and small formations of bombers all over below–picking out rocket installations near the coast. They broke up any hopes the Jerries had of breaking up a Merry Xmas in London. We're starting a binge now. Merry Christmas!" The squadron members celebrated with the knowledge they would not be flying in the morning. The next day Don reflected on the party and what it felt like to be away at Christmas: "Did it up fair well last nite. Day off for everyone today. Need it. Doesn't seem much like Christmas is actually here! It will seem more like it when letters from home come up to their Christmas. It seems that things like this move more according to what I read from home than by what the date shows me it should be."

Christmas in northern Aitkin County, Minnesota, came and went much like it had in other years, except so many young people were away. Week after week the letters of these loved ones appeared in the *Hill City News*. The newspaper also ran notices during December from Clarence Beerbower, Gay Huntley, and Joe Sailer expressing appreciation for the patronage of their customers in 1943. Each of their families had one or more sons away this Christmas. Consequently, they did what was necessary to spend the holidays with remaining family members nearby. Clarence and Josie Beerbower made the long drive to Marshall and Lavaun Hankerson's home at Medford, Minnesota, an hour south of the Twin Cities, where they were joined by Darrel and Arlene Beerbower.[7] Marshall had resigned his teaching position a few weeks earlier and was now home on a short leave from Great Lakes Naval Station in Chicago. Darrel anticipated his induction into the Army Air Forces on January 5. After Christmas he and Arlene returned to Hill City for a few days. While there, they had frequent contact with Elayne and Bonnie, who were living at the Kutcher farm.[8]

On December 26, Don sent Gay Huntley a V-letter. He limited what he wrote, because all outgoing mail was censored for security reasons.

> Dear Sir:
> I don't know quite how to start this. I feel guilty at being so long overdue. We're finally doing what we spent all that time in the States training for. . . . We're really in on the Berlin Mail Run for sure! It's exciting work to say the least. We've been at it almost a month now and have made us a good record, though not without some small losses. One that hit us hard was that of our Squadron C.O. I watched him go down in the North Sea.
> We had a swell Christmas dinner, turkey and all. Knocked ourselves out on it. Had the day off too. I'm getting The News swell, in less than a month and enjoy it ever so much.
> As ever, Don.[9]

The death of Major Owen Seaman was a significant loss for the squadron, especially for those who had worked the closest with him. Don had served as one of Seaman's flight leaders through the training in Nevada, California, and Oregon, and on the first combat missions in the P-51 Mustang. Seaman had become a respected leader who, during his eleven months as commanding officer, laid the foundation for the squadron's accomplishments against the Luftwaffe. Group Commander Martin had no one in mind to promote within the squadron as a replacement for Seaman. Instead, he gave the position to Operations Officer Robert L. Priser of the 355th Fighter Squadron, an American pilot who had transferred into the 354th Fighter Group after flying eighty-eight missions with the Canadians and British.[10] Martin made a good choice when he selected Priser. The man had a wealth of experience, like the 355th's George Bickell and the 356th's James Howard. Martin's selection, however, caused Don some uneasiness. He commented about it in his diary on December 28: "Got our new Squadron Comm. today. Capt. Priser. An [RAF] transfer with a fair amount of experience. It's going to be hard to condone to some one coming from somewhere else to come in & take over. He may be all right though. Just hope that he isn't the weak sister he looks like."

Squadron Commanders Robert L. Priser and George R. Bickell

Part of the problem for Don was getting comfortable with an outsider. In addition, Priser had the misfortune of being a small man with a slight build. Seaman would have towered over him. The straight-laced Priser had been around English pilots long enough that he acted and talked like one of them. For instance, he referred to an airplane as a "kite."[11] As with any new commanding officer, Priser would need to prove himself to the Fighting Cobras.

The squadron's mission on December 30 called for its deepest penetration into Germany in 1943. Lieutenant Colonel Martin again commanded the 353rd's lead flight, as Priser had not yet reported for duty. The group had orders to support the bombers attacking Ludwigshaven in the Palatinate, Don's ancestral home province along the German-Swiss border.[12] Because the target was in southwest Germany, the P-51s' flight path took them across Belgium. Fifty minutes after linking up with the bombers, Martin directed Blue and Green Flights to attack two twin-engine Dornier Do-217s spotted flying above the bomber formation.[13] Don described what happened when he engaged his first enemy aircraft flying above a ten-tenths overcast near Mannheim, east of Ludwigshaven.

> I was leading Green Flight toward box of friendly bombers when I observed a Do-217 flubbing along above and in front of the big friends. E/a started what appeared to be a poorly executed frontal attack from above and passed directly below us. I executed a tight turn to the right and dived for a stern attack, dropping my wing tanks at this time. At 300 yards I took a quick burst for correction, closed to 150 yards and opened fire, continuing until breaking away at extremely close range. I observed strikes along the fuselage and left engine burst into flame, pieces flying off. I broke left and up circling to give my wingman cover during his attack. Leader of my second element, which had remained above to give us cover, called in, unable by this time to locate us. I ordered the two elements out [the] bomber route enroute home.[14]

Don's wingman Carl Lind explained his role in the destruction of their first German warplane in the encounter report he wrote after returning to Boxted:

> I observed the leader firing as I was in trail and saw smoke, then flames pouring from the left engine. Leader closed rapidly, breaking up to the left. E/a started a gentle turn to the right at this time so I gave him a half ring lead and started firing at about 300 yards range. I saw my tracers go by his right wing so corrected my lead and saw hits on the wing. I corrected lead and observed white smoke coming from the right engine. I broke up to the left, observing e/a rolling over into what appeared to be a spin. I last saw it going into the deck below us. . . . I had pulled off e/a at about 15,000' and rejoined my leader about 8,000' above.[15]

When Don returned to his quarters after the mission, he could hardly contain his excitement as he scribbled down additional information in his diary about his shared victory with Lind.

RED Letter Day. Got myself a Dornier 217! First enemy plane I've seen close enough to get at and I did a half turn spin to be sure not to lose him. Lind, my wingman followed me but lost the second element in the maneuver! I closed to about 800 feet & fired a burst just as the rear gunner started firing. I knocked him out & knocked some pieces off which flew past me! Twang! Then I just sat there & closed up to about 200 feet, no deflection & opened up on him. Knocked off a radio contraption that almost hit me & put his left engine on fire and thoroughly sprayed him. We were down to 17,000 . . . from 25,000 & I was so close & so much stuff flying off him that I pulled up not knowing that Lind was behind me as I wanted to clear my tail. He was about 1000 feet behind me though, so I stayed up & he closed on in for a minute and says he put the right engine on fire. I think it already was but we're sharing the claim. They say that's the best way to get a wingman who'll really stick with you so I figure it's a good investment to very cheerfully share it rather than raise a stink & prove otherwise by our pictures.

The pictures Don refers to were from his gun camera film. American fighters carried cameras that automatically began recording when the guns commenced firing. The film verified damage or destruction of enemy aircraft. This footage proved its value especially when pilot lacked an eye witness to his claim.

In Don's encounter report he mentions being in Green Flight. American fighter groups used color coding to help identify participants in air warfare. The 353rd Fighter Squadron identified its four flights with red, white, blue, and green. Red always designated the lead flight, where the squadron commander flew. Green designated the flight tasked with engaging bandits endangering the fighters prior to rendezvous with the bombers. The pilots in red and green flights usually had more opportunities to mix it up with the Luftwaffe.[16]

The second Dornier Do-217 that Martin had ordered pursued turned out to have been damaged by Blue Flight's Bradley, Cannon, and Silva. Cannon made the final pass at the twin-engine fighter-bomber. In his encounter report he wrote, "I could see a burst of gunfire from tail of e/a which ceased shortly after I opened fire. I fired a 1½ second burst, and all my guns jammed but one. I opened fire with one gun continuing to dive below e/a. I observed strikes along fuselage near tail section and saw pieces flying off. I pulled up to the left and rejoined formation. E/a was still diving straight ahead."[17]

The Do-217 was an outgrowth of the twin-engine Do-17. The newer model, first used by the Luftwaffe in late 1940, could carry a heavy bomb load, or be used as a night fighter. With a maximum airspeed of three hundred ten miles per hour, it couldn't compete against single-engine fighters. It saw limited action against the large daylight formations of B-17s and B-24s.[18]

Major General Lewis Brereton waited at Boxted for the pilots returning from their mission on December 30. He was concerned that the Ninth Air Force only had forty percent of the fighters, medium bombers, and troop carriers it needed to support the invasion of France. Of the five fighter groups Brereton had in Britain, only the 354th presently engaged in combat. The other groups only had a total of ten airplanes. Brereton stayed for the debriefing of the pilots. He seemed pleased with the veteran group's results even though the attacks led by Beerbower and Bradley against the Do-217s inflicted limited damage on the Luftwaffe.[19]

The following day Brereton learned that Major General James H. "Jimmy" Doolittle was replacing Ira Eaker as the commanding officer of the Eighth Air Force.[20] Doolittle, a well-known figure in American aviation during the twenties and thirties, had established numerous speed records while serving in the Army Air Corps and as a civilian. After leading the raid on Tokyo from the aircraft carrier *Hornet* in April 1942, he was awarded the Congressional Medal of Honor. Doolittle's future decisions regarding the use of fighter aircraft would eventually affect the pilots of the 353rd Fighter Squadron.[21]

James H. "Jimmy" Doolittle

The record-setting mission on December 31 gave Captain Robert Priser his first opportunity to lead the squadron. Eight P-51s provided escort and target support for B-17s and B-24s striking airdromes at Bordeaux and St. Jean D'Angley in southwest France. Glenn Eagleston protected Priser's wing, with Wally Emmer as the second element leader. Grant Logan flew his first mission and provided wing cover for Emmer. Don had Wah Kau Kong on his wing, with Ridley Donnell and Felix Rogers paired in the second element. This mission offered an opportunity for the pilots to gain additional combat experience in an area of the war zone that was new to them.[22] It proved to be a successful mission. The pilots reported excellent bombing results, with smoke rising three thousand feet over the airfields. Don arrived back at Boxted after a long flight, tired but happy to be home.[23] He summed up his tenth and final mission of the month in his diary with these words:

> We really rounded out the old year right. Longest raid yet for us. A new record established for fighters. To Bordeaux in France. It's 510 miles straight to the target & we were over it protecting the bombers for 35 minutes. Weather stinko when we got back. I was up for 5 hours and 10 minutes. My crew chief had to pry me out of the cockpit when I got down! Not a sputter out of the Bonnie "B" all the way either. Saw a couple of Jerries but they were down too far & no bother to the bombers. Couldn't afford to lose all that altitude to go after them when there may have been Jerries in the sun, as there always is, ready to jump the bombers if we went down. Most I got from this raid is a darned tired Butt!!
> It's a quiet New Year's Eve I'm spending for I'm hitting the hay pronto.

Don had developed confidence in *Bonnie "B"* and in his crew chief, Leon Panter. A sound ship and solid mechanic were crucial to his well-being. Missions meant running the risk of drowning in the sea or being captured on land when an engine failed. Don was the only pilot to complete all of the squadron's December missions, nine of them in *Bonnie "B"*.[24] He would not have been able to achieve this record without a well-maintained Mustang. Moreover, the strong collegial bond with Panter augmented Don's competitive spirit as the squadron's assignments took him deeper and deeper into the Third Reich.

However, flying an average of a mission every three days began to wear on Don. When he wasn't escorting bombers, he had training responsibilities for new pilots and other duties associated with being a flight leader. The loss of Eaves, Kerley, and Seaman, not to mention the ongoing tension of combat flying, took its toll. Captain Priser recognized this. Shortly after the first of the year, he authorized an R-and-R for Don in London. Don immensely enjoyed the simple pleasures he experienced in his brief respite away from Boxted:

"Knocked myself out in the Park Lane Hotel between their soft beds, the hot tub and the good Scotch whiskey. It was a relief to get away from the work for a change!"[25]

By January 1944 Don had been in the Army Air Forces for two years. His desire to serve his country as a fighter pilot had become reality. Not only was he a proven combat leader, but he had also developed into an excellent flyer. His experience in a variety of aircraft and the hours logged in *Bonnie "B"* had brought him to the objective all pilots strive to achieve—Don could now maneuver his ship in difficult situations with ease; *Bonnie "B"* had become an extension of himself.

P-51 over England U.S.A.F. PHOTO

19

LITTLE FRIENDS

I was flying Green Four on way in to target when Lt. Owen called in a JU 88 closing in on the tail of an aborted B-17, at about one o'clock low. Lt. Eagleston put the flight in string and made a partial overhead pass on the JU 88 and went below on his pass. The JU 88 then made a steep turn to the left and down into the overcast with Lt. Nall on his tail about 30 yards behind. Lt. Eagleston said, "Do not follow him down." We broke off but green 2 followed the JU 88. We reformed and circled twice but Lt. Nall did not appear again.

Edward R. Regis, P-51 pilot
(Missing Air Crew Report)

By January 1944 the momentum of the worldwide conflict had shifted to the Allies. U-boat activity in the North Atlantic had been severely restricted. Soviet armies were in possession of much of the territory lost to the Germans earlier in the war. North Africa, Sicily, and most of Italy south of Rome had been cleared of Axis forces. In the Far East, the Japanese had been pushed out of the Aleutians and the Solomon and Gilbert Islands in the southwest Pacific. Most importantly, American factories and shipyards were producing the airplanes, guns, submarines, surface craft, and tanks needed by the Allies to overwhelm their enemies.

In the European Theater of Operations (ETO), the aerial war against the Luftwaffe intensified as the Allies strove to achieve air supremacy prior to the spring invasion of northern France. By night, the Royal Air Force attacked Axis targets; during the day Eighth Air Force heavy bombers and Ninth Air Force medium bombers did the same. A series of German ports, naval bases, and shipbuilding facilities along the North Sea and the Baltic attracted a great deal of Allied attention. These included Bremen, Emden, Hamburg, Kiel, and Wilhelmshaven. Hamburg had already been nearly obliterated. During an eleven-day period between July 24 and August 3, 1943, air crews dropped an estimated 165,000 high-explosive and incendiary bombs and phosphorus canisters on the city, seriously damaging port facilities, industrial plants, and private property. At least forty thousand people perished in the attacks. Civilian morale throughout Germany plummeted because of the destruction of Hamburg.[1] German port cities unknown to most Americans prior to World War II; by early 1944 they had become household names to anyone following the progress of the strategic bombing campaign in the ETO.

On January 4, 1944, Captain Robert Priser led the 353rd Fighter Squadron on its eleventh mission, a return trip to Kiel on the Baltic Sea. Felix Rogers flew off Priser's wing. Don Beerbower and Wah Kau Kong made up the second element of Red Flight. Jack Bradley, Jim Cannon, and Glenn Eagleston led the other three flights. Of the sixteen aircraft scheduled to fly, four aborted.[2] During this escort and target-support mission, few enemy aircraft interfered, except with Eagleston's flight. He and Ed Regis damaged a pair of German fighters. In the process, the squadron lost its fourth pilot, recent RAF transfer John Nall.[3] It had been Priser's second opportunity to lead the Fighting Cobras. Don's brief diary entry on January 4 indicated his changing view of Priser: "Oh boy–another Kiel Deal! It was a longtime over water again! No shots again today. Captain Priser is working out okay! He's a pretty good leader in the air. Used to be in the 'Eagle Squadron.' "

John B. Nall in RAF uniform

Jack Bradley had been the squadron's operations officer since the early days at Tonopah. On January 4 Priser reassigned him to the position of senior squadron flight commander. Bradley's assistant, Arthur Owen, received a promotion to operations officer.[4] For whatever reason, Priser had decided to move Bradley out of the number-two spot in the squadron, a position the Texan had held for nearly a year.

The following day, Priser gave Bradley the responsibility of leading the Fighting Cobras on a mission back to Kiel. The three squadrons would escort the bombers over the port facility and on their outbound course from the target. The 353rd left Boxted with the rest of the group shortly before 1000. By

1055 its eleven Mustangs had entered enemy territory over Tessel Island, Holland. After flying north of the Zuider Zee, Bradley sliced through clear sky to the group rendezvous point with the bombers southwest of Kiel. En route they noticed the Germans were screening their larger cities with smoke. As the pilots crossed the Jutland Peninsula, they flew over the Kaiser-Wilhelm Canal, the all-important waterway used by the German navy to move warships between its bases at Wilhelmshaven and Kiel, thereby saving hundreds of miles of travel on the open sea. By 1150 the 353rd and its sister squadrons were in place protecting the bombers. Flak grew heavy and accurate, and the Luftwaffe sent many fighters into the fray. The 355th and 356th claimed eighteen enemy aircraft destroyed or damaged. The 353rd tallied only single victories by Hunt, Eagleston, and Beerbower.[5] Don's kill took place at 1205 near Amrum Island in the German Bight. He described the engagement in the following report:

> I was White Flight Leader covering bombers on route . . . from target with Red Flight in vicinity of southern tip of North Frisian [Islands] when encounter occurred. We were cruising at about 23,000 feet east along bomber course. I noticed we were over running the bombers so started crossing over to the other side. About half way across the formation No. 4 called in a bogey at 8 o'clock from the bombers and 1000 feet below the formation, flying a parallel course. Closing in I recognized bogey as an Me-110 and took my wingman in throttles open in a sliding diving pass on to his tail, second element remaining up and to one side for cover. I took a long burst from 200 yards 10 degrees deflection. I observed strikes along the right wing and saw pieces fly off. I corrected my lead to the canopy when I was at 0 degrees dead astern from about 125 yards, closing fast. His left engine started smoking and he appeared to be just flubbing along out of control. I closed on in until I nearly flew through him and broke down and to the left. E/a seemed pilotless by this time. I circled twice to let the second element have some shots and saw him roll over on his back, going straight down. I saw e/a crash on edge of a small island. I assembled flight and headed back toward target area.

Don did not hesitate to bring his guns to bear on the most dangerous component of an enemy aircraft—the pilot. Ethically, pilots and crew inside an aircraft were considered fair game; free-floating outside, their vulnerability protected them from harm. When Jackknife 39 arrived back at Boxted, he had clocked nearly four hours in *Bonnie "B"*. As Don noted in his diary on January 5, victory was sweet.

Two days in a row over Kiel! And this time, not for nothing! I got me an Me 110. Damn!–I almost flew thru this one. Up to within 20 feet of his tail before I dumped my stick & went under him. I'll never forget the nose on that baby as I passed under it and broke off and up. It had four cannon and four machine guns stacked into it. Wow!! He had no rocket guns of course with that load. I'm anxious to see those pictures. Had Kong, Donnell and Meserve along. We all saw him hit a little island west off the Danish Peninsula and go up in sand and smoke! Pretty site to see him roll over and spiral almost straight down. He must have been going 500 mph he got down from 20,000 so fast.

Captain Priser guided the squadron to Ludswigshaven on January 7 for an uneventful mission, except for Lieutenant Harry Baer; he flew for the first time in combat as wingman for James Parsons. Don and Glenn Eagleston experienced mechanical problems with the high blowers on their aircraft and returned after an hour-and-a-quarter and two-and-a-half hours respectively.[6] This third group mission in a row, led by Majors George Bickell or James Howard, achieved Lieutenant Colonel Kenneth Martin's purpose of giving his subordinates the opportunity to gain more extensive command experience.[7] Rotation of leadership positions was worthwhile at the squadron, flight, and element level as well. This practice gave Martin, Bickell, Howard, and Priser some choices about which pilots to promote if a key leader did not return from a mission.

The squadron's fourteenth mission on January 11 provided escort and target-support for heavies hitting Oschersleben, Germany. It was the maiden flight for Albert Ricci and Glenn Pipes. Jack Bradley led the squadron with Thomas Varney on his wing.[8] The Eighth Air Force had its sights on three aircraft manufacturing centers: the Junkers factory at Halberstadt, the Messerschmitt factory at Brunswick, and the Focke Wulf factory at Oschersleben. These cities were major industrial centers in Saxony, west of Berlin. The January 11 raid marked the beginning of a concentrated Allied effort to destroy German fighter production and to eliminate as many of these aircraft as possible in the air and on the ground. The ultimate goal was to gain unlimited access to German targets without serious interference from the Luftwaffe.[9]

The squadron departed Boxted at 0957 behind the group leadership of James Howard. When the formation crossed the enemy coast about an hour later, Howard had trouble determining their exact position because of the heavy overcast, but the P-51s continued on, cruising at twenty-six thousand feet, until they joined the bomber stream at 1115 near Munster.[10] Bradley described what happened after Howard assigned the 353rd its area of responsibility:

> Group leader dispatched our squadron to cover the last three boxes into the target area. I assigned Blue Flight to the right of the boxes, White Flight to the left and Red Flight, of which I was the leader, to the rear, all members of Green Flight having previously aborted. We effected target cover until about 1145 hours uneventfully. At this time Blue Leader called bandit at rear of bomber formation. I observed a Me-110 out of range but closing in on big friends from astern. As my flight was in better position for attack than the other two I peeled off for attack. As flight dived toward e/a, he broke down and to port. I fired a short burst from 45 degrees deflection at 400 yards closing to 200 yards at approximately 15 degrees with only two guns in operation, one gun jamming almost immediately.... Last seen, e/a was in steep dive, doing approximately 500 indicated.... At about 1210 I saw two FW-190s about 3000 feet above and approximately ½ mile to starboard. I dived to the right to get directly beneath them and started to climb with everything forward.... The FW-190s were in trail about 100 yards apart at about 23,000 feet. I closed fast to about 100 yards on the rear e/a opening fire with about 15 degrees deflection. E/a seemed to shudder momentarily and burst into flames immediately. I believe he exploded as I passed him as some force jarred my airplane rather violently. In range of lead e/a at this time, I held my fire until 50 yards astern, pulling slightly to one side for small deflection. I fired a short burst and e/a caught fire. As pilot attempted to split-s I caught him with a second burst while he was on his back with nose down. I broke left to clear my tail and was rejoined by my wing man who had been on my tail during combat. E/a last seen was engulfed in flame in vertical dive....[11]

The Focke-Wulf FW-190, one of two mainline single-engine Luftwaffe fighters, could achieve a speed of four hundred and eight miles per hour with its air-cooled, radial engine. It possessed good maneuverability in a dog fight, but lost some effectiveness at high altitude. Armed with four twenty-millimeter cannon and two seven-point-nine-millimeter machine guns, the FW-190 was a formidable foe in combat. The Me-109, the other primary fighter, had seen initial service in Spain in 1937. Once the premier fighter in the world, by 1944 the '109 couldn't hold its own against the faster, more agile P-51 Mustang. Although the liquid-cooled engine of a clean G-model produced a top speed of four hundred twenty-nine miles per hour, most Messerschmitts carried heavy armor and an array of machine gun and cannon options that affected the plane's maneuverability and speed.[12]

Focke-Wulf FW-190

Smithsonian Air and Space Museum, photo by Summer S. Johnson

Messerschmitt Me-109

Nat'l Museum of the Air Force

While Bradley deftly handled enemy activity in his sector on January 11, so did most flights in all three squadrons. Before the day was over, the group claimed fourteen destroyed and twenty-seven probably destroyed or damaged FW-190s, Me-109s, Me-110s, along with several Do-217s, Ju-88s, Me-210s, and Me-410s.[13] Other groups involved in the mission posted claims for a additional one hundred forty-one destroyed enemy aircraft. Though bomber losses for the Eighth Air Force were high, with fifty-five B-17s and B-24s lost, only five American fighters failed to return home.[14] In his diary that evening, Don described in detail the part he played in this major air battle.

> Had a big raid. And what a raid. We went clear in to 3 targets southeast of Magdeburg. Within 40 miles of Berlin! We'll get there yet! This was really "B" Flights day! If we'd have had any guns, we'd have gotten 6 or 8 of them I'm sure.
>
> I had Pipes on my wing for his first mission and he still hasn't gotten his breath! Rogers & Lind in second element. The other two flights went down after the first 110 we saw—which was too far down and that was the last we saw of them. I kept the flight over the wing of bombers over the target with no opposition till we got about 10 min. north of the target and I started seeing what looked like half the G.A.F. down below the bombers just following along. About that time they started coming up in separate attacks, but 2 or 3 at a time. Had to split up in elements to keep them off. But Rogers knew we had to keep in contact with each other and it worked out perfect. I shot at 5 Me 110's and bluffed off two more from the bombers by flying up their tails till they broke away and down. One of my guns didn't fire at all and two stopped after 50 rounds. So I was shooting most of the time with just one gun! More damn fun. Lind's guns gave one short burst & quit. Rogers' all stopped half way thru but we still stayed and bluffed them off. It was a running battle for about 30 min. and the 4 of us kept all of them off.
>
> Ordinarily if 4 ships got caught that far in Germany all alone, they'd bat butt for home but I couldn't see leaving the bombers there alone with all those e/a down below waiting for us to leave. The bombers were almost on our course home and we had lots of gas so we just hung around. It seemed like we were just 4 ships against half the German Air Force! It was really comical, the bluff we pulled and got away with! I destroyed 1 Me 110, damaged 2 others and one Do 217. I could have stacked up a triple today if

all my guns had fired out. I never had any thing so disappointing happen to me before in my life! . . . We still know that that wing of bombers are thankful to 4 P-51's who stuck with them even though we won't get the credit for it most likely.

Donnie's score is now 2½ destroyed! Half an ace! Not bad.

Don Beeerbower and Bonnie "B" *at Boxted*

The bomber crews had an affectionate name for fighter pilots. They called them "little friends," a name Don and his mates had certainly proven to be on this mission.

In the melee of the fighting, James Howard ended up separated from his wingman. All alone, he tagged on to an isolated B-17 group. The bombers suddenly came under attack by at least thirty bandits, and Howard did all he could to protect the formation. In the process, he destroyed two, probably destroyed another two, and damaged two more enemy aircraft.[15] The "big friends," as fighter pilots referred to them, this day were from the 401st Bomb Group (H) stationed at Deenethorpe Airdrome. After the mission, Colonel Harold W. Bowman of the 401st sent Howard a letter through Major General Jimmy Doolittle thanking him on behalf of his men for saving many of them from being shot down. Howard's bravery later earned him the Congressional Medal of Honor, the only fighter pilot in the ETO to be so recognized.[16]

James Howard in Ding Hao! U.S.A.F. PHOTO

Howard and the other pilots returned to Boxted between 1400 and 1430. Some of the aircraft had sustained battle damage. The 353rd's Carl Frantz brought in his P-51 without a tail wheel. It had been shot off. He lost control of his Mustang shortly after landing when the tail made contact with the tarmac. As Frantz skidded to a stop on the runway, a landing plane struck his aircraft. Frantz suffered head lacerations and shock.[17]

Like Don, many pilots reported gun stoppages on this mission. As maintenance personnel struggled to fix this vexing problem, the matter was pushed upstairs to Major General Brereton, who arranged for Washington to send technicians from Wright Field, Ohio, to England. It took time to find a solution, but eventually the angle of the gun mountings was changed and booster motors were installed on the feed chutes to the four Browning fifty- caliber machine guns.[18] Felix Rogers experienced the frustration of jamming many times: "[I] had one of those four gun B's to the end. And all you had to do was pull a reasonable amount of g's and the guns would stop firing." Rogers didn't believe the problem was ever totally solved.[19] Donald J. Chisholm, armorer on Charles Koenig's Mustang, *Little Horse*,[20] recalled another issue with the gun system: "We did have some trouble with the guns freezing up, if the planes flew too high."[21] Eventually, heater kits were installed to keep the weapons warm.

On January 14 Don had a hand in solving another vexing problem when he flew *Bonnie "B"* north of London to Poddington Airdrome, home field of the 92nd Bomb Group (H).[22] All knew that aircrews mistook the P-51 for the Me-109, resulting in friendly fire damage to American aircraft. A captured Messerschmitt was on hand, so Don and another pilot did some flybys for the B-17 gunners. Because both fighters had liquid-cooled engines, their profiles in flight appeared much the same. To help aircrews distinguish between the German and American planes, the three P-51 squadrons ended up having a white lateral stripe painted on the upper portion of each Mustang's vertical stabilizer and rudder for quick identification. This stripe matched nicely with the existing white nose and white lettering on the Mustangs, and the single white stripe on each wing, horizontal stabilizer and elevator. That evening, Don made

Bonnie "B" at Poddington Airdrome January 14, 1944. U.S.A.F. PHOTO

Captured Messerschmitt Me-109 in RAF markings - very likely the aircraft that flew with Bonnie "B". DON BEERBOWER PHOTO

a brief reference to his unusual visit to the bomber base and the unfortunate loss of another pilot in his diary entry for the day: "Flew formation with an Me 109 at Poddington for pictures. Mission this afternoon. Just over France a ways. But lost Logan on a bad engine. A damn good kid too. He should be OK though. Maybe we'll see him again." Don held out hope that Grant Logan would receive assistance from the French Underground and evade capture. Logan disappeared on the squadron's second Crossbow mission over France. He had been flying with Jackknife White Flight led by John Mattie. As their four Mustangs approached the coast of Belgium, James Keane radioed Mattie that he needed to abort. As Keane headed back across the North Sea, the remaining fighters stayed on course at twenty-four thousand feet and then turned south. Near Cambrai, Jerry Leach and Grant Logan informed Mattie they were also experiencing serious trouble. The high blower on Leach's ship stopped working properly so he ran out of oxygen, while Logan's engine couldn't maintain adequate manifold pressure. Mattie banked around to assist them.

> I made a 180 degree turn to the right and headed toward the two planes which had fallen back about one-half mile. As I approached to within one-quarter mile, one ship started a steep spiraling dive while the other ship continued on a course of approximately 315 degrees. I followed the ship down to 4,000 feet in its dive and upon coming abreast of the ship, I learned it was Lt. Leach, who stated he was light headed from lack of oxygen and was forced to hit the deck. I then called Lt. Logan and received the reply that he was at 13,000 feet and still having trouble. I called him several times, but received no replies. Lt. Leach and I then proceeded to come home crossing out two miles SW of Dunkerque.[23]

N. Grant Logan

Logan had been in the squadron since its days in Portland. Prior to going in the service he'd worked as a commercial artist and industrial designer. Both officers and enlisted men had liked Logan very much. Squadron Historian William Moneta wrote that Logan's "sparkling personality and generous sense of humor" would be missed by everyone.[24]

On January 21 Major General Brereton and Brigadier General Quesada participated in an awards ceremony at Boxted. Don, along with Bradley, Eagleston, and Emmer received clusters for their Air Medals. The generals were also present to recognize those receiving promotions. Lieutenant Colonel Martin accepted the silver eagles of a full colonel. In addition, Don, Bradley, Cannon, and Emmer finally received the rank commensurate with an officer having their responsibilities. Their promotions to captain were made retroactive to January 15.[25] In his diary entry that evening, Don expressed his pride, crowing, "[It's] now–Captain Beerbower. We kind of knocked ourselves out on wine at the club. Feels pretty good with the old railroad tracks on the shoulder. Best damn rank in any army for a pilot. I feel pretty good about it even though we have waited so long. Have a devil of a cold in my head & chest."

The weather turned foul in mid-January, not at all conducive to combat flying. In one respect this was timely, because throughout the month the squadron received replacement P-51Bs and Cs. The B and C models were identical except North American Aviation manufactured the former in Inglewood, California, and the latter in Dallas, Texas. The new aircraft came with an internal auxiliary fuel tank that promised to increase the fighter's range by three hundred miles. The ground crews took advantage of the down time to prepare their used aircraft for transition to other units and to set up the new Mustangs. Each P-51 required a thorough inspection, sighting of guns, radio check, and test flight. The pilot, crew chief, assistant crew chief, and armorer all took part in this. In addition, many of the planes were christened with names. William Moneta wrote that John Mattie's, *My Buddy*, "done in large white letters; edged in red, and sporting a background of shooting stars, was an outstanding example of the pilots' creative work."[26] Mattie named *My Buddy* in honor of his brother, David, who was still in high school back in Pennsylvania. Mattie had developed a friendship with Staff Sergeant Nathan Glick, a Ninth Air Force artist and illustrator assigned to the 354th.[27] Glick had the responsibility of recording "the group's activities by doing portraits [of pilots] and action drawings of their missions."[28] One of his best pieces was a drawing of *My Buddy* that captured the attractive nose art design on Mattie's Mustang.

Nathan H. Glick's sketch of John Mattie's My Buddy.

Richard E. Turner, unknown observer, and Nathan H. Glick U.S.A.F. PHOTO

Don turned in *Bonnie "B"* for another P-51B, #43-12375. The new ship had been manufactured at North American's Inglewood plant, eighty-two planes ahead of *Bonnie "B"* [#43-12457]. The Army received the aircraft on August 6, 1943, and then shipped it via Newark, New Jersey, to the British, on loan as FX886. On December 31, 1943, the plane Don would name *Bonnie B II*, was transferred to the Ninth Air Force.[29]

The additional capacity of the new internal auxiliary tank, along with that of the existing external drop tanks, would allow the P-51s to provide air support over Berlin and other more distant targets in Germany. But extending the fighter's range in this manner forced a trade-off. The weight of the eighty-five gallon internal auxiliary tank, located behind the cockpit, shifted the airplane's normal center of gravity, thereby affecting the Mustang's flying characteristics. The pilot had to be extra cautious when departing, landing, and making abrupt in-flight movements until the fuel was burned off.[30]

Despite the poor weather, training for the newer pilots continued. Most of them had not gone out yet on combat missions, so they used the time to maintain and increase proficiency in their aircraft. One of these pilots was John Rody. On January 23, Don described in his diary what happened when Rody nearly lost his life attempting to land at Boxted: "Rody washed out an airplane today trying to land in a very bad haze. Lost his head & hit the trees. Be ok in a week or so I think. Lucky as hell."

During the month, two new pilots joined the squadron: John H. Arnold, who arrived on January 7, and Technical Sergeant Dennis L. Johns, who arrived on January 24. Johns became the unit's first non-commissioned flying officer. The day he arrived, five pilots transferred out: Baer, Culbertson, Hanson, Read, and Skenyon.[31]

Don did not fly on January 24 when the squadron went to Frankfurt, Germany. Captain Priser led the mission. Flying on his wing was Captain Joe Giltner, the commanding officer of the 363rd Fighter Squadron, 357th Fighter Group.[32] The 357th was Major General Brereton's second unit to receive P-51s. For some time the Eighth Air Force had been trying to get the 354th Fighter Group and its Mustangs permanently transferred to VIII Fighter Command, but Brereton hesitated to give up the only combat-experienced fighter group in the Ninth Air Force. Instead, a deal was struck whereby Brereton exchanged the 357th for a new P-47 outfit from the Eighth Air Force.[33] While the generals negotiated, key pilots from the 357th needed to gain combat experience. For this reason, Captain Giltner joined the squadron on January 24. The mission did not attract enemy aircraft except for a brief encounter with a flight of Focke-Wulfs. Jim Cannon witnessed what happened:

On 24 January 1944, I was leading Jackknife White Flight of four in mutual support, providing escort to a box of forts enroute home. Captain Priser with Captain Giltner of the 363rd Fighter Squadron on his wing, was leading two members of the Red Flight, the Green and White Flights, flying line-abreast and in mutual support. He was weaving back and forth in front of the formation. We were flying just above the cloud level, approximately 25,000 feet, when at 1145 in the Brussels, Ghent and Antwerp area, four white nosed FW-190's made an attack on Captain Priser's two-ship [element] from 4 o'clock and below. After a short burst from one of the e/a, they split-s'd back into the overcast as my flight turned into them. I saw Captain Priser and his wingman break right and drop their wing tanks, but did not see any strikes on him. I lost Captain Priser when I turned into the FW-190's and broke off as they went into the overcast. Green Flight and White Flight with the two members of Red Flight went [into] a Lufberry [circling] looking for the captain and the e/a's, but were unsuccessful. I then brought my plane home. The attack by the e/a's was apparently well planned as they appeared suddenly and disappeared as rapidly.[34]

The enemy aircraft may have been directed up through the overcast by radar in a manner typical of German night-fighter operations. Whatever the cause, the two squadron commanders did not return to Boxted.

Robert Priser had served well in his role as the replacement for Owen Seaman. With many combat missions to his credit, he brought much-needed experience to the squadron. Priser had been married on Christmas Day, 1943. His wife, whom he visited nightly, lived in nearby Colchester. The squadron members' "sympathies were extended to [her]."[35]

For the second time in a little over a month, Colonel Martin faced the task of finding a commanding officer for the 353rd Fighter Squadron.

20

It's a Dangerous Game

We had a [debriefing] after every mission and if it were a long mission . . . they served us a little, oh, some kind of whiskey or bourbon in a tin cup. You can imagine how refreshing that was, and the object was to loosen us up so we could talk a little bit. I guess it maybe had some effect. But, anyway, we'd meet in the briefing room and . . . if [we'd] been engaged, write whatever [we] could remember of the whole thing. . . .

Jack T. Bradley, squadron commander
(interview with the author)

On January 26, 1944, two days after Captain Robert Priser disappeared over Belgium, Colonel Kenneth Martin appointed Captain Jack Bradley as the new commanding officer of the 353rd Fighter Squadron. In the five weeks since Major Owen Seaman had drowned in the North Sea, Bradley had gained the combat experience Martin wanted in a squadron leader.[1] The two men now knew and trusted each other after a year of serving together. During the few weeks Priser commanded the squadron, Bradley had been given the opportunity to lead it on several missions, of which Martin undoubtedly received positive reports. Moreover, Bradley had proven to be skillful and bold as a fighter pilot, having destroyed or damaged a number of enemy aircraft since his first kill on December 20. Martin was satisfied that Bradley could handle the additional responsibility.

Bradley was born in Brownwood, Texas, on June 6, 1918. He completed grade school and high school there and went on to attend a year of college at the University of Texas and another at Hardin Simmons University. He then returned to Brownwood and settled into an accounting position with the Walker Smith Company. When the war broke out, he signed up for the aviation cadet program, graduating with Class 42-H on August 27, 1942.[2] A little older than most of the pilots assigned to the 353rd Fighter Squadron, Bradley completed flying school a month ahead of many of them. Jim Cannon believed Bradley's age and seniority influenced his selection as the unit's first operations officer. Cannon respected Bradley's leadership skill. Long after the war, Cannon portrayed his old commander this way: "He was a Texan. You knew it from the very beginning. He was a decent sort of fella himself. You didn't horse around with him either. He held a pretty firm hand as operations officer. . . . Bradley had a way of making you feel foolish about walking in late at a meeting or if he saw an airplane on the flight line that wasn't flying, he wanted to know who in the hell wasn't out there flying it. . . . He was a strong leader and deserves a lot of credit for his leadership in running the squadron."[3]

John Mattie described Bradley as "a very personable guy. [We] called him Smiling Jack, of course."[4] The nickname came from the popular aviation comic strip, *The Adventures of Smilin' Jack.* Bradley was handsome, confident, direct, and aggressive in the air. He emphasized discipline in the squadron; he was a leader who had expectations of those serving with him. Sometimes, however, he could rub people the wrong way. Felix Rogers looked beyond this abrasive style to credit Bradley for his contribution to the unit: "I never really cottoned to Jack Bradley but Jack Bradley was a hell of a combat leader. I mean his personality bothered me I suppose because I was the only Bostonian in the group and he was all Texas. . . . But Jack was a really good combat leader. . . . I think we played by the book the way it should be written and we learned, all of us, learned to be leaders."[5]

Jack T. Bradley

The Adventures of Smilin' Jack

The Texan named his Mustang after his wife, Margie, and the Japanese word for ship, Maru. He had first used the name *Margie Maru* for a P-39 Airacobra when stationed on the West Coast.[6]

Bradley's promotion to commander of the 353rd Fighter Squadron created an opportunity for other pilots to advance within the organization. The new chief acted quickly to fill key positions. On January 26, Arthur Owen was relegated to his former position as assistant squadron operations officer, and James Parsons and Ridley Donnell were appointed squadron flight commanders to serve with Jim Cannon and Wally Emmer.[7] To complete the reshuffle, Bradley moved Don Beerbower into the positions he once held under Owen Seaman. Don commented ambivalently about the change in his duties several days later: "I am now Operations Officer, Ass't Sqdn. C.O. and Senior flight commander. Don't know whether I like it too well or not. It's a hell of a lot of work, worry and responsibility."[8] In his new role, Don would not be flying as often as he had in the past. Typically, he or Bradley would remain at Boxted while the other led the squadron, although both participated in the 353rd's next mission.

On January 29 the weather cleared enough for Bradley to lead the Fighting Cobras alongside the 355th and 356th on a target-and-withdrawal support mission to Frankfurt, Germany. The fighters departed Boxted at 0926, and by the time they made landfall near Flushing on the Dutch coast, they'd worked their way up to thirty thousand feet. The group cruised above a solid ten-tenths overcast at lower altitudes all the way to Frankfurt and back.[9] Don did not see enemy action until he turned from the target area with the bombers. At 1215 he noticed a lone B-17 outlined against the white backdrop of the clouds, nearly three miles below his position.

> I was leading Green Flight, comprised by three ships, in withdrawal support for bombers of 1st [Air] Task Force from target area. We were in the vicinity of Kirchberg at about 27,000 feet when I spotted 6 s/e [single-engine], e/a attacking a straggling B-17 flying below bomber formation at about 10,000 feet. I dived and closed in on a FW-190, firing a short burst with 15 degrees deflection at very short range, closing rapidly. I observed no strikes. I pulled up sharply to 13,000 feet and rolled over to press attack on a Me-109 which appeared to be setting up for a stern attack on big friend. I attacked from 30 degrees from above and behind e/a, firing a 2 second burst from 200 yards closing rapidly to zero range. I saw strikes along fuselage and canopy. I observed e/a to explode as I pulled up and circled to the left. At this time I also saw another s/e, e/a going down in flames off to front and below me. I then saw a FW-190 about 700 feet above me. I pulled up under his tail, firing with one gun from 10 degrees at 150 yards. After a 3 second burst at 100 yards my one gun jammed. E/a rolled to right and split-s'd. I saw strikes about middle of fuselage and

along left wing root. As I broke off attack I observed a s/e, a/c [single-engine aircraft] in flames going straight down through overcast. I circled back over bomber which went into overcast in shallow glide. Big friend seemed under control. I reassembled my flight, climbed back to 18,000 feet and returned home.[10]

Don provided more detail about the engagement in his January 29 diary entry:

> Nice show today to Frankfurt. Took Munger on my wing for his first show. Meserve led second element with no wingman. After we'd been on the bombers about 30 minutes I saw a lone B-17 way down below with 2 jerries attacking. I dropped belly tanks and down we went and <u>really</u> in a hurry! Almost 600 mph. I tore into the first, a 190 but overran him too fast of course. About that time we saw six of them all trying to get at the fort, so we really settled into a battle. I exploded the second one I fired at, a Messerschmitt 109 and damaged the third one with only one gun and Munger damaged one. Meserve destroyed a 109 too. They all turned tail then and the B-17 went into the cloud deck it was heading for. Don't know if it got home or not but we did our share. That was all the e/a we saw.

Robert Meserve caught his foe off guard, and his fire proved deadly. The pilot of the Messerschmitt was concentrating on shooting down the crippled B-17 and seemed unaware of Meserve's Mustang, *Scampy*, swiftly approaching him.

> I pulled off to the left to engage a Me-109E which was preparing to make a stern attack on the straggling Fort and half-rolled down on the tail of the e/a. I fired a short burst from about 300 yards to zero yards and saw strikes on the cockpit, fuselage and wings. As I broke left, I saw pilot slumped over in the cockpit, the canopy missing and the e/a burst into flames. E/a then went down in a moderate diving turn to the right and into the overcast. I cleared my tail and rejoined my flight. We were in visible distance of bombers until 1300 hours and saw no further attacks by e/a.[11]

The only other action favored Glenn Eagleston, who damaged a Focke-Wulf 190. The squadron's thirteen ships and the rest of the group crossed the North Sea near Dunkirk and began dropping in at Boxted at 1330.[12]

"Shooting the Breeze" after a mission. Left to right: Wally Emmer, Ridley Donnell, James Parsons, James Burke, Don Beerbower, and Glenn Eagleston. (name source: Ed Regis)

Don did not fly the following day, January 30, when Jack Bradley in Red Flight took the squadron to Brunswick where they engaged sixty enemy aircraft. Bradley and Eagleston claimed single kills, while Wally Emmer and Cannon put in claims for damaging two Me-110s. Eagleston and Wah Kau Kong sustained damage to their Mustangs,[13] Kong's plane having taken a hit in the right wing tip by a twenty-millimeter cannon shell during Red Flight's encounter with several FW-190s. The puncture made the wing feel heavy to Kong, so he had to handle the P-51 gingerly to avoid going into a stall. Finding himself alone, he tacked onto a box of bombers from the 2nd Air Task Force as they returned from the target area. Eventually, Kong attracted the attention of a flight of twin-engine P-38s. As he banked to identify himself as a friendly aircraft, he saw four Me-410s in close echelon formation less than a quarter mile off to his left. Kong, harboring an aggressive streak like many of the pilots in the 353rd, decided to maneuver his wobbly Mustang in behind the Messerschmitts. He made this report after returning to Boxted:

> I positioned myself for a stern attack but was seen by the last enemy plane who peeled down while the other 3 e/a went into a gentle turn to the right. I led the last plane and fired from about 300 yards. The planes went into a steep dive, still in formation and as the last plane flew through my tracers all except one of my guns stopped firing. I then skidded to the second plane and fired again,

but still didn't observe any results. After my remaining gun jammed, I pulled off and saw the P-38's follow the e/a where I broke off.[14]

The Me-410 heavy fighter was the Luftwaffe's improved version of the Me-210. Its twin engines projected ahead of the nose of the warplane, making it easy to identify in flight. The crew consisted of a pilot and a gunner. The gunner faced the rear of the aircraft, handling two remote-controlled thirteen-millimeter machine guns located in barbettes on either side of the fuselage between the wing and the tail assembly. With two twenty-millimeter cannon and four seven-point-nine-millimeter machine guns in the nose, the Me-410 could project a hail of deadly armor-piercing rounds against straggling B-17s and B-24s. Its best cruising speed of three hundred and seventy-three miles per hour in high, thin air made it best suited for attacking bombers. However, this was not enough speed to compete well against Allied fighter planes.[15]

Messerschmitt Me-410
Drawing by Major Joseph J. "Jay" Sailer

Colonel Martin flew with the squadron to Wilhelmshaven on February 3. The first mission of the month proved uneventful except for Richard Klein, who reported trouble with a leaking oil line during the return trip from Germany. After dropping from twelve thousand to five thousand feet, he bailed out into the cold embrace of the North Sea, seventy-five miles from Boxted. Klein, now missing in action, had been with the Fighting Cobras since Portland. Always "helpful and cooperative," he'd served as the special services officer. The following day, two new pilots joined the 353rd: James G. Burke and Billy B. Bronston.[16] One man lost at sea, two men filling empty bunks—the flux of death and life became almost as predictable as the changes in weather.

Richard M. Klein

Don did not participate in the uneventful mission to Frankfurt on February 4. He also missed the raid on February 5 when bombers attacked an airfield at Romilly-sur-Seine, sixty miles southeast of Paris. On this mission Lieutenant Colonel Don Graham, a visiting pilot from the 357th Fighter Group, damaged a FW-190. Other than his encounter, no other enemy contact occurred except for several P-51s fired upon by P-47s. No one took a hit.[17] Don commanded the squadron for the first time on February 6, when the bombers hit airfields southeast of Paris, but again, "no action at all."[18]

Brigadier General Pete Quesada from the Ninth Air Force's IX Fighter Command visited Boxted on February 7 to confer with Colonel Martin.[19] Most likely, he wanted to address recent changes in fighter tactics. The push emanated from General Henry H. "Hap" Arnold. In a directive to his Army Air Forces commanders on New Year's Day, he implored, "Destroy the Enemy Air Force wherever you find them, in the air, on the ground and in the factories." The targeting of aircraft manufacturing centers had been underway since early January. In addition, Eighth Air Force's Major General Jimmy Doolittle and VIII Fighter Command's Brigadier General William Kepner had been experimenting with a new method of providing protection for the B-17s and B-24s. Instead of tasking fighters to fly close to the bombers along an assigned section of the route, fighters would now be protecting an area the heavies would traverse on their way to and from the target. This gave pilots more flexibility to attack enemy aircraft before they closed on the bomber stream. As the only active P-51 unit, the 354th Fighter Group was already providing area support or coverage at the target end of the bomber route. The plan to attack enemy airfields was implemented the day before Quesada's arrival at Boxted, when Kepner authorized the 78th Fighter Group to machine-gun ground targets on its return from an escort mission.[20] Now Quesada wanted to discuss with Martin plans to attack targets of opportunity on the way home from their next mission.

That night the alert-officer at group headquarters received a field order informing Martin to ready his three squadrons for a return mission to southwest Germany on February 8. In the early morning darkness, thunder reverberated over the tarmac as ground crews warmed engines, preparing their Mustangs for the upcoming raid. Roused earlier than usual, pilots traded their snug bunks for a cold latrine, then hurried off to the officers' mess where they pushed down an uninspiring breakfast before assembling at the operations building. On a large wall in the briefing room, maps and charts identified the target for the day—Frankfurt. Martin and Lieutenant Colonel James Howard, who would be leading the group, gave an overview of the mission. Intelligence, operations, and weather officers covered their portions of the briefing. The men were told they would be strafing ground targets on the return leg of the mission. The whole process took twenty to thirty minutes. As the pilots left for the flight line, Martin and Howard huddled in the war room with the squadron and flight leaders for "last minute plans and instructions." The order to fly low level shooting at anything that appeared useful to the enemy had the Fighting Cobras pumped up. This excitement caused some concern, however. Squadron Historical Officer William Moneta wrote, "One could almost see the men lick their chops as they filed out of the Briefing Room–so much so that there was a slight feeling of apprehension on the part of the ground staff despite the fact that caution and possible pitfalls had been especially stressed by all officers who briefed that morning."[21]

Don guided the squadron's sixteen Mustangs from the Red-Flight-leader position on the Frankfurt mission. Carl Frantz headed White Flight. Captain Lloyd Hubbard, a visiting pilot from the 357th Fighter Group, covered Frantz's wing. John Mattie, also in a flight leader role, had Blue Flight. Wally Emmer led Green Flight. Another 357th pilot, Captain Bud Anderson, watched his wing.[22] Hubbard, Anderson, and the four flight leaders were all graduates of Class 42-I, so they knew what to expect from each other. Don had not seen his friend Anderson since the fall of 1942 when they were together at Hamilton Field, California.[23]

Clarence E. "Bud" Anderson

C. E. ANDERSON PHOTO

The P-51s started clearing Boxted at mid-morning. The fighters moved down the runway in pairs, flight leader and wingman, then second element leader and wingman, until each flight and squadron was airborne. Shortly after takeoff, each element leader joined with his flight leader. The flight leader and his wingman were in the number-one and number-two positions, respectively, in the flight. To their right, in the number-three and number-four positions were the second element leader and his wingman. This was called a finger-four formation. It can be visualized by placing the fingers of the right hand on a flat surface. The tip of the middle finger represents the flight leader, number one. The index fingertip to the left is his wingman, number two. The fingertip to the right of the middle finger is the second element leader, number three. The little fingertip is the wingman, number four. This pilot flew the farthest back in the finger-four formation and was known as "tail-end Charlie."

Don had Glenn Pipes on his wing with Wah Kau Kong as second element leader when he departed the airdrome at 0955. Donald Munger took Kong's wing in the tail-end Charlie position.[24] By the time the three squadrons crossed the Dutch coast south of Vlissingern at 1035, they were widely dispersed in a line-abreast formation at twenty-one thousand feet. In a line-abreast formation, the squadrons, flights, and elements spread out so that pilots could provide mutual support to each other if they came under attack. By 1110 the squadrons had staggered themselves between twenty-seven thousand and thirty thousand

North American P-51B/C Mustangs - An element leader and his wingman. U.S.A.F. PHOTO

feet over Selters, Germany, and were in position to provide support to the bombers hitting Frankfurt. After an hour-and-a-half elapsed with little enemy activity, the Fighting Cobras moved on to their ground-strafing assignment.[25]

There is something exhilarating about flying at treetop level. The sensation of increased speed and the suddenness with which new objects come into view produces a rush of adrenalin that can be quite addicting. The squadron's pilots had all experienced low-level flight in training situations; now they were experiencing it in real combat with four fully armed fifty- caliber Browning machine guns under their thumbs; and they had been given the freedom to destroy any target useful to the enemy.

With the exception of Emmer's Green Flight, everyone saw action on the return trip. John Mattie indulged in perhaps the most exciting shooting when he decimated two locomotives. The gun film was "exceptionally interesting." William Moneta summed up the activity of the other pilots:

> 1st Lt. Carl M. Frantz and 2nd Lt. Carl A. Bickel shot up a hanger and other ground installations at an unidentified aerodrome near Aresnes. 2nd Lt. Donald J. Munger and Wah Kau Kong damaged several unidentified red brick objects on an apparently abandoned aerodrome west of St. Omer, while 2nd Lt. David O'Hara shot up a radio station and tower at Gravelines. During the attack on the field near Aresnes, however, Capt. Hubbard . . .

was hit by A/A fire at point-blank range, and his ship was seen to explode. This 5th mission, 8 February, has been talked about ever since, as the most exciting affair so far–all the pilots enjoyed it, and would like more of the same, please.[26]

Kong and Munger had been with Don and Pipes near St. Omer, France. Don enjoyed their new assignment, recounting that "[We strafed] a Jerry airfield on the way home. New Deal on today's mission. More damn fun."[27] By 1405 all remaining P-51s had returned to Boxted. After the pilots debriefed with the intelligence officers of each squadron, a head count determined that in addition to Hubbard's death the group had lost three other pilots, all from the 355th.[28] Bud Anderson burned with anger after learning what had happened to his close friend and fellow flight leader. He blamed Frantz for exposing Hubbard to the dangerous ground fire associated with enemy airfields. Anderson felt his friend had lacked the level of combat experience for this type of assignment.[29]

When Major General Brereton and Brigadier General Quesada, waiting at Boxted for the pilots' return, learned the group had only destroyed one FW-190, the two generals and Colonel Martin concluded that the little gained in strafing targets of opportunity wasn't worth the risk to the pilots. Ground attacks were "dropped from future missions until further notice."[30]

The squadron did not fly again until February 10 when several pilots tangled with the Luftwaffe on a penetration-and-target support mission to Brunswick. The considerable enemy activity resulted in the destruction of one Me-109 by Felix Rogers and another by Ed Regis. Jack Bradley, Glenn Eagleston, and James Parsons damaged one aircraft apiece. For Eagleston, however, the mission proved memorable for another reason. The three squadrons were "inexcusably attacked numerous times" by red-nosed and white-nosed P-47s.[31] The friendly fire rounds from one of the big Thunderbolts caught up to Eagleston, but he nursed his disabled Mustang back to England before the engine seized up, forcing him to bail out. He landed safely and soon made it back to the squadron. The day ended much differently for Donald Munger.[32] Poor landing conditions at Boxted had forced him to continue flying west until he could drop in at Debden Airdrome, home of the 4th Fighter Group. After remaining on the ground for over two hours, Munger contacted operations and received permission from Don Beerbower to return to Boxted. He filed a flight plan and departed Debden at 1530. Twenty-two minutes into the flight and only three miles from his home field, Munger hit the top of a small hill and was killed. The ceiling at the crash site was estimated at a thousand feet with twenty- to twenty-five-mile-an-hour winds and visibility limited to three-fourths of a mile because of a snowstorm. After receiving confirmation of Munger's crash, Crew Chief Ben C. Richardson prepared the ship's flight record. Don sent it and a statement to the Aircraft Accident Investigation Committee, saying he had authorized Munger's return to Boxted. Four days later Colonel James McCauley, commanding officer of the 70th Fighter Wing, issued an order supporting a committee recommendation for all combat groups in the wing. McCauley wrote, "The practice of pilots, directed to other fields after combat, flying in to home airdrome under conditions of poor weather or approaching darkness must be discontinued."[33]

Munger had developed into a competent fighter pilot during his two months in the squadron. When he left Debden for the forty-mile hop over to Boxted, he was tired from his mission to Brunswick. A thousand-foot ceiling is normally adequate clearance for a low-level, cross-country flight of this nature. But Munger apparently became disorientated by the snow and the low cloud base that concealed the hill he struck. Don referenced the accident in his diary entry on February 10: "Had a mission today. Brad led the sqdn so I stayed home for a rest. Lost Munger. He got back and landed at another field and then took off in the poor weather to come on home & hit a hill and really washed up."

Donald J. Munger in flying suit

It appeared to be a routine mission on February 11 when the Fighting Cobras revisited Frankfurt, except that Don and Jack Bradley both participated instead of one remaining behind at Boxted. Jim Cannon and Ridley Donnell led the other two flights. In addition to putting up a full complement of sixteen P-51s, the squadron incorporated two radio-relay aircraft for enhanced communications. David O'Hara and Thomas Varney were told to fly high over the North Sea and provide a transmission link between Boxted and the mission leaders.[34]

The eighteen Mustangs departed their home base shortly after 1000, intent on guarding the bombers into, over, and out of the Frankfurt area. With this much time protecting the heavies, the likelihood of enemy contact skyrocketed. The anticipation of action may have been why Don and Bradley joined forces on this raid. The squadron made landfall over Walcheren Island, Netherlands, at 1055, short several aircraft that had aborted. Rendezvous occurred at 1140. From Cologne to Frankfurt, and during the time they spent in the target area, both fighters and bombers experienced "vicious and concentrated" attacks by approximately one hundred single- and twin-engine enemy aircraft. Over Frankfurt, "intense and accurate" flak focused on both fighters and bombers. Bickel, Beerbower, Bradley, Fox, Kong, and Rogers all scored kills. Meanwhile, in the radio-relay aircraft over the North Sea, O'Hara and Varney were harried by P-47s. Somehow, they evaded the friendly fire and later returned safely to base. The fighters left the bombers at 1225, cleared the enemy coast near Ostend, Belgium, at 1345, and began landing at Boxted by 1443.[35] A severe loss to the group

Wally Emmer and Don Beerbower congratulate Wah Kau Kong.

on this mission occurred when Colonel Martin and a German pilot collided in mid-air. Martin's wingman Glendon Buer described what happened near Koblenz: "At approximately [1222] an ME 410 came diving from 12 o'clock low and we dived to meet him head-on. Col. Martin met him head-on and I could see both of them firing. I looked back to clear the Colonel's tail and just then saw a bright flash. The ME 410 was a solid mass of fire and Col. Martin's ship was snapping over and over but apparently not on fire or smoking. All that remained of the 410 was a puff of black smoke hanging in the air. . . ."[36]

Ironically, both Martin and the German pilot survived the collision. Later in the day, the two seriously injured pilots met for a brief moment in a village hospital. (At the end of the war, Martin told Lieutenant General Brereton that the plane he collided with was an Me-109).[37] Martin had preached to the men–and now put into practice–the mantra he had learned from Lieutenant Colonel Donald Blakeslee: "never break" from a head-on pass. Martin had provided the group with exceptional leadership. Group Historical Officer Frederic Burkhardt tried to describe the feelings of Martin's men when he wrote, "It is not possible to put into words how greatly the loss of Col. Martin is felt by everyone who has served under him and it is the prayer of every man of this command that Col. Martin is a prisoner of war and that we shall all serve under him again."[38]

Kenneth Martin

Although the squadron and the group as a whole had performed admirably over Frankfurt, the implications of being without the commanding presence of Martin played on Don's mind after returning to Boxted. Seaman was dead, and now the other stabilizing force he had known since Tonopah was gone, as well. Don sensed his own vulnerability, but he couldn't bring himself to lay this burden on Elayne. He didn't want to worry his wife. Instead, he left her a message in his diary on February 11 describing the hazardous nature of his work.

> Bradley led the squadron again today and I led the second section & after 4 aborts, I wound up leading his second element. And it was a good flight of 4 that we made up! I got me another Me 110 and damaged at least one more! Bradley got one also. That puts him a half one up on me. I'll have to get out here & get a double to cinch things up. Ha.

We lost Col. Martin in a head on crash. I'm going to kind of sum things up here now so that in case something does happen, maybe it will help Elayne to understand a little. First; to date, we've lost 9 pilots in the squadron. It's a dangerous game we're playing. They've given us this plane and because we're the only group with them, we set way out over the target alone on the long missions. We've gotten along good so far but 40 to 50 planes in an area that far into Enemy territory is not much. The Jerries could put 300 up there anytime they really want to and they may do it one of these fine days: after just us.

Aside from that, these 1000 mile trips in a single engine aircraft are something that just invites trouble. Engine trouble is bound to turn up in time.

It all boils down to this—It's a matter of time for a large percent of us. And a golden opportunity for those of us who . . . live to tell about it. I plan on being one of those. We're going to miss Col. Martin a lot. We're lucky to have Lt. Col. Howard now to take over the Group.

The following day it became official. Brigadier General Quesada and Colonel McCauley came to Boxted for the ceremony appointing James Howard as the new commanding officer of the 354th Fighter Group. Quesada also brought a promotion elevating Howard to full colonel. The tall, gangly veteran pilot known as "Big Jim," received a warm welcome from the men. In his brief speech to them, he asked that they be patient and "bear with him." The unassuming Howard appealed to their pride and loyalty and then thanked them for their cooperation and closed by saying, "I hope I have appealed to your minds; if not, then to your hearts." Captain Richard Turner replaced Howard as the commanding officer of the 356th Fighter Squadron.[39]

James Howard

21

Damn!

Once you takeoff there are airplanes everywhere. You are constantly on the alert. The airfields were pretty close together in England. There were airplanes in the sky all the time so you had to be very, very alert to make sure you knew where your flight leader was, where your element leader was and where the [squadron] and group was. You were constantly scanning the sky and you could not see all the airplanes that were there. If we joined the bomber stream in the middle or the end you never saw the beginning of it, there were so many airplanes up there, over a 1,000 bombers. And then I don't know how many fighters. Each group would send up at least 50 fighters. There were a lot of P-47 groups. Then with the ack-ack [flak] bursting around and then looking for enemy aircraft, it was an awesome sight. You didn't have much time to go ahead and think about it because you were so busy checking behind, on sides, where your flight leader was, and so forth.

John D. Mattie, P-51 pilot
(interview with the author)

Poor weather hovered over England and the Continent in mid-February 1944. The 353rd Fighter Squadron had not flown a mission for eight days when RAF Air Chief Marshall Sir Trafford Leigh-Mallory, Major General Lewis Brereton, and Brigadier General Pete Quesada paid an unexpected visit to Boxted Airdrome on February 19. After addressing the pilots and ground officers of the 354th Fighter Group, Leigh-Mallory talked informally for some time with many of them. The men relished the opportunity to "speak on such intimate and pleasant terms with such authority."1 Leigh-Mallory knew the Allies were about to launch a prolonged assault on the enemy's aircraft industry. This mattered to him in his role as the overall air commander for the spring invasion of France. The Allies were planning to take advantage of a high pressure system moving southeast toward central Germany. Good visibility would allow American bombardiers to hit the Dornier, Focke-Wulf, Heinkel, Junkers, and Messerschmitt manufacturing plants. The development of the long-range P-51 Mustang made it possible to challenge the Luftwaffe with this strategy. The combined Allied day-and-night heavy bomber missions that took place during the week of February 19 to February 26 came to be known as Big Week (Operation Argument).[2]

On the cold, damp, snowy morning of February 20, over a thousand bombers lifted off the numerous airfields of eastern England. Each squadron turned toward designated assembly areas where it and two other squadrons formed a group (or box of 36 aircraft), and then groups blended into wings, and finally, wings into three divisions. The air armada now began streaming across the frigid, unforgiving waters of the North Sea in defensive boxes of B-17s or B-24s, four miles apart. Further behind, the first of eleven hundred fighter escorts began leaving their airfields. The pursuit planes needed only to assemble into individual groups. These swift aircraft could easily catch the Flying Fortresses and Liberators in time to fend off an attack. On this mission the heavies split into a northern and southern strike force. The smaller northern force was dispatched toward Denmark in a feint at targets on the North German Plain. Although these bombers eventually turned back because of weather conditions, the diversion served its purpose by attracting enemy fighters from the Kiel area. Eighty minutes behind the northern force, the southern force entered enemy territory over the Netherlands and headed for Brunswick, Germany, where the bomber train split into individual combat wings to attack designated manufacturing plants.[3]

The 354th Fighter Group was ordered to provide penetration-and-close-target support for the bombers assigned to hit aircraft factories at Leipzig, seventy-five miles southwest of Berlin. The 353rd Fighter Squadron and its two sister squadrons began leaving Boxted at 1057. The group launched fifty-four P-51s under the leadership of the 355th's commanding officer, Lieutenant Colonel George Bickell. Two of the ships would serve as radio relay aircraft while four others tagged along as spares. As Don Beerbower and the other pilots climbed away from the English countryside, they had to contend with an eight-tenths cumulous cloud barrier until they emerged from the overcast at six thousand feet. By 1150 the group had leveled out at twenty-five thousand feet as it made landfall at Gravenhage on the Dutch coast. Moving inland south of the Zuider Zee, the cloud cover improved to four-tenths coverage. Visibility at altitude remained excellent except for traces of contrails at twenty-four thousand feet and thirty thousand feet. At 1245, thirty-five minutes ahead of schedule, the group rendezvoused at Bockenem with the six boxes of bombers tasked to hit Leipzig. Learning that the Luftwaffe had just pounced on the lead elements of the unprotected formation, Bickell immediately ordered his squadrons forward. A few minutes later, the Mustangs of the rookie 357th Fighter Group arrived, and relieved them. Now the 354th's squadrons swung around to cover the three boxes of bombers originally assigned to them.[4]

Don was leading the 353rd's Blue Flight with Edward Hunt on his wing and

Wally Emmer in the second element leader position. Emmer's wingman Ed Regis had aborted shortly after takeoff because of engine trouble. Thirty minutes later, spare pilot Felix Rogers did the same after his cockpit frosted up and his P-51's engine began throwing oil. A frustrated Rogers, who had destroyed an Me-109 on each of his two previous missions, also returned to Boxted.[5]

The Americans continued moving with deadly determination toward Leipzig. At 1310 near Oschersleben, Don spotted four Me-109s at 8 o'clock, fifteen hundred feet below the heavies. S-turning behind the lumbering bombers, Don called out the bandits to his flight, dropped his wing tanks and instantly dove left from twenty-two thousand feet toward the unsuspecting Jerries. At the post-mission intelligence debriefing, Don described what happened as he rapidly approached the enemy:

> I positioned for attack on element leader and closed dead astern to 200 yards. I fired a 4 second burst and hit the canopy direct with all four guns. He started smoking and exploded just as I broke left to avoid collision. I broke into the other Me-109 just as he rolled over in a split-s. I fired a 2 second burst with only one gun from 100 yards and 25 degrees deflection. I saw strikes along the right wing root. I think I got a few hits in the cockpit as he started smoking as he went down. I broke off attack at about 18,000 feet. I then circled in an attempt to pick up my flight but couldn't find them so climbed back to bombers. I stayed with bombers through the target area, trying to join with other P-51s but they were all going too fast as I had to conserve gas, having dropped my wing tanks early.[6]

Over Merseburg Don "tacked on" to a flight of four P-51s providing withdrawal support. At 1345, as they cruised at twenty-two thousand feet near Mulhausen, a pair of twin-engine Me-110s came into sight a thousand feet below and about a mile and a half to the right of the second box of bombers. Don watched as the flight commander and his wingman banked toward their foe.

> The first element of the Mustang flight made a pass at the nearest Me-110 but did not close nearer than 200 yards. E/a made a slow turn to the right which brought him under my nose and I crossed over and attacked from his left and above with about 15 degrees deflection. I fired several long bursts with one gun from about 250 yards, closing slowly. I hit the left engine which exploded, throwing the aircraft up on the right wing. I pulled my line of fire into the canopy which came apart in an explosion. It looked like half the top

of the ship came away. I flew through pieces of the plane. E/a seemed to stop in mid-air and flipped over on its back. I saw a black object fall free and I pulled up and saw two chutes open. I was joined at this time by a P-51 . . . and continued home.[7]

By 1450 remnants of the group cleared the Continent over North Holland. The trip back to England proved uneventful except for a light, milky dusting of rime ice on the leading edges of the aircraft as they eased through a layer of supercooled water droplets hidden in the clouds. The touchdown at Boxted was officially listed as 1600. Don had put four hours and fifty minutes on *Bonnie "B"*.[8] It had been quite a day. His first victory tied him with the only P-51 aces in the European theater, James Howard and Richard Turner from the 356th Fighter Squadron. His second moved him ahead of them and the 353rd's C.O. Jack Bradley, who had also achieved his fifth victory on February 20.[9]

The other pilots in Blue Flight, Edward Hunt and Wally Emmer, each destroyed a '109. Bradley's second element leader John Mattie picked off a Messerschmitt and shared another with his wingman Robert Silva. With Don's two kills, the squadron ended up with seven enemy aircraft destroyed against no losses. The rest of the group claimed an additional eight victories.[10]

Don expressed his satisfaction with the mission in his diary entry that evening: "I did just exactly what I said I would. We had a lay off due to weather till today and this was our longest raid yet. To Leipzig with a lot of time over the target too. 560 miles to the target. And I got my double. An Me 109 and an Me 110. And damaged another 109. . . . It was a good mission except that I lost Emmer and Hunt on the first attack and was alone for an hour way over the target. More fun!! That makes ace for sure."

Don had every reason to feel proud of his accomplishment. It was the hope of every fighter pilot to achieve ace status. To do so was not easy. It required a pilot to destroy five enemy military aircraft in aerial combat. In the Ninth Air Force, each of its three tactical air commands established a Victory Credit Board. The pilot typically initiated the process for a claim by writing a combat or encounter report after completion of a mission. Experienced pilots serving on the Victory Credit Board reviewed gun camera film and eyewitness statements. A determination was then made as to whether the enemy aircraft was destroyed, probably destroyed, damaged, or in the case of the Ninth Air Force, listed as an unconfirmed victory. The Army Air Forces would not accept an unconfirmed claim as an official victory credit. The process of determining claims could be particularly frustrating for the pilot when the aerial combat took place without a witness. Because the gun camera only recorded when the guns were being fired, the telling evidence of a plane's destruction often occurred after the firing stopped.

Don Beerbower: *"When I first became an Ace."*

At other times the film was blurry, and therefore the claim was disallowed.[11]

The pilots in the squadron who later became leading aces exhibited unique characteristics. Jack Bradley described them this way: "We had a dozen guys in that squadron that were all good flyers, which is number one. And number two, they were all good shots. Number three, they all had good eyesight. Number four, they were aggressive and brave. It was a combination of what makes a good fighter pilot. And we were just blessed having that many guys in one squadron that had all those attributes."[12]

When Bradley refers to good fighter pilots as being aggressive and brave, he means they wanted to destroy the enemy pilot and his airplane. Not every fighter pilot in World War II felt comfortable killing, or risking being killed. Avoiding engagement was common. Consequently, the number of American aces remained few. Historically, aces make up only five percent of all U.S. combat pilots. The benefit of having aces in a unit was that these pilots usually made very good leaders, and their leadership improved the quality of the unit as a whole, thereby producing more aces and more leaders.[13]

Bradley made an internal leadership decision on February 20. He relieved Arthur Owen of his duties as assistant squadron operations officer and replaced him with Ridley Donnell. Owen, who Captain Priser had originally promoted to the position of operations officer by replacing Bradley, now found himself effectively out of the operations section. Bradley cut orders for Robert Meserve to replace Donnell as the leader of Don's old flight. None of the changes would have occurred without Don's knowledge. As operations officer and senior flight commander, he was expected to produce four flights of well-trained pilots and well-maintained airplanes for each mission. The flights were now led by Jim Cannon, Wally Emmer, Robert Meserve, and James Parsons. Meserve, who had helped train the Fighting Cobras during their brief stay at Greenham Common, became the first person promoted to a flight-leader position who was not from the original Tonopah group of pilots.[14]

James Cannon

Wallace N. Emmer

Robert L. Meserve

James J. Parsons

The group had a late departure from Boxted on February 21. Colonel James Howard sped down the runway at 1144, climbed to altitude, formed up his three squadrons, and led them east across the North Sea in anticipation of joining the bombers inbound to Brunswick. Howard's view of the enemy coast was obscured by a solid layer of strato-cumulus clouds. These decreased to three-tenths coverage as the Mustangs entered Germany. Good visibility diminished only when they passed through contrails. Shortly before rendezvousing with the heavies northwest of Minden, Howard dispatched the 353rd Fighter Squadron to deal with a potential threat to the formation. The Luftwaffe appeared intent on disrupting the impending attack. The pilots later reported seeing over two hundred single- and twin-engine bandits between Dummer Lake and the target area.[15]

Don led Red Flight this day with Don McDowell on his wing. Robert Meserve and Jim Cannon were in charge of White and Green Flights. Blue Flight

Leader Wally Emmer had gotten sick, and with Ed Regis as his escort, had returned to Boxted. With their departure, Blue Flight's Glenn Eagleston and his wingman slid over to fill in for two aborts in Red Flight.[16]

Since Green Flight had the responsibility to engage any enemy aircraft endangering the squadron prior to rendezvous, Don directed Cannon to carry out Howard's order. The twenty-five-year-old, no-nonsense former catcher for the Long Creek, Nebraska, baseball team was flying his ship, FT-K, *Cannon Ball*. John Mattie, leading the second element of Green Flight, had been so "hyped" about his victories the day before that he volunteered to replace Thomas Donohoo on this mission.[17]

The formation had just passed northeast of Dummer Lake at 1340 when Cannon came face-to-face with twenty Focke-Wulf 190s preparing for a high-side attack on the Fighting Cobras. At the post-mission debriefing Cannon reported, "The group had just completed a wide left turn prior to RV [rendezvous] with bombers. . . . They dived for attack on our flight which was on the outside of the squadron formation. I turned into them, dropping wing tanks at the same time."[18] As Cannon did so, he called out, "Bogies high at 1 o'clock!" Mattie could see they only had one course of action: "When you're out manned and they've got the high altitude advantage, you've got to break them up. And that's what Jim did." Mattie continued,

> I just dropped my wing tanks and we turned into them and scattered them out. Cannon made no explanation as to what he was going to do, see. I assumed that we were going to go ahead and have a dogfight in there once we scattered out and so I got on the tail of a '190. I could see I was getting hits when all of a sudden I looked back. I didn't know I didn't have a wingman [James Keane] . . . so I was open game to those Germans. I got hit in the left wing. Then I got hit in the right wing, and I looked back and there were two German aircraft . . . firing at me.[19]

While Mattie was attempting to escape destruction, Cannon and his wingman Jerry Leach had climbed above the danger. As Cannon looked down he observed the Germans flying in a circular pattern, involved in some sort of aerobatics. Puzzled by this, he checked his flight and noticed both Mattie and Keane missing. Cannon discovered later that Keane's engine had cut out when he dropped his wing tanks. Keane had unaccountably failed to switch over to his internal fuel supply. Cannon and Leach promptly returned to the bombers. They did not see Mattie again.[20]

By now Mattie had a fire in his cockpit. He had no choice but to bail out.

[I] trimmed my aircraft into a climb position, jettisoned my canopy and unstrapped myself and tried to get out of the airplane. I couldn't get out so I tried to stand up. As soon as I tried to stand up why it seemed like I was lifted right out of the plane. The first thing I know I'm coming down in the sky. I didn't realize I was burned across the eyes. I didn't like to fly with goggles down, I kept them up. The fire in the cockpit burned my eyebrows. The gloves had space between the jacket and the wrist, both hands were burned there. When I got out my eyes were closed. Once I felt I was free of the aircraft I pulled my lanyard and my 'chute expanded and I was floating down. Three Focke-Wulf 190s made a couple of turns around me. I was fairly high. I guess when I opened the 'chute I must have been about 18,000 feet because I know I got cold. I was not without oxygen as I had the portable oxygen canister attached to my parachute.[21]

After the three Focke-Wulfs departed the area, Mattie listened to the fading sound of the big radial engines as the bomber stream moved further east toward Brunswick. As he descended slowly and quietly from the winter sky, the Pennsylvanian contemplated his situation. His options depended on where he landed, but he knew one thing for sure—he was in trouble.

John D. Mattie and R. S. Johnson

There was a little town underneath me which later I found out was Wunstorf. I practically landed on the Burgomaster's office. In fact my 'chute draped up over this two story building. I was just hanging there for a while against the wall and a crowd started to gather. I kept tugging at my 'chute and I finally came down on the ground. They were pretty roused up and ready to do me mayhem. . . . I was only a mile away from a German fighter airport and they saw me coming down. Soldiers came on bicycles and fortunately they got there before the crowd got after me. Then they took me out to the airfield for interrogation.[22]

After Green Flight's engagement with the Focke-Wulfs, the remaining flights in the squadron joined the bombers. Several minutes later Don noticed an enemy aircraft as he led the squadron from his position in Red Flight. He responded at once.

[We were] providing close escort for heavies over target at Braunschweig [Brunswick]. We [rendezvoused] with bombers at 1345 and I positioned my squadron on the second box of bombers. On course to target in the vicinity of Steinhuder Lake I saw a FW-190 [at 1400] below the bombers and peeled off for attack. I closed to about 200 yards and fired several short bursts, observing flashes near the cockpit. Before I could close for more effective shots, e/a dived into a thin cloud deck at 18,000 feet. E/a seemed to slow up after I fired and before going into cloud deck.[23]

Reassembling his flight, Don climbed back up to the bomber stream. At 1415 as White Flight cruised at twenty-one thousand feet southwest of Hannover, Robert Meserve noticed four Mustangs pursuing a twin-engine aircraft six thousand feet below. Before the lead P-51's guns stopped chattering, the Jerry began smoking badly. Suddenly Meserve's wingman Billy Bronston dove toward the enemy ship.

Lt. Bronston pulled up near me and did a half-roll, diving after the Ju-88 which was, at this time, going straight down. Both aircraft disappeared into a cloud bank which was at about 10,000 feet. I followed to the top of the overcast and began circling. A FW-190 came up out of the overcast and I executed a 360 degree turn and it went back into the overcast. I started to climb in a tight spiral and saw a Me-109 come zooming up out of the overcast. I executed about a turn and a half and the Me-109 half-rolled into the overcast. I climbed back to 23,000 feet and continued circling, remaining in the area for about five minutes, but Lt. Bronston did not appear.[24]

Bronston's highly unusual action violated the squadron's rules of engagement. The wingman's job obligated him to protect his element leader. Bronston had not only failed to do this, but he had left the formation without permission. When Meserve returned to Boxted, he reported Bronston as missing in action.

Billy B. Bronston

Bandits remained in the area. At 1430 Don spotted two flights of twin-engine aircraft.

> Enroute out in the vicinity of Hildesheim I saw eight Me-110s below and north of bomber box heading east toward two boxes of bombers which were just rounding the target area. There were no e/a in sight of our bomber box so I dived toward them. I settled below them and dead astern of the right section of four. As I closed to 300 yards, two of the e/a dived for the deck. I closed to 200 yards of e/a on right and fired several short bursts. The left engine exploded and smoke poured out of the right engine. The canopy flew off and a large section of empennage [tail assembly] broke up. I passed over his left wing within 20 feet of e/a and saw the pilot slumped over in the cockpit. As I pulled up and circled for my flight to reform, I saw e/a skid crazily and flip up on one wing, going into a vertical dive out of control.[25]

In their initial engagement with the lone Focke-Wulf, Don McDowell, flying on Don's wing, provided protection for his flight leader. Now, as they approached the Me-110s, McDowell received the green light to clobber one of the Messerschmitts. He later reported his success:

> The two rear e/a in the lower flight peeled off and down as we closed and we attacked the next two. I observed flight leader getting strikes on one Me-110 from astern. As I closed e/a began a slow turn to the left and rear gunner opened fire scoring .30 cal. strikes in my oil scoop, coolant and wing. I pulled through my lead in a slight bank and fired several short bursts, striking flashes all over the fuselage. I saw the left engine explode and begin smoking badly. E/a split-s'd and I followed him straight down. I fired several more short bursts and knocked the right engine out. There was an explosion in the cockpit, and the canopy flew off and went over my right wing. I broke off at 15,000 feet and pulled up to the left to clear my tail. E/a was spinning straight down and aflame and smoking. I saw two chutes open. I climbed back to 20,000 feet and rejoined Red leader.[26]

Over in Red Flight's second element, Glenn Eagleston noticed one Me-110 pull away from the others. He closed within a hundred yards and gave it a four-second squirt hitting the fuselage and both engines. The last he saw of the Hun "it was spinning straight down at 8,000 feet, smoke and flames coming from both engines, obviously out of control."[27]

The engagements had taken place south of the bomber course. Reforming Red Flight, Jackknife 39 pointed the nose of *Bonnie "B"* to the northwest. At 1450 as the Mustangs closed on the heavies, Don spotted several single-engine enemy aircraft:

> As we approached bombers I saw four Me-109's completing overhead passes through bomber formation. They pulled out under bombers as we came into range of them from dead astern. I closed to 200 yards of e/a on right and opened fire with only one gun, scoring strikes along engine and fuselage. E/a made a slow, right turn with engine smoking badly. I pulled up and circled, attempting to pick up my flight but with no success. I joined a flight of P-51's from another group and started home.[28]

Meanwhile McDowell faced a situation requiring a double punch. As one element of the German flight banked to his right, the remaining two Messerschmitts continued straight ahead. Surprisingly, all of McDowell's guns were still working, so he closed in on the '109 to the right, spraying it with a three-second blast from his four Brownings. He described what happened next:

> E/a burst into flames and started smoking. There was so much smoke pouring from e/a I couldn't see him and was afraid I was going to ram him, so I fired another short burst point blank and pulled off to the right. E/a on left broke to the left and I swung behind him. I followed him in two 360 degree turns to the left, closing slowly. [While turning] I saw the pilot of the other e/a bail out and the plane crash below. The e/a finally straightened out and I closed from astern and below. I fired a short burst from 20 yards and saw hits all over the fuselage. E/a exploded, throwing oil all over my canopy. I popped the stick forward to avoid hitting the flying pieces. I pulled up trying to find him and all I could see was smoking pieces going down. I climbed up to 32,000 feet and returned home.

McDowell had expended five hundred and thirty-four rounds of fifty-caliber ammunition while scoring his three victories.[29] Lady luck had been on his side in each engagement. Any of the strikes on his aircraft from the Me-110 rear gunner or the flying debris from the '109s could have disabled his Mustang. The tin of whiskey at debriefing probably never tasted so good.

After nearly four-and-a-half hours of escort duty and skirmishing, the squadron could claim five enemy aircraft destroyed and two damaged. All had come from Red Flight. Two pilots had vanished. Don both lamented and celebrated in his diary that evening: "Another good raid to Brunswick. I led the squadron today and it was a good raid except that we lost Mattie and Bronston (new boy). It's going to be quiet . . . for a while without Mattie around. Got me an Me 110, damaged an Me 109 [and an FW-190]. That makes me 7 destroyed and top man in the whole group. Folks should get to read about me on that one!"

John Mattie had joined Don's flight at Tonopah in January 1943. In England, Mattie served as assistant squadron intelligence officer. He spent many hours of his own time helping out in the S-2 section. He enjoyed "pottering" around *My Buddy*, which he knew inside and out. His ship was still at Boxted, as Mattie had borrowed someone else's P-51 on February 21. Squadron Historical Officer William Moneta expressed the feelings of the men when he said about Mattie, "He was a quiet man, who enjoyed working and being of service. Undoubtedly one of the most well-liked pilots in the squadron, his loss was deeply felt on all sides."[30]

Jack Bradley led the mission on February 22 when the squadron escorted bombers to Oschersleben and Halberstadt, southeast of Brunswick. Don stayed behind at Boxted. The Fighting Cobras experienced terrific enemy activity prior to the rendezvous and en route to the targets. The numerous aerial battles broke up the squadron to such an extent that it was unable to remain with the bombers all the way to the two German cities. Jim Cannon, Ridley Donnell, Glenn Eagleston, Carl Frantz, and Charles Koenig all made claims for destroyed aircraft. Jack Bradley and Wah Kau Kong shared in the downing of an Me-410. Their victory, however, came at a price.[31] Bradley and Kong were southwest of Brunswick when they saw the Messerschmitt attacking a straggling B-17 below them at sixteen thousand feet. Without hesitation, the pair dove to engage the enemy aircraft. In Bradley's ensuing description of the account he reported: "I fired a long burst from 300 yards, observing parts flying off the tail assembly and smoke pouring out of the right engine. All my guns stopped except one and I broke off attack to let my wingman finish off e/a. I circled and saw Lt. Kong fire at e/a from close range. The right engine of e/a burst into flames. As Lt. Kong broke off over e/a, the rear gunner must have hit him as his plane exploded and disintegrated in the air."[32]

Wah Kau Kong

But the wingman's plane had not totally broken apart. Somehow Kong found the will to bring what remained of his P-51 to rest five hundred meters east of the village of Kamerun, near Blomberg. But in the process, he had suffered numerous bone fractures and a crushed skull.[33] The news jolted Don. Kong had joined his flight in Portland. As with John Mattie, Kong had been a man Don respected and would deeply miss. That evening, a four letter word in his diary expressed the depth of his sorrow: "Had a mission today & lost Kong–Damn! I stayed home for a rest. We couldn't have lost two better moral[e] builders than Kong & Mattie. Rear gunner on a 410 got Kong."

Don Beerbower

William Moneta described Wah Kau Kong as "a good sport, an excellent flier and a determined fighter." Kong had recently received press attention for being the only Chinese-American fighter pilot in the European theater. This encouraged him to advertise himself as the "handsomest and hottest Chinese pilot in the ETO!" His Mustang, in which he flew his last mission, bore the name *No tickee-No washee* on one side of the nose and *Chinaman's Chance* on the other.[34]

Kong had died doing the right thing. He had not hesitated a moment to protect the lives of ten fellow Americans aboard a crippled B-17.

Nat'l Memorial Cemetery of the Pacific, Honolulu, Hawaii

The squadron had the day off on February 23. Don did not participate in the raids on Schweinfurt and Nuremberg on February 24 and February 25. No enemy aircraft strayed within firing range of the Fighting Cobras on these missions, nor did the unit lose any pilots. Edward Hunt did have a close call when one of the wing tanks on his ship took a twenty-millimeter cannon round, but he returned safely to Boxted. His buddies considered him "a very lucky fighter pilot."[35]

Big Week was history. Ironically, although the bombing of German manufacturing centers temporarily slowed the production of aircraft, the Nazi regime would produce more airplanes in 1944 than any year of the war. Hitler accomplished this by relocating twenty-seven large industrial facilities to seven hundred twenty-nine well-dispersed, smaller sites. More critical to the Luftwaffe was the loss of experienced pilots. Its ability to replace these men had been dwindling since the autumn of 1943. As ongoing combat reduced its flying corps, the Luftwaffe had no other choice but to shorten the training period for new pilots to fill the vacancies caused by attrition. After Big Week, more and more evidence surfaced that the Allies were making significant progress in their goal of gaining air superiority. With increasing frequency, the Luftwaffe was forced to be selective about which industrial plants to protect from bomber attacks.[36]

22

YOU MUST PERSEVERE

From a distance a dogfight looks like a giant ball. When you are approaching an area where there is a dogfight you see planes going every direction. Up close you see flashes of airplanes going by. Rule number one for successful fighter pilots is to check your tail. So if you're in a fight and do tack onto an enemy aircraft you want to make sure nobody's done the same to you, and then you go for it.

Clayton Kelly Gross, P-51 pilot
(interview with the author)

On February 29, 1944, Captain Jack Bradley led the 354th Fighter Group to Brunswick. It was the first time he had been given the responsibility for all three squadrons.[1] The "Pioneer Mustang Group," as it was known, no longer held sole responsibility for escorting bombers to distant targets in Germany. Captain Don Beerbower, commanding the 353rd Fighter Squadron along the familiar route over Dummer and Steinhuder Lakes into the Nazi heartland, had expressed concern in the past about their vulnerability to attack when alone with the heavies deep inside enemy territory. Yet he knew that being out on this limb increased the odds of mixing it up with the Luftwaffe, something he wanted to do. Nevertheless, from now on he would see more Mustangs in the sky and have fewer encounters with the defenders of the Third Reich. After the completion of the mission on February 29, Don wrote in his diary, ". . . We had too much support & nothing showed up so it was a dry run. There are 3 other P-51 groups going now so we get some help over the target."[2] One of these units was the 4th Fighter Group headed by the 354th's old mentor, Colonel Donald Blakeslee. After flying Mustangs with them in December, Blakeslee jockeyed with the higher ups to have his group's P-47s exchanged for long-range P-51s. He succeeded in time to participate in the first raids on Berlin.[3]

The Fighting Cobras did not have a mission on March 1. However, the next day each squadron was assigned an enemy airdrome to monitor while the heavies went after targets south of the French capital. Their orders directed them to "shoot down anything that [takes] off while the Bombers [are] below Paris." But as Don noted in his diary, "Nothing showed."[4] The mission was uneventful except for the ongoing problems with attacks by friendly fighters. Wally Emmer returned to Boxted with an aircraft shot up by a careless Thunderbolt pilot who mistook his Mustang for a Messerschmitt. Two days earlier one of the flights had been attacked by Lightnings as it returned home over the Zuider Zee.[5]

With four P-51 groups available to provide area support to the most distant targets in Germany, the Eighth Air Force set its sights on Berlin. Its objective in missions launched between March 3 and March 9 was straightforward: strike targets of military value in and around the Nazi capital, and engage and destroy enemy aircraft. These raids, if successful, could boost the morale of those back home; Americans would be encouraged by the ability of our bombers to hit Berlin at will.[6] The Nazi capital, symbol of Hitler's power, had been on the receiving end of the RAF's night bombing campaign since 1940, but indiscriminate bombing of the city had not eliminated important manufacturing sites. The Americans believed they could hit these targets with the precision bombing capabilities of the Norden bombsight used on B-17s and B-24s.

The weather appeared favorable for the attacks to begin on March 3 but, over the Continent, the bomber train encountered heavy, turbulent cloud formations with tops towering as high as thirty-five thousand feet. Tense pilots fought to hold their positions as they flew in and out of the soup. Finally, the crews were ordered to return by VIII Bomber Command. The recall caused a massive traffic problem as hundreds of ships, many flying on instruments, turned back toward England in the congested sky. Numerous explosive collisions added to the edginess of every participant in this tragic false raid.[7]

Lieutenant Colonel George Bickell commanded the 354th Fighter Group on March 3. Twenty minutes prior to rendezvous, he noticed two boxes of bombers on a parallel course heading west. Because Bickell had not received a recall transmission, he continued in an easterly direction. At the rendezvous point, he found one box of B-17s on a heading to hit their assigned target. Bickell dispatched the 353rd to escort the big friends and sent the 355th and 356th back to Boxted.[8] Don, leading the Fighting Cobras this day, shadowed the bombers on to Oranienburg, a city about twelve miles north of Berlin. They didn't see any enemy aircraft or experience any losses.[9]

The Allies made a second attempt to reach the German capital on March 4. This time Group Commander James Howard led his escort ships away from Boxted at the head of the 353rd Fighter Squadron.[10] Establishing a bearing of eighty degrees, he shepherded the group out across the North Sea. Forty minutes into the flight, the pilots confronted a giant cumulonimbus cloud formation. Entering the gray mist, the forty-six Mustangs soon encountered severe turbulence. Many pilots couldn't maintain visual contact with their element or flight leader in the billowing thunderclouds. Instead of remaining in a tight formation, planes lost contact and became scattered. Carl Frantz was trying his best to lead the second element in Green Flight. When he climbed above the clouds and looked around, his wingman, Edward Fox, was missing.[11] Over in White Flight, David O'Hara had been trying desperately to maintain contact with Robert Silva.

> I was flying Jackknife White 4 on 2nd Lt. Robert G. Silva's wing. He held a good position the whole flight and for the first two minutes in the overcast at 22,000 feet. [In] the approximate vicinity of 5205-0300E at 1125 hours, he started to oscillate, more-or-less a pendulum motion, from one side of the formation to the other. I stayed on his wing until he suddenly went up on his left wing and shot upward at least 100 feet. I tried staying with him by hitting full throttle and yanking the stick. Result, I snap-rolled, probably spun, and lost him. My speed was 120 mph or less. Lt. Silva was stalled out when I attempted to stay with him. Shortly before Lt. Silva's difficulty, I heard Goodall [controller] call "63" [Lt. Fox] and told him to switch to "B" channel for a fix. After I'd recovered and headed back to base, I switched to "B" channel, thinking I could have been of some assistance. I heard a faint "Mayday" twice. I went to the deck, but could not find anything. This was apparently 2nd Lt. Edward F. Fox.[12]

Edward G. Silva U.S.A.F. PHOTO

Edward F. Fox U.S.A.F. PHOTO

Both Silva and Fox disappeared in the all-consuming waters of the North Sea. Because of the heavy overcast, Howard couldn't be sure of his location when light flak marked the enemy coastline. When the three squadrons arrived at the rendezvous point, no big friends greeted them. Howard pushed on to Berlin anyway. After patrolling the area until 1330, he turned his Mustang, *Ding Hao!*, west and led the group home. Unbeknown to Howard, the bombers had again been recalled. When he later learned what had happened, he "complained bitterly . . . that his group was forced to make this perilous trip without having been advised of any change of plans on behalf of the bombers."[13] The poor weather conditions had again caused VIII Bomber Command to direct hundreds of B-17s and B-24s to return to base. Three squadrons from the 95th and 100th Bomb Groups, however, did not receive the message. They flew unescorted to Berlin, dropped their ordnance through the overcast, and returned to England after losing five bombers. It was another botched mission.[14]

That evening Don wrote a letter to Gay Huntley letting him know how much he enjoyed receiving the *Hill City News*. Two and a half weeks later, Huntley commented about the hometown ace in the newspaper: "Captain Don Beerbower seems to be making quite a reputation for himself. . . . A recent AP dispatch credits him with 9½ Nazi planes in his bag." The editor went on to report to his readers that Don "is the same lad we knew when he was playing ball on the [town] team as the following letter . . . shows." Don's letter read:

> Dear Mr. Huntley:
> I have received five copies of The News in the last two days, which brings me up through Feb. 3 and catches me up. I think that calls for a short line at least. I read them all through when they first came in and again tonite–and I'll probably go through them again tomorrow.
>
> We actually got "over" Berlin today for the first time. We've gone as far before but not actually to the capital.
>
> The RAF heavies can be heard droning out for Germany tonite as most nites. Germany is taking an awful beating and it's building up every day.
>
> My roommate, the squadron C.O., is in the hospital with the flu, which made me pretty busy this past week. I've led the squadron on the last four consecutive missions and it is too much to keep up when we're going almost every day. If he doesn't hurry and get out he'll be having company.
>
> We haven't been having much action on the last few raids. About all I have to show for them is a tired seat! You can't imagine

how sore one gets after being strapped to the seat with no room to move for five hours at a crack.

I'm itching now to get some action on a raid so I can catch up with my painter. He keeps one extra cross on my plane to "make me work harder," he says. It's a conspiracy that my crew chief worked up with the painter. He has 8 on now and it looks pretty nice. With seven victories I'm high scorer in the whole group. Now I'm bragging.

Got a letter from Archie Sailer today. I'm going to try to contact him and see if we can't meet somewhere.

Thanks a million for The News.

Don[15]

Sailer was now a chemical warfare officer with the Eighth Air Force Service Command stationed at Huyton in western England. On March 6 he transferred to the 1576th Quartermaster Battalion, a trucking outfit that transported bombs between Liverpool on the Irish Sea and heavy bomber bases in East Anglia.[16]

The first full-scale raid on Berlin took place on March 6, when weather conditions improved enough for the bombers to hit the targets in the city hard. Don led the squadron again from the Jackknife Red Leader position. James Burke protected his wing as Red Two. Ridley Donnell, Red Three, had Edward Hunt flying his wing as Red Four. Robert Meserve, Jim Cannon, and Carl Frantz were in charge of White, Blue, and Green Flights. Six of the squadron's planes aborted, including all four from Green Flight.[17] Lieutenant Colonel Bickell led the Mustangs off Boxted at mid-morning, made landfall over Noordwijerhout on the Dutch coast at 1115 at twenty-five thousand feet, and joined with the bombers five minutes early at 1224. Shortly after meeting the heavies, the Fighting Cobras spotted a gaggle of approximately fifty enemy aircraft at thirty-two thousand feet approaching the bomber stream from the southeast.[18] Don described what happened next as Red Flight slowly S-turned near the heavies.

At 1250, March 6, 1944, in the area between Burg and Graben, I was proceeding toward Berlin giving close escort to bombers at 22,000 feet at the lead of Red Flight. I saw Lt. Ridley E. Donnell, Jr., leading my second element in mutual support with my lead element, make a sharp break to the left toward a FW 190 which was bearing in on him. He stalled out of the break but controlled the spin to almost a one-turn barrel roll and looked like he was under control at the bottom, having lost less than a thousand feet. At this time I turned back to head off e/a coming into position for attack on bombers and did not see Lt. Donnell again.[19]

Ridley E. Donnell   U.S.A.F. PHOTO

Ridley Donnell and fellow Class 42-I graduate John Mattie, had been members of "D" Flight at Tonopah. Now only Wally Emmer remained from this original group of pilots who had served under Don from their first days together in Nevada. Willie Y. Anderson was chosen to replace Donnell as assistant squadron operations officer.[20] Anderson hailed from Chicago and had served in the same section with Don at Luke Field, Arizona. One time at Tonopah, the two young pilots were fooling around in a Jeep chasing wild ponies across the bleak countryside when Don suddenly ran into something he wasn't expecting. Anderson figured they were lucky the windshield was down when it happened: "We're screaming along there and all of a sudden we hit a rivulet and the front wheels go down. We must have been doing 50, 60. The front wheels went down in this thing and [we] hit on the other side. They stayed there and the Jeep just kept going. And, of course, we left the Jeep and rolled around a bit and got up. 'You okay?' 'I'm okay.' 'You okay?' 'Ya, I'm okay. . . .' He was aggressive."[21]

Only two squadron members got any shooting on March 6. Glenn Eagleston had a field day destroying an Me-109, probably destroying another, and damaging a third. Edward Hunt also claimed a probable on a '109.[22]

On March 7 the 353rd received its largest influx of new pilots since mid-

December. The depleted ranks made it tougher on the veterans. It not only meant they flew more often with less rest, but it changed how they related to the new men. Having a close friend die or be captured increased the emotional strain on pilots. Ed Regis had had a bunk right next to Wah Kau Kong at Boxted. Regis used to borrow his good friend's 1934 Ford when he wanted to drive from Portland across the Columbia River to Vancouver to visit his future wife, Mary. When Kong was killed, it hit Regis hard.[23] Willie Y. Anderson remembered avoiding close relationships with new pilots because he had learned how painful it was to lose a friend. He didn't pay much attention to replacements; "They just filled up a bunk until they were gone because they didn't last very long."[24] Within weeks, many of these men—Ralph A. Brown, Philip D. Cohen, William B. Dehon Jr., William T. Elrod, Vincent J. Hart, David W. Henley, Frederick W. Jersig, Robert R. Kegebein, Billy J. Lamb, Edward V. Parnell Jr., William J. Phillips, Robert Reynolds, Orville L. Scott, Woodfin M. Sullivan, Edwin D. Urquhart, and Frank E. Weber—would be dead or in POW camps.[25]

One of Don's responsibilities involved integrating new pilots through a training regimen so they could move quickly into combat operations. But with Bradley sick, Don's focus had to be on leading the squadron, which he did again on March 8. He made a brief comment about the mission in his diary: "We went to Berlin today and the bombers really hit it. We saw no e/a at all tho there were some around some of the bombers–there were none around ours. Almost went to Russia with some B-24's–I was 20 miles the other side of Berlin before I realized they weren't coming around to bomb. Must have been a ferry trip! Some Trick!!"

Don did not go to Oranienburg with the rest of the squadron on March 9, the final mission to the Berlin area in the operation that had begun on March 3.[26] The weather now intervened. Flying conditions over the Continent turned too nasty for combat operations, and a week would pass before the Fighting Cobras went out on another assignment.

When the pilots had downtime at Boxted, their options for off-base entertainment were limited. The men usually headed to the Red Lion Inn in nearby Colchester for food and beverage. At this pub in early February, they had had a "long planned, long expected, long awaited" squadron party.[27] Ed Regis enjoyed the place. He remembered it this way: "The Red Lion was popular with the 353rd. It [had] an open room with a bar as you entered the front door. There was a large side room with tables for eating. They had a warm beer which I did not like. I liked the ale and the very friendly waitress. We had numerous dinners there. In fact, Dick Klein had paid for a steak dinner for 10 or 12 but did not attend as he never returned that day [February 3] from a mission."[28]

Colchester was large enough to attract the attention of the Luftwaffe. On still nights that winter, the men could hear air raid sirens wailing in the distance as enemy aircraft approached the city, but the attacks in the area were more of an irritant for the pilots than anything. If Jerry strayed near Boxted, Army Air Forces gunners responded with antiaircraft fire.[29] This affected everyone's rest, especially for those scheduled to go out on a raid the following morning.

Missions no longer concerned John Mattie. After being held several days at the German airdrome near where he had been captured, he and other prisoners were transported by train to the main interrogation center at Frankfurt. Many prisoners, bandaged and in pain from injuries, had to walk about a mile from the train station through the heart of the city to the interrogation center. Mattie described the experience: "It was all desperate ruins and people there began to taunt us and make remarks about us, spit at us and everything else." Mattie spent a week in a jail cell. Every day interrogators questioned him for an hour. He was surprised to learn how much the enemy knew about him. They told him where he had graduated from high school, when he joined the Army, and what training he had taken. They knew his squadron and flight designation at Boxted. From Frankfurt, the authorities sent Mattie and many other captives by train to Barth, Germany, on the Baltic Sea. He characterized the ride as slow, cold, and difficult; "There was no place to lay down. The car was full of prisoners. . . . One stove they had there in the middle." The cars clacked and jostled along, day and night. The rail network had been bombed in numerous places. Delays impeded their progress. Mattie could see Russian prisoners working on the tracks. Finally, in mid-March, they arrived at Barth. Mattie described a touching reunion with an old squadron mate: "When we got to camp there were all these *kriegsgefangen*, which is the name in German for prisoner of war, and we shortened it to kriegies. And all these krieges are in there waiting to see if they had any friends coming in. And right away I saw Buford Eaves. He was one of the first ones shot down in our squadron. He yelled my name out, and I saw him and, of course, once we got in the gate I ran towards him. . . . Oh, it was a feeling of joy to see somebody you didn't know was alive. I was very happy to see him and besides Bu and I were pretty good friends."

The pair had restless feet. On Mattie's third night in camp, he joined Eaves in the first of several escape attempts.[30]

On March 16 the Fighting Cobras were back in the air. This time the bomber boys attacked Augsburg and Gabligen in southern Germany, where the Luftwaffe waited to pick a fight. Anderson and Hunt, Arnold and Leach accommodated Jerry with shared claims, while Beerbower, Eagleston, Emmer, and Ricci got credit for destroying one enemy aircraft apiece.[31] That evening

Don recapped his tangle with a Messerschmitt at very high altitude: "Got an Me 109 today. Led the squadron to Augsburg. We got into a dogfight with 3–109's. My flight had fun for a while. I finally got a shot at one from right over him & raked him from [the] nose right into the canopy. He spun from 30,000 feet to the ground straight down."

Dogfights on escort missions typically began as a general melee involving numerous aircraft. Planes careened in every direction, zooming about, "attacking, being attacked and warding off attacks," friends and enemies taking hits, garbled radio traffic, bombers going down, fighters trailing smoke, and white parachutes drifting toward the ground—John Mattie remembered it as a "pretty horrific picture."[32] Willie Y. Anderson described the engagement of large forces this way: "You know the sky is pretty big and when you put a couple of hundred airplanes up there all of a sudden the sky is crowded, and then all of a sudden you and one other airplane is up there and you're all alone." It immediately sank home for pilots in dogfights that only one of them was returning to his base safely. Anderson continued, "[You] realize this guy in the other airplane is going to kill you so you do your best to keep him from killing you, and it is quite frightening at the time. But if you want to continue you must persevere and forget everything except getting this other fella. . . . You come back with red eyes when you'd bunt, push stick and rudder in one corner, because you'd break all the blood vessels in your eyes. You'd come back crying blood, but you got away from him, whoever was after you."[33]

The squadron revisited Augsburg two days later, March 18. Don found himself in a new role as backup to Lieutenant Colonel Bickell, who was leading the group. Lousy flying conditions confronted the pilots when they cleared the runway around noon. The fully loaded Mustangs had to plow through layers of cirrus clouds and snow until they reached thirty-one thousand feet and good visibility. Landfall occurred somewhere over the hidden Dutch-Belgian coast.[34] A few minutes before the scheduled rendezvous, a large enemy force suddenly materialized out of the clouds. James Keane, leading the second element in the 353rd's Blue Flight, described what happened: "2nd Lt. Albert J. Ricci was my wingman. At 1345 hours, near Reutlingen, our flight bounced a formation of 16 Me-109s and FW-190s at about 17,000 feet. In the dogfight which followed I lost contact with my wingman and did not see him again. As we went in for the bounce, Lt. Ricci was with me, but after Blue Leader fired on the rearmost flight of e/a, the formation broke in all directions and when we reformed a pilot from another squadron had tacked onto my wing." Fifteen minutes later, Ricci briefly joined several fighters from the 355th Fighter Squadron before departing for another flight of P-51s. Alone and vulnerable, Ricci disappeared.[35]

Albert J. Ricci U.S.A.F. PHOTO

The run-in with the enemy delayed the group's arrival at the rendezvous point by ten minutes. When the little friends joined their big friends over Ulm, the heavies were already under attack by a gaggle of at least twenty Huns. The Mustangs raced toward the Messerchmitts spitting lead at their bolting foe. Four of the Fighting Cobras' shots rang true. Beerbower, Eagleston, Keane, and McDowell each claimed an enemy aircraft destroyed. Newcomer Billy J. Lamb had damaged an Me-109.[36] Don proudly summed up the day in his diary:

> Led squadron to Augsburg again–Also deputy group leader!!! And–got me another Me 109 for my 9th. That really put me out in the lead of the group. Pilot bailed out.
>
> 16–109's tapped the group just before rendezvous to split it up but we broke it up with only our squadron, shot down 4 of them & dispersed them so quick & got on with the group that it didn't but cost them. Col. Bickell, leading the group said tonite that he couldn't see how I directed all my flights so well & got them back together so quickly & still got a Jerry myself! Quite a compliment. Col. Howard also complimented me on it tho he wasn't along.

For this and future missions, Don's call sign, Jackknife 39, changed to Jackknife 31, the designated operations officer number Jack Bradley had been using. Bradley now began using Jackknife 30, the call sign of former squadron commanders, Owen Seaman and Robert Priser. Beerbower's Red Flight and

Eagleston's Blue Flight enjoyed all the victories on March 18. Lamb had flown on Don's wing. James Parsons, second element leader, and his buddy "Doc" McDowell rounded out the flight.[37]

The squadron did not fly on March 19. Don used the down time to schedule practice missions for his newest pilots. He delegated this training responsibility to the individual flight leaders. That afternoon Don's classmate from 42-I, "Snapper" Parsons, planned to take Edward Parnell and William Phillips up on a local-area, simulated-bomber-attack mission. Doc McDowell would lead the second element. The foursome left the hardstand area with a crew chief on each wing, guiding the pilots along the taxiway. Parsons stopped adjacent to Runway 34, checked magnetos while waiting for incoming traffic to land, and then led the flight out on the runway for the planned northerly departure from Boxted. He and Parnell taxied into takeoff position fifteen yards from the airfield controller, Corporal C. E. Lawrence. McDowell and Phillips stopped twenty yards behind the lead element. When Parsons was cleared to go, he increased his ship's throttle and began rolling down the runway. Parnell did the same and the first two P-51s were on their way. However, after "some distance" Parsons slowed to a stop, checked his watch (it read 1443), and then turned to look at other squadron aircraft moving along the taxiway. McDowell had observed Parsons' and Parnell's initial movement along the runway; and, thinking they were departing, glanced at his crew chief, Staff Sergeant Kenneth Spillman, for the all clear. Then he signaled Phillips, increased his engine's power and turned toward the center of the runway. Phillips, just off McDowell's wing, straightened out and together they advanced throttles. Corporal Lawrence, alarmed that Parsons and Parnell had stopped, tried to signal McDowell and Phillips, but his emergency biscuit gun failed. The two ships gained speed. Parnell caught a glimpse of the oncoming fighters and instantly swung his aircraft to the right in an attempt to avoid being hit. McDowell and Phillips did not realize the danger dead ahead until the tails on their P-51s popped up. When the pair saw the stalled Mustangs, they automatically cut power, slammed on their brakes, and turned sharply to the right. Phillips missed both planes, but McDowell's left wing smashed into the tail of Parsons' ship and went up and over the fuselage, canopy, and right wing. The collision knocked off McDowell's propeller and left wheel assembly. His aircraft spun ninety degrees to the left and came to a stop. Parsons' Mustang swerved a hundred and eighty degrees and rolled back off the runway toward Phillips. Parsons' crew chief, Staff Sergeant Robert D. Reagan, and others raced to the accident scene to provide assistance.[38]

For several hours it appeared that Parsons would survive, but he died from cerebral hemorrhage while being transported by ambulance to 136 Station

Hospital. Four days later Parsons' colleagues paid their last respects at his burial in a temporary grave at the Cambridge American Military Cemetery. James Parsons was survived by his wife, Jeanette, of Seattle, Washington.[39]

James Parsons "Old Snap"

Don McDowell

In less than a month the squadron had lost Mattie, Bronston, Kong, Fox, Silva, Donnell, Ricci, and now Parsons, one of the old guard. That evening, five of the original Tonopah pilots went to Colchester intent on remembering their comrade and using the elixir alcohol to blunt combat stress. Very likely, they went to the Red Lion Inn. After Don returned, he recorded his daily activity, as was his habit, and then closed the dark-green, hardcover diary, never to write in it again.

Don Beerbower's diary

We lost "Snapper" today on a takeoff accident for a practice squadron mission. McDowell ran over him with his wing. He was unconscious for 3 hours before he let go. I was with him in the accident reception room & he seemed to be coming out pretty good but he didn't make it. Tonite, Bradley, Eagleston, Emmer & Koenig & I went to town and drank toasts and good wishes to him for 3 hours & tried to do it up–with fair success. I have a skinned knuckle for putting my fist thru a door!? Never realized how much I liked old Snap till he'd bought it.

Don Beerbower in reflective pose

As a consequence of the fatal accident, Willie Y. Anderson and three other officers were appointed to serve on an Aircraft Accident Classification Committee. Their report, completed on March 31 and sent up through channels to Colonel James McCauley at 70th Fighter Wing, in part said,

> The Committee feels there was no aircraft material failure involved but does feel justified in attributing the cause of the accident to more than 50% pilot error. There were extenuating circumstances. The runway control was inoperative at that time; Lt. Parsons applied throttle and moved down the runway as if to takeoff and Lt. McDowell interpreted the Crew Chief's signal as meaning the runway was clear. The Committee does feel that pilot error was involved inasmuch as the pilot did not turn the aircraft 45 degrees to the runway and personally ascertain that the runway was clear.

<u>Recommendation</u>: That all practice and operational takeoffs be controlled by a flag man and that all pilots be reminded in a forceful manner that it is their responsibility to see that the runway in use is clear for takeoff.[40]

Anderson expressed sympathy for McDowell in this case. Standard operating procedure required pilots to verify the runway as clear before takeoff, but this requirement had been ignored by squadron pilots at Boxted. As Anderson recalled, "We used to takeoff two at a time. . . . Snapper was rolling down the runway and then Doc McDowell straightened her out and rolled right down behind him. . . . [For] some reason Snapper aborted takeoff, pulled the power off. Well, hell, Don didn't know that, crawled right up him, chopped him up with the prop. They were pretty close [friends]." The unfortunate mishap had a jarring affect on McDowell, and he never got over it.[41]

23

ON THE BEAM

To compare the two in some respects is like comparing salt and pepper. On the ground I found Beerbower a little reserved but [Eagleston] very outgoing. We did not associate much with the flight leaders so I am not fully aware of how Beerbower was in most private conversations, etc. On the other hand, everyone knew when Eagle was around. . . . In the air, I believe they were very similar. Both were very aggressive and looking for a fight. I never flew wing for Beerbower or in his flight but was aware of some of his accomplishments. On the other hand, I probably flew wing for Eagle on about twelve missions and I believe I confirmed about six or seven of his victories. I found out very quickly to stay in position to protect his butt as he concentrated entirely on what he was doing. My job was to clear him at all times.

Edward R. Regis, P-51 pilot
(interview with the author)

    By late March 1944 it seemed less like winter and more like spring in the countryside around Boxted Airdrome in East Anglia. For Captain Don Beerbower and the other pilots of the 354th Fighter Group, the hint of English balminess represented a fresh start. In nearly four months of combat operations from this British base, they had been fighting two enemies, the Luftwaffe and the weather. It was a welcome relief to contemplate leaving behind the chilly air, poor visibility, and moisture that had influenced their daily routine for so long. As the seasonal transformation followed its annual pattern, other changes were afoot as well. Within several weeks the group's flying duties, command structure, and base of operations would all be different.

    The improved weather enabled the 353rd Fighter Squadron to participate in four missions between March 20 and March 24 in support of heavy bombers hitting targets at Frankfurt, Barsdorf, Brunswick, and Schweinfurt. Limited enemy action on these raids chalked them up as milk runs compared to most of their previous jobs. However, a fatal accident occurred shortly after takeoff on March 24. Arthur Owen, with replacement pilot David Henley on his wing, and Carl Lind, with rookie pilot Vincent Hart beside him, had just departed Boxted. Owen described what happened as Colonel James Howard broke trail for the Fighting Cobras, followed by the other two squadrons, up through a three-thousand-foot layer of overcast.[1]

> I was leading Green flight in the lead squadron on the mission on March 24, 1944. We set course at 0807 at 2,300 feet and started our climb out, entering the overcast at 2,500 feet. I checked the positions of the flight as we started our climb through. My wingman was tucked in close and 2nd Lt. Carl Lind, leading the second element, and his wingman, 2nd Lt. Vincent J. Hart, were in close position. The cloud layer was very dense and when I looked back several times on the climb, Lt. Lind was in position but I could just barely see him. The climb through was in smooth air, and at 5,500 feet I broke through on the right of Blue flight. On coming out of the cloud layer I looked back to see if the second element was still in position, but Lts. Lind and Hart were not there. I continued on, thinking that they had lost me in the clouds and would soon be coming up. However, Lts. Lind and Hart did not join our squadron or either of the other two squadrons. They did not at any time say anything on the R/T, to my knowledge.

Carl Lind

No one had received a radio transmission from Carl Lind or Vincent Hart. The mid-air collision occurred before they reached the coast.² The climb through the three-thousand-foot layer of overcast should have been a routine maneuver. Hart had joined the squadron on March 7, but Lind was an old hand. He had been assigned to Beerbower's new "B" Flight at Portland in June 1943. Now only Felix Rogers remained from the group of seven pilots Don took under his wing when he returned from his emergency leave in Minnesota.

On March 25 the squadron welcomed back John Montijo, one of the original flight leaders from the early days at Tonopah and Santa Rosa. Montijo transferred to the 356th Fighter Squadron in April of '43. Most recently, he had been attached to group headquarters.³ On this same date, Allied Supreme Commander Dwight D. "Ike" Eisenhower ordered attacks on the railway systems in France, Belgium, and Germany. The success of Operation Overlord, the code name for the invasion, hinged on Allied success in slowing the enemy's ability to move troops, equipment, and supplies to Normandy. Hundreds of large railway junctions and marshaling yards had been identified for destruction.⁴ In addition to disrupting the Nazi transportation network, Eisenhower ordered his air power to bomb and strafe airfields. From this point on, the Luftwaffe was to be given no safe quarter. Lightnings, Mustangs, and Thunderbolts returning from escort missions would seek out German bases, and fighters and bombers would set out regularly from England to attack enemy airdromes in France and Belgium. With D-day only a few weeks away, victory on the beaches could not be assured without control of the air.⁵

Allied Supreme Commander Dwight D. Eisenhower

The 354th Fighter Group felt the effects of Eisenhower's order on March 26, when all three squadrons headed out on their first dive-bombing mission. Jack Bradley, Wally Emmer, Robert Meserve, and Don Beerbower led the 353rd's four flights. All but Don's Green Flight carried two five-hundred-pound bombs. Green Flight would provide top cover for the other aircraft. Replacement William Elrod covered Don's tail. Another new man, William Dehon, did the same for Second Element Leader David O'Hara. The squadron crossed the English Channel near Pas de Calais and then darted to Creil, France, twenty miles northeast of Paris. They pounded the marshalling yards, railroad equipment, and associated buildings of this transportation hub.[6] No enemy aircraft interrupted their fun. As with their first strafing assignment a few weeks earlier, the men enjoyed the thrill of hitting ground targets with bombs after the long, tiring, and often tedious escort missions to Germany.[7]

Staff Sergeant Nathan Glick decided to commemorate the Creil event. The illustrator had spent the winter recording the 354th Fighter Group on paper. Now he concluded it was important to create an action drawing of the first dive-bombing mission. He chose to use Squadron Commander Jack Bradley and his *Margie Maru* as the foreground for his work, and the damage caused by the attack at the rail hub as the background. Glick's drawing recorded an important event in the unit's history.[8]

Margie Maru *at Creil, France*

This mission marked a turning point for the pilots from Boxted. From now on their duties would gradually shift from escorting heavy bombers to attacking ground targets. It also served as a reminder that, although they were attached to the Eighth Air Force to help achieve its strategic objectives, they were first and foremost part of the Ninth Air Force, whose responsibilities included tactical support for the soldiers preparing to go ashore at Normandy.

In late March, Colonel James Howard received an order informing him that the group was being transferred to the 100th Fighter Wing. As part of Major General Lewis Brereton's preplanning for Operation Overlord, the 354th would be joining the 358th, 362nd, and 363rd Fighter Groups to form one of two wings of the XIX Tactical Air Command (TAC), effective mid-April.[9] Brereton's choice to command the XIX TAC was Brigadier General Otto P. Weyland, a Texas A & M graduate who had transferred to the Ninth Air Force on January 31. His most recent experience had been as a fighter wing commander in Italy. Weyland preferred the P-47 Thunderbolt for fighter-bomber support. He believed its eight fifty-caliber machine guns and air-cooled radial engine provided more fire power and could endure more punishment than the P-51 Mustang with its four fifty-caliber machine guns and liquid-cooled engine. Weyland would prepare his new unit to support the future deployment of the Third U.S. Army in France.[10]

The final mission of the month, on March 27, turned out to be a long, quiet affair escorting heavies to Biarritz, France, near the Spanish border. It was anything but quiet on April 1 when the squadron went to Ludwigshaven on the upper Rhine River in southwestern Germany. Jack Bradley had a very close call when *Margie Maru's* "right flap, left elevator, left engine cowling, horizontal stabilizer and fuselage" took a spray of shell fragments near Ostend, Belgium. Green and Blue Flights engaged a gaggle of at least twenty-five enemy aircraft, with Glenn Eagleston and Edward Hunt downing an Me-109 apiece. On April 5 the squadron participated in its first strafing attack in nearly two months, providing top cover for the 355th and 356th Fighter Squadrons while they dive-bombed airdrome installations at Bourges, Châteauroux, and Chartres, south of Paris. The Fighting Cobras had "one hell of a good time" when they joined in the low-level shooting, releasing their wing tanks as if they were bombs. Jack Bradley put in the only claims; he destroyed three Me-110s on the ground. Bradley's Red Flight emerged unscathed from some light but concentrated ack-ack.[11]

April 5 also brought big changes for the 354th Fighter Group. On this date the squadrons initiated their transfer to an airdrome in Kent, forty miles southeast of London. A detail of men departed Boxted by truck convoy for Lashenden Field near Headcorn, while the pilots entertained themselves over France.

Lashenden was sixty-five miles closer to Normandy than Boxted. For the first time in the group's history, it did not make a transfer by rail. Since trains would not be available after they crossed the English Channel, some in the 353rd Fighter Squadron wondered if the move using vehicles was meant to test their mobility. When the men arrived at Lashenden, they started setting up tents, digging a latrine, building cinder paths, and erecting a mess hall and the other structures that would be needed in a few days by the remainder of the squadron.[12]

Don Beerbower

The Fighting Cobras experienced a transfer of a different sort in early April when First Lieutenant William Moneta left for a new assignment with the 70th Fighter Wing. Moneta had joined the squadron at Hamilton Field, California, on January 16, 1943. He had served as its historical officer, intelligence officer, and mail censor. Moneta's many responsibilities always kept him in close contact with the pilots, and he knew them well. He left behind a fine written record of the unit's operations and the men who served with it during the fifteen months he worked in the organization. Moneta closed his historical report for March with these comments: "Squadron losses during March were not particularly high, [Donnell, Fox, Hart, Lind, Ricci, and Silva] but each was a tragedy to those of us who had come to know and appreciate these pilots. . . . We knew that our victories were far more numerous than our losses, but that knowledge failed to make it easier. We learned that every man who wears wings is entitled to every courtesy, every consideration. [The pilots] <u>write</u> their history, while we on the ground merely write it."

Moneta left Boxted on April 8. His duties were given to a replacement, Second Lieutenant Albert J. Feigen, who would become a very capable officer.[13]

After a week of unstable air and limited activity, six hundred forty-four B-17 Flying Fortresses and B-24 Liberators left England on the morning of April 8, intent on destroying aircraft depots and manufacturing sites in central Germany. The target was Brunswick, a city the Luftwaffe often defended with fierce determination. A well-respected German unit known as the "Battling Bastards of Brunswick" patrolled this area. These "bastards" typically provided stiff opposition to the bomber force.[14]

Late in the morning, Group Commander James Howard gave his crew chief a parting nod, and then initiated the penetration-target-area-and-withdrawal support mission to Brunswick. Jack Bradley flew at the head of the Fighting Cobras. Don tagged along on this mission, leading one of the flights. Howard formed-up over the East Anglian countryside and then guided his charges out across the white-capped North Sea. Climbing to altitude, the squadrons moved into a line-abreast formation. As they approached the coast, pilots switched on guns and gun sight lights and began scanning the sky ahead for bandits. At 1236 Howard's three squadrons made landfall at IJmuiden near Amsterdam. Continuing in an easterly direction, they crossed the Zuider Zee on their way to Dummer Lake, where Howard planned to intercept the bomber stream at 1311. Visibility aloft was good except for five-tenths to seven-tenths cirrus clouds and nonpersistent contrails between twenty-eight thousand and thirty thousand feet. When contrails became persistent at thirty thousand feet, they provided cover for any enemy aircraft seeking a height advantage over their foes. The bombers showed up four minutes behind schedule at 1315. Five minutes later, seventy-five-plus Focke-Wulf 190s and Messerschmitt 109s attacked the heavies. Many of the enemy aircraft carried rocket guns. In their initial pass, the bandits exploded three bombers and sent three more spinning earthbound out of control. White parachutes suddenly dotted the springtime sky.[15] Red Flight Leader Jack Bradley didn't reach the action until the enemy fighters had gone through the formation and were swinging around for a second broadside on the bombers. Ed Regis, flying in the second-element-leader position in Red Flight, described what happened next: "By then we were in a position to attack them, which we did. Bradley went in and I followed him down about 150 yards behind him trying to give him some protection. . . . Don heard our radio chatter . . . and was on there asking where we were and how far ahead of him we were and so forth. He got up there I guess about the time I knocked down an Me-109 because he got on the horn and said, 'Who just shot down that [Messerschmitt]?' And I told him, 'Red Three.' "[16]

Beerbower and his wingman, Technical Sergeant Dennis Johns, had immediately responded to the initial attack of the daring Luftwaffe pilots. Nearing Wittingen, they banked toward the action.

> T/Sgt. Dennis L. Johns was flying my wing as No. 4 in White Flight when, at 1320, the bombers were tapped by 50 plus FW 190s. Our flight was below and in front of the bombers at the time and we turned sharp left to intercept the e/a. He followed [me] but just as we hit the melee, I pulled up sharp and to the left and started to circle to pick up something and keep our tails clear at the same time. I had only made about 180 degrees of a circle and [Johns] was gone. Nothing had been near shooting at us and I can only believe that he saw an e/a off alone and took after him. It was the last I saw of him.[17]

These early engagements blossomed into a giant dogfight that extended from the squadron's position near the bomber stream all the way to the ground. With aircraft veering in every direction, Don could only get off a couple of quick shots at the first two Jerries that came within range of his guns. A moment later, he tacked onto a Focke-Wulf, ripping into it with several good bursts. The plane flipped over on its back and fell like a lead weight straight down.[18] By now Ed Regis had joined the fray on the deck, pursuing an Me-109, when *Bonnie "B"* roared by him on his left. As he later recalled, "To my amazement, Don not only caught up with me but passed me just as the '109 hit a line of trees. . . . He got about 50 yards in front of me, something like that. The '109, I don't know what he did, neither one of us was shooting. He hit a row of trees and went in a ball of flames across the field up to some farmer's back yard."[19]

Back at Boxted, Don reflected on the Messerschmitt pilot's last moments: "He ploughed right into the [trees]. I just pulled up in time myself. He hadn't done anything but try to run away."[20]

Don later recounted his final engagement of the day, a tense dogfight, for Gordon Gammack, a staff reporter for the *Des Moines Register*:

> On the first two, the pilots didn't get out but I didn't care about that. The third one was different. That fellow put up a real fight. It must have lasted 10 minutes. The first time I hit him, he dumped his cockpit canopy and I sort of let up to give him a chance to bail out. Usually when a pilot dumps his canopy, he does it so he can bail out. Then he went at me again. And he was really

flying around there, too. But I got his engine and then he did jump. But the chute never opened. I really felt bad about that. Normally we don't think about this business on a personal basis. You don't dare. But that time I got a bit of a twinge. He gave me the best fight I ever had.[21]

While Don stalked these planes, Blue Flight Leader Jim Cannon got himself into serious trouble. He was flying Carl Frantz's plane *Joy*, his own ship sat in the squadron hanger back at Boxted. Cannon had just destroyed a Focke Wulf when he noticed a bandit coming in overhead and others to his left and right, which concerned him. He ruled out the pilot barreling down from 12 o'clock high.

> I wasn't worried about him. I figured he couldn't hit me from . . . a 90 degree angle. That's where I made my mistake. All of a sudden, "Boom!" A shell missed my cockpit by about two inches and went through the wing. He got my tail with an explosive shell. He hit a trim tab cable. I was at a pretty high speed and the stick pressure was such that I couldn't handle it. I started to roll. I must have rolled that thing 50 times before I released the canopy to bail out, being near the ground. But I finally got the rolling stopped and started going back to England. I lowered some flaps which reduced the stick pressure for better control of the stick. It turned out that the main reason I had such high stick pressure was because I had no trim tabs. It took all the strength I had to keep the nose down. . . . The rudder was jammed between the elevators where that shell had exploded. The elevator would hardly go up and down. I had a hell of a time getting the elevators to work. . . . Frantz had one of those Malcolm canopies and he was a little unhappy about my ruining his airplane for him. One 20 millimeter went right through the gas tank, straight down, perfect 90 degree shot. The gas tank didn't leak a drop. That's pretty good.

Fortunately for Cannon, American fighters had self-sealing fuel tanks. He also lucked out in that the Luftwaffe didn't discover him on his long flight to England. When Cannon radioed Goodall while inbound to Boxted, the message "The oranges are sweet" couldn't have sounded sweeter. With good landing conditions at his home field, the only challenge remaining was setting *Joy* down safely on the ground. Cannon's odds improved when the landing gear functioned properly. Coming in slowly and under power, he mustered all his remaining strength to land the shackled Mustang.[22]

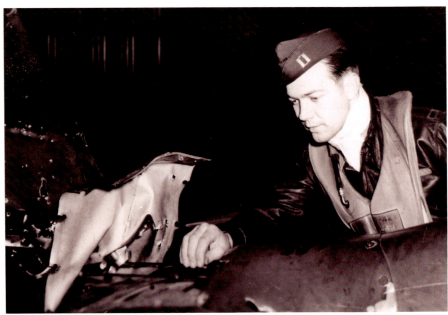

James Cannon and wing damage to Joy   JAMES CANNON PHOTO

On the return trip from Brunswick, several Fighting Cobras escorted a straggling B-24 until it was hit by flak and exploded over Oldenburg. They watched as five of the ten crewmates bailed out of the descending Liberator. Only three parachutes opened. These aircraft and other small groups from the squadron returned home, crossing the Dutch coast between Walchern Island and Zanvoort. The first pilot landed at Boxted by 1615. In addition to Don and Jim Cannon, several other squadron pilots had tallied kills: Jack Bradley, David Henley, Edward Hunt, David O'Hara, Ed Regis, and Robert Reynolds. Only Dennis Johns failed to return from the mission.[23]

Major General Lewis Brereton was proud of the accomplishments of the Ninth Air Force's Pioneer Mustang Group. On April 8 he made the following entry in his diary: "Escorting the heavies to Brunswick, the 354th [Fighter] Group ran into a swarm of FW-190s and Me-109s and shot down 20 for a loss of four Mustangs. Capt. Don Beerbower bagged two FW-190s and one Me-109, raising his score to 12½ German planes destroyed. Capt. Jack Bradley destroyed three FW-190s, making his score 8½. Colonel Howard got an FW-190 in a dogfight in which both planes flew upside down."[24]

One of Don's victims had been a long-nosed Focke-Wulf.[25] This fast, streamlined, stretch version of the FW-190A had an inline, liquid-cooled engine instead of an air-cooled radial engine. It served as the prototype of the soon-to-be-manufactured FW-190D-9 "Dora-9."[26]

When he saw the condition of his aircraft, Carl Frantz realized it was going to the salvage yard. He and several others, including Don, had had the new Malcolm sliding hood installed on their planes. He regretted that his was now ruined.[27] The British-made, bubble-shaped canopy resembled the one the RAF used on the Spitfire. The British refitted all of their Mustangs with the Malcolm hood, an important upgrade to the P-51B and C models, because it greatly improved cockpit visibility and allowed the pilot more room to maneuver his upper body as he searched for enemy aircraft.[28]

Don did not fly on April 9 when the group went to distant Gdynia, Poland. Jim Cannon also remained at home, but Flight Leader Carl Frantz spent over five frustrating hours during this bomber raid enclosed in the greenhouse canopy of his friend's ship *Cannon Ball*. The only squadron member to claim a victory happened to be one of the new pilots, Frank Weber, who'd been asked to fill in with the 356th.[29]

The three squadrons experienced something new on April 10 when they received two assignments in one day. In the morning they dive-bombed the railway marshaling yards at Hasselt in eastern Belgium. The Fighting Cobras dropped sixty-six general purpose five-hundred-pound bombs on its tracks, rolling stock, and buildings; then the pilots made "uneventful sweeps over airfields at St. Trond and Tirlemont" before heading back to Boxted.[30] Don mentioned the mission in a letter to his brother that evening. Darrel now served in an aircrew training pool at South Plains Army Airfield near Lubbock, Texas.

> Got a letter from you today so will answer right now. I guess I haven't quite kept up to schedule but I've done my best and haven't missed too bad. I wish you wouldn't keep blowing me up & bragging about me in my letters–I know how wonderful I am!! (Maybe that will keep you from it) Ha. . . .
>
> Had a dive bombing mission today–this morning–and escorted B-26's this afternoon. I led the squadron this morning & stayed home this afternoon & Bradley led.
>
> On dive bombing we work it by squadron and have just a few ships without bombs for escort. Today we hit a railroad yard just this side of [censored] valley. My navigation was "on the beam" and it sure made me feel good to run it off perfect.
>
> Now to brag a little!! Saturday, April 8, was a big day! I got 3 Jerries in one day! Is that good enough? Boy, we had a balls-out affair for a solid hour. . . .
>
> [Don]

Darrel Beerbower

In the afternoon raid, the group escorted the Ninth Air Force's twin-engine B-26 bombers for the first time. The penetration-withdrawal-and-support mission was to Namur, Belgium, a city in the Meuse River Valley, forty miles southwest of Hasselt. Jack Bradley and Edward Hunt scored victories when Focke-Wulfs bounced the rear box of bombers. On the 353rd's return, the pilots strafed the airdrome at Mons.[31]

The Martin B-26 Marauder served as the mainstay medium bomber of the Ninth Air Force. It fit in well with the tactical responsibilities required of Major General Brereton and his pilots in northwest Europe in the spring of 1944. The Marauder's two Pratt and Whitney R-2800-43 radial piston engines allowed the plane to fly at a maximum speed of two hundred eighty-two miles per hour, carry a bomb load of four thousand pounds, and a crew of five to seven men. For the bomber to have speed and carrying capacity, it needed a specially designed wing. This made takeoffs and landings touchy. The Ninth Air Force had eight groups of Marauders which they deployed extensively during the buildup to the landings at Normandy.[32]

Lieutenant Colonel George Bickell flew with the 353rd's Red Flight on April 11 when the group's orders required them to escort the heavies over targets at Cottbus and Sorau, near the Polish border in eastern Germany. Don led Green

Martin B-26 Marauder Nat'l Museum of the Air Force

Flight in what became a mission that pushed pilots and aircraft nearly to the limit of their endurance.[33] The action began when Thomas Varney's White Flight tried to dodge flak as they passed over Munster. Second Element Leader Carl Bickel described what happened to his wingman, replacement pilot Edward Parnell:

> At about 1045 hours, my wingman, 2nd Lt. Edward Parnell, Jr., was hit in the scoop. His plane began smoking and he called that he was going back. I turned and joined him to provide escort out. We maintained our altitude for about ten minutes. He called that his cockpit was full of smoke, and he began to lose altitude. I dropped 20 degrees flaps and throttled back and S'd over his line of flight. I asked how he was when he got to 5,000 feet. He replied he wouldn't make it. I advised him to jump before he got too low. By this time his engine was smoking badly. At 3,000 feet he bailed out. This was at 1105 hours about ten miles south of Utrecht. I followed him down and saw him get out of his 'chute harness and walk in a northerly direction. He was hobbling slightly, as if he had turned an ankle on landing. I regained altitude and returned home.

Germans quickly apprehended Parnell, who'd touched down in good condition except for a wound on the right side of his face and a left thigh peppered with some shell fragments.[34] When Bickel circled over Parnell, he'd looked for a place to land, hoping to pick up his wingman. He knew a P-47 pilot had recently done this. Bickel thought he could make enough room in the cockpit for Parnell by dumping his parachute. However, he scratched the idea when all he saw below him were small, fenced-in fields. Later, the group commander gave him a chewing out for making it easier for the Germans to find Parnell. In hindsight, Bickel decided it had probably been a foolish thing to do, but at least he discovered Parnell's condition. He later wrote to the pilot's parents explaining what happened and assuring them their son landed safely.[35]

At 1105, as the rest of the squadron cruised over Graben, three Me-109s bounced Jim Cannon's Blue Flight from above and astern. Flying in mutual support formation was Second Element Leader James Burke, a spare pilot filling in for someone who had aborted. Burke had no wingman. When he saw the attacking bandits, he called out over his radio transmitter, "Break!" The enemy aircraft closed so rapidly, however, that Cannon's wingman Ralph A. Brown couldn't respond before he took fire. As Brown called for assistance, Cannon pursued one of the Messerschmitts. The radio transmission from Brown to Cannon was garbled, but Burke understood Brown's message and prepared to retaliate. But first he had to deal with a Jerry on his own tail. He glanced quickly at Brown, whose Mustang spewed smoke as it descended slowly from twenty thousand feet.[36] Cannon now swung around and noticed a P-51 with a '109 on its tail. He closed immediately, getting hits and breaking up what he interpreted as an attack on Brown. Cannon's radio had died completely by now. It wasn't until the flight leader returned to Boxted that he learned Burke had been the pilot he'd saved from possible destruction, not Brown.[37] Brown did not make it home.

Fifteen minutes later the rest of the squadron rendezvoused with the bombers at twenty-three thousand feet south of Stenda.[38] The fighters that had been escorting the heavies up to this point now peeled off as the 353rd moved into position. The Mustangs began S-turning to better maintain their place in relation to the slower-moving formation. With good visibility above five-tenths cumulus cloud tops at eighteen thousand feet, Don had no difficulty picking up a bandit in front of Green Flight. At 1140 he moved into position to fire.

> I was leading Green Flight, 353rd Fighter Squadron, on escort mission for bombers of the 1st Bombardment Division, 3rd Air Task Force, with targets at Cottbus and Sorau. Just after rendezvous, I spotted a Me-109 ahead and about 2,000 feet above us. I led the flight right up under and behind this e/a and, keeping our auxiliary tanks on, started to pull up behind him without his seeing us. Just as I got up level with the e/a and about 250 yards behind him, he started a slow left-turn and I fired a 2-second burst getting a few hits but not seeming to do much damage. The e/a broke on to the left then and right in front of 1st Lt. Don McDowell, who

was leading my second element. Lt. McDowell fired and pulled on around, crossing under me and got good hits. As the Me-109 came on around, we were both firing and he snapped into a spin with both of us firing. I didn't see the pilot bail out. I watched the ship spin in all the way to the ground and crash. I believe Lt. Don McDowell got the engine on his first shot and I confirm his claim of destruction on the Me-109.[39]

After leaving the bombers at 1225, the pilots strafed an airfield on the south side of Wittenburg, destroying three Henschel Hs-129 antitank aircraft and damaging six others. Crossing Germany they observed aircraft on airdromes at Schernickau, Rathgow, and Teltow. The pilots returned to East Anglia via Haarlem on the Dutch coast. They landed low on fuel and ammunition at 1500, five and a half hours after departing Boxted.[40] The distance of six hundred and eighteen miles to the target constituted a record for their longest mission to date.[41] It came at a cost to the squadron of Brown and Parnell. Cannon and McDowell claimed the only victories.

The targets for the bombers on April 12, Leipzig and Schweinfurt, didn't matter because the weather conditions deteriorated en route to the rendezvous point, and the fighter escorts were recalled. On the way home, Lieutenants Meserve and Moran spotted a Focke-Wulf and "blasted him to hell."[42]

For five days VIII Bomber Command had been pounding German aircraft manufacturing plants in another one of its concerted efforts to interrupt the flow of fighters and bombers to the Luftwaffe. This intense period ended on April 13, when the bulk of the heavies concentrated on the Messerschmitt factory at Augsburg in southern Germany.[43]

Orders for the 353rd Fighter Squadron and its sister squadrons on this mission diverged even further, to escorting two hundred forty B-17s assigned to splinter off from the main bomber stream to hit Schweinfurt. The name of this city aroused fear among many crew members on the big four-engine Flying Fortresses, due to the widely known fact that in the summer and fall of 1943 the Luftwaffe had shot down a high percentage of bombers attempting to destroy this city's important ball-bearing industry. Although the effort to protect Schweinfurt had been more intermittent since then, its reputation remained. On April 13 the Luftwaffe would defend the city with a vengeance.

Shortly after takeoff, Lieutenant Colonel George Bickell prudently decided to return to Boxted because of a rough running engine on his P-51. He handed the reins over to Captain Maurice Long of the 355th Fighter Squadron. The new group leader rounded up his remaining Mustangs and made the hundred-mile run in clear skies across the North Sea. As the pilots made landfall at

Blankenburg, Belgium, another penetration-target-area-and-withdrawal-support mission lay ahead of them. This kind of assignment improved the odds of a good scrape. Visibility remained fine except for persistent contrails above twenty-six thousand feet. Moments after rendezvous, the Luftwaffe executed a frontal assault on the lead box of bombers. Three different gaggles of Focke-Wulfs and Messerschmitts, ranging in size from forty to as many one hundred fighters, struck the formation in swarms before it reached Schweinfurt. At one point south of Darmstadt, over forty parachutes floated in the air at one time.[44] Squadron Leader Jack Bradley hurried forward from the rear of the formation when the first attack occurred in the vicinity of Worms. With him in Red Flight were seasoned veterans Carl Bickel, Glenn Eagleston, and Willie Y. Anderson. Bradley pounced on an FW-190 at once only to have two of his guns jam after inflicting several strikes on the aircraft. Diving after the Jerry, he got off another burst before his remaining guns failed. At the same time, Bickel tried to lock on another '190, but the enemy's "evasive action was terrific." After several tight, high-speed turns, his guns locked-up as well. Unable to fight, the pair headed for home. Meanwhile Eagleston and Anderson had been pursuing the same '190s when Anderson saw a fighter bearing down on his friend. Heeding a sharp radio warning, Eagleston broke in time to evade the German. Eagleston then noticed at least fifteen more Focke-Wulfs bearing down on the lead box of B-17s. He and Anderson immediately diverted to break them up. From a good hundred yards, Eagleston deftly sprayed a short burst over the engine and wing root of a '190 as he and the Jerry zoomed past each other. Then Eagleston and Anderson banked sharply to chase the trailing flight of bandits. Eagleston's guns barked at one of the Huns from fifteen degrees deflection at a hundred yards, scoring on the fuselage. Another quick squirt at fifty yards astern scored again. This forced the pilot of the severely damaged plane to bail out. Simultaneously, Anderson had his way with another '190, his first kill. Eagleston, too far away to observe strikes, could see the Jerry smoking badly and in a "violent spin." The triumphant pair now returned to the bomber formation, staying with them until relieved of their escort responsibilities. This done, Eagleston decided to drop below the cloud level and look for targets of opportunity. He soon spotted an airdrome with exposed aircraft begging for fire. Attacking at low level, he blew up an Me-410, then crossed the field and strafed what appeared to be a multi-engine transport or flying boat. He and Anderson circled the field observing the damage, then climbed up to six thousand feet and set a course for Boxted. Five minutes west of Frankfurt, Eagleston noticed a locomotive pulling a train of cars. Without hesitation, he attacked, exploding the boiler on his first pass and riddling the train with more strikes in another pass before leaving the area and returning home.[45]

Don Beerbower was leading Blue Flight when the Luftwaffe made its initial attack on the bomber formation. He abruptly banked *Bonnie "B"* toward the diving Huns.

> Just after RV, our squadron was coming up the left side of the bombers, working toward the front of their formation. When we were about in the middle of the formation, the bombers were attacked from head-on by about 40 FW-190s and Me-109s. We couldn't intercept them before they hit the bombers, but we contacted them just after they broke through. I picked up a FW-190 and dove with him, but couldn't gain very fast so I started firing from about 300 yards from dead astern to get him before he hit the clouds. I fired two bursts of about three seconds each and observed good hits on the left wing and they moved over into the fuselage just as the aircraft hit the clouds. I pulled off and circled, climbing back toward the bombers. I contacted two more FW-190s but I had only one gun and they got into the clouds before I got a good shot in. I went on back to the bombers and went around the target with the bombers. Just as we came off the target, I picked out an Me-109 starting a pass at a straggling B-17 about 6,000 feet below. I cut him off and fired a burst from about 300 yards and 25 degrees deflection from above and to his left. I think I saw a few strikes but am not sure so I make no claim. He broke left and down without firing at the straggler and I pulled off and accompanied the Fort for about twenty minutes before starting home.[46]

The three squadrons remained with the B-17s until P-38s took over near Berg. The group claimed fifteen destroyed planes, seven of which were made by the 353rd's Anderson, Cannon, Eagleston, Emmer, Frantz, and Sullivan.[47]

The poor weather conditions that followed at mid-month provided much-needed rest for the bomber crews and a time to refit and replace the numerous B-17s and B-24s damaged or lost between April 8 and April 13. The squadron's pilots and their ground crews were tired as well. They had flown seven missions in six days. On April 14 the men rested.

Don did not fly with the squadron on April 15 when it revisited northwestern Germany on a fighter sweep. The weather turned unusually bad. Two of the replacement pilots, Robert Kegebein and Billy Lamb, became separated from their flights as they descended through a heavy cloud bank near Cape Arkena, Germany. It was so dense, Carl Bickel later reported, "I could not see my wing tips." Many pilots responded to Squadron Commander Jack Bradley's order to get out of the weather by climbing above the clouds. Kegebein and Lamb descended. When they broke through, the pair joined up, soon coming across an airdrome which they strafed. An antiaircraft gunner promptly found Kegebein's Mustang, forcing him to bail out. As he drifted down under his parachute, he saw a "blast of smoke" from a nearby airfield. The Germans later told him they had shot down Lamb and that he was dead.[48] Six of the fourteen replacement pilots who had joined the squadron on March 7, had now been lost.

Robert R. Kegebein

The April 15 mission turned out to be the squadron's last combat operation from Boxted. Most of the men and equipment were already at Lashenden Field. All they needed now was a break in the weather, and they could join the other two squadrons at their new home in Kent, fifteen miles north of Rye Bay on the English Channel.

24

Flak Galore

Statistics show that if you get over the first seven or eight combats, you generally survive pretty well except against flak.

Felix Michael Rogers, P-51 pilot
(interview with the author)

    Lieutenant Colonel George Bickell, a small-featured, twenty-seven-year-old fighter pilot from Nutley, New Jersey, was the only surviving squadron commander from the original officer cadre of the 354th Fighter Group. This fact and his extensive experience as a combat leader resulted in a new assignment for him in April 1944. Rumors had been afoot for several weeks that Colonel James Howard would be appointed to a higher headquarters position. Credence to this talk gained legitimacy when Bickell became Howard's deputy on April 6. His promotion created a commanding-officer vacancy in the 355th Fighter Squadron; Captain Robert W. Stephens filled it. On April 17 the men learned that Howard had been relieved of duty and transferred to Headquarters, IX Fighter Command. The Congressional Medal of Honor nominee had provided two months of timely leadership after Colonel Kenneth Martin went down over Germany in February. Now Bickell got the nod to lead the group. His first job, to complete the movement from Boxted to Lashenden, was slated to happen on April 17, but low clouds intervened, keeping many aircraft

George Bickell

grounded. Conditions improved the following day, thus allowing all pilots to arrive at Lashenden in time to be briefed for the first combat operation from their new base.[1]

For those who had been in the 353rd Fighter Squadron since early 1943, southeastern England reminded them of their time at Santa Rosa, California—mild climate, springtime, and fruit trees in bloom. In fact, the squadron's tents at recently constructed Lashenden Field stood in an orchard adjacent to one of the two landing strips. Nearby were the medical and supply facilities, mess hall, and squadron headquarters, with hangars and hardstands next to the perimeter track. The wire net and matting that concealed uneven spots on the surface of the L-shaped runways could provide inattentive pilots a "thrilling" experience on takeoffs and landings. The closest village was Headcorn. When the men sought entertainment, they went to Maidstone, "a large clean city" twelve miles to the north. Unlike Colchester, where there had been a military presence for several years, the squadron members found the civilians in the Maidstone area "friendly and polite, eager to welcome American soldiers into their midst." Southeastern England was different in another sense as well: fighters dominated the air instead of bombers. Having fighters at these advanced bases made it easier to fly two missions a day over France and the Low Countries. Landing strips were only a few miles apart. A nearby P-47 base was so close that Thunderbolts passed nearby at "low altitude, just having taken off from their airfield." The density of aircraft in the sky kept all pilots extra vigilant as they climbed away from or descended to Lashenden.[2]

For Captain Don Beerbower, the transfer to Headcorn meant the Allies were one step closer to ending the war in Europe. In a letter to his brother Darrel he wrote, "This theatre [ETO] won't last too much longer now. . . ." Don had been at Boxted four-and-a-half months. Leaving there satisfied in him a desire for momentum, to complete the series of transfers that he had been making since joining the Army Air Corps at Fort Des Moines, Iowa, in January 1942. He sensed that these moves were all designed to prepare him to help eliminate the Nazi regime in Berlin. But all the progress had come at a price. Now, leaving Boxted forced him to close another chapter and begin anew, to leave behind the feelings of loss for the many aviators he'd been close to, commanding officers like Martin and Seaman, and fellow pilots such as Eaves, Kerley, Kong, Mattie, and Parsons. Don carried forward his confidence about returning home to Elayne and Bonnie. This, he concluded in his letter to Darrel, might happen after they defeated the Germans.[3]

The mission on April 18 from Lashenden was the group's fifty-sixth combat operation. It involved providing withdrawal support to two hundred seventy-three B-24s returning from a raid on Berlin. The only thing that caused an adrenalin rush on this mission turned out to be the intense and accurate flak over Bremershaven and Harlingen, Germany. On April 19 and April 23 the pilots flew dive-bombing missions against the railway marshaling yards at Namur, Belgium. British Typhoons mistakenly fired at one of the squadrons on the return from the April 23 raid. All ships made it home to Lashenden by early afternoon.[4] Several hours later the group took to the air again for a fighter sweep over western Germany. Since Squadron Commander Jack Bradley had already flown to Namur, Don took charge of the 353rd's second operation. Wally Emmer, Carl Frantz, and Felix Rogers led the other flights. For some pilots like Frantz and Don McDowell, pulling both missions that day meant they would clock over six-and-a-half hours of combat flying on April 23.[5]

B-24 hit by flak

U.S.A.F. PHOTO

Late in the afternoon, the group sent up forty-five Mustangs plus one radio relay aircraft. Off the Belgian coast near Ostend, the pilots counted twenty-one naval ships in parallel columns heading in a southwesterly direction. When they entered the Netherlands north of the Hook of Holland at fifteen thousand feet near Gravenhage, extensive flooding could be seen along the coastline as far south as Dunkirk, France. Further on, at least fourteen balloons hung in the atmosphere at eighteen thousand feet south of Korbecke, Germany. As the pilots continued east, the broken clouds below them became a solid overcast. With potential ground targets obscured, the Mustangs turned for home. But unbeknown to the group commander, the winds aloft had changed. The formation gradually drifted off course over the important steel-producing Ruhr Valley and its concentrated, radar-controlled flak emplacements.[6] Don described what happened to *Bonnie "B"* in a letter published two-and-a-half weeks later in the *Hill City News*: "Got the Bonnie B all beat up Sunday. We went to [Hannover] and it was all overcast and we got too far south on the way back and came over the Ruhr Valley. (Flak galore) The devils let us get right in the middle before they opened up and then all hell broke loose. 400 mph in a shallow, weaving dive sure seemed slow! Got four holes. We didn't lose anyone but had a lot of patching to do."[7]

Don's plane and the aircraft flown by William Dehon suffered "considerable" damage. They had avoided injury, death or a POW camp by only a matter of inches. The following day, Dehon and Carl Frantz struck back at the enemy by combining to down an Me-109 while escorting bombers to southern Germany. Edward Hunt also destroyed a Messerschmitt.[8] A noteworthy accomplishment of the bomber force on this raid was the destruction of the first production run of the new twin-engine Me-262 jet fighter manufactured at

Don Beerbower astride his Mustang. Bonnie "B" *is showing the wear and tear of combat*

U.S.A.F. PHOTO

Leipheim near Munich. The Luftwaffe desperately wanted to have these high-speed aircraft so they could go on the offensive against the massive aerial attacks on their homeland. Although the Nazi war machine eventually produced the Me-262 and other jets, the Luftwaffe never had enough of these advanced aircraft in combat to gain air superiority. Pilot shortage continued to be the most a serious problem for the Germans. In the four months from December to April, they lost a thousand flyers in daylight raids. During a stretch of ten missions in April, the Allies shot down five hundred aircraft and killed or wounded four hundred pilots. With losses of this magnitude, the Luftwaffe had no choice but to use young, poorly trained replacements.[9]

Messerschmitt Me-262 jet fighter

NAT'L MUSEUM OF THE AIR FORCE

When Gordon Gammack, staff writer for the *Des Moines Register*, interviewed Don in April, he found him irritated with the "extremely wary" German pilots he met in the air. Don was blunt about his views of the Luftwaffe.

> Hell, we're willing to jump them when they've got us out numbered. The other day there were 30 of them up above a flight of our bombers. I took eight ships up to 35,000 feet to take a crack at them. They had every advantage, altitude, speed and everything. But they ran. . . . The trouble with the German air force is not so much their planes or their pilots but the frame of mind of the pilots. Even when they take the offensive in a fight–and that's mighty seldom, it's only for a couple of minutes and then they change.

Gammack reported to his readers that the former Iowa State College student doesn't have "a speck of doubt in his mind that he can win any fight with the Luftwaffe he wants to pick." Don's diminishing respect for enemy pilots was tempered by two aspects about combat operations that did concern him. He told Gammack, "The only things I really worry about ever are flak and engine trouble and there's nothing you can do about that anyway except keep your crew chief on the ball."[10] Don had no doubts about the capability of Staff Sergeant Leon Panter. He told Ninth Air Force Public Relations Officer Donald Dresden that he thought his crew chief among "the best in the Air Corps." Panter's admiration for the group's top ace was mutual. "He has plenty of guts," the sergeant said, "I've seen him come in with the engine running pretty tough, but he didn't turn back on account of it."[11] Panter's last comment is very likely an overstatement or a misstatement. Don realized the certainty of capture or drowning if *Bonnie "B"* experienced engine trouble. Rarely did his ship have problems, but when it did, he aborted like everyone else.

On April 25 the 353rd participated in a group fighter sweep southeast of Frankfurt. They found the airdromes at Boxberg and Assanstadt loaded with Me-109s and twin-engine Do-217s, Ju-88s, and Me-110s. The squadron destroyed eight and damaged at least sixteen more planes in the strafing attack. Anderson, Arnold, Bickel, Cannon, Eagleston, Elrod, Emmer, Henley, Meserve, Pipes, Reynolds, and Rody made claims. On April 26 the squadron went back to escort duty when the group provided support to heavy bombers hitting Brunswick. Not a single enemy plane opposed this mission, but the P-51s flown by Anderson, Cohen, Hunt, Regis, and Weber were struck by flak. All but Ed Regis returned safely to England.[12]

The trouble began when the Flying Fortresses failed to meet the Mustangs west of Brunswick at the appointed time. The three squadrons orbited the area at twenty thousand feet for fifteen minutes and then started flying various courses trying to locate the bombers. Because of a solid overcast, the group commander miscalculated his location and inadvertently drifted across Hannover's antiaircraft batteries. Regis described what happened as black puffs of flak began appearing near Squadron Commander Jack Bradley's *Margie Maru*.

> I didn't even feel it when I was hit. . . . Brad was in front of me with an eight ship flight and I was over to the right a little bit. He was turning to the left and the damn flak followed him right around behind his flight. I don't know if they were using radar or what but it was pretty accurate. I know they hit me and they hit Willie Y. He crash landed at Manston. I knew something was

wrong [when] Hunt called me and said I was streaming oil. I looked down and my oil pressure went to zero. I called Bradley and told him I'd lost my oil pressure. I don't know how long I flew, maybe five minutes, then the coolant popped. Bradley called me and said, "Bail out of the damn thing!" So I unplugged the radio so I wouldn't have to listen to him. I kept flying and then the engine just got so bad that I wasn't going any place so I got out.

Edward R. Regis

Regis was hoping to reach Belgium or Luxembourg before jumping from his aircraft. Normally, he would have been flying his own ship, *Rigor Mortis*, but it was in the shop.[13] The Blue Flight Leader left his aircraft at twelve thousand feet. Bradley circled nearby wondering why Regis didn't open his parachute. Finally, at seven thousand feet it blossomed. As the squadron commander banked around the descending pilot, Regis adjusted his harness. Then, as Bradley later reported, "[Regis] waved to me and gave our OK signal just before he disappeared into the overcast at 4,500 feet. I last saw his ship going straight down, trailing heavy black smoke. This was at 1020, about 20 miles southwest of Hannover."[14]

Regis' departure from his P-51 actually had been far more difficult than it appeared to Bradley. He had slowed the aircraft down to about a hundred miles per hour before attempting to bail out. When he tried to go over the side, the wind slammed him back into the cockpit. Out of desperation Regis pushed as hard as he could with his legs, but as he popped out his standard issue dinghy "caught on the top of the armor plate behind the seat." He was momentarily hung up. "The plane was going straight down and I was banging against the fuselage when I broke loose," he recalled. Luckily he missed the stabilizers as he sailed past the Mustang's tail, but his troubles were not over: "I was tumbling like mad." Remembering his training, he put out an arm and a leg, which stopped the tumbling, but now he found himself descending back first. Extending an arm, he promptly turned over and commenced falling face down. Then he pulled the rip cord on his parachute but nothing happened—"That's when I panicked." He made another attempt and this time it opened. When Regis dropped out of the overcast, he saw his destination would be the middle of a small village of perhaps fifteen houses. As he tugged on his 'chute's risers to slide away from the buildings, a small boy came out of a house and looked up. "I could see his mouth and it was going like mad and people started coming out of all the houses." At the last moment, a gust of wind pulled him away from the village. Moments later he came to rest near a farmer who was working his field. This fellow "looked about as shook up as I was at that particular time." A soldier in a green Wehrmacht army uniform and the villagers soon corralled Regis. He had little choice but to cooperate with his captors. About thirty minutes later an official came by with a horse and buggy and took him to Holzminden. Regis characterized the ride as uncomfortable; "he had his gun out pointing the thing at my head. It was bumpy and so forth and that bothered me quite a bit." Regis and an English flight officer were held in the local jail overnight and then transported by train to the interrogation center at Frankfurt. Ultimately Regis wound up in *Stalag Luft III* at Sagan, near the Polish border. The POW camp was a long way from his boyhood home in Rimersburg, Pennsylvania.[15] Regis had joined the squadron at Portland in June 1943 with Bickel, Hunt, Kong, McDowell, Lind, Logan, O'Hara, Rogers, Silva, Varney, and others. The ranks of these veterans had worn thin. Now another old hand was gone.

The Fighting Cobras returned to dive-bombing on April 27 when the group found targets at Charleroi, Belgium, in the morning and Amiens, France, in the afternoon. Don and forty-seven other pilots attacked near Charleroi, a city located south of Brussels on the Sambre River. This was familiar territory. The P-51s carried seventy-five-gallon wing tanks, and all but the top cover planes were loaded down with two five-hundred-pound general-purpose bombs to sprinkle around the city's important railway marshaling yards. Flying over the Belgian coast, the pilots noticed heavy flooding between Knocke and Ostend, extending as far east as Ghent. As they approached Charleroi from the west, they observed a large concentration of railroad cars. On the east side of the city, numerous P-47s pounded a target. This held up the group's fighter-bombers for seven minutes. Once the Thunderbolts cleared the area, the Mustangs lined up for a bomb run from the northeast to the southwest. Diving at an angle of seventy-five degrees, they made direct hits in the middle of the rolling stock. They also obliterated a large, oblong structure.[16] Don mentioned the attack in a letter home. He wrote, "Got a direct hit on a big roundhouse in [Belgium] with my two 500-lb bombs. My wingman hit it too, blew the top right off. I was leading the squadron and we knocked out those railway yards."[17]

After seven missions in five days, the squadron stood down on April 28 for a well-deserved rest. Several days earlier, the *Saturday Evening Post* had published an extensive article about the group, one of many stories about America's first P-51 unit that had appeared in national magazines after Colonel James Howard's noteworthy mission on January 11. Not surprisingly, writers emphasized the pilots who were commanders or had many victories.[18] This irritated Jim Cannon, who felt the press ignored the important work of the other men. He complained, "They weren't concerned about the guy who did his ordinary job. There were a lot of people that flew in our outfit that were not aces but they did a hell of a good service for the team. They kept the team together." Cannon believed this media interest encouraged leading pilots to strive for more victories and that it led to competition. He added, "We had a lot of groups over there that were publicized about aces and their home town. . . . Once that gets in your blood I think it gets catchy. I think you want to stay ahead of the other guy."[19]

As the top ace in the group and in the Ninth Air Force as a whole, Don received his share of the attention. Although his correspondence indicates he enjoyed being recognized for his skill, notoriety did not seem to change his outward behavior. Flight Leader Clayton Gross of the 355th Fighter Squadron attended regularly scheduled evening group meetings with Don. He described his contemporary as having a "very military bearing" and being "a quiet man." He did not deem that fame and achievement had affected his colleague, saying, "Some successful pilots would let everybody know about it, but I never heard Don ever say a thing about how good he was. He didn't have to, we all knew how good he was. But he was quiet and unassuming, a very nice guy."[20] Don also displayed a very hard-charging attitude when his blood was up. Hill City Coach Floyd Kaslow had observed this "very spirited" aspect of Don's character back in high school. Now it showed itself in his aggressiveness in combat. And as Jack Bradley noted, "He was very competitive, too. Even though we were not conscious of it at the time, I'm sure there was a certain amount of competition going on in the squadron. It's not something anybody talked about."[21] Major Donald Dresden commented about other facets of Don's demeanor in a public relations piece he wrote that spring:

Outwardly Captain Don Merrill Beerbower has none of the characteristics usually associated with fighter aces. The concentrated ego, the extreme extroversion . . . and the many other superficially true and apocryphal hallmarks of the top flight fighter pilot are completely lacking. In fact, he is the antithesis of the type Hollywood normally casts for the part. A medium built lad in his early twenties, dark complexion and well featured, he looks, talks and acts as though he were an intelligent, personable young man from Minnesota, maybe interested in the creamery business. He is. Above all, he gives the impression of never being ruffled; he is surrounded by an aura of deep and abiding calm.

The pilots told Dresden that Don seldom raised his voice to others around the squadron area, and that he behaved the same way in the air. He refrained from shouting over the radio when they were engaging the enemy. Dresden described it this way: "His conversation is no more animated than it is on the ground, and his decisions seem to have the same quality of thorough thinking that characterize his orders as operations officer and deputy commander of his squadron."[22] Overall, Don's personality seemed unchanged by his accomplishments. His temperament served him well as he and the other members of the Fighting Cobras transitioned through a period of diversified flying. None of the pilots knew from day to day whether they would be escorting bombers, strafing airfields, or dive-bombing railroad marshaling yards. But they did know the steady hand of Captain Beerbower would be with them.

On April 29 VIII Bomber Command sent four hundred eighty B-17s and two hundred sixteen B-24s in three air task forces against targets at Berlin. The

Don Beerbower before leaving Boxted

354th Fighter Group would fly with the three combat wings of the 2nd Bombardment Division, 3rd Air Task Force. Each wing consisted of approximately seventy-two B-24s. Lieutenant Colonel Bickell received word through group headquarters at 0220 of the pending mission. The operations order directed the three squadrons to cross the North Sea and the Netherlands, then fly on to Berlin using Lingen, Dummer Lake, Hannover, and Magdeburg as geographical check points. The orders stipulated that the 354th relieve a P-47 group when they rendezvoused with the B-24s over Dummer Lake, and then "render penetration support to the limit of their endurance." Withdrawal support would be provided by a P-38 group, followed by two RAF Mustang squadrons and two P-47 groups, one covering each of the last two legs of the mission.[23]

The 353rd Fighter Squadron, with Don in command, departed Lashenden at 0900. His flight leaders were friends he had flown with since January 1943: Jim Cannon, Glenn Eagleston, and Wally Emmer.[24] Forming up with their sister squadrons over the Kent countryside, they turned east toward the dark blue expanse that lay between them and the Continent, and gradually climbed to twenty-two thousand feet. They crossed the Dutch coast at Noordwall at 0950. The fighters crept up to twenty-four thousand feet as they flew past the Zuider Zee. Rendezvous with the 3rd Air Task Force took place at Dummer Lake at 1035. As the P-47s peeled away to the west, the squadron maneuvered into its assigned position. The bomber stream soon passed Steinhuder Lake and skirted the antiaircraft emplacements at Hannover and Brunswick. Suddenly near Gardelegen, northeast of Brunswick, thirty-plus Me-109s and FW-190s attacked. The P-51s' immediate response allowed the task force to brush aside the enemy and maintain course for Berlin. Northeast of Magdeburg, in the vicinity of Stendal, the Luftwaffe struck again. This time fifty-plus Focke-Wulfs dropped down from eleven o'clock high, making two overhead passes at the bombers. The Jerries took advantage of the great speed they had gained on the first pass to climb quickly into position for a second diving attack. In the wake of their two passes, five B-24s were sent spiraling toward the earth, four-and-a-half miles below, but the bomber stream flowed relentlessly toward Berlin as the P-51s pursued the FW-190s.[25] A massive melee ensued with individual dogfights raging between thirty-four thousand feet and treetop level.

After the initial attack on the bomber formation, White Flight Leader Jim Cannon in *Cannon Ball*, and his second element leader Felix Rogers in *Beantown Banshee*, joined forces as both had lost their wingmen. Cruising at sixteen thousand feet at 1120, they intercepted two retreating Me-109s. Rogers thought this occurred near Brandenburg, when in reality they were closer to Brunswick.[26] The Americans caught the German pilots in a loose formation just above the overcast at thirty-five hundred feet. Rogers, closer to the '109 in front of him when they came within firing range, pulled the trigger first. Cannon marveled at what happened when Rogers struck the Messerschmitt with a solid burst from his four fifty-caliber machine guns: "He hit it with so many APIs [armor piercing incendiaries] that it lit up so brightly I considered it destroyed beyond a doubt." Cannon fired at the fighter in front of him as it disappeared into the clouds.

> The first thing I saw when I got below the clouds was a lone '109 tooling along down there. I figured that was the one I shot at because the one [Felix] shot at couldn't go anywhere because he had put holes in it all over the place. So I decided to give it a short burst. There was no effect whatsoever. It was going pretty slow about that time so I pulled up along the left side of it and looked in it to see if the pilot might be incapacitated. The canopy was gone. . . .
>
> I was surprised to see the pilot with no helmet and his medium length, lightly colored hair flowing straight back in the slipstream. Despite my being on his left wing and about ten feet away, he never looked my way but I clearly remember seeing his very light complexion and prominent pointed nose profile that left me with a deep and lasting impression. . . .
>
> We were at about a 1,000 feet of altitude. I thought he'd bail out when I shot at him but he never did. So I thought, "Hell, he's not going to bail out." I was going to watch him. I figured his engine was about ready to quit. . . .
>
> By now being near and approaching the ground, I made a climbing left turn and saw the Me-109 crash land in a cloud of dust in an open field and the pilot running away from his plane toward some debris or cover of some sort. . . .
>
> About that time I heard a big click in the back of my airplane like somebody dropping a rock on the floor or a steel ball on a tin roof. All of a sudden I felt a lot of pain and my eyes were starting to burn so I put my goggles on. It was getting hotter than hell in there . . . I realized I was on fire so I pulled the canopy and bailed out. I was really low, probably 400 or 500 feet, maybe more I don't know. I couldn't get out of the airplane very fast. It's difficult to get out of an airplane. It seemed like the slipstream caught my helmet. All of a sudden I was out there in the clear, quiet as can be. I looked down and the ground was coming up real fast. I hit the ground and rolled a couple of times. . . . [I] crashed four kilometers southwest of Broitzem, Brunswick's airfield.

I wasn't far from the German pilot that had just crash landed. I got burned pretty bad. . . . I was going to hide the parachute. About that time a German with a Mauser came over a little knoll and hollered, "*Comrade!*" I thought, "He thinks I'm a German pilot. I won't say anything." He got closer and closer, looking at me, and he had his gun pointed at me. He got real close and saw I was a captain. He said, "*Hauptman?*" . . . I got captured right on the spot. I wasn't ten feet away from where I landed. My right hand was burned pretty bad. The German soldier got a bucket of water from some place. There must have been a little stream there. He motioned to put my hand in there, which I did. It felt better. About that time a German officer came on the scene. Of course, the civilians had gathered from all around. I don't know where they came from. There must have been 50 of them around there. They started beating me up. The German officer stopped them. He put me in a car. We went down the road a ways and, "Bang!" The old tire blew out. . . . We got out and went to another car that was around there, it had a dead battery. We finally walked up to a beer hall of some kind. The German officer was talking to the civilians in charge in that building. He talked to the man who said, "No, no." He talked to the wife. She looked at me and started nodding her head, "Yes." Apparently he was trying to borrow their car. So we got into a third car and they took me to a collection of buildings right out of Brunswick.

The B-17s were flying overhead. You could see the contrails and all the heavy artillery was going off, heavy guns of all types. You could hear shrapnel coming down. We went to an underground place where they had a medical facility. Civilians were on both sides of the corridor. They looked at me something fierce. They took all the English money I had and my watch. I was searched and treated for burns.[27]

Rogers had lost radio and visual contact with Cannon below the broken overcast. He circled under and over the clouds for twelve minutes, but the ground fire from the airfield southwest of the city grew so intense that he felt he needed to leave the area. Rogers climbed to the safe altitude of thirty-six thousand feet and returned to Lashenden.[28]

The P-51s still protecting the bomber formation left the heavies west of Berlin when relieved by the P-38 group at 1140. North of Brunswick the pilots watched as a pair of Lightnings collided with each other. Two parachutes descended from the impact area. By the time the Mustangs reached Dieppe on the French coast, it was 1315 and they had descended to eighteen thousand feet.[29] One of the squadrons flying farther north noticed "five parallel tracks composed of rectangular appearing posts running the length of the beach" between Dunkirk and Nieuport. At low tide, the pilots could easily see the hundred-yard-wide, twenty-mile-long invasion barricade. With this intelligence, they proceeded on to Lashenden, arriving at 1435. Of the six enemy aircraft destroyed, four fell to the guns of the 353rd Fighter Squadron. Those putting in claims included Beerbower, Eagleston, McDowell, and Rogers. Cannon and Eagleston gained credit for damaging one aircraft apiece.[30]

Jim Cannon's luck had finally run out even though he was a person who believed, "It can't happen to me." This attitude had buoyed his spirit in his sixteen months as a flight leader. It had given him the self-assurance to approach every mission with the expectation he would return home later in the day. Perhaps it was naïve to view flying in combat this way, but his optimism did remove from his mind the fear that he would be captured or killed, making him a more confident pilot and leader. Moreover, his fellow pilots benefited from this attitude. His mistake on this raid was lingering too long at low altitude.

A day or two after Cannon's capture, the Germans took him from a holding cell at the airfield to the main interrogation center at Frankfurt. From there he was transported east to *Stalag Luft III* at Sagan, where he joined Robert Kegebein, Kenneth Martin, Edward Parnell, and Ed Regis.[31]

The last mission in April involved accompanying bombers to Lyon in southeastern France. Although no enemy aircraft intervened, heavy flak created some work for the ground crews. The Mustangs flown by William Dehon, Don McDowell, and David O'Hara sustained damage, but all returned safely to Lashenden.[32]

On May 1 the group got another crack at dive-bombing. During the first mission of the day, Bradley led the Fighting Cobras to the railway marshaling yards at Namur, Belgium, a town which sat astride the confluence of the Sambre and Meuse Rivers. Early in the evening, Don, along with Flight Leaders Carl Frantz and Glenn Eagleston, took thirteen Mustangs across the English Channel to strike the airfield at Orly on the south side of Paris.[33] The pilots experienced a tense ascent to their assigned altitude when they had to climb blindly through twelve thousand feet of overcast before reaching the brilliance of blue sky. Once over France, the cloud cover began to thin. When the three squadrons reached Orly, the air-to-air visibility had diminished moderately because of haze. All ships carried two five-hundred-pound general-purpose bombs, except those from the 355th Fighter Squadron, which provided top cover. The bomb run was initiated at twelve thousand feet. Each pilot had to control his airspeed and the angle of attack in the long dive to the release point at three thousand feet. The specific targets were the aircraft dispersal points and hangars. After bombs away, the pilots' forward airspeed brought them within fifteen hundred to two thousand feet of the antiaircraft batteries guarding the facilities. Fortunately, on this day, ground fire came up light and inaccurate. No enemy aircraft pestered Don's squadron. Eleven-and-a-half tons of bombs hit the aircraft dispersal area; however, none of the hangars were damaged. The gunners at nearby Bretigny Airdrome threw up light but accurate flak when the squadrons flew too close to them, so the group leader guided the Mustangs around the west side of Paris. Near Versailles the pilots noticed a heavy concentration of rolling stock. They passed this observation along to intelligence staff upon their return to Lashenden.[34]

The dive-bombing fun continued on May 2 with a strike at an airdrome northeast of Lilburg, Germany. Later in the day, the railroad marshaling yards at strategic Charleroi, Belgium, took a pounding again. On May 4, the 354th escorted heavies to Berlin, but poor flying conditions caused a recall of all ships. The Eighth Air Force made another attempt on the German capital on May 5, but bad weather caused the bombers to miss their rendezvous with the group.[35]

Later that evening, Don wrote a letter to Darrel and Arlene. They had been able to stay together because Arlene had found work and housing at the bases where Darrel was stationed. Don began to write at 9:30 p.m. He told them *Bonnie "B"* had a "really sweet" new engine. He was proud of his Mustang, proclaiming, "I'm sending a couple of snaps of the best ship in the world! Ha–Course that's just one man's opinion." But above and beyond anything else, Don missed his family, his wife, his home. He longed for a couple of days by a Minnesota lake, away from the daily grind of combat operations. Don didn't have a reputation for excessive drinking, but he knew how he wanted to celebrate his first night home: "Wish more than anything almost–that the two couple's of us could go for a weekend to some cabins and really have a party! You'd probably all have your hands full the first nite getting me home to bed. Cause I'm thinkin' I'd be all for drinking myself under the table–And good old U.S. Bourbon would probably knock me for a loop after the watered scotch we get over here."

Don's thoughts had shifted from *Bonnie "B"* to having a good time at home. As dusk settled around him, he concentrated for a moment on the view out his window. Poignancy flowed from the simple words he used to express what he glimpsed through the glass pane: "It's raining out tonite & dampening the apple blossoms outside the window. And getting dark early. . . ." Without realizing it, Don had created a metaphor of his own generation's youthful effort to survive amid a world consumed by the misery of war. It would succeed, but only after Death, who roamed the orchard beyond his shelter, grimly reaped its share of young men.

25

A Desperate Will

[Eagleston] caught one [locomotive] and the guy saw him coming and the black smoke was pouring out of that thing. And as Eaggie came down on him he looked and it had entered a tunnel and Eaggie went up over it and he said, "The son of a gun came out the other end of the tunnel and the wheels [are] turning backwards. . . ." Eaggie spun around and got him before he got back in the tunnel.

Willie Y. Anderson, P-51 pilot
(interview with the author)

In May 1944 recently promoted Lieutenant General Lewis Brereton sent a lengthy report to General Hap Arnold in Washington describing the status of his command and stating that the Ninth Air Force was prepared for the coming campaign in France. By now the Eighth and Ninth Air Forces and the Royal Air Force had nearly eleven thousand aircraft at their disposal to support the invasion. Brereton shouldered specific responsibility in the month leading up to the assault on Hitler's western defenses to use his fighters and bombers to maintain air superiority over northwest France and to isolate Normandy. During a twelve-day period in May, the Ninth Air Force flew fourteen thousand sorties across France, the Low Countries, and Germany, attacking airfields, bridges, railroad marshaling yards, trains, and communication lines. Allied pilots destroyed over two hundred locomotives and numerous aircraft.[1] Captain Don Beerbower knew he played an important role in the buildup to a monumental amphibious assault. What he did not know was when it would occur or where it would occur. Writing to family members on May 5, Don slipped an oblique conclusion past the censors: "We're going to see some action soon. . . ."[2]

On May 7 and 8 the three squadrons of the 354th Fighter Group ran into a communications breakdown for their scheduled missions to Berlin. The field orders stating the specific rendezvous times did not arrive by teletype or telephone until after the pilot briefings. Consequently, on May 7 the squadrons failed to locate the correct air task force and came home without engaging the

Luftwaffe. The group did better on May 8 when the fighters found their big friends in time to join them at the target. Once over Berlin, the flak bursts proved to be very accurate. The pilots described them as white puffs of baseball-size explosions a hundred feet apart.[3] Later, as they returned home, Felix Rogers and his wingman David Henley were flying in mutual support of each other between Steinhuder and Dummer Lakes when they noticed a gaggle of Focke-Wulfs and Messerschmitts climbing beneath them. Henley dove toward the formation, followed by Rogers. They were soon fighting for their lives. Rogers later reported, "About 10 [e/a] were making passes at Lt. Henley who was in a Lufberry firing at an Me-109. By that time they had me on the run and I tried to out climb them. Lt. Henley called and said he had one. An Me-109 right beneath me rolled over flaming from nose to tail and went straight down from 6,000 feet. . . . We finally succeeded in losing the e/a which split up in groups and went down through the overcast." Henley called Rogers saying he had been hit "in the wing tank, tail and . . . windscreen from a cannon burst." Henley was alright but losing fuel and reaching the point at which he would have to bail out. The two pilots stayed in radio contact for twenty minutes before Rogers lost reception. Henley went on the record as missing in action.[4] The 353rd scored the only victories on this mission. Glenn Eagleston and Charles Koenig put in claims; and Felix Rogers filed one for himself and David Henley.[5]

The squadron had an early morning assignment on May 9 when they and the rest of the group went to Florennes, Belgium. Although enemy aircraft attacked and destroyed several B-24s, the Fighting Cobras couldn't claim any victories. The only serious incident occurred when a flak battery hit Wally Emmer's Mustang as the formation crossed the coastline. He arrived home safely.[6] That evening Don wrote a letter to Darrel and Arlene. He expressed excitement that his brother had finally been transferred from a training pool in Texas to primary flying school in Arkansas: "I sure am glad you are getting a break, Darrel–you'll never know how happy it made me!" Don also mentioned his disappointment for failing to bag a Focke-Wulf on the mission to Berlin on May 8: "Damn–I missed getting a F.W.–190 yesterday. Makes me mad–don't see many any more & I don't often miss getting one I spot any more, but it was hazy as heck & I took my eyes off him to clear my tail before I started after him and he just disappeared."

Late in the afternoon on May 10 the three squadrons flew uncontested to the Ardennes in northern France to bomb a railroad bridge. The group crossed the English Channel near Cape Gris-Nez at fourteen thousand feet, and then headed toward the target along the French-Belgian border. Once the pilots had the railroad bridge connecting Charleville and Mezieres in sight, they descended with their deadly payload to their bomb run commencement altitude of eleven thousand feet. As the 356th circled overhead, the other two squadrons screamed earthbound from north to south at an angle of sixty degrees. The pilots released their five-hundred-pound armor-piercing bombs at thirty-five hundred feet. Two shattered the south end of the bridge; one struck the south approach; and most of the others blew up on either side of the river. Although the flak barrage was moderate, one of the 353rd's fighters didn't make it through.[7] As Edward Hunt and wingman Frank Weber barreled toward the bridge at forty-five hundred feet, a twenty-millimeter antiaircraft burst found Weber's plane. The explosion almost killed Robert Reynolds flying a hundred yards behind the pair. As he watched, "The wings came off, barely missing my aircraft." The dive-bomber crashed in flames north of the target. Weber's charred remains were found on the railroad right-of-way.[8]

Frank E. Weber

The May 11 escort mission to Saarbrucken cost the squadron another pilot when William Dehon bailed out near Lommersweiler, Germany. Carl Frantz had been leading Blue Flight with Dehon on his wing when they spotted fifty-plus enemy aircraft maneuvering to strike the bomber formation. Frantz reported the outcome of their attempt to break up the attack:

> As I gained position, two Me-109s broke off from the main gaggle and came at my flight from 12 o'clock high. I called these two e/a in to my flight and did an Immellman and came out at 6 o'clock high to the e/a. At this time they must have seen my flight because they broke in opposite directions, the e/a to the right going

down. I positioned myself on the e/a on the left as he went into a tight turn and, in the ensuing encounter, shot the e/a down. Lt. Dehon was with me as we went into the Immellman, but that is the last I saw of him.

Glenn Pipes was tailing Frantz and Dehon, but because of the heavy haze he had trouble seeing the pair as they tangled with the Messerschmitts. He did see an aircraft explode and go down in flames. Neither he nor Frantz could establish further contact with Dehon.[9] Frantz's kill marked the squadron's one hundredth aerial victory. Pipes took the only other Fighting Cobra credit for destroying an enemy aircraft. As he was pursuing a Focke-Wulf at low level, it suddenly crashed into a "copse of trees." The pilot seemed to lose control of his aircraft before Pipes could fire at him.[10]

William B. Dehon

On May 12, the 1st, 2nd, and 3rd Air Task Forces sent up nine hundred Flying Fortresses and Liberators. The 354th was commanded to protect the two hundred forty B-17s in the four combat wings of the 3rd Air Task Force, targeting Zeitz and Bohlen, south of Leipzig, in eastern Germany. When the squadrons rendezvoused with the bombers, their orders would direct them to deploy "sufficient fighter strength ahead of the formation to offset frontal attacks." Once relieved, they would "fall back toward the rear of the formation" and contribute support to the limit of their endurance, paying particular attention to stragglers.[11]

Jack Bradley led the 353rd Fighter Squadron from the Red Flight Leader position. Don Beerbower, Thomas Varney, and Willie Y. Anderson were responsible for White, Blue, and Green Flights, respectively. Philip Cohen, Don McDowell, and William Elrod comprised Beerbower's White Flight. These pilots, with the exception of Elrod, who was replaced by Woodfin Sullivan shortly after takeoff, clocked an hour more flight time on this mission than others in the squadron. Each accumulated from five to five-and-a-half hours in the air.[12]

As the Mustangs taxied along the perimeter track behind new deputy group commander Lieutenant Colonel Charles G. Teschner, a number of "would-be fliers" from the group's ground complement began lining the runway to gaze at the squadrons leaving Lashenden for Germany.[13] This happened with every mission. The men enjoyed the excitement of watching the aircraft depart. They came for another reason as well: the men couldn't help mulling over the possibility that some of the pilots and planes would not return. Might this be a final goodbye to a comrade?

Bradley's flight of Fighting Cobras roared into the air first. After its departure, White Flight moved into position for takeoff. Once cleared, Don, with Cohen at his side, increased the throttle on *Bonnie "B"* and began to move her heavily down the runway, her wings sensing the burden of full ammunition compartments and topped-off fuel tanks. As the pair lifted off, McDowell and his wingman Elrod turned their P-51s into the wind, added power, and left the spectators behind as well. Soon, the rear wheel on each Mustang came off the ground, and shortly thereafter the planes transitioned to flight. With all the noise and activity, no one standing beside the runway heard or noticed anything unusual as the P-51s started gaining altitude. Elrod was ascending west of the field at about a hundred fifty to two hundred feet when his engine, under maximum stress, suddenly quit. Trained for this type of emergency, he immediately glanced ahead of the aircraft's flight path for a level place to land. Then, as Elrod later reported, "I switched tanks and flicked the fuel pump to emergency and jockeyed the throttle a little. . . . I had kept the plane in a glide straight ahead losing altitude rapidly. On the way down my right wing clipped a tree and the plane burst into flame immediately." Elrod had flown nearly three miles off the end of the runway when the burning plane "hit the ground fairly easily."[14] It skidded across two fields and tore through a hedgerow along a roadway before finally coming to rest. The black smoke from the burning aircraft quickly caught the eye of the men at Lashenden. Realizing what had happened, they grabbed any transportation they could find and raced to the scene. To the relief of everyone, they found only the charred remains of a Mustang at the crash site. Elrod was "discovered calmly smoking a cigarette and watching, from a safe distance, his plane burning to a black ruin."[15]

As the squadron bore east across the Strait of Dover, Bradley directed Woodfin Sullivan, available as a spare on this mission, to replace Elrod in White

Flight. The formation was flying in a layer of haze at twenty thousand feet when they made landfall south of Dunkirk. The group gradually climbed to twenty-five thousand feet en route to their rendezvous with the B-17s north of Frankfurt. Overhead three-tenths cirrus clouds drifted at twenty-eight thousand feet and persistent contrails scored the sky above thirty thousand feet. Shortly after joining the bomber stream, the fighters were challenged by seven bandits sneaking in right below these contrails. In the ensuing engagement, two enemy aircraft went down, along with one Mustang.[16] Carl Bickel described the enemy bounce that occurred when Blue Flight was attacked: "I was flying Green Three of the 353rd Fighter Squadron on a penetration, target and withdrawal support mission. . . . We were in mutual support with Blue Flight, making a climbing interception of some e/a. Five e/a jumped Blue Flight. We called break but the flight did not break until attacked. I saw strikes on the engine of Blue One, 1st Lt. Thomas S. Varney, and he went into a spin. Later, we heard Lt. Varney on the R/T say, 'This is Varney. I'm OK . . . I'm bailing.'" The veteran pilot went over the side of his P-51 at fifteen thousand feet, forty miles northeast of Frankfurt.[17]

Twenty-five miles west of Leipzig three single-engine fighters made a pass at the heavies. The B-17 gunners destroyed one of these ships. As the bombers withdrew, two more enemy aircraft fell victim to American marksmanship and went down north of Wurzburg. When Don spotted four more Jerries near Bad Nauheim, White Flight doggedly pursued the Messerschmitts north for a hundred miles. South of Bielefeld they cornered the Me-109s, destroying three and damaging one. The remainder of the fighter escort was relieved east of Cologne. White Flight's detour north held up their arrival at Lashenden until late in the afternoon. It was a good hunt for the squadron and White Flight in particular. Of the nine aircraft shot down, all but the lone Focke-Wulf destroyed by Captain Lasko of the 355th were Messerschmitts credited to the Fighting Cobras. Five of the '109s fell victim to the hot shots in White Flight. Beerbower, Cohen, and Sullivan each claimed one, and McDowell two. From the other flights, Bradley received credit for two destroyed and wingman John Arnold for another. Don put in a claim for a damaged aircraft for his hit near Bielefeld.[18]

Don's excellent shooting skill had much to do with his leading the Ninth Air Force in victories. He learned marksmanship at a young age, hunting deer, grouse, and ducks in the second-growth timber, brushland, and sloughs around Hill City. But aiming and firing at a moving target from a moving airplane was far more difficult than sighting and shooting from a hunter's stationary position. The complexity of the coordination was especially noticeable when a pilot tried to hit an enemy airplane flying at an angle to the pilot's line of flight. The attacker had to adjust his lead as he sped closer to his prey, instantaneously calculating a hit on an airplane based on deflection. Don had scored several victories in this manner, when firing from astern the target was not an option. Chicagoan Willie Y. Anderson admitted he never developed into a good marksman. He explained his deficiency this way: "My shooting was confined to the fact I'd get behind some poor bastard and I put the bull, gun sight, below'em and get as close as I dared and then pull the nose up through them so the bull went through'em and walk rudder pedals while I squeezed the trigger. And I just blasted the shit out of them with everything I had and sometimes I'd be ducking pieces and parts. One pass was usually all it took, and I went after somebody else. I never stayed with'em because he was all through."[19]

The skill it took to shoot accurately did not come naturally to Felix Rogers, either. Unlike Don's rural exposure to hunting, Rogers had grown up in the Boston area. He portrayed himself as a "city boy [who] never got off the pavement. And one thing I'd never done in my life was shoot. . . . My hand, eye coordination was not as good as it ought to be. . . . But the fact of the matter is I never was a really good shot."[20]

Jack Bradley and Don talked about shooting often. They discussed it hoping to improve their own success and the success of the men who served with them. As Bradley recalled, "We started out taking deflection shots but as we became wiser we would save our ammunition and try to get as close to the enemy aircraft as possible. . . . We had our guns bore sighted, harmonized . . . at 1,000 feet and Don and I both moved ours to 700 feet. Then all our guns would converge in one spot out there hopefully within about a six foot pattern. And [when] you hit somebody with that, you almost always had a destroyed airplane."[21]

Amorers' bore sighting a P-51

U.S.A.F. PHOTO

The four fifty-caliber Browning machine guns in the P-51B and C models could each fire between seven hundred fifty to eight hundred fifty rounds per minute of armor-piercing, incendiary, and tracer rounds. The air-cooled, belt-fed, short-recoil-operated Brownings weighed sixty-four-and-a-half pounds apiece. Firing long bursts would quickly use up the ammunition and burn out the thirty-six-inch barrel.[22] The armorer assigned to each aircraft watched for wear and other maintenance issues with the guns and gun sights. He also loaded the bombs under the wings and set the fuses. Sergeant Don Chisholm, armorer for *Little Horse* (the Mustang flown by Charles Koenig), had been trained to break down and reassemble the fifty or so parts of the machine gun in total darkness. One of his favorite tasks as an armorer was bore sighting. He recalled, "We would jack the planes up to level flight, line it up with the target, and adjust the guns to sight on the target. I happened to be on that crew as I was a sharpshooter myself. It was always fun to do this job; of course, we got to fire the guns."[23]

Donald J. Chisholm (wearing sunglasses) with friends.

Good shooting skill paid off for several pilots on May 13 when the squadron mixed it up with seventy-five-plus enemy aircraft on a five-hour mission escorting B-17s to Politz near Stettin in Pomerania. Lieutenant Colonel George Bickell led the group from the Jackknife Red Flight Leader position. Bradley and Beerbower stayed home on this raid to eastern Germany, but all four of the squadron's flight leaders—Glenn Eagleston, Wally Emmer, Carl Frantz, and Robert Meserve—went along to support Bickell. Frantz flew in the second element leader position of Red Flight.[24] Eagleston and Frantz had been promoted to flight leaders after the loss of James Parsons and Jim Cannon.

May 13 turned out to be an outstanding day for Frantz. He shot down three Me-109s and damaged a fourth. Emmer downed two and James Keane claimed another '109. Meserve earned credit for damaging an FW-190.[25]

After several weeks of flying numerous missions, the squadron found itself idle for five days in mid-May when the weather over southern England remained wet and overcast. But by 0440 on May 19, conditions had improved enough for IX Fighter Command to issue orders to the 354th Fighter Group and others to participate in a mission to Brunswick and Berlin involving nine hundred B-17s. The well-rested pilots were assigned the duty of protecting the four hundred twenty Flying Fortresses of the 1st Air Task Force, the three P-51 groups of VIII Fighter Command shadowing the heavies into and over Berlin, and the 354th specifically covering the bombers' withdrawal from the German capital until relieved by two P-38 groups from VIII Fighter Command.[26]

Jack Bradley led the 354th from the Red Flight Leader position of the 353rd Fighter Squadron.[27] Robert Meserve flew with Bradley in the second element leader position, and Glenn Eagleston, Wally Emmer, and Don Beerbower led White, Blue, and Green Flights. Don would put in a long day, clocking over five-and-a-half hours before the mission ended.[28]

The group made landfall at twenty-three thousand feet over Schouwen Island, south of Rotterdam, Netherlands. The flight remained uneventful as the formation followed the Rhine River east to the German border. Visibility remained good except for non-persistent contrails between twenty-six thousand feet and thirty thousand feet. By the time the three squadrons had penetrated a hundred miles inland, cumulus clouds were five-tenths with tops at twelve thousand feet. They cruised past Dummer Lake, Steinhuder Lake, and Brunswick, finally rendezvousing with the returning bombers near Rhinow, west of Berlin. Here they encountered flak but no enemy aircraft. Bradley stayed with the big friends until reaching Putnitz on the Baltic coast. Below, an airdrome with a number of enemy aircraft out in the open tempted Bradley to dispatch part of the group to seek out other targets of opportunity, and then to send Mustangs from the 355th Fighter Squadron against the airfield. Lieutenants Allen and Moran destroyed a Fieseler Fi-156 Storch, a Junkers Ju-88 in the air, and another on the ground; they also damaged five trainers. Meanwhile, the Fighting Cobras' Red and Blue Flights strafed seaplanes in the harbor north of Putnitz. Red Flight members Bradley, Meserve, Pipes, and Rody each riddled a twin-engine Heinkel He-115 float plane, while Emmer blew up a Dornier Do-26 flying boat. More kills followed when Blue and Green Flights attacked additional exposed aircraft at an airdrome near Westrow. Emmer and

Don McDowell each decimated an Me-110, while Beerbower and Robert Reynolds both blew up FW-190s. Pilots found two locomotives to strafe at Bad Segeberg and another at Neustadt; they destroyed all three. With ammunition low and distance from home a concern, Bradley and the pilots with him climbed to twenty thousand feet and continued west along the sea. Below them they counted thirty-plus flying boats in Trave Estuary and seven destroyers, along with numerous freighters and tankers, at anchor in Lubock Bay. Crossing the base of the Jutland Peninsula, they noticed the Germans were using smoke to conceal the harbor at Kiel and the Kaiser-Wilhelm Canal. The pilots also observed about thirty cargo ships sailing on a westerly course out of Wilhelmshaven. Flying on at an altitude of twenty-five thousand feet, Bradley could see Norderney Island in the East Frisians, the resting place of James Kerley, off to the north. Finally, the formation began descending over the Zuider Zee, crossing the Dutch coast at seventeen thousand feet near IJmuiden. All ships crossed the sea safely before letting down at Lashenden.[29]

The squadron lost an aircraft on this mission when John Montijo, low on fuel, made an emergency landing at West Malling, an RAF airdrome at Maidstone. As he taxied from the runway along the perimeter track toward the parking area, a fuel lorry pulled out from a wooded area and stopped in front of him. Montijo, emotionally drained from the stress of the mission, abruptly slammed on his brakes to "avoid hitting the truck." In the collision that followed, the driver and several passengers were killed. Montijo was angry with "the stupid driver." He later reported to the Aircraft Accident Classification Committee, "All I could do was slap on the binders, which caused my ship to rack up on its nose." The sudden stoppage of the propeller damaged the engine, and it had to be replaced. The committee found Montijo fifty percent responsible, feeling he "should have used his brakes sparingly; had he done this the nose-up probably would not have occurred." They recommended all pilots be cautioned to "taxi slowly and to 'S' [S-turn, weave] their ships constantly." Better yet, they wanted the crew chief to ride on the wing whenever possible to guide the pilot while moving the aircraft.[30]

The following day, May 20, Don Beerbower's thoughts undoubtedly drifted back home to his wife and daughter. It was Bonnie's first birthday. Don could not afford much distraction, however, as he was leading the squadron on an escort mission to Reims in northeastern France. While he and other Red Flight members—Charles Koenig in *Little Horse*, Willie Y. Anderson in *Swede's Steed*, Carl Bickel in *Z-Hub*—and the rest of the squadron participated in the group raid, Glenn Eagleston and John Montijo slipped into Belgium on a reconnaissance mission scouting for future targets along the Tirlemont-Liege railway line.[31] Both missions turned out to be anticlimactic, as the Luftwaffe chose to hold back its forces. Even though May 20 had been a quiet day for the pilots, the date held importance for the three squadrons, because on that day the Ninth Air Force changed the group's name to 354th Fighter-Bomber Group. This signified the shift in responsibilities already underway as the Fighting Cobras transitioned from their primary duty of escorting heavies to strafing and dive-bombing ground targets.[32]

Elayne Beerbower had been staying at the Kutcher farm in Spang Township northwest of Hill City since Don's departure for England in October 1943. As Bonnie's birthday approached, Editor Gay Huntley informed the readers of the *Hill City News*, "It is being urged that the day the invasion of Europe begins be made a day of prayer for the men engaged in the great struggle against the aggressors. It's a fine idea and should be adopted by the whole nation." All Americans sensed the great importance of the Allies breaching Hitler's Western Wall. To what degree Don would be directly involved in this action, no one knew for sure. Elayne and others in the family realized from articles about him in the local newspaper and from the letters he sent that his duties had been

Bonnie's first birthday - at Beerbower's home
Left to right: Clarence, Bonnie, and Josie Beerbower, and Bill and Anna Kutcher

shifting away from aerial escort work to ground attacks. The danger Don faced created in them a lingering fear no one could shake. The family found comfort in dealing with this by continuing to go about their normal routine. On the second Sunday of May, Bill and Anna Kutcher invited Clarence and Josie Beerbower and Don's grandmother Lula out to the farm to help celebrate Elayne's first Mother's Day. On May 20 the Beerbowers returned the courtesy by having a birthday party for Bonnie at their home in town. The little girl had made great strides in her development in the past year. Bonnie did not remember her father or understand conversations about him; nevertheless, she, like many other children whose parents served overseas, would have been sensitive to the underlying emotions of the adults around her. Often family members made reference to something mentioned by Don in a letter, or perhaps to an article about him in the newspaper. An example of this was a story and a photograph of Don published in the News a few days before Bonnie's birthday. The front page article lauded Don as "Hill City's ace," dodging flak in the skies over Germany, dive-bombing a railroad hub, and meeting and shaking hands with King Peter of Yugoslavia.[33] Although press coverage like this filled all with pride, nothing would make them happy until Don returned home.

On May 21, 22, and 23, the group participated in raids in France designed to weaken the German response to the upcoming assault on the Normandy beaches. Don led the squadron on May 21 when it escorted B-26 Marauders to Abbeville at the mouth of the Somme River, eighty-five miles from Lashenden. The following day Wally Emmer was Jackknife Red Flight Leader when the group flew two hundred fifty miles due south across the Channel to dive-bomb a target at Tours on the Loire River. Jack Bradley took his turn with the squadron on May 23 when the group escorted heavies to Bourges in central France.[34] With the exception of destroying five locomotives on the Tours mission, these three days of flying lacked action for the Fighting Cobras.[35]

On May 24, the 353rd contributed fifteen Mustangs, including one radio relay aircraft, to the group's total of forty-nine ships ordered to provide routine withdrawal support for heavies returning from Berlin. The cloud cover over the Continent on this mission measured eight-tenths to ten-tenths with tops at twelve thousand feet. Another layer of five-tenths to six-tenths cirrus clouds drifted along between twenty thousand feet and thirty thousand feet. The group met the returning bombers at twenty-nine thousand feet between Kiel and Hamburg. They provided support to the main force and to numerous stragglers until relieved north of Juist Island in the Frisians. Heavy flak exploded in the skies over Bremen and the western tip of Norderney Island, frightening anyone caught in it.[36] Neither Jack Bradley in Red Flight nor Don in Green Flight nor anyone else engaged enemy aircraft. However, on this mission William Elrod's fate was sealed. The recent survivor of the crash on takeoff at Lashenden was flying on the wing of Blue Flight Leader Carl Frantz.[37] At 1315, above a tentenths overcast north of the mouth of the Elbe River and east of the Frisian Islands, Blue Flight's James Keane noticed a problem with Elrod's aircraft. He later reported,

> I saw Blue Two spewing coolant from stacks on both sides and called Blue Leader to head south to make sure we were over land if [Elrod] had to bail out. We did head south and Blue Two's engine cut out completely at about 20,000 feet. We all overshot him directly on top of the overcast and he had no choice but to let down through it. We circled over and then let down on a south heading, we were well inland but could not find Blue Two. We believe he bailed out 'O.K.' If he did, we are sure he was not over water.

Keane thought they were near Jever, Germany, ten miles northwest of Wilhelmshaven, when his colleague slipped into the clouds. Although Keane presumed Elrod parachuted to safety, Blue Two in fact did not survive what was very likely flak-induced damage to his aircraft's engine.[38]

The sobering loss of Elrod greeted five replacement pilots when the squadron returned to Lashenden in the afternoon. The new men were Harlow R. Eldred, James B. Forrest, Hayden H. Holton, Leon A. C. Huffman, and John S. "Jack" Miller. Flight Officer Bruce W. Carr also joined the unit later in the month. The previous influx of fourteen pilots had arrived on March 7. Nine of these men were now dead or captured. After two-and-a-half months of combat flying, only Cohen, Phillips, Reynolds, Sullivan, and Urquhart were still with the squadron.[39]

Over the next three days, Beerbower and Emmer shared the leadership of the Fighting Cobras. Don took the squadron to Mulhouse, France, on May 25, and a similar heavy bomber mission to Konz Karthaus, Germany, on May 27. Emmer went with B-26 Marauders to Chartres, France, on May 26.[40] The only action during these raids occurred on an early morning mission to Mulhouse, a city in the old French province of Alsace, twenty-five miles north of the Swiss border. Don led the squadron southeast from Lashenden across the Channel to Abbeville on the Somme, and then to Reims, Epinal, and the Vosges Mountains, before arriving with the heavies over Mulhouse. At one point Carl Frantz alerted Don he needed to abort because of a malfunctioning high blower on his aircraft's engine. This mechanical breakdown didn't affect his ship's performance at low altitude, so he decided to seek out targets of opportunity on the way home. At Arras, Frantz caught up with a locomotive, demolishing it and a flak tower. He was the only one in the squadron or group to strike enemy forces on this mission.[41]

When Lieutenant Colonel Bickell returned with the three squadrons from Mulhouse that day, he learned the group had been placed on alert status. This meant Operation Overlord could happen at any time. Bickell needed to have the group prepared to respond within six hours of receiving an alert. The next day good news arrived: like Kenneth Martin and James Howard before him, Bickell had been promoted to the rank of colonel. The following day, May 27, Bickell hosted an important dignitary at Lashenden. This was none other than the commanding officer of the Third U.S. Army, Lieutenant General George S. "Blood and Guts" Patton, Jr.[42]

Patton had been brought to England by General Eisenhower after successful campaigns in North Africa and Sicily. The supreme commander placed him in charge of a dummy force in southeastern England that had been created to fool the Germans into thinking the Allies intended to attack across the narrow Strait of Dover near Calais. This assignment delayed his seeing action on the Continent until after the breakout at Normandy. The purpose behind Patton's inspection of the men and their Mustangs at Lashenden did not take a genius to fathom. Once in France, Third Army's armored and infantry divisions were slated to receive ground support from the 354th Fighter-Bomber Group.[43] Squadron Historical Officer Albert Feigen captured the flavor of Patton's visit:

> [Patton] made his way through the crowd and stepped up to an improvised speaker's stand. We were hardly prepared for his manner of speaking, but quickly became attached to it, for it was the speech of a G. I. Joe, and [we] thoroughly enjoyed the brief address.
>
> Battles are not won by long range artillery fire or high altitude bombing. "You must have a desperate will to close with the enemy," General Patton said. Ground and air forces, working harmoniously and co-operatively, will come to direct grips with the enemy and destroy him. We were urged to keep the aircraft in perfect operating condition, with all mechanisms clean and in good repair. "I don't know much about airplanes," the General asserted, "but I do know a hell of a lot about machines. Our job is to keep those airplanes flying, if they fly 5 or 6 missions a day. Let's do the best possible job we can to complete those missions, day after day."
>
> We liked General Patton. He spoke to us "straight"—without the fancy trimmings. His language was that of a soldier rather than

that of a desk-man. And we appreciated the fact that he had visited us rather than another Group.⁴⁴

George S. Patton, Jr.

Patton talked about the need for the pilots to be the "eagle eyes" for his advancing tank columns, communicating with his ground forces about potential targets over specific radio frequencies. As Carl Bickel listened to Patton's remarks, he thought the officer's language the "most vulgar" he had ever heard spoken by anyone. Yet, as the steely-eyed Patton stood before the crowd in a smartly cut uniform, he seemed "invincible." Language aside, Bickel felt compelled to follow this general anywhere the war took them.⁴⁵

Don remained at Lashenden on May 28 when Bradley led the squadron on a penetration-target-area-and-withdrawal-support mission escorting heavies to Magdeburg, Germany. Bradley chose to fly as Red One in Glenn Eagleston's flight. Eagleston dropped back to the Red Three position. Carl Frantz led Blue Flight with Don McDowell as Blue Three. White Flight Leader Wally Emmer had Edward Hunt as his second element leader. In Green Flight, Felix Rogers filled in for Robert Meserve; Rogers borrowed *Bonnie "B"* for this mission. Glenn Pipes was Green Three.⁴⁶

The three squadrons left the English countryside behind them on a beautiful, unwarlike spring morning. They crossed the warming waters of the North Sea and were approaching landfall at Breille, Netherlands, when Frantz received a radio transmission from McDowell:

> I was leading Blue Flight with squadron enroute to rendezvous with B-17s which were bombing target at Magdeburg. At about 1247 hours, 1st Lt. Don McDowell, who was leading my second element, called me on the radio and said he would have to go back.

> We were at about 22,000 feet at this time, which was approximately five minutes before we crossed the enemy coast at Brielle. I said, 'Roger,' and he dropped out of formation and turned back on course. This was the last I saw of him.[47]

The Mustangs continued on to Wittingen, north of Brunswick, where they joined the bomber stream. The mission appeared to be another dry run until they reached Neuhaldensleben near Magdeburg. Suddenly, the Luftwaffe struck the front and rear of the B-17 formation with a force of sixty-plus Me-109s and FW-190s. Bradley ordered the squadron into battle. The melee that followed spread the Fighting Cobras from twenty-five thousand feet down to the treetops. In Red Flight, Bradley and Eagleston shot down two Jerries apiece, while Willie Y. Anderson bagged one. Frantz picked off a '109 and James Burke damaged two others for Blue Flight. In White Flight, Emmer showed off the best shooting of the day, claiming three victories; and Hunt destroyed a '109 and damaged a second. The only member of Rogers' Green Flight with a kill was Pipes. When the air clash ended, Pipes found himself alone near Magdeburg. He soon spotted Bill Perkins from the 356th Fighter-Bomber Squadron.[48] Perkins later reported what happened when the two Mustangs turned southeast to rejoin the train of heavies coming off their bomb run:

> I was flying along in the Magdeburg district when 1st Lt. Glenn H. Pipes formatted on me. We were at an altitude of about 18,000 feet. We let down to 15,000 feet and headed south with the intention of picking up the bombers on their way home. This was at approximately 1415 hours. Ten minutes after setting course south, Lt. Pipes called in and said, "There are two aircraft taking off the field off to our right." I looked but could not see them so told Lt. Pipes to go after them and I'd follow him down. We went right down to the deck and came into the field as if to strafe. I was behind him when we crossed the field. I saw Lt. Pipes shoot up a FW-190 on the far side of the field. The aircraft caught fire and burned fiercely. We then climbed up and set course south again. We encountered a Ju-88 at 4,000 feet and I shot it down. Again we set course south. It was about 1530 hours then and we were between Magdeburg and Dessau. I saw white smoke trailing from Lt. Pipes' ship. I called and told him. He said, "God damn it! They got my coolant." He said he'd have to get out. I told him to stick with the ship until the last moment. He started losing altitude. We were at 9,000 feet. He called and said he had to set it down

and for me to strafe his plane after he bellied it in. Over the R/T I directed him to a clear field. By then he was too low to see any distance. He put it down on the outskirts of a little village. He did a good job. The plane didn't break up or strike any obstacles. I circled the ship at about 1,000 feet. I did not see Lt. Pipes get out of his ship. I was too far away. But within 15 seconds after it came to rest I was over him at 1,000 feet and saw a man running away from it. Flame and black smoke were coming from the cockpit, so I did not go down and strafe it. The man running away from the plane had a bright colored vest on. It was an orange color like a Mae West. I assume that was Lt. Pipes. I set course for home directly without watching further activities.

Glenn H. Pipes

Pipes' Mustang had succumbed to the inherent defensive weakness in aircraft with liquid-cooled engines. A small break in a water line had finished his P-51, FT-X. Pipes crash-landed on a sloping meadow four hundred meters north of Ruppersdorf. He fled to the nearby woods but was soon captured by the local Home Guard. They transferred him to the police in Saalburg.[49] From there he was passed along to the Luftwaffe for interrogation and later imprisonment in the West Compound at *Stalag Luft III,* where colleagues Jim Cannon, Ed Regis, and other members of his outfit greeted him.[50]

The pilots still accompanying the B-17s arrived over the target five minutes before Pipes and Perkins joined forces. Heavy, intense flak harried every ship. The group remained with the bombers until they reached Kemburg, southeast of Magdeburg. Swinging west, they flew directly to Dunkirk and then crossed over to Lashenden. Of the nineteen aircraft the Luftwaffe lost on this mission, the Fighting Cobras claimed nine. Although the squadron had accounted for nearly half of the victories, they also suffered all of the group's losses for the day. When newly promoted Major Jack Bradley counted heads back at Lashenden, he discovered Pipes and McDowell were absent.[51] Perkins accounted for Pipes, but McDowell had not been heard from since his radio transmission to his flight leader near Breille. Both veteran pilots, Pipes had joined the 353rd at Boxted in late November 1943. McDowell, an ace who laid claim to the squadron's first triple victory, had arrived at Portland on June 8, 1943. Both men had exhibited the aggressive behavior associated with the fighter pilots under the leadership of Jack Bradley and Don Beerbower.

The failure of McDowell to return to Lashenden concerned Don. No calls came in from Air-Sea-Rescue or from other airfields. McDowell's close friends grew anxious as well. Replacement pilot Jack Miller remembered Willie Y. Anderson, Carl Bickel, and Charles Koenig "were pretty upset over it." They had all served together for nearly a year.[52] Part of Anderson's concern was McDowell's lingering despondency over the accident in March when James Parsons died as a result of their collision on the runway. McDowell still blamed himself for his role in the death of his friend. Soon stories began to circulate that he had taken his life.[53] Circumstances surrounding her son's disappearance were difficult for Clara McDowell to find out. She received a notice from the War Department in June regarding his MIA status. Later, the authorities confirmed his death, that it was the result of combat, and that he had died in England after crossing the North Sea. In 1948, when her son was permanently interred at the United States Military Cemetery in Cambridge, England, Clara McDowell was still seeking the details of his death in vain.[54]

Don McDowell

26

BIG FRIENDS

What I remember best was the wonderful relaxation of coasting back down [in a B-17] to the lower altitudes where it was warm instead of arctic and you could take off your oxygen mask, with little chance of fighter attacks, and watch the green fields of East Anglia appear just over the Channel. And then, after landing and taxiing to the revetment, those wonderful words, "Switches off."

William C. Healy, B-17 pilot
(interview with the author)

On May 29, 1944, the 354th Fighter-Bomber Group received orders to provide withdrawal support for B-17s striking Leipzig, Germany. Colonel George Bickell assigned Captain Don Beerbower, operations officer of the 353rd Fighter-Bomber Squadron, the responsibility of serving as group commander on this mission.[1]

B-17 Day's Pay

PAINTING BY J. PABLO SOTO FROM "RETIREMENT FOR OLD THUNDERBIRD" BY KEITH FERRIS

Long before Don led the group's three squadrons of P-51 Mustangs from Lashenden Field, the bombers were forming up over East Anglia. One of the units flying on this mission was the 94th Bomb Group (H), "The Big Square A," a B-17 outfit based at Rougham Field near Bury St. Edmunds, a town twenty-five miles north of Colchester. The 94th's nickname came from the white letter A over a black square on the tail of each of its Flying Fortresses.[2] Every Eighth Air Force heavy bomber group had an emblem identifier in the same location on its aircraft. The emblem made it much easier for crews to identify each other during airborne assembly.

Leading the 94th to Leipzig was twenty-seven-year-old Captain William C. Healy. The experienced aircraft commander had witnessed the Japanese attack at Pearl Harbor, flown fifty missions in B-17s in the Pacific theater, and served at the Pentagon before his transfer to England in the spring of 1944. His knowledge of the Luftwaffe, however, consisted only of bombing targets at Osnabruck on May 13 and Berlin on May 19. When Healy had looked down at the German capital, the flak had been so heavy immediately below the group's assigned altitude that he had felt like they were flying "on a blanket of antiaircraft" fire. This mission left a lasting impression on him for a another reason: "I remember [it] vividly because one of our planes dropped a bomb on the tail of Lieutenant Reid's aircraft resulting in a catastrophic dive and loss of that crew over Berlin, the only one that day."[3]

William C. Healy

On May 29, the Eighth Air Force dispatched three air task forces consisting of nine hundred ninety-three B-17s and B-24s against nine primary targets in eastern Germany and Poland. These included aircraft component and assembly plants, an airfield, and an oil installation. The VIII and IX Fighter Commands provided twenty-seven groups totaling one thousand sixty-eight P-38s, P-47s, and P-51s. The 94th Bomb Group joined one of four combat wings of the 3rd Bombardment Division, 2nd Air Task Force. The IX Fighter Command would provide ten groups, including the 354th, to protect this force. If the mission went according to plan, Beerbower's fighters would provide withdrawal support for Healy's combat wing after the bomb run. They were scheduled to rendezvous at 1250 near the town of Grimma, southeast of Leipzig.[4]

Healy, with lead pilot First Lieutenant G. S. Smith, flew in #42-32020, *Five Grand*. They departed Rougham Field with twenty-one B-17s between 0745 and 0802. Once airborne, Healy initiated the arduous task of coordinating the movement of the 94th from Bury St. Edmunds to the main bomber stream. He directed Smith to begin a gradual banking climb as two wingmen slipped in on either side of their ship to form an element. Soon, another element joined them to form a squadron. By the time they reached two thousand feet, all three squadrons, plus three spares, had completed normal group assembly. The twenty-one B-17s steadily spiraled upward within sight of the airfield to fifteen thousand feet, each loaded down with fuel, ammunition, five thousand pounds of general purpose bombs, and a crew of ten men. The rough throbbing sound of their big radial engines thundered across the landscape below. The excellent weather allowed pilots unlimited visibility. At 0908 Healy told Smith to turn the formation northwest toward Depham Green, where the 94th would unite with two other groups to form the 45th B Combat Wing. Once at Depham Green, the 94th executed a rectangular course to complete this phase of the assembly; the course ran from Depham Green to Barton Bendish to Ely to Newmarket and finally to radio beacon, Buncher #12.[5]

Decades after this mission, Healy explained the important role of the lead pilot in joining the groups into a combat wing: "We'd get the guy we thought was one of the best pilots and he'd be the lead pilot, then I'd take the place of his co-pilot." It was critical that the lead pilot be gentle with the controls, especially when he closed in on another group. Healy continued,

> [He] had to be so careful, do it so slowly, like docking the *Queen Mary*. Every time you move your throttle . . . the guy in back has to use a whole bunch, so just very, very gingerly, get up there, finally, assemble in position. . . . [Once,] instead of merging at a shallow angle, [a group] came out of the clouds at a right angle collision course. Twenty-one aircraft can't be turned except very gradually. You can't move, you can't do anything and here they were on course, just like that, at our altitude. How we ever did it, I don't know. They flew through us, we flew

through them. We all dodged individually, and nobody got killed. But how utterly helpless we were; [we] couldn't do a thing.[6]

Wing assembly complete, they turned east at 0945, the 45th now joining three other wings to become part of the 3rd Bombardment Division. When Healy and Smith crossed the English coastline at Great Yarmouth at seventeen thousand feet, lead navigator First Lieutenant Judah H. Modansky noted they were one minute behind the briefing time for this point in the mission due to "slightly stronger" winds than anticipated. It was 1001. Assembly had taken two hours.[7] Though a pleasant spring day, the cold at seventeen thousand feet pressed in on them. The cabin in the noisy, drafty B-17 was not pressurized, and the bomber's four big, air-cooled radial engines emitted little heat. Healy wore layers of clothes including long underwear, uniform, electric suit, coveralls, and a fleece suit. Over all that he'd donned a Mae West and a parachute, "And over that you wore a flak vest, so you were just like the Michelin Man." As they gradually began climbing to their cruising altitude, the temperature dropped well below zero, and as usual, Healy felt "so damn cold."[8]

The four combat wings of the 3rd Bombardment Division, spaced in boxes four miles apart, now took on the designation of 2nd Air Task Force. In the skies over East Anglia and beyond, other B-17 and B-24 crews had been going through the meticulous process of forming the other two air task forces. The largest of these formations, the 1st Air Task Force, targeted Tutow north of Berlin, and Stettin, near the Baltic Sea. The 3rd Air Task Force would attack facilities near Cottbus and Sorau, southeast of Berlin and Posen, Poland. Healy and the 2nd Air Task Force would be on the right side of this three-pronged operation, skirting south of Berlin to Leipzig. The VIII and IX Fighter Commands had one of their most experienced fighter groups with each task force. Colonel "Hub" Zemke and the Thunderbolts of the 56th Fighter Group provided penetration support for the 1st Air Task Force. Beerbower and the 354th had the assignment of withdrawal support for the 2nd Air Task Force. Colonel Donald Blakeslee and the Mustangs of the 4th Fighter Group were providing withdrawal support for the 3rd Air Task Force.[9]

As the bombers crossed the North Sea, their crews felt secure under the protection of friendly fighters and the watchful eye of Allied radar. Since none of the 94th's aircraft aborted, the three unneeded spares turned back to England. *Five Grand* and the remaining eighteen B-17s held high-group position in the 45th B Combat Wing, in the second box behind the 13th Combat Wing. The trailing boxes of bombers consisted of the 4th and 92nd Combat Wings respectively.[10]

The great air armada of nearly a thousand bombers and their escorts followed an easterly heading toward the mid-section of Holland's Zuider Zee on a direct course for Berlin. The Luftwaffe apprehensively monitored the progress of the rampaging stream pouring across its radar screens. It could only speculate as to where the Allies intended to strike.

B-17s heading for Germany U.S.A.F. PHOTO

Healy had a few minutes to relax before they entered enemy territory. As command pilot for the 94th on this mission, he bore responsibility for orchestrating communications with and between other bomber and fighter units.

> My job was sitting in the co-pilots seat with a console in front of me with the radio frequencies, communicating with the fighters, with headquarters back in England, with the groups maybe in front, getting information from them and then determining what we were going to do. Are we going to hit target A or target B, depending on the cloud conditions, all that sort of thing. I flew with different lead pilots. . . . One communication on my console was the fighter circuit. I'd give a call, "Little friends, this is Hot Shot Red. Where are you?" (Our call sign was Hot Shot Red.). . . . If I was having some problems I'd say, "I've got some bandits coming in. Can you get over here in a hurry?" Sometimes they could, but the main thing they did for us was when we didn't see them. Because what they were doing was suppressing, disorganizing the German fighters coming in, going in on their fields, strafing them, getting them as they were getting off and so forth. Lots of times they were helping us but we didn't even realize it.[11]

Healy and his retinue made landfall on the Dutch coast at 1033, two and a half hours after takeoff. At twenty-one thousand feet, visibility remained good.[12] Don Beerbower had departed Lashenden several minutes earlier with forty-five Mustangs plus two radio relay aircraft. After Don assembled the three squadrons, he banked *Bonnie "B"* to the east and began climbing for the group's assigned altitude. Before them lay the sparkling blue waters of the North Sea. Don easily recognized familiar landmarks along the French coast. The Fighting Cobras quickly passed Calais and then Dunkirk, site of the British rescue of its defeated land forces in 1940. Soon they could see Knocke, Belgium, where combat flying had begun for the senior veterans six months earlier. At 1125, the 354th penetrated enemy territory at Westhoofd Island in Zeeland, the southernmost province of the Netherlands. In line-abreast formation at twenty-two thousand feet, the pilots were feeling more comfortable with the minimal heat coming off the liquid-cooled engines of their Mustangs than the bomber crews ahead of them. They scanned the sky for any sign of the Luftwaffe. Visibility was very good. Some haze persisted up to ten thousand feet, but the only clouds so far in the flight were two-tenths cirrus above thirty thousand feet. Away to the north Don had no trouble making out the wide expanse of the Zuider Zee. The group sliced along the Dutch-Belgian border and so entered the Third Reich. Bypassing the heavily defended industrial plants of the Ruhr Valley and proceeding high over the line of foothills bounding the southern edge of the North German Plain, the warbirds soared amongst cirrus clouds that increased as they crossed the ten-degree-east meridian near Kassel. By now Don could mark confirmation of the bomber force by the ominous easterly advance of white contrails against a blue backdrop above thirty-three thousand feet.[13]

The 2nd Air Task Force, north of Magdeburg at control point four, seemed to be heading directly for Berlin when they abruptly dropped their right wings and changed course from a true heading of eighty-nine degrees to one hundred thirty-two degrees. At 1151 Lead Navigator Modansky recorded the 94th nine minutes ahead of schedule. Now at an altitude of twenty-five thousand feet, the bombers remained on a southeasterly heading until 1208, when they turned again to further confuse the Luftwaffe about their intentions. The new heading of one hundred seventy-two degrees gave them the option of striking at Dresden or Leipzig.[14] Healy could see "funny streaks in the sky. . . . I couldn't see the fighters, as they were too far away. But you could see at the end of each long tail of flame, a B-17."[15] The 45th B Combat Wing's three groups arrived eleven minutes early at the initial point (IP) where they would begin their bomb run. Suddenly, the Luftwaffe struck the few friendly fighters nearby, scattering them in every direction. At this crucial juncture in the mission, the heavies would be unprotected for the next twenty-five to thirty minutes. The

Luftwaffe immediately dropped several gaggles of Focke-Wulfs on the exposed bombers. In the confusion of this ambush, the 13th Combat Wing flew through the IP without turning southwest toward Leipzig for its bomb run. Healy and the 45th had no choice but to follow the lead wing, which they grudgingly did for twenty miles. Over the town of Riesa, the 45th broke ranks and returned to the IP. Modansky described their reasoning in his post-mission report: "At that point, in order that we might take interval and space ourselves correctly, we decided to go back to the original Initial Point . . . since the low group peeled off in front of us." The two remaining groups arrived at the IP one minute late. Fortunately for them, the Jerry pilots' attention had been drawn to the low group, which they hit twice with waves of twelve to twenty FW-190s. Their frontal attacks destroyed five B-17s. Modansky recorded that the 94th crossed the IP at 1227. The airspace, now confused and congested

Last mission of a Flying Fortress

because of the earlier snafu and the ongoing enemy attack, deteriorated further when the 45th found itself out of order behind the 4th Combat Wing, which was catching hell in heavy flak as its groups flew over Leipzig. One of their aircraft exploded. Further back at the IP, Modanksy gave Smith and Healy a heading to fly for the bomb run. As they banked *Five Grand* to the right on a course of two hundred forty-three degrees, lead bombardier First Lieutenant M. E.

Spangle began searching for the group's assigned target. Smith received new coordinates and turned the ship left to two hundred thirty-six degrees. At 1231, with winds aloft registering twenty miles per hour out of the southeast, Spangle began the bomb run. By now the Luftwaffe had withdrawn, perhaps to avoid the antiaircraft fire over Leipzig. The group suffered through "accurate, intense and heavy" flak, but the exploding shrapnel did not significantly interfere with the bomb run. Smith held the ship steady, but Spangle couldn't find their target, the Allgemeine Transport Anlagen, because of haze, "clouds of dust," and the enemy's smokescreen over the city. A tense Spangle gave Smith a heading correction to two hundred forty-two degrees as he searched for their secondary aiming point, the Heiterblich Single Engine Factory, a component manufacturer for Messerschmitt 109s. At 1235, while flying at twenty-six thousand fifty feet over the target, Spangle finally called bombs away. Following Spangle's example, the majority of the group's B-17s immediately dropped their ordnance of five-hundred-pounders by salvo. Two aircraft in each of the three squadrons were also taking photographs of the hits on and around the factory. From Spangle's observation point, "the general results looked very good." The heavies now banked sharply to the left as they headed away from Leipzig, and England, on a course of one hundred thirty-seven degrees to their rally point. The big Forts less the weight of their bombs also rolled up and down and rocked from side to side as the pilots took evasive action to dodge the flak. The 94th had lost contact with the other groups in the wing somewhere back near the IP. As they approached Grimma, Healy noticed that the nearby 13th Combat Wing was short its top group, so he directed Smith to slip the eighteen bombers into this vacant position.[16]

The 354th, scheduled to rendezvous with the heavies south of Grimma, did so at 1250. The irregularity of some of the boxes clearly suggested that the bombers had been attacked earlier in the mission. Don immediately directed the three squadrons into position to protect the ragged formation from further assault by the Luftwaffe. The beat-up train of bombers, some carrying seriously wounded or deceased crewmembers, now made a large arcking wheel to the southwest, putting northern Bavaria in their path home. As they approached the city of Coburg, some fighter pilots could see an airdrome loaded with forty-plus Me-109s and FW-190s, and numerous twin-engine aircraft. Twenty miles south of the city, others saw a previously unmolested, well-constructed runway complex. Several rows of buildings containing at least twenty big hangars stood partially concealed in the adjacent woods. The site appeared to be a bomber base. Soon a third *flugplatz* appeared on the edge of a wooded area ten miles west-southwest of Coburg, "situated on a slope, the opposite of which dropped off into a sheer valley." Thirty-plus Me-109s were parked next to the woods.

The airstrip appeared "well defended topographically and by flak emplacements." Don was not authorized to release any flights to strafe these fat targets. His first responsibility was to provide for the safety of their big friends. So the fighters continued on, duly noting the coordinates for later action as determined by intelligence staff. The group's responsibility for withdrawal support ended at 1350, southwest of Koblenz in western Germany. On the way home, two locomotives served as compensation for juicy targets passed over; a good strafing run left the boilers "emitting dense clouds of steam." An hour after leaving the bombers, the formation made landfall outbound at Nieuport, Belgium. Don led the ships in at 1522. It had been a five-hour mission. Lashenden Field and the village of Headcorn proved a welcome sight.[17] Don didn't realize it, but with the upcoming changes in the group's assignments, he had just participated in his last long-range escort mission to Germany.[18]

Healy and the other two groups in the 13th Combat Wing were still in the air. They began descending from twenty-one thousand feet over the French coast near Dunkirk. *Five Grand* and the rest of the 94th struck landfall over Clacton, England, at 1523. Using Buncher #12 as a homing beacon, the weary group set course for Bury St. Edmunds. The eighteen B-17s landed at Rougham Field between 1540 and 1603, eight hours after takeoff. The gun crews had expended over thirty-two hundred rounds of fifty-caliber ammunition defending the wing. Although no ships were lost, eleven of the group's bombers suffered flak damage. As one of Healy's pilots eased in #42-31788, the number-two propeller, which had been windmilling, overheated and seized on the shaft. It fell off as the plane landed on one good tire. The other tire had been pierced by shrapnel.[19] Such "miracle" homecomings were not unheard-of for bombers.

The VIII and IX Fighter Commands' claims for the day included the destruction of thirty-eight German planes. The VIII Bomber Command claimed sixty-eight downed fighters by its bomber crews. Since gunners from different ships often shot at the same enemy aircraft, this last claim was probably inflated. A total of eleven American fighters and thirty-five bombers failed to return from the mission. The intelligence summary for the operation included a comment about the lack of enemy air activity; "It was the smallest opposition ever seen to [a] major raid in Berlin and E of Berlin areas in good weather."[20]

The responsibilities of Healy and Beerbower on the Leipzig mission serve to illustrate the inherent difference between bomber and fighter pilots in general. The 94th was tasked with delivering its bomb load on target no matter the enemy opposition. The 354th was required to do whatever necessary to prevent the Luftwaffe from interfering with the bombers after hitting their target. The big friends had less flexibility than their little friends in meeting their goal. Healy believed this distinction affected the mindset of bomber and fighter pilots. At a party he attended at a Mustang base near Bury St. Edmunds, Healy reached an understanding of the cause-and-effect relationship:

> When we had a party at our place, some people would get drunk, just sodden drunk. Often there'd be arguments and people would go to bed mad. They were just a mess. But I'd go up there [P-51 group], they're all light hearted, all having a great time, you know, talk, talk, talking about the fighting. We never did too much talking about that at a party, just an entirely different attitude. And the different attitude I think was because of the fact they could control their situation. We couldn't. We just had to sit and get shot at. After I'd been up there I wished I'd been a fighter pilot instead of a bomber pilot. Not that they didn't have casualties and so forth. They did, but at least you had the feeling you could do something about it.[21]

Don had successfully handled the difficult task of guiding and coordinating three squadrons of aircraft across a thousand miles of hostile territory. Although mostly uneventful, the mission did not end on a dull note. The pilots reached home in time to join Colonel Bickell at the officers club, where he was throwing a party to celebrate his recent promotion. Group Historical Officer Frederic Burkhardt described it as "one of the best parties ever experienced (the word is carefully chosen) by the Group officers."[22]

The next morning, the after-effects of the party manifested themselves in the 353rd's sloppy mission to Rotenburg, Germany, east of Bremen. Wally Emmer drew the short straw. Consequently, the St. Louis ace found himself at the forefront of twelve Mustangs plus a spare and a radio relay aircraft. Rookies Hayden Holton and Bruce Carr aborted fifteen minutes out of Lashenden when Holton realized the engine on *Bonnie "B"* had "loaded up" and because Carr lost the clip on his oxygen mask. Old hands James Burke, Carl Frantz, and John Montijo lasted a few minutes longer but soon they dropped away as well. The rule against pilots having alcohol in their systems when flying combat missions was not strictly enforced. The officers assigned to fly on May 30 had obviously indulged themselves at Bickell's party. The proof lay in the number of aborts compared to those on other missions.[23] Pilots had a trick to help clear a hangover. To gain alertness they breathed one hundred percent oxygen at takeoff instead of waiting until they climbed to ten thousand to twelve thousand feet.[24] Luckily for Emmer, the raid on Rotenburg turned out to be lackluster. And on May 31 when Don led the squadron in Jack Bradley's *Margie Maru* to Luxeuil in eastern France, he had the same luck. The overcast made it impossible to observe where the pilots rendezvoused or where they later left the B-17s.[25]

The 353rd flew a record twenty-five missions in May. This exceeded the previous high of twenty-one established in April. Historical Officer Albert Feigen recognized the important contribution made by mechanics, radiomen, and ordnance-armorers to the unit's effort when he wrote, "The greatest credit possible is due [the ground crews] whose work on the line keeps a squadron of

A huddle of the 354th Fighter Group's Top Aces—Counter-clockwise starting in the lower left-hand corner: Don Beerbower, Jack Bradley, Glenn Eagleston, Robert Stephens, Richard Turner, Edward Hunt, Carl Frantz, Lowell Brueland, Frank O'Connor, Robert Goodnight, and Wallace Emmer.

ships . . . able to withstand the stresses of 5 hours or more in the air, with all the violent maneuvers which combat requires." Victory confirmations and gun camera footage were convincing testaments to the quality of their work. The men enjoyed watching the dogfight films of each squadron. These served as an engrossing prelude to the Monday, Wednesday, and Friday evening movie schedule established for the group's personnel.[26]

The squadron gained two pilots on June 1: Russell S. Brown and Harvey H. Chapman. Two days later, the Fighting Cobras went out on their first assignment of the month, a dive-bombing mission against targets in northern France.[27] Don flew *Margie Maru* once again at the head of a full complement of sixteen Mustangs. The only abort during this operation was Glenn Eagleston's wingman, John Montijo.[28] The three squadrons left Lashenden early in the afternoon in ten minute increments. Their targets were a choke point east of Compiegne, embankments, railroad tracks, and rolling stock in the Laon area, northwest of Reims, and two small bridges west of Soissons. Montijo dropped out of the squadron over the French coast near Calais after he sustained flak damage to his cockpit. He dropped his two five-hundred-pound general-purpose bombs in the Channel on the way home. Don and the rest of the 353rd arrived near the target area forty-five minutes after takeoff. The pilots released their bombs on this mission at a much lower altitude than usual, between one hundred and three hundred feet,[29] trying a technique known as skip-bombing or low-level bombing. It required the pilot to use a shallow line of attack on his approach, which exposed him to more ground fire but hopefully bought him better results in hitting the target.

As Don led Red Flight across a railroad target near Laon, he lost his second element leader to the new bombing method. Blue Flight Leader Carl Frantz observed a parachute landing on the edge of an airdrome at 1510. He later reported, "We were the only ships in the area and Second Lieutenant John H. Arnold was the only pilot lost and, since this was the time he went down, I believe this was Lt. Arnold's chute." A German antiaircraft battery had peppered the aggressor. Arnold, a steady, reliable squadron member since January 7, landed safely in a meadow near the Athies Airdrome, four kilometers east-northeast of Laon. He was captured three hundred meters west of the base. Local authorities held him for three days and then transported him to a prisoner collection center at Brussels for further processing.[30]

The squadron reported fair results against its targets in the Soissons-Laon area. In addition, Felix Rogers, who had recently replaced Willie Y. Anderson as assistant operations officer, picked up credit for making mincemeat out of a German weather balloon. Montijo had returned to the base safely after being hit by flak; Arnold would sit out the remainder of the war in a POW compound. When Albert Feigen compiled the unit history for the month of June, he lamented the loss of the veteran pilot: "Lt. Arnold . . . established a superior record as an excellent pilot and a 'good joe.' His tall and erect figure and strong face have been sincerely missed in the outfit."[31]

During early June Don and Leon Panter orchestrated a makeover of their Mustang; *Bonnie "B"* needed a paint job. The ship's outward appearance had deteriorated from the general wear and tear of many hours of flight and exposure to the elements. They painted over the white nose cone and white strip on the tail's vertical stabilizer, or dorsal fin. *Bonnie "B"*[*II*] lettering, painted white, replaced *Bonnie B II*. From a distance, *Bonnie B II* appeared to read *Bonnie Bill*. Don wanted the emphasis on *Bonnie "B"*. Her nose, fuselage, wings, and tail were coated with the dark, semi-gloss green used by the squadron. A white prancing mustang appeared on either side of the dorsal fin, with the aircraft's tail number, #312375, painted in yellow across the base of the pony. They printed Don's name immediately below the cockpit, and listed the names of Leon Panter, his assistant James Downes, and armorer Donald Langran on the side of the engine cowling—all names painted white. Under the pilot's name, fifteen black swastikas over white diamonds, along with a white symbol of a locomotive, represented Don's kills. The swastikas were in three staggered rows. The squadron's letter designation for *Bonnie "B"*, FT-E, remained white,[32] as did the white stripe on each horizontal stabilizer. The American star symbol retained its standard blue and white coloring. In addition, three invasion or zebra stripes (an Allied requirement) appeared on the top and bottom of each wing and between the cockpit and tail assembly. These wide, white bands separated by black bands would make it easier for soldiers and sailors to identify friendly planes over Normandy. Also, the ground crew had recently added an extension to the front of the dorsal fin on *Bonnie "B"*. This was an experiment to see if it made the P-51B and C models more stable and easier to trim in flight. The dorsal fin extension, the Malcolm hood, and the new paint scheme gave *Bonnie "B"* a very streamlined, fresh appearance. Don couldn't help admiring his "new" ship.[33]

A week or so before *Bonnie's* makeover, former group commander James Howard had come down to Lashenden to get some flying time. New Fighting Cobra pilot Jack Miller was sent up on a "test hop" with Howard on just his second day with the squadron. Years later, Miller remembered his impressions of the flight: "We all had to be checked out by somebody, [so Howard] took me up. . . . He was a tall guy and I was a little bit in awe of him because he had just been given the Congressional Medal of Honor." Miller had been helping build submarines at Manitowoc, Wisconsin, before he enlisted in the Army Air Corps. After graduating from flying school at Napier Field, east of Dothan, Alabama, he married and then moved on to Bartow Army Air Base, in Florida,

A freshly painted Bonnie "B" at Lashenden Field in early June 1944. Invasion or zebra stripes have been added to help Army and Navy gunners identify friendly aircraft.

for training in P-51s. He came to the group after a short training stint at Goxhill in Lincolnshire. When Miller arrived at Lashenden, he and four of the five replacements with him were assigned to the Fighting Cobras, "because that was the squadron that needed pilots the most." He ended up in "A" Flight, the alpha designation for the pilots assigned to Glenn Eagleston's flight. After Miller returned from flying with Howard, Willie Y. Anderson and Carl Bickel took him out along the coastline to familiarize him with the area. As Miller later recalled, "The check points had headings back to the field, like when you came over the white cliffs of Dover you took heading such and such. They kind of orientated me that way. I must say this, as a group of pilots go, they were top notch. I think part of it was the training they got from the original members. By the time they came overseas, they were pretty well trained. And then they passed it on to us. . . . I remember my first mission. I flew on Bradley's wing. After that it was Eagleston and then Willie Y. after Eagleston left." Miller appreciated the value of being in a solid organization with experienced leadership and combat-tested pilots.[34]

The men of the 354th received a commendation in early June when Lieutenant General Lewis Brereton issued an order from Ninth Air Force Headquarters to the first P-51 group assigned to heavy bomber escort missions in the European theater. It cited them for their outstanding performance between November 4, 1943, and May 15, 1944:

> The 354th Fighter Group was instrumental in the eminently successful development and execution of long-range penetration and target support missions in the protection of heavy bombardment aircraft participating in daylight assaults upon objectives deep in enemy territory . . . where, despite hazardous weather conditions, formidable antiaircraft fire, and strong enemy fighter opposition, the valiant pilots of this group, though frequently out-numbered, destroyed a record number of enemy aircraft while providing vigilant and aggressive support for the bombers. The brilliant achievements of the 354th Fighter Group constitutes an important contribution to the furtherance of the war effort, and is demonstrative of the aggressive teamwork which is in keeping with the highest traditions of the Army Air Forces.[35]

Within a few days, Franklin D. Roosevelt elevated Brereton's order to a Presidential Unit Citation for the Pioneer Mustang Group.[36]

Further recognition for the men came on June 4 when the lead story in the British edition of *Yank* magazine was a "comprehensive write-up" about the group. The cover featured a photograph of a 356th pilot and an armorer loading a Mustang's wing guns.[37]

Morale was high on the eve of the invasion. The men were proud to be associated with an organization whose honors included having had a former commanding officer receive the Congressional Medal of Honor, having won a unit citation, and having been the focus of ongoing press coverage. Albert Feigen crystallized the unit's character in his monthly historical report: "People are interested in what we are doing. Further, having recently inspected a new Mustang (a P-51D) which put in at this field, we know that technical skill of the finest sort is behind us, helping us, putting superior equipment at our disposal. Most important, we feel confident that we are doing a good job—we're not cocky (that would be dangerous)—we're confident, and that insures even better work for the future."

As Feigen put closure on the 353rd's first six months of combat, he looked forward to the coming task that would bring victory and a return to normalcy. He concluded, "We want work. We want an invasion. And we want 'back to America.' "[38]

PART THREE

On August 5 it became known that Captain Don M. Beerbower, squadron commander in Major Bradley's absence, had received his majority.... The former operations officer, whose battle experience includes the destruction of 18½ enemy aircraft, is undoubtedly one of the squadron's most popular officers. His decorations (recommended as well as already awarded) include the Air Medal with 24 bronze oak leaf clusters, the Distinguished Flying Cross with two bronze oak leaf clusters and the Silver Star with one bronze oak leaf cluster, while his "Bonnie B" ranks . . . as one of the outfit's most colorful aircraft, certainly one of its staunchest.

Albert J. Feigen, squadron historian/intelligence officer
353rd Fighter Squadron Unit History

    As Major Don M. Beerbower led the sixteen Mustangs of the 353rd Fighter Squadron past the old provincial capital of Reims, he could see an enemy installation several miles in the distance. Nestled in among vineyards and wheat fields and the small villages of St. Thierry and Courcy lay former French aerodrome *Base aerienne 112*. This large complex had been under German control since 1940 and went by the Luftwaffe name *Flugplatz A213*.[1]

    Cruising at an altitude of six thousand feet, Beerbower gently guided *Bonnie "B"* northeasterly as the squadron rapidly approached the potential target three miles beyond the city. As the pilots scanned the airfield below, they noticed at least thirty twin-engine aircraft parked in revetments.[2] The squadron commander made the decision to attack.

27

Unbelievable!

Tuesday morning the news came over the radios the long awaited assault by the Allied forces upon Hitler's European Fortress had begun. The attack was made on the Normandy coast of France, some of the most heavily fortified of what has come to be known as the "Invasion Coast."

Hill City folks received the news quietly and soberly. There was no cheering or rejoicing. The lives of too many of our dear ones are at stake in this greatest of all military operations. Many boys from this community have been in England waiting and preparing for D Day and H Hour, and the thoughts of our people went out to these loved ones, and all the other boys with them, in earnest prayers for their safety.

This is no time for flag waving or cheering. It is the time for prayers—humble, devout acknowledgement of the supreme allness and goodness of God, whose loving care is ever with His children, protecting them from all evil. . . .

Gay C. Huntley, editor/publisher
Hill City News

A great armada of Allied ships assembled in the English Channel on June 5, 1944. Rear Admiral Carleton F. Bryant, on board his flagship *Texas*, had orders to form the bombardment group for Omaha Beach along the south coast of Cornwall. Texas had been pulled off Atlantic convoy duty in April and sent to Britain to prepare for the invasion. Bryant's group consisted of one other battleship, *Arkansas*, the oldest in the U.S. Navy; light cruisers *Bellona, Georges Leygues, Glasgow, Montcalm*; and twelve destroyers. After coming together in a column formation, the group proceeded east under gray overcast skies past Plymouth and Dartmouth, where it joined more ships to become Force "O". Late in the day, off the Isle of Wight, the formation turned southeast in two columns. As the columns began crossing over to the Norman coast, the lead ships entered narrow, well-marked channels Three and Four, which had been swept clean of German mines. At 0130 Ninth Air Force twin-engine Douglas

UNBELIEVABLE! 291

Battleship Texas *off Virginia Beach, Virginia, December 21, 1943*

C-47 Skytrains began discharging their cargo of paratroopers from the 82nd and 101st Airborne Divisions behind Utah Beach. Comparable drops simultaneously took place on the eastern flank of the British and Canadian landing areas. Less than an hour later, at 0220, Bryant's group led Force "O" into a transport area ten to twelve miles off Omaha Beach. Here *Texas* and *Arkansas*, along with the cruisers and destroyers, separated into western and eastern groups, respectively. *Texas* slipped into position off Pointe du Hoc while *Arkansas* cruised east to within range of Port-en-Bessin. The fire-support ships from these two groups took up positions between five thousand and ten thousand yards offshore. At 0430, an hour-and-a-half before sunrise, the landing craft began the slow difficult task of moving from the transport area to Omaha Beach. At dawn a German battery at Port-en-Bessin commenced firing on *Arkansas*. When the warship's spotter plane reported the enemy's position, naval gunners soon bracketed and then silenced the threat. At 0550 *Texas* started shelling Pointe du Hoc, a high prominence overlooking the landing areas, its main batteries ultimately expending two hundred fifty rounds of fourteen-inch shells on this target. By H-hour, 0630 on June 6, soldiers of the 1st and 29th Infantry Divisions pushed forward under the protective guns of *Texas* toward a strip of beach that would be forever known as Bloody Omaha.[1]

By June 1944, the Allies fought the war on many fronts. In the Pacific, the invasion of Guam, Saipan, and Tinian in the Marianas and the Battle of the Philippine Sea were near. From the Marianas, the new Boeing B-29 Superfortress would be within bombing range of Japan. In western China and Indochina, the Allies continued to tie up enemy resources in a war of slow attrition. Allied infantry progressed sluggishly up the Italian peninsula as well, even though Rome was liberated on June 5. Stiff German resistance, masterfully led by *Feldmarschall* Albert Kesselring, continued until the end of the war. In the east, the Soviets had recaptured much of the land they had lost to the Germans three years earlier. They were now poised for a massive attack along a line running from the Gulf of Finland south along the Dnieper River to Odessa on the Black Sea.

Two other fronts were significant. The first was the air war over Western Europe. Although the Luftwaffe continued to defend the homeland against massive round-the-clock bombing, it couldn't counteract the loss of experienced pilots. Therefore, Allied aerial attacks in France in the late spring of 1944 met little German opposition. The second front was at sea, where the U-boat threat, although still real, had diminished to such an extent in the North Atlantic that *Großadmiral* Karl Doenitz's underwater craft did not detect the invasion fleet.[2] The Nazis were far from defeated, however. Their development

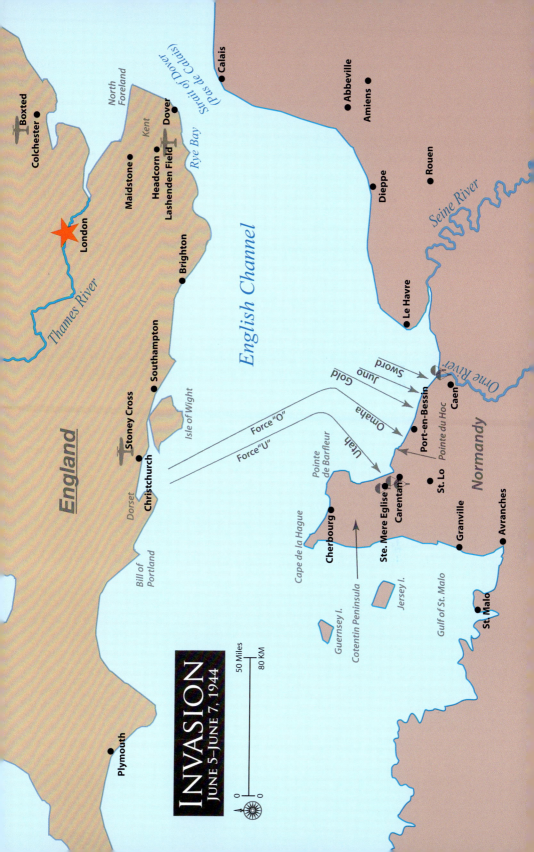

of rocketry and jet propulsion had put them significantly ahead of the Allies.

Rumors of D-day's imminence had been circulating among the members of the 354th Fighter-Bomber Group at Lashenden Field for several days. The appearance of an officer and two enlisted men from the 4th Combat Camera Unit on June 3, followed by late-night meetings in the war room trailer, had everyone keyed up for the coming battle. Pilots expected to be sent out on June 5, but the call did not come. That evening, as ships massed in the Channel and C-47 Skytrains prepared to takeoff with their cargo of paratroopers, the men watched a lengthy USO show, *In The Grove*. Afterwards, the flying officers answered a summons to a briefing where they received information about the impending attack. The pilots also learned the group had been placed on standby for a possible mission on June 6.[3] The men retired for the evening knowing the final push to defeat Hitler was at hand.

D-day dawned peacefully for the pilots of the 353rd Fighter-Bomber Squadron, except for the arrival of nine replacements. They included John E. Bakalar, Richard H. Brown, Ira J. Bunting, Franklin D. Chamberlain, Kenneth H. "Ken" Dahlberg, Clifford H. Dean, Edwin H. "Pink" Pinkerton, Orrin D. Rawlings, and Theodore W. Sedvert.[4] But tension grew as the day progressed. Operations Officer Don Beerbower and other pilots in the squadron "spent several hours in the cockpit," wrote war correspondent Gordon Gammack, "waiting for a takeoff order, but at two in the afternoon none had come in and pilots were hopeful that meant things were going all right."[5] The fighting had not been going well for the soldiers and sailors on Omaha Beach or for the paratroopers behind Utah Beach; elsewhere the troops were making progress toward their objectives. Allied fighter groups had established air superiority over the landing areas. Only a handful of German aircraft attempted to strafe or bomb the ships or troops. The afternoon came to a close with no call for the Mustangs at Lashenden.

After chow some of the pilots started to complain about the prolonged alert status, when for the second night in a row they were called to a briefing, this time about an unusual night assignment. The orders directed the group to help escort a forty-mile-long train of a hundred Horsa and Waco gliders and their C-47 tugs as they delivered reinforcements, equipment, and supplies to the paratroopers on the Cotentin Peninsula. The rendezvous was to take place over Portland Bill, a prominent, narrow strip of land off the Dorset coast that formed the southern tip of the Isle of Portland. With the briefing over and the evening light "fast-fading," Colonel George Bickell and his pilots hurried to the flight line.[6]

Bickell filled the Red Flight Leader position in the 353rd Fighter-Bomber

Squadron. Jack Bradley, Wally Emmer, and Robert Meserve led the other three flights.[7] Bickell and forty-six other Mustangs were soon airborne for Portland Bill. An hour later the group rendezvoused below a three-thousand-foot cloud base with the second section of the troop carriers.[8] All pilots had been told to fly with their aircraft's running lights off and to maintain radio silence to help conceal the blended formation's position from the Luftwaffe. The low ceiling remained unchanged as the gently swaying, ribbon-like stream continued out across the black waters of the Channel. The tugs plodded along, each providing a tethered life line to a Horsa or Waco loaded with supplies or paratroopers. The P-51s had to fly at near stall speed to avoid outrunning them. Veteran Carl Bickel looked at the "ghostly figures of those big old gliders" and felt thankful not to be piloting or riding in one of them, especially when they later began taking flak hits over Normandy. Occasionally, a Mustang engine would throw off exhaust sparks, causing the pilots to think they were being shot at from below. Everyone was jumpy.[9] Richard Turner, commanding officer of the 356th Fighter-Bomber Squadron, led a flight of four Mustangs escorting a box of sixteen tugs. As the fading light from the high latitude evening turned to an inky darkness, his only way of keeping track of the C-47s was by the blue exhaust flames from their engines. He feared the tow ropes and the occasional aircraft that strayed near his ship. He knew of no way to differentiate between a friendly fighter and a German night fighter. Fortunately, they encountered no enemy aircraft. In mid-channel the formation swung southeast, staying well clear of the northern tip of the Cotentin Peninsula. Finally, it turned southwest, crossed Utah Beach, and dropped paratroopers and gliders in the general area of the 82nd and 101st Airborne Divisions several miles inland. Turner realized they were over land when tracers erupted from the ground below, but within a few minutes his role in the mission ended. He banked the flight away from the formation and headed back to southern England through airspace congested with homebound fighters. Turner had six near-collisions as he sought out a pundit light (hooded searchlight) by Christchurch, the checkpoint they'd been directed to pass before landing at a nearby airfield. He considered the night mission a "cliff hanging mess!"[10]

The weather at Lashenden had deteriorated so much that Colonel Bickell was ordered to use the airdrome at Stoney Cross. As the group's planes closed in on the field from the south, Flying Control Officer Jerry Neil cleared them for landing on Runway 33. John Rody, flying in the 353rd's White Flight, had just settled into his final approach behind two Mustangs when he found himself in trouble: "I realized I was too low and decided to pull up. As I gave it the gun I hit telephone wires. The engine failed to catch and, having no alternative, I decided to glide the ship in. I made a fair landing, but short of the runway.

While still rolling, my left wing hit a bush and caused me to swerve to the left, damaging the left wing and the right wing slightly. After cutting the switches, I crawled out unharmed."

The weather conditions at the time of Rody's landing were considered fair. The investigating officers later determined the accident a result of pilot error. They issued no recommendations for further action against Rody.[11]

Willie Y. Anderson also experienced a tense finish to the mission. A red warning light in his cockpit indicated a problem with his landing gear. After waiting until everyone cleared the runway, he landed near midnight without incident. The warning light turned out to be faulty. After taxiing to a parking area, Anderson located the other pilots at "kind of a mess hall." Cold, hungry, and tired, Anderson also found creature comforts: "So I had a Spam sandwich and a cup of coffee. And I crawled under the sink because it was the warmest spot in there 'cause they were washing dishes and the warm water was keeping everything warm. So I crawled under the sink and went to sleep."[12]

Colonel Bickell also felt tired, but rest for him would have to wait. He had to coordinate a scheduled early morning mission. After consulting with headquarters staff back at Lashenden, he decided the mission would have to originate from Stoney Cross. Bickell made one exception: he directed the 353rd to send four ships from Lashenden first thing in the morning to join the group once it got airborne. The Mustangs were replacements for a flight from the June 6 mission that risked coming down through a low ceiling at Lashenden instead of landing with the rest of the planes at Stoney Cross.[13]

Operations Officer Don Beerbower woke before dawn on June 7. He had the responsibility of delivering the four replacement aircraft to a pre-selected rendezvous point for the morning's mission to Normandy. After breakfast and a short briefing, he went out to his ship's hard spot to confer with crew chief Sergeant Leon Panter. A walk-around of the fighter satisfied Don that his freshly painted, sleek Mustang stood ready. Soon Don, with Panter sitting on a wing, led three other P-51s along the perimeter track. By daybreak Jackknife 31 charged down the runway at Lashenden and lifted off in *Bonnie "B"* with wingman Carl Frantz sliding up beside him in *Joy*. Glenn Eagleston followed closely behind in *Feeble Eagle*, with Woodfin Sullivan in *Rigor Mortis* taking his wing.[14] Rarely did the Ninth Air Force's two future leading aces, Beerbower and Eagleston, fly together in the same flight.

All through the previous day and night, equipment, supplies, and troops had been pouring into the five American and British beachheads and flank areas where scattered groups of paratroopers were fighting to achieve their objectives. To support these isolated soldiers, the Allies launched another long string of C-47s and gliders. The 354th departed Stoney Cross at 0530 to escort these aircraft. Over their heads at three thousand feet a ninth-tenths ceiling spawned occasional showers. The three squadrons and the flight from Lashenden intercepted their charges from IX Troop Carrier Command off the Dorset coast between 0555 and 0605.[15] The rising sun revealed to the 353rd's Carl Bickel another "seemingly endless string of gliders." His squadron continued across the Channel to the American sector where he was treated to a panoramic view of massed ships and landing craft along the invasion beaches. Bickel watched as men off-loaded from Higgins boats and then struggled ashore among the dead floating in the surf. To one side he noticed a destroyer sinking, victim of a German coastal battery. As they proceeded inland, Bickel saw gliders struck by ground fire: "[We] would see them cut loose and be hit before they even struck the ground. We could see all kinds of bodies and equipment spewing out of the ruptured craft." Surprisingly, he discovered no enemy aircraft interfering with the mission.[16] By 0700 the pilots felt vulnerable to small arms fire as they poked along under a fifteen-hundred-foot ceiling of five-tenths stratocumulus clouds. To the northeast, three cruisers were pounding enemy targets. To the west of the drop zone, he could see thin strips of flames a quarter mile long. As the P-51s turned with the C-47s to retreat to England, they encountered "intense light flak" off Pointe de Barfleur on the northeast tip of the Cotentin Peninsula. The fighters left the glider-free tugs at 0750 over the lighthouse at Portland Bill. Peeling off to the east, they headed for home, where all aircraft arrived safely at 0850.[17]

The twin-engine C-47 Skytrain was the military version of the Douglas DC-3 airliner. This gracefully designed aircraft served the Ninth Air Force in a variety of roles, including as a transport, tug, and troop carrier. It became one of the most important Allied aircraft of the war.

Douglas C-47 Skytrain

ESTRELLA WARBIRDS MUSEUM – PHOTO BY PAUL SAILER

Back at Lashenden, the pilots met with the intelligence staff and ate another meal; most then had the day off. But Don learned the 353rd and the 355th were scheduled for a mid-afternoon mission. He would be leading the squadron, as Jack Bradley had taken the last two operations. Even though Bradley and the experienced pilots who had flown with him needed rest, there were still enough veterans available for most of the leadership positions in the upcoming mission. Beerbower, Glenn Eagleston, and Carl Frantz took Red, White, and Green Flights. Don needed Edward Hunt and Carl Bickel to fly a third mission in a row in the Blue Flight Leader and Red Flight Element Leader positions, respectively. The other element leader assignments went to James Keane, John Montijo, and Edwin Urquhart. The remaining pilots, mostly replacements, had only been with the squadron a few days.[18]

In short order, thirty-one Mustangs bore down on Normandy. Each carried two five-hundred-pound general-purpose bombs to drop on bridges north of Carentan, an important French crossroads town nine miles inland from Utah Beach. Carentan sat astride the main road between Caen, on the east flank of the British advance, and Cherbourg, a large port on the Cotentin Peninsula. The Allies planned to capture Cherbourg so its facilities could be used to handle the supplies and equipment needed to support the ground forces. A railroad ran through Carentan paralleling the highway between Caen and Cherbourg. In addition, the Vire-Taute Canal and the Douve River joined the Taute River north of town. A series of bridges crossed the highway, railroad, and waterways. On June 6 these spans had allowed two battalions of the German 6th Parachute Regiment to counterattack elements of the American 501st and 506th Parachute Regiments of the 101st Airborne Division, who had lodged themselves between Carentan and Utah Beach. By the afternoon of June 7, the parachute regiments were still fighting north of town. The objective of the two dive-bombing squadrons was to block the enemy from reinforcing its isolated regiment north of the Douve and Taute Rivers, or from escaping south across the bridges to Carentan. If the mission succeeded, it would expedite the capture of this key town, thus allowing the two wings of the First U.S. Army on the Utah and Omaha beachheads to link forces.[19]

To reach Carentan, the two squadrons flew southwest from Lashenden across the Channel to the Bay of the Seine, a distance of one hundred fifty miles. One of the new pilots, Jack Miller, looked down on all of the sea craft and thought the sight "unbelievable!" As they flew past a battleship, Miller thought he recognized the *Texas* firing fourteen-inch projectiles inland: "It was amazing to see those big guns go off."[20] When they arrived over the target, the conditions favored success—good visibility, only a slight haze, and two-tenths scattered clouds between three thousand and six thousand feet. Each squadron planned to destroy three bridges.²¹ As Don surveyed the terrain between the beachheads, all forces appeared dug in or in hiding. He could see supply parachutes and broken gliders, their black and white zebra-stripe markings clearly visible, scattered about among the hedgerow-bordered fields. Glancing north of Carentan, he saw little movement.²²

Horsa gliders scattered among parachutes – Normandy, June 1944   U.S.A.F. PHOTO

The Fighting Cobras had never provided close air support for ground forces, so they were uncertain about the amount of small arms fire they would encounter from the enemy soldiers concealed below. Don directed the flights to make their bomb runs from north to south as friendly troops controlled the area to the north, and to begin their approach to the target at three thousand feet using a ten-degree angle of attack. On bridges 419872 and 424876, pilots planned to release their bombs at one hundred feet, and on bridge 410860, at three hundred feet. As the flights initiated their dives, they encountered "meager light flak." Those releasing their bombs from three hundred feet completely missed bridge 410860. The flights assigned the other two bridges dropped their bombs much closer to the target, punching fifteen-foot gaps in each of them.[23] This success, however, came with a cost. Partway through the attack, Jack Miller observed a Mustang crash.

> I was flying White Four, 353rd Fighter-Bomber Squadron, on a bombing mission. We arrived at the target and on my first bomb-run one of my bombs hung on. Seeing there was no flak, my flight leader, Captain Glenn T. Eagleston, told me to go in and make another pass. I still did not get rid of my bomb so I made another pass. As I was pulling up from my third pass I saw a P-51 pulling off the target and starting to turn to the left. Suddenly, the ship started to roll to the right and [lose] altitude fast. His right wing hit the ground and the ship cart-wheeled across a field. I observed a small explosion and fire with a lot of smoke. The pilot did not jump or attempt to leave the ship. Since I understand our Group was the only P-51 outfit on this target and there was but one ship from the Group lost, I believe the ship I saw go in was that of 2nd Lt. Leon A. C. Huffman.[24]

Huffman had arrived in the squadron on May 24 with the group of new pilots that included Miller. On the June 7 mission, he had Hunt's wing in Blue Flight. He and Miller lacked skill in skip-bombing. Carl Bickel had another replacement pilot on his wing, James Forrest.[25] Their deficiencies, Bickel knew, stemmed from lack of experience. Bickel believed Huffman was killed by one of his own explosive devices. A bomb could skip over the intended target if not released at the proper dive angle. If angled too shallowly, the device bounced into the line of flight of the aircraft. With a time release fuse, the bomb's explosion sent shrapnel skyward toward the climbing fighter. Even though Bickel hardly knew Huffman, he felt bad about the pilot's untimely death. As Red Flight led the squadron away from Carentan, Bickel looked over at *Bonnie "B"* through "very sore and bloodshot eyes." He was worn out. Turning his gaze toward Lashenden, he followed Don home where Flight Surgeon Leonard Snydman later treated him for conjunctivitis.[26]

Don brought the four flights in at suppertime.[27] In three difficult Operation Overlord missions, the squadron had surprisingly suffered the loss of only one pilot. But the toll of the dead and missing in the past two weeks now totaled five: Elrod, McDowell, Pipes, Arnold, and Huffman. This put added pressure on Don and the four flight leaders—Eagleston, Emmer, Frantz, and Meserve—to hurry along the recent influx of replacement pilots.

In the hubbub of June 7, a young lieutenant arrived at squadron headquarters and reported in to Jack Bradley. This was twenty-one year old Nebraska native Frederick B. "Bud" Deeds. A graduate of Class 43-F at Luke Field, Arizona, in July 1943, Deeds had followed the same route as Don Beerbower to England. His assignments took him from Luke to Hamilton Field, California, then Tonopah, Nevada, and the San Francisco Bay area. Eventually, he ended up at Camp Kilmer, New Jersey. His trip across the North Atlantic was on the converted ocean liner *Queen Elizabeth*.

Deeds had left Ninth Air Force headquarters at Reading early on the morning of June 7. Now, standing before Bradley and Flight Leader Carl Frantz, he heard his squadron commander say to the double ace, "He's to go into your outfit. Get a plane and take him up and see if he's ready." Frantz grabbed *Joy* and Deeds another ship. The future high school chemistry teacher, who later christened his own fighter *Joy* after a girlfriend back home, went up with Frantz for a half-hour of rat racing. "In rat racing you try to get on each other's tail and then try to stay on it," Deeds recalled, "You do all the maneuvers that you can. The one in front is trying to shake the other. Frantz was in front and I was trying to stay on his tail. That's the way they decided if you were ready to fly with the outfit or not. . . . We [came] in and he told Bradley, 'He's ready.' "

Five days later, Deeds would be sent out on his first mission.[28]

Frederick B. Deeds   BUD DEEDS PHOTO   *Carl M. Frantz*

28

OVER MY PROTEST

When flying as Don's wingman [on June 14], we were attacked by German fighter planes. One enemy plane dropped down on his tail, and seeing this, I turned into the attacking plane and fired a burst. Seeing me, the [pilot] broke off into a diving turn which took him below and in front of Don, who then dropped behind him and shot him down. I don't know whether my fire ever hit the plane or not. Don said it had done some damage and over my protest, insisted that I share the kill with him. At the time he was the top ace in the Ninth Air Force. And, of course, I couldn't argue with him . . . there was nothing selfish about him.

Frederick B. Deeds, P-51 pilot
(interview with the author and letter to the author)

Within thirty-six hours of D-day, the Luftwaffe was transferring large numbers of aircraft from Germany and southern France to pre-invasion prepared airfields within striking distance of Normandy. Poor flying conditions over the next several days hampered the Allied effort to interfere with the Germans as they strengthened their tactical air units. By June 10, 1944, they had a thousand fighters and bombers in the region. The weather also slowed the resupply and reinforcement of Allied ground forces, and thus impeded the progress of the First U.S. Army and Second British Army in meeting their objectives. With the capture of Carentan on June 12, the Utah, Omaha, Gold, Juno, and Sword invasion beaches were linked across a fifty-mile bridgehead.[1] This allowed the Americans to concentrate on the crossroads town of St. Lo to its immediate south, and on sealing off the Cotentin Peninsula to the west, thereby isolating the enemy forces protecting the sought-after port of Cherbourg.

The 353rd Fighter-Bomber Squadron remained idle from June 8 to June 11. The officer cadre used this unexpected period of downtime to prepare the replacement pilots for the rigors of combat flying. Squadron Commander Jack

Bradley turned most of this responsibility over to Operations Officer Don Beerbower. Bradley and Beerbower had been training pilots together since January 1943. Their influence in the development of flying officers was significant, but flight leaders and element leaders played an important role as well. Bradley believed the qualities exhibited by key individuals within the organization set a standard which new pilots tried to meet. Many years later he recalled, "None of us were particularly outstanding so much that we warrant special talent, we just had about a dozen guys in there, they were all very qualified, good pilots, good shots, good courage and we were fortunate in that respect. And I think we had a little hierarchy there. . . . The new kids would come in and with training and encouragement by us they tried to emulate what we were doing."[2]

One of the replacements was Ken Dahlberg, a Wisconsin farm boy who had migrated to St. Paul, Minnesota, and later other Midwestern cities where he worked in the hotel industry before being drafted.[3] The twenty-seven-year-old first lieutenant was already an experienced instructor pilot when he joined the squadron on D-day, but he had much to learn from the veterans in his unit. Looking back over the years, Dahlberg knew what made the outfit better than other squadrons.

> [It] is a combination of whatever makes companies or countries or whatever, better. . . . The landscape is the same. The equipment is the same. The adversary is the same, so what is it? It's the people. Okay, the people are the same. They're random, right? So we have just said everything is the same. The 353rd [didn't have] the first choice or first pick, you know, it was random. So if everything was the same, what makes one group better than another group? There is only one thing left and that's leadership, isn't it. If everything else is the same, somebody inspired that group to do better.[4]

By June 1944 Bradley had become the most experienced squadron commander in the 354th Fighter-Bomber Group. His squadron surpassed the 355th and 356th in aerial victories, and it possessed the most aces in the organization. The squadrons had trained and fought together over eighteen months, so naturally they had developed a certain amount of friendly rivalry. Long after the war ended, Jim Cannon remembered, "Bradley had a lot of pride in the squadron. Being a Texan, he was always kidding the other two squadrons all the time. We had a lot of competition between squadrons."[5] Like all good leaders, Bradley tried his best to engender and nurture *esprit de corps* in his unit. Sometimes it came at the expense of the sister squadrons. He did not discourage the repetition of the following few lines of verse concocted by someone in the 353rd:

> Oh, the 355 had plenty
> The 356 had more
> But the one who kept the skies so free
> Were the guys from the 353.

Clayton Kelly Gross

To his everlasting chagrin, 355th Flight Leader Clayton Kelly Gross could not erase the sting of these four lines from his memory.[6]

The weather cleared enough by June 12 for all three squadrons to be assigned ground targets in northern France. Before departure, commanders briefed their pilots about the increased presence of the Luftwaffe in the area. Squadron Leader Richard Turner had the briefing in mind when, after the 356th destroyed its target, a railway bridge near Rouen, he began scouting around for enemy airstrips. One of his pilots soon spotted a large pasture with many FW-190s partially concealed in the hedgerows lining the makeshift airfield. Attacking with a fury, the 356th left behind twenty burning '190s plus a Ju-88 that Turner caught flatfooted as it attempted to take off from another field ten hedgerows away.[7]

The 353rd had also been directed to disrupt the movement of enemy troops to Normandy on June 12. Jack Bradley led the squadron to a stretch of railroad tracks running between Rennes and Laval where the pilots unloaded seven tons of high explosives, then sought out targets of opportunity on the way home. Coming across a German convoy, they tore into it with their fifty-caliber

Browning machine guns, riddling a gasoline truck, five half-tracks, and a supply vehicle. After Bradley's return, Don Beerbower led the squadron on a second mission scouring the airspace over British forces near Caen. He then took the squadron south past Falaise and Argentan and finally to the railroad junction at Bonnetable, northeast of Le Mans. Along the way Flight Leader Wally Emmer shot down a Focke-Wulf in a "thrilling battle" on the deck. After the squadron bombed a railway bridge, the flights separated and began searching for ground targets to strafe. Ken Dahlberg shot up a German staff car on this, his first mission, while Phil Cohen and Bruce Carr incapacitated a couple of locomotives and twenty wagons.[8] Jackknife 31 and *Bonnie "B"* saw action on this mission as well. Don described it in a letter to Darrel and Arlene on June 13.

10:30 a.m.

Dear Sis & Bro

Just a line to let you know everything is okay. And to send these few pics.–How ya' like the one of Bonnie B in the distance? She was just newly painted all over. Now she's back in the hanger! I got a little too low yesterday trying to be sure to knock out a railroad bridge (got it too)–and I hit the top of a tree with my right wing–Needs a new tip & another big section–maybe a new wing–hope not! I don't like to fly other ships while it's out. Got a Me 109 on the ground on the way home, found a little grass strip with 2 on it–
Makes 16.

Those marks sure sound good Darrel–I think I'm gaining my weight back lately too! Ha!! Haven't weighed since I've been over here. Afraid to. I've been up since 4:15 a.m. so I'm going to see if I can grab a short nap. Write lots.

Don

Hitting the wingtip of his ship reminded Don of his fallibility—how his willingness to close with the enemy had brought him within inches of death. Don's reference to his brother's grades was his way of encouraging Darrel, who continued in flying school in Arkansas.

On June 13, an especially busy day for the group, Colonel George Bickell led the morning mission, a pounding of the railroad marshaling yards at Rennes. After returning to Lashenden, Bickell received orders to send the 354th's air echelon to France. Preparations began at once to have this advance team ready to leave the following morning. In the meantime, the Fighting Cobras had another mission to fly. Jack Bradley filled in for Bickell when the three squadrons went after ground targets that evening between St. Lo and

Avranches.[9] Bradley flew in the Red Flight Leader position of the 353rd Fighter-Bomber Squadron. Don, who hadn't participated in the first mission of the day, commanded Blue Flight.[10] Forty-eight P-51s, each armed with two five-hundred-pound bombs, formed over Lashenden and then departed into the evening twilight. Visibility favored them with a three-tenths cumulous cloud base at thirty-five hundred feet and tops at fifty-five hundred feet. After the Mustangs blasted their targets south of St. Lo, the squadrons scattered out by flights to strafe anything they could find that supported the Axis forces. Before the mission ended, the group had attacked trains, railroad choke points, bridges, buildings, ammunition dumps, mechanized vehicles, trucks, wagons, and machine gun emplacements. They met no enemy fighters but did experience heavy concentrations of antiaircraft fire from an airfield south of Caen, and along the highways leading from Argentan north to Falaise, and Vire north to Aunay-sur-Odon. All aircraft arrived safely back at Lashenden by midnight. At debriefing the pilots reported to intelligence staff that they saw many motor convoys near Argentan: "Trucks are camouflaged & drawn off along the side of the roads but can be seen from 2,000 ft easily."[11] Allied air supremacy was making it very costly for the Germans to reinforce their fighting units. Darkness offered the only safe time for them to move troops and supplies, and this was limited by the long summer days of the high latitudes.

The first section of the air echelon departed Lashenden by convoy at 0700 on June 14. At 0900 the second contingent marched off to the railway station at Headcorn. By nightfall both groups had rendezvoused at "a marshalling area in a pine grove near Southampton." Here, they relaxed for several days while waiting for ships to transport them across the Channel to an airstrip named A-2 at Cricqueville-en-Bessin, Normandy. After weeks of preparation, the men anxiously anticipated establishing flying operations in France. As the air echelon marked time at Southampton, everyone was encouraged to get plenty of rest and to eat well before departing for the war zone. Most of the men more than happily complied with this request.[12]

The building of airstrips in Normandy, and consequently having aircraft stationed near ground operations, gave the Allies a crucial advantage in their ongoing invasion campaign. By nightfall on D-day, aviation engineers from the Ninth Air Force had scraped out a two-thousand-foot emergency landing strip at St. Laurent-sur-Mer on Omaha Beach. This was A-1. Six days later Lieutenant General Lewis Brereton landed in a B-17 at A-1 to look over the work of his men. After visiting with Major General Pete Quesada at IX Tactical Air Command headquarters, and with Lieutenant General Omar Bradley at First U.S. Army headquarters, Brereton went to inspect three airstrips under construction. At Cricqueville-en-Bessin, thirty-six-hundred-foot A-2 neared completion. Brereton ended his day by reconnoitering the beach area. He observed Liberty ships being sunk to form a breakwater, or Gooseberry. He also watched engineers move sections of floating docks, or Mulberries, into position. The Allies intended to use these temporary facilities to shuttle supplies and material inland until they could capture the deep-water port at Cherbourg. Satisfied with the progress he had witnessed, Brereton departed for England.[13]

On June 14, at about the same time the air echelon was preparing to leave Lashenden, Colonel Bickell received an order from Ninth Air Force headquarters changing the unit's name back to 354th Fighter Group, but the modification in name would not affect dive-bombing operations.[14] Ten minutes after the truck convoy left for Southampton, pilots assigned to the first mission of the day took off from Lashenden, each carrying a half-ton of bombs earmarked for targets in northern France. The 353rd Fighter Squadron dropped its ordnance on a highway and railroad crossing near Pre-en-Paul. The flights then split up and attacked several locomotives and a variety of vehicles, including fifteen trucks pulling howitzers, and a large convoy of three–to–five–hundred trucks foolishly exposed near Laval. Wally Emmer lost a wingtip diving on one of his targets. Once the flights returned to Lashenden, they were re-armed with bombs and sent out to the area around Laval and Rennes. As with the morning mission, pilots were directed to begin their bomb runs at four thousand feet, using thirty-degree dive angles, with release at a thousand feet. Although this approach had worked well in the morning, it failed in the afternoon. The pilots completely missed a railroad bridge across the Rance River, another bridge near Rennes, and a single railroad track north of Beaufort. The Fighting Cobras found better luck strafing ground targets. They demolished or damaged gun emplacements, trucks, armored vehicles, and two buses transporting about sixty German officers.[15] Don Beerbower tagged along as a flight leader behind Jack Bradley on this mission flying Willie Y. Anderson's plane FT-T, *Swede's Steed*. But not until the third operation of the day did enemy aircraft challenge the American fighters. For this mission, Bradley placed Don in charge of a short squadron of three flights. The Fighting Cobras' job reverted to escort duty, this time a formation of Ninth Air Force B-26s to St. Hilaire-du-Harcouet. *Bonnie "B"* still sat in the shop, so Jackknife 31 borrowed Glenn Eagleston's FT-L, *Feeble Eagle*. On Don's wing in the Red Two position was replacement pilot Bud Deeds. Wally Emmer and Willie Y. Anderson led White and Blue Flights.[16]

The 353rd cleared Lashenden at 1925, fifteen minutes behind the rest of the group. Each squadron was escorting a separate formation of bombers on a penetration-target-and-withdrawal mission to targets in northern France. The 355th set out for Alencon and the 356th for Argentan. None of the Mustangs carried bombs or auxiliary fuel tanks. It was a lovely evening for flying, and perhaps hunting; the air felt delightfully stable and smooth. With the wartime double daylight savings time in effect, the sun still beamed fairly high in the June sky. As Don led the P-51s out over the Channel, he could see for miles in every direction. By the time the Fighting Cobras made landfall at Port-en-Bessin at 1955, they'd climbed to eleven thousand feet. Below them, partially obscuring the bridgehead, hung puffy, cotton-ball-shaped cumulous clouds. Their northwestern sides reflected patterns of brilliant white against a backdrop of rich earth-toned colors from the checkerboard fields two miles below. The six-tenths cloud cover extended from twenty-five hundred to four thousand feet. High overhead at twenty thousand feet, a thin blanket from a wispy cirrus formation suggested a change in the weather. After passing St. Lo, the three flights picked-up the B-26s at 2000 near Avranches. Turning southeast, they descended to ten thousand feet as the formation followed the main highway to St. Hilaire a short distance away. The medium bombers released their ordnance at 2005. The billowing destruction below told the fighter pilots that the bombing results were excellent. As Don scanned the sky, he noticed a box of unescorted B-26s approaching the town. He decided to detach Blue Flight to provide protection for the Marauders. Red Flight and White Flight remained with the original formation as it climbed back to eleven thousand feet and banked northeast toward Caen. As they flew past this German-held city into the area controlled by the British army, Don spotted a flurry of activity near Colombelles, which turned out to be twelve Me-109s bouncing a formation of B-26s. Don did not hesitate to assist the unprotected bomber crews, immediately ordering White Flight Leader Wally Emmer to join Red Flight in attacking the Messerschmitts. The dogfight that ensued began at 2020 and ended abruptly after Don destroyed a '109 and shared another kill with Bud Deeds. Wally Emmer and James Keane downed two more, with Bruce Carr getting credit for a probable and Keane for one damaged. The plucky Americans made landfall outbound over Cabourg at 2030, and by 2105 they were taxiing off the runway at Lashenden. Don soon learned that the 355th had dropped two more of the Messerschmitts in the same area a few minutes after the victories scored by the 353rd pilots.[17] He later summed up the mission in a letter to Darrel and Arlene, writing, "By the way–I got 1½ Me 109's on the [14th]. Okay? Right over the beachhead! More Fun. Guess we'll be moving on over to a base in France soon. That should prove exciting. At least we won't have 100 miles of channel to cross each time–I don't like that."[18] Don couldn't forget the image of his first squadron commander, Owen Seaman, disappearing beneath the cold, rolling surface of the North Sea; it was a haunting reminder of the inherent danger of flying over water.

Perhaps not wanting to worry his family members, Don did not mention in his letter the timely "burst" from Deeds that prevented a Jerry from shooting him down.

The squadron did not fly on June 15, but the day did not pass without incident. Some of the men who'd risen early in the morning noticed what appeared to be a plane on fire flying north of the field. It made an odd sound as it angled away from Lashenden. No one gave it any further thought. As night approached, men retired to their tents to sleep. The clear evening sky sparkled with bright stars seemingly within arm's reach. An occasional airplane hummed in the distance. At 2345 this tranquility suddenly ceased with an eruption of firing from batteries south of the field. Scrambling out of their tents, men watched tracers and searchlights chasing to a target streaking across the sky and emitting a peculiar noise. As it disappeared into the night, knots of anxious men in "white underdrawers and undershirts" talked excitedly about what this phenomenon might be. They wondered if bombers were overhead or whether the enemy might be parachuting troops into the area. Things had just begun to settle down when another bogey approached the area at a thousand feet on course for Maidstone and London. The bandit appeared to be smaller than an airplane as it sped past ahead of a stream of tracer bullets from frustrated gunners. Moments after passing, more fire erupted away to the southeast, and another "thing" approached Lashenden. This time the searchlights and the antiaircraft fire tracked true. "All of a sudden, there was a blinding flash followed seconds later by a terrific explosion," Group Historical Officer Frederic Burkhardt later reported. "No one was asleep by this time and everyone was completely dressed and, though obviously worried, enjoying the show and display of fireworks." As the sleepless night wore on, intelligence staff passed the word that these projectiles were Hitler's secret weapon, an unmanned flying bomb.[19] For months the Allies had been aware of an unusual amount of German activity along the French coast adjacent to the Pas de Calais. Operation Crossbow, the effort to disrupt the launching areas, had failed. The Germans named their new weapon the Fieseler Fi-103. This twenty-six-foot-long, winged cruise missile had a rear-mounted, pulse-jet engine capable of speeds in excess of four hundred miles per hour. The first one had struck London in the early hours of June 13.[20] One hundred fifty more had been launched from France during the night of June 15-16. Almost one third of these hit London. Variously known as V-1s, buzz bombs, and doodlebugs, only sixteen had been shot down by antiaircraft batteries or by the swift RAF twin-engine De Havilland DH-98 Mosquitoes.[21]

A V-1 that did not reach its target.   MIKE TRIVENTI PHOTO

Don did not fly on the June 16 when Jack Bradley led the squadron on a dive-bombing mission near St. Lo. His turn came on the morning of June 17 when he flew *Bonnie "B"* for the first time since damaging its wing.[22] The squadron sought, and had no trouble finding, targets of opportunity in the Cherbourg area. They bombed and strafed radar stations, trucks, armored vehicles, artillery, airdrome installations, and thirty–to–forty horse-drawn vehicles between Bricqueville, Havre de Pontbail, and Barneville.[23] During this mission, John Rody developed engine trouble near Cherbourg, fell behind his flight, and ended up in the unforgiving sea. His wingman, Ken Dahlberg, could not locate him in the water, ran low on fuel, and had to return to base. Rody, the survivor of two earlier landing accidents, disappeared before he could be located by Air-Sea-Rescue.[24]

John Rody

Carl Bickel had grown up around horses like those attacked in the German convoys during this operation. The idea of firing at these beasts of burden disturbed him. He later wrote:

> Shooting up the columns of men and equipment along those narrow, tree-lined roads caused lots of evident confusion and panic. I could see men scattering and horses rearing and fighting against their traces. Some were obviously killed. This only added to the confusion and the blocking of the roads. It was sad to see those animals being slaughtered. Strange that I had more compassion for the animals than the men, but it was probably because they represented less of a threat than the enemy and their guns.[25]

The squadron's second mission on June 17, to the Bayeux area south of the Allied lines, was led by Jack Bradley, with Thomas Donohoo on his wing. Carl Frantz, Willie Y. Anderson, and Robert Meserve manned White, Blue, and Green Flights.[26] As the squadron approached the coast south of Lashenden, the pilots picked up a radio transmission. Long afterward Anderson described what happened: "The controller called and said, 'There's a bandit crossing the coast.' Up near Hastings, I think. I said, 'I see him. I'll go get him.' So I went after him. . . . I pulled up behind it, gave him a blast and the tube came off and nosed down and hit [what] appeared to be an apple orchard. . . . These were pulsers. They had a pulse tube on top of the bomb load. We were on our way out. After I got him I returned to the group and completed the mission."[27]

Anderson had clocked the V-1 at an air speed of four hundred miles per hour. After shooting down his first of what would eventually be several doodlebugs, he hurriedly returned to the 353rd, joining Bradley in time to participate in the dive-bombing of an important road junction near Caumont, south of Bayeux. As the Mustangs struck the target, Donohoo's ship was hit by flak.

Thomas L. Donohoo

After having recently returned to the squadron from several months of detached service with a fighter training group in England, now Donohoo had to bail out of his damaged aircraft near St. Lo. Following the bombing phase of the mission, the other pilots ran into a gaggle of enemy aircraft. In the ensuing engagement, Meserve and Orrin Rawlings each destroyed a Focke-Wulf, and Bradley, Richard Brown, Bruce Carr, and Robert Reynolds downed two more '190s. The victories were bittersweet because of the loss of Rody and Donohoo, two pilots who had joined the squadron together the previous December.[28]

Mike Triventi, a member of the 353rd's air echelon, had a close call of his own on June 17. The crew chief of James Keane's *Skibbereen* nearly drowned off-loading on Omaha Beach.[29] The diminutive staff sergeant, the last of thirty-five men to debark from their Higgins boat, was weighed-down with a field pack, steel helmet, canteen, Thompson sub-machine gun, and fourteen clips of forty-five-caliber ammunition. When the five-foot-four-inch, hundred-twenty-three-pound noncom stepped off the landing craft, he was immediately in trouble: "My feet hit bottom and I took a couple of steps forward, popped up, my neck came out and I was able to gulp some more air. The waves knocked me down once, and I went through the same process. I walked under water. . . . It took me three tries to get to shore by walking and if it wasn't for my buddies helping me along I don't think I would have made it." Once on land, the men hiked across the beach and then climbed about a hundred feet to a plateau where a road paralleled the coastline. Finally, they boarded trucks for the short ride to their new home, an airstrip named A-2, south of the hamlet of Cricqueville-en-Bessin. Aviation engineers had already scraped away the sod and laid down rolls of steel wire on the runway and taxiways. Now the air echelon would finish preparing the base for flight operations.[30]

Crew Chief Michael F. Triventi

As darkness fell that evening, the men at Lashenden gathered around to watch the V-1 activity. In a letter Don began to Darrel and Arlene at 11:05 p.m., he mentioned the benefits and drawbacks of this form of entertainment: "We're watching the pilotless rocket planes tonite again. Most of them go over in sight of our field and you ought to see the antiaircraft fire that's thrown up! Best 4th of July fireworks ever. Lots of them tonite. Hope I can get to sleep. I can if our own field's batteries don't open up."

The German aerial assault quickly became a dire concern. Each missile carried a large warhead which caused significant damage when it struck a populated area. In the forty-eight-hour period between June 16 and June 18, three hundred V-1s crossed the English coastline. Half of these reached London. In response to this threat, the Allies went after its source. Orders came down from General Eisenhower to give the buzz bomb launching areas top priority. Eight of the suspected sites were delegated to the Ninth Air Force.[31]

The fast-moving reprisal hit the Fighting Cobras on June 18, but not until their third mission of the day. The squadron first attacked the railroad infrastructure around Saumur in the Loire Valley. After returning and bombing up, the ships took off again, but by now a ten-tenths cloud cover made it difficult for the pilots to locate railroad targets from Arras south through Amiens to Paris. Few bombs were dropped.[32] Don did not fly until evening, leading three flights escorting medium bombers to V-1 launch sites in the Pas de Calais area. Edward Hunt and Carl Frantz, well-rested after the morning mission to Saumur, led White and Blue Flights.[33] Leaving Lashenden on a forty-five degree heading, the 353rd climbed through three thousand feet of overcast before joining the B-26s at fourteen thousand feet near North Foreland, a distinctive chalk headland on the sea northeast of Dover. Don had been briefed on the ominous low pressure system that slowly spun over England, northern France, and the Low Countries. In addition to the solid blanket of condensation below them, more clouds rolled above fifteen thousand feet. At Furness, Belgium, near the French border, deteriorating conditions forced the Marauder commander to turn back for England. With this decision, Don turned for home. The anticlimactic mission accounted for only one victory—a doodlebug Carl Frantz and replacement pilot John Bakalar shot down as it raced toward London.[34]

The developing weather system played havoc with the ground offensive. By the evening of June 18, the Allies had poured 95,000 vehicles, 218,000 tons of supplies, and 629,000 troops into the bridgehead. During the night, the worst June storm in forty years struck the Norman coast, raising cane with the ships and small craft using the man-made port facilities that had been created shortly after D-day. By mid-afternoon on June 19, the wind was gusting to thirty-two knots. Unloading came to a standstill. The high tides pushed many of the smaller vessels and barges onto the beach. The floating Mulberry docks serving Omaha Beach began to break up. The wind and rain blasted friend and foe for several days, finally letting up on June 22. Although the storm caused a serious disruption in the flow of materiel to the drenched troops, by June 24 the unloading was moving at a fast pace. The tricky weather in the Channel and the destruction caused by the tempest created a sense of urgency among the military leaders to secure the deep-water port at Cherbourg. The Allies were making limited progress east and south of the bridgehead. However, the day before the commencement of the storm, American forces under Major General J. Lawton "Lightning Joe" Collins had worked their way west across the Cotentin Peninsula to the Atlantic. Three days later, after securing his southern flank, Collins issued orders to move north on Cherbourg.[35]

During the height of the storm on June 20, conditions east of the Rhine had improved enough for the squadron to accompany the rest of the 354th to Magdeburg, as escorts for heavy bombers. The group followed this with a June 21 raid against Berlin. During the Berlin operation, the 353rd mixed it up with fifteen Me-410s caught harassing a box of B-24s. Willie Y. Anderson shot down two of the Messerschmitts, James Burke destroyed another, and replacement pilots Richard Brown and Ira Bunting claimed one together.[36]

The missions to Magdeburg and Berlin were the first raids by American bombers this far into Germany since D-day. For two weeks the heavies had been supporting the Allied landings in Normandy. The June 21 mission was a first for the Eighth Air Force. Colonel Donald Blakeslee and the 4th Fighter Group escorted one hundred forty-four B-17s to their target at Berlin, then continued across Poland to Russia for refueling and rearming instead of returning to England with the rest of the strike force. Blakeslee and his pilots sat in their cockpits for seven-and-a-half grueling hours.[37] The random daylight bombing of Hitler's capital on June 21 was unusual for another reason: it was done in direct retaliation for the relentless, indiscriminate German bombing of London using V-1s.[38]

The squadron's last mission from Lashenden took place on June 22, when the pilots were assigned targets of opportunity in the Chartres, Rambouillet, and Le Perray area west of Paris. After dive-bombing railroad cars parked in a wooded area and a newly constructed thousand-yard concrete railway bridge, the flights strafed a variety of vehicles and a high tension power line. Near Rambouillet, the pilots spotted three Me-109s approaching them from below. In the engagement that followed, Ken Dahlberg destroyed one Messerschmitt, Glenn Eagleston and Charles Koenig shared another, and Carl Bickel took credit for a probable.[39] It was Dahlberg's first victory. He got so excited while shooting at the '109 that he didn't let up on the firing button even though the pilot was attempting to bail out. Dahlberg's adrenalin had him so pumped up that he began circling his descending victim. An abrupt radio transmission from the acting squadron commander, ordering him to immediately return to his flight, put an end to Dahlberg's exuberance.[40] The 353rd took pride in its aerial discipline. Careless behavior put the pilot and those who depended on him at risk. Dahlberg learned an important lesson that would eventually result in his becoming one of the top aces in the Ninth Air Force.

Jack Bradley and Don Beerbower did not fly between June 19 and June 22. They were busy preparing for the move across the Channel.[41] The squadron ferried its aircraft to Normandy on June 23. The 354th's ground echelon did not leave Lashenden until a week later. To complicate the logistics of the move, three pilots joined the squadron during its last hours in England: Loyd J. Overfield, Andrew J. Ritchey, and Franklin Rose, Jr. Well-regarded flight leader Robert Meserve stayed behind to prepare to leave for the States. Meserve had completed two hundred hours of combat flying and was therefore entitled to a thirty-day leave at home. Other flying officers would soon follow.[42]

29

GALLANTRY IN ACTION

During these first days in France, the enemy was only ten miles or so away from our strip and the days and nights were filled with the sound and fury of war to an extent which our personnel never experienced before or afterwards.

Frederic S. Burkhardt, group historian
History in the Sky

Lieutenant General Lewis H. Brereton had been preparing the Ninth Air Force for months to carry out its mission in northern France. Now that the Allies were ashore, his aircrews had critical objectives to fulfill:

- Support the action of field armies.
- Protect these field armies from air threats.
- Isolate the combat zone by destroying enemy reinforcements and disrupting their lines of communication.
- Be an aerial strike force at the disposal of ground commanders.

By June 23, 1944, the 354th Fighter Group's aircraft lay hidden around a runway south of the tiny village of Criqueville-en-Bessin, Normandy. Within three days, four more groups would be operating from nearby airstrips.[1] After months of preparation, the Ninth Air Force was finally able to meet its last responsibility: close air support of ground troops.

Shortly after the 353rd Fighter Squadron joined its sister squadrons at A-2 on June 23, Commanding Officer Jack Bradley received orders to prepare three flights for an evening mission to La Loge on the Cotentin Peninsula. Their task: to provide top cover for P-47 Thunderbolts assigned to dive-bomb concrete gun emplacements in that area, strafe targets of opportunity, and return home.[2] The Allied push north toward Cherbourg needed critical support from the Ninth Air Force, which exacted a high cost. The previous day, twenty-four fighter-bombers and one twin-engine bomber had been shot down.[3] Airstrips in France provided a clear advantage over the Ninth Air Force's bases in England. With less time required to complete a mission, units could fly more sorties each day. When Bradley returned to A-2 on June 23, he had only clocked an hour-and-a-half in *Margie Maru*.[4]

Bradley had stuck with his old ship even though a few pilots in the squadron now enjoyed flying new P-51Ds. He saw some clear advantages to the new Mustang. Years later he commented, "We were getting those D models about the time of the invasion. They had six guns instead of four. Most importantly, they had that teardrop canopy which gave you great visibility, back, sideways and so forth. . . . When you went from the B to the D that's a pretty quantum jump, different the way it feels, the way it flies and so forth."[5]

The rearward-sliding teardrop canopy gave the new model a very streamlined appearance. The P-51D had more stability, especially with the addition of the dorsal fin extension. It also had increased range. One of the most important improvements was the wing configuration of the six fifty-caliber Browning machine guns. North American Aviation engineers had fixed the jamming problem that was never totally resolved with the four- gun design in the P-51B and C models. In addition to the two extra guns, the new Mustang had more armor than its predecessor. As a result of this extra weight, the earlier models maintained a slight airspeed advantage over the P-51D.[6]

Charles Olmsted's North American P-51D Polly   MIKE TRIVENTI PHOTO

Four-man pyramidal tents like the ones they had at Lashenden served as the sleeping quarters for the pilots at A-2. When Carl Bickel perused the 353rd's bivouac area on June 23, he discovered his crew had dug him an oblong foxhole large enough for his cot. They had also scrounged up a wide board to partially cover it. As Bickel prepared to go to bed that evening, the sky occasionally flickered with light from shell explosions several miles away; Bickel decided it made sense to spend his first night below ground in his foxhole. Although the new accommodation felt safe, he couldn't sleep. Heavy vehicles rumbled around the area delivering supplies or moving on up to the front. The artillery and gun fire, not quite distant enough for comfort, persisted in troubling him; but somehow Bickel finally fell asleep. He woke the next morning stretched out flat on his back. Bickel's tent mates, who did not have foxholes, had folded his arms across his chest and placed poppies in one of his hands. He felt like someone on display at a "funeral parlor."[7] One of the pilots sharing the tent with Bickel was Willie Y. Anderson. After Anderson played his part in the mischief, he wandered off to the latrine, but soon discovered it wasn't a very private place. "It was a slit trench with a pole over it. You just straddled the pole and then went potty. [When] I looked up there were about 10 or 12 Frenchmen standing there smiling and nodding. I was pretty embarrassed but they all nodded and clapped their hands and said, '*Bonjour,*' or something like that, 'Good morning.' We didn't have much to do with the French."[8]

Clowning around at A-2—Charles Koenig, Carl Bickel, and Willie Y. Anderson

Breakfast consisted of boxed rations, as did lunch and supper. Until the arrival of the ground echelon, the men did not have a field kitchen to provide them with a hot meal. The chow in the olive drab cans got old in a hurry.[9]

The runway, taxiways, hard spots, and bivouac areas at A-2 were carved out of a "huge, old Norman farm." The 353rd spread itself around the edges of a pasture on the north side of the strip. The runway itself ran north and south, perpendicular to the beach. Tall trees paralleled one side of the runway. The tower operator sat in a Plexiglas enclosure atop a vehicle parked next to the strip. He had little protection from out-of-control aircraft or enemy air attacks. The three squadrons were in separate hedgerow or tree-ringed fields. By placing hardstands close to the wood line, the engineers had made it easier to camouflage them with netting. According to Carl Bickel's aerial observations, the Mustangs were now "virtually invisible."[10]

A-2 lay one mile south of Cricqueville-en-Bessin and approximately two miles southwest of Pointe du Hoc, the promontory hammered by the battleship *Texas* on D-day. A-2 stood for Advanced Landing Ground Number Two or Advanced Landing Strip Number Two. The squadron used both names to describe the tactical airfield.[11] Stockpiles of all kinds of materiel had been cached between the base and Omaha Beach. Sergeant George Chassey, who crewed *Little Horse* for Charles Koenig, expressed amazement at how much there was on hand:

> There was a fuel dump up the road that was just off the beach. We had to run our fuel trucks up to this fuel dump and fill the fuel trucks out of five gallon jerry cans. That was a little difficult to do. It took a while. We finally figured a way to do it more efficiently but that's how we did it. There was this huge field that was just piled high with five gallon jerry cans of 100 octane gas and along there on the trip from the airstrip to the fuel dump you passed ammunition dumps, you passed supply dumps of all types. It was incredible the amount of materiel that they brought in within days after the original invasion.[12]

Crew Chief George I. Chassey

Operations Officer Don Beerbower flew his first mission from A-2 on June 24, when he along with Felix Rogers and Glenn Eagleston led twelve P-51s on a three-hour fighter sweep in the St. Lo area. After their return, Wally Emmer with Carl Bickel led a second fighter sweep of eight Mustangs to St. Lo and then up the Cotentin Peninsula to Cherbourg and back.[13] The purpose of this new type of mission: to seek out and destroy enemy aircraft or targets of opportunity in a designated area. Of the two fighter sweeps, only Beerbower's "bore fruit" when the three flights caught trucks, locomotives, and railroad cars out in the open. They left in their wake raging fires, explosions, and death.[14]

The squadron flew three missions on June 25. Jack Bradley and Carl Frantz initially took eight Mustangs northwest of A-2 where they escorted dive-bombers hitting a target at Tourlaville, near Cherbourg. Don and Edward Hunt followed in the afternoon with a two-flight fighter sweep in the vicinity of St. Lo, the pivotal crossroads town south of Omaha Beach still held by the Germans.[15] Twice the squadron's radar controller, code named Sweepstakes, vectored them to unidentified aircraft. In both instances, the bogies turned out to be P-47s. The two flights successfully peppered a large camouflaged bus hidden in some brush alongside a road, and they damaged one of two trucks caught out in the open on a highway. The pilots cut short their attack because of intense small arms fire. In the evening, David O'Hara, John Bakalar, James Keane, and Bruce Carr set out in search of a downed aircrew in the Bay of the Seine, east of A-2. As the four Mustangs cruised at two thousand feet seven miles northwest of Caen, a British battery opened up on them with fairly accurate, light flak. Moments later, the gunners identified the American aircraft and stopped firing. The pilots continued the search and soon located the dinghy off the mouth of the Orne River. Numerous Allied ships and aerial balloons cluttered the coastline. O'Hara came up with an ingenious idea; he decided to seek help from the crew of a nearby LCI (landing craft infantry) by blinking an SOS message to them with his wing lights. The LCI commander understood the signal and soon was picking up the occupants of the dinghy.[16] The four pilots later received a commendation from the 70th Fighter Wing for the efficient manner in which they carried out the rescue mission. (The group had been placed under the operational control of the 70th Fighter Wing when they arrived in France.)[17]

Jack Bradley's last mission before leaving for a thirty-day furlough in Texas occurred on June 25. Soon, Glenn Eagleston, Carl Frantz, and Edward Hunt would be sent home as well. Like Robert Meserve, these pilots, along with Don Beerbower and Wally Emmer, had logged over two hundred hours of combat time.[18] Bradley had been notified of his stateside leave when Colonel George Bickell called him and Richard Turner, commanding officer of the 356th

Fighter Squadron, to his office. Bickell told them they had far exceeded the Ninth Air Force's quota of combat hours and that one of them was going back to the United States. Both pilots had the same seniority date and almost identical flying time. Bickell put the onus on the two commanders to decide between themselves who would be granted leave. Turner, a bachelor, argued that Bradley should receive the furlough because he was married and had a family. But Bradley at first declined to accept Turner's logical and generous offer. In the end, Bickell and Turner convinced Bradley he should take this opportunity to return to America.[19]

Squadron Commanders Jack T. Bradley and Richard E. Turner

A damp, rainy low pressure system rolled in off the English Channel the night of June 25 and 26. This grounded all squadron combat flights until June 28, when Glenn Eagleston and Carl Frantz led eight Mustangs on an area patrol. This turned out to be their last mission prior to leaving for the States. Don Beerbower participated in the third of the four assignments given to the squadron that day, a fighter sweep in the Avranches area.[20] The mission of Eagleston and Frantz was the first area patrol for the squadron. An area patrol differed from a fighter sweep because of its defensive nature to protect shipping and amphibious operations from interference by enemy aircraft. Thus, they flew at four thousand feet from the coast north of Bayeux to Le Havre on the eastern edge of the British sector. The two flights then turned west, climbed to eight thousand feet, and patrolled from the coastline north of Bayeux inland to St. Lo and then across the base of the Cotentin Peninsula to St. Malo on the Atlantic. Turning north they flew to Valognes, south of Cherbourg, then back along Utah Beach to Bayeux, where relief arrived in the form of eight ships from the 355th Fighter Squadron.[21]

During the four lackluster missions on June 28, the pilots neither fought a single enemy aircraft nor attacked a single ground target. The most serious incident of the day involved Harvey Chapman, a replacement pilot who joined the unit on June 1. Red Flight Leader James Keane and White Flight Leader Willie Y. Anderson had the last mission of the day. The plan called for the eight Mustangs to fly together to Bayeux and then split up, with Keane turning southeast to patrol along the beaches toward Caen and Anderson swinging northwest to cruise up the coast to Pointe de Barfleur on the Cotentin Peninsula. Chapman was flying on the wing of James Burke in the tail-end Charlie position in White Flight.[22] His ship, FT-U, #43-12461, a P-51B that had been flown earlier by Woodfin Sullivan, Edwin Urquhart, and Wally Emmer, had performed normally all day, other than Emmer not being able to keep the ram air control handle in place. This problem had been repaired by Crew Chief William R. West before Chapman taxied out on the runway for a southerly departure. All instrument readings appeared fine as FT-U sped down the runway, but once airborne Chapman noticed black smoke coming out of the exhaust stacks. He reached for the fuel mixture to adjust it from rich to lean. The engine wasn't missing, instruments all read in the green, yet the smoke remained heavy. As Chapman turned to form up with the rest of the flight, the engine missed once. He thought it was an ignition miss, but soon the engine sputtered again. White Four quickly scanned his instruments paying special attention to the coolant temperature, which read a comfortable hundred degrees. Even though his instrument readings reassured him, Chapman knew something was wrong. As he turned back toward A-2, the engine started to run very rough. White smoke poured out from under the cowling in numerous places. Chapman's training kicked in as he analyzed his dangerous situation. He did not have much altitude, his airspeed was low, and his tanks were full of fuel. The situation had become critical. Chapman later reported:

> The engine rapidly became increasingly worse, and the quantity of smoke became very great. Then the engine quit running altogether except for an occasional "spit" during the descent to the ground. I considered the altitude too low to bail out and decided to make a 270 degree left turn into air strip #4 with the intention of landing west to

east. I had crossed the west end of this strip in my turn and was now headed away from it. I let the wheels and the flaps stay in the "up" position. I had to turn at a near stall all the way in order to make it. I didn't have enough altitude and had to go through a tree off the northwest corner of the strip. I couldn't quite line up with the runway and finally fell in flat diagonally across the west end of the strip. The left wing dropped just before hitting. The tip caught the mat and threw the ship up on its nose a bit as it started to slide. The slide was very brief, not over 150 feet. The aircraft was badly damaged. I received very slight injuries (because of a locked shoulder harness).

The airfield Chapman reached was A-4, an advanced landing strip less than a mile southeast of A-2. The investigators blamed the accident on power plant failure, noting the one hundred seventy-nine hours on the engine and two hundred twenty-four hours on the airframe. They stated that attempts had been made to replace the plane because it "was too old for combat." However, the squadron had been forced to use it on this operational mission "due to a shortage of available aircraft." The investigators commended Chapman for locking his shoulder harness before taking off, feeling it helped him avoid injury. They recommended that "war weary aircraft should be replaced by new tactical aircraft, as such aircraft should be flown only in necessity."[23] Beerbower's *Bonnie "B"* classified as one of these older ships, but it had recently received a new engine.

The squadron flew twice on June 29 and once on June 30 before weather restricted combat activity until July 4. Of the three missions, only the fighter sweep southwest of St. Lo on June 29 paid dividends. Red Flight Leader Wally Emmer, with White Flight Leader Carl Bickel off to his side, led the eight-ship formation. Robert Reynolds and Ken Dahlberg (in Felix Rogers' *Beantown Banshee*), handled the second element leader positions as Red Three and White Three, respectively.[24] The first leg of the mission took them southwest to Granville on the Gulf of St. Malo, where they encountered rain showers below the six thousand foot overcast. As they turned southeast toward St. Hilaire, conditions improved. Less than an hour into the flight, the squadron's controller Sweepstakes contacted Emmer, directing him to investigate several bogies north of their position. The Mustangs turned northeast, passing Vire as they climbed to nine thousand feet through a broken ceiling of eight-tenths cumulus clouds. Moments later they made contact with three bandits. The two flights immediately fell in trail behind the yellow-nosed Focke-Wulfs. Emmer, Bickel, and Reynolds all tagged on to an enemy aircraft. The tense fifteen-minute dogfight that followed went from nine thousand feet to the deck. With the exception of one enemy pilot, the Germans behaved aggressively and used "violent evasive tactics."[25] Dahlberg had his hands full with a fourth German pilot he intercepted closing in on Bickel. Twisting and turning, each trying to gain an advantage over the other, they spiraled down to treetop level where one of them would likely die. As they banked sharply in a tight circle, Dahlberg scored a few hits on the '190. With the plane trailing black smoke, the pilot attempted a snap roll to escape, but he ran into a hail of fifty-caliber bullets from *Beantown Banshee* and crashed.[26] After downing all four of the German planes, the eight ships regrouped, completed their fighter sweep, and returned to A-2.

On June 30, Jack Bradley, Glenn Eagleston, Carl Frantz, and Edward Hunt left France for England and the slow voyage back to America. All four had achieved ace status. Bradley had officially shot down fourteen enemy planes, Eagleston thirteen-and-a-half, Frantz eleven, and Hunt six-and-a-half. Don Beerbower's tally was fifteen-and-a-half (His May 12 victory was later considered an "unconfirmed destroyed" aircraft and not credited by the U.S. Air Force in his official score.).[27] As difficult as the squadron found it to lose these skilled pilots, the problem of how to fill their vacated leadership positions presented an even greater challenge. The military's answer was to promote qualified individuals based on their date of seniority. In addition, Colonel Bickell and his predecessors had made every effort to allow the flying officers opportunities to gain command experience in combat. Therefore, when Bickell sent Bradley home, his selection of Beerbower as the temporary squadron commander did not surprise anyone. Don had seniority, and as the operations officer since late January, he was second in command. His experience in handling large numbers of aircraft in combat also made him the obvious choice. Don's replacement was double-ace Wally Emmer, originally a member of Don's first flight at Tonopah. The determined, hard-fighting Emmer had been a flight leader for over a year. His victory total had reached ten-and-a-half. With Emmer's promotion, and Eagleston, Frantz, and Meserve gone, all four flight leader positions needed to be filled. Doodlebug killer Willie Y. Anderson and steady Charles Koenig, who had also joined the squadron at Tonopah, moved into two of these vacancies. The other "Bickell," Carl Bickel, and mustachioed Felix Rogers, pilots who had been together since Portland, were promoted into the other two positions. From all appearances, this was a significant makeover of the squadron's command structure. However, these men had flown together in combat for seven months under the leadership of Martin, Howard, and Bickell at the group level, and with Bradley and Beerbower for the past five months at the squadron level. The 353rd wouldn't miss a beat. Don officially took over command of the squadron on June 30.[28]

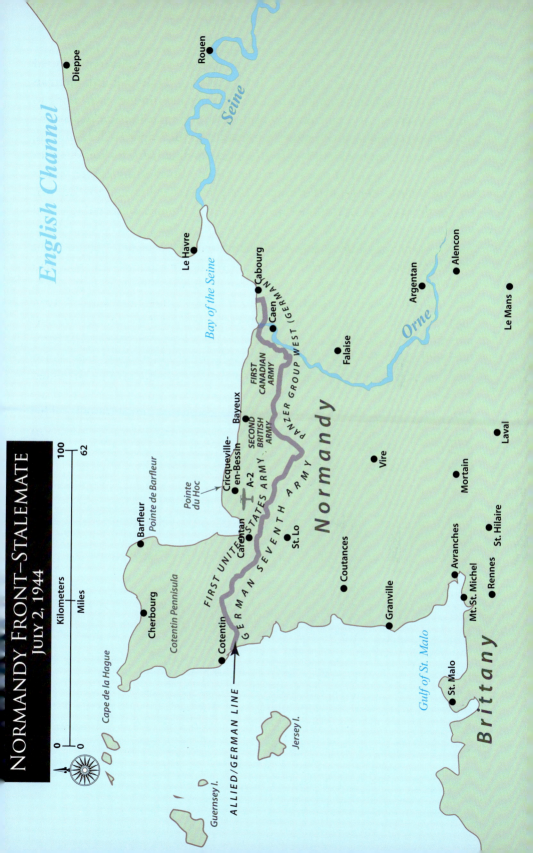

By the end of June, the fighting on the Cotentin Peninsula began to peter out. German forces in and around Cherbourg could no longer withstand the combined aerial bombardment of the Ninth Air Force, the incoming artillery rounds of Major General Collin's advancing army, and the naval gunfire led by battleships *Arkansas*, *Nevada*, and *Texas*. The Allies liberated the city on June 29 when thirty-nine thousand Germans surrendered. The last remnants of the enemy retreated to Cape de la Hague on the northwest tip of the peninsula. They gave up on July 1.[29]

The low, gray skies over Normandy on July 1 did not prevent Lieutenant General Brereton, British Air Marshall Coningham, and General Eisenhower from crossing the Channel late in the day in Brereton's personal C-47 Skytrain, *Debonair Duke*. In the morning they joined General Montgomery in Bayeux as his guests for Sunday worship services. Brereton now commanded the world's largest air force. It included 4,270 fighters, twin-engine bombers, transports, troop carriers, and reconnaissance planes.[30] After church Brereton visited A-2 to participate in an awards ceremony honoring the men of the Ninth Air Force's

Awarding of the Silver Star – left to right, Lewis Brereton, Don Beerbower, James W. McCauley and George Bickell

most successful fighter group. Because of Don's status as top ace, he was given special attention at the event. A motion picture crew filmed the removal of camouflaged netting from *Bonnie "B"* and Don taxiing the ship a short distance before shutting it down, climbing out of the cockpit onto the wing, and jumping to the ground. Brereton awarded many of the pilots with medals. Don was filmed receiving the Silver Star from the commanding general for his victories on April 8.[31] The next morning he wrote to Darrel and Arlene about this good news and other matters on his mind.

> July 3, 1944
> 10:50 [a.m.]
>
> Dear Sis and Bro.
>
> It's been raining for 4 days now and our runway is out of commission! Great, eh? We should be & would be busy now too. Sure doesn't seem like tomorrow is the 4th of July.
>
> Have I told you about my hope for a leave?–30 days in the states! Should be home right near my birthday! Sure hope you can be there some. I'd hate to have to spend some of the time traveling to see you– But reckon I would!!
>
> Just finished a letter to Dad & Mom and told them of Lt. General Brereton stopping in yesterday and giving me the Silver Star! "Gallantry in Action"–it says on the back–sure is a beauty! It's for the time I shot down 3 in one day! April 8. They made movies of me too. More fun! You'd enjoy it if you get to see it!

Don Beerbower's Silver Star front and back

I've been Sqdn. C.O. for 5 days now and getting along okay. Bradley is home now. Emmer is my operations officer.

Did I tell you about my trip to Cherbourg the day after it fell? Got a helmet, canteen, rifle, ammo belt and bayonets, etc. I'm cutting the rifle down for a hunting gun. It's going to be okay too. Has the same action as a Springfield. It'll be nice.

Gosh, Darrel, I sure hope your knees get okay. I don't know what to say cause it's not much you can do if it is that way–I know how tough it would be if you had to give up now.

I'll have to close now. Hoping to see you in not too long.

Don

As Don mentioned in his letter, the runway underpinning used to secure the wire mesh in place did not work well in mud. Nor was it easy for a pilot to control an aircraft on wet steel. He needed to be extra careful when he gave the engine power. The torque generated by the increased speed of the turning propeller blades made it difficult to control the aircraft on a slippery surface.

The low ceiling began to break up by midday on July 3. When the 354th ground echelon arrived on Omaha Beach after a damp, cold crossing from Southampton at 1500, a pleasant summer afternoon surprised the men. Group Historical Officer Frederic Burkhardt later waxed eloquently: "As the shore was reached there lay ahead the steep shoreline silhouetted against the billowing white clouds floating before the deep blue curtain of the Normandy day." Sunshine and fields of red poppies welcomed them to France as the men crested the embankment above the beach.[32] The cheery display of bobbing, delicate wildflowers reminded the thoughtful of another generation of American soldiers whose sacrifice stained this blood-drenched land.

John Paul Sailer

By 1700 the ground echelon reached A-2. To their satisfaction, the men discovered the new airstrip lay adjacent to an apple orchard, just as at Lashenden. By dusk they were settled into their new "army home." The group's strength now totaled one thousand thirteen officers and enlisted men. Of these, three hundred one fell under the command of twenty-two-year-old Squadron Commander Don Beerbower.[33]

Don Beerbower at A-2

On July 4 General Eisenhower came by A-2 to pay his respects and to take a ride in a modified, two-seat P-51B. He was interested in an aerial view of the German-controlled terrain around the critical crossroads town of St. Lo. With Eisenhower came IX Tactical Air Command's Major General Quesada. The group had been placed under Quesada's temporary operational control when it arrived in France. The 356th Fighter Squadron had the honor of escorting the two generals for the flyover. It was a rare privilege for the Pioneer Mustang Group to have someone as important as the supreme allied commander in its presence. Richard Turner worried about the danger involved in the mission; he did not like seeing Eisenhower in the cramped backseat (no parachute) of a modified, war-weary Mustang. The flight only lasted about thirty minutes, but Turner, who had to abort in his brand-new P-51D partway into the mission, couldn't have been more relieved when the generals arrived safely back at A-2.[34] Carl Bickel watched Eisenhower climb out of the ship someone had specially named *The Stars Look Down*. He thought the flight risky and unwise, conjecturing how the war would have been altered significantly had the Luftwaffe surprised Ike in the "old two seater."[35] News reporters tagged along in the general's entourage. When Eisenhower shook hands with Don, he asked the Ninth Air Force's leading ace about his victory total. This question and follow-up compliments to Don about his fine record were carried in the States by radio and wire services.[36] Although everyone enjoyed mingling with the top brass, the highlight of the day was the issuance of the first white bread anyone had seen since the men had sandwiches on the train ride between Camp Kilmer and *Athlone Castle* back in October 1943. Burkhardt wrote of the white bread, "Let no one underestimate the greatness of this occasion."[37] What a morale booster! With the arrival of the ground echelon, everyone expected to eat better.

Having Eisenhower at A-2 did not interrupt combat flying. The three-day stretch of poor weather had allowed the pilots an opportunity to rest and the ground crews time to catch up on the routine maintenance of the aircraft. Crew Chief Mike Triventi only accomplished basic repairs on his and James Keane's *Skibbereen*. The amount of servicing he could do was limited by what he carried in his tool box. As a tactical unit at an advanced landing strip, the squadron did not have the hangars and heavy maintenance equipment they were accustomed to in England. Still, Triventi, the assistant crew chief, the armorer, and the radioman gave the Mustang's different systems a good going over. As the men worked on the aircraft, cattle quietly observed them. Triventi smiled at the gentle manner of the cows as they grazed contently around *Skibbereen*, intent on the lush Norman grass.[38]

Cows graze at A-2 near Skibbereen

MIKE TRIVENTI PHOTO

James P. Keane

The squadron flew a fighter sweep and two patrols on July 4. All were two-flight missions. Don decided to lead the sweep in *Bonnie "B"*. Early in the flight, Charles Koenig turned for home when his ship developed a voltage regulator problem. Later in the day, Carl Bickel and Felix Rogers went out on beach patrol in the area around Bayeux and Caen. Willie Y. Anderson and John Montijo led a second patrol in the same vicinity.[39] The Luftwaffe did not challenge any of the flights.

The squadron's missions had morphed again. Escorting heavy and medium bombers and dive-bombing had been significantly reduced. It was also becoming unusual for the 353rd to leave A-2 with a full squadron of four flights, let alone setting out on a mission as a group of three squadrons. With minimal movement by the ground forces, the Fighting Cobras were more often asked to protect the beach area from aerial attack or to strafe targets of opportunity when flying fighter sweeps.[40] These humdrum operations required only an hour-and-a-half to two hours, and coverage of only a fifty-mile radius around Cricqueville-en-Bessin, thus making it possible to fly several missions per day.

Back in Minnesota on July 4, Elayne and Bonnie had a quiet holiday with none of the festivities of the pre-war celebrations in Hill City. The parade, games for the youngsters, and baseball would wait for another time. At the William Kutcher farm in Spang Township, the family enjoyed the company of Bill's mother and his sister, Adeline, who were visiting for a few days. Clarence and Josie Beerbower drove out from town and spent a few hours with their friends, daughter-in-law, and granddaughter. A somber mood permeated the community this Fourth of July. In two days the *Hill City News* would publicly state what everyone already knew—Sergeant George K. Boleman had been killed in New Guinea. Kenneth, as people knew him around town, was ten years older than Don and Elayne.[41] He had helped build the Kutchers' new home before the war.[42] His brother, Paul, now in the Army, had been Don's boyhood friend. Kenneth had married Grace Christensen, Don's high school classmate, in 1942. He would never meet their son, LeeRoy. Kenneth's was the third Hill City death of the war. Editor Gay Huntley, commenting in the obituary, noted the "kindly, generous nature" of this man, and then added, "As we mourn the loss of our friend, let us re-dedicate ourselves to the task that remains to be done, in the determination that he and his comrades who have made the supreme sacrifice, shall not have died in vain."[43]

In a town small enough for everyone to know everyone else, Boleman's death affected the whole community. It also brought home to every parent, every sister and brother, and every wife and girlfriend, that heartbreaking news like this was only a telegram away.

George K. Boleman

30

AN INEFFICIENT USE OF RESOURCES

We were very pleased with our new set-up when Don Beerbower was made CO and Wallace Emmer was made our new Operations Officer. This was a very happy arrangement, as we all worked very well together. (There had been a bit of friction sometimes before.)

Carl G. Bickel, flight leader
Before the Contrails Fade Away

The 353rd Fighter Squadron lost sixteen pilots in May and June 1944. Eleven went down in combat and five returned to the United States for rest and recuperation. To replace these flying officers and others lost earlier in the spring, the squadron had received twenty-one new pilots since May 24. Three additional replacements arrived on July 4: Omer W. Culbertson, George W. Hawkins, and Charles A. Olmsted. Culbertson was back for a second stint with the Fighting Cobras.[1] Over half of the squadron's complement of pilots had less than six weeks of combat experience. With the large turnover of key personnel and new leadership, the squadron could easily have slipped backwards and lost its fighting edge. Captain Don Beerbower, the new commanding officer, would see that this did not happen. It began with Don projecting the qualities that had made the 353rd so successful: aerial discipline and aggressiveness. These he instilled in the pilots through his own example, and by the example of the experienced officers running the day-to-day operations: Wally Emmer, Willie Y. Anderson, Carl Bickel, Charles Koenig, and Felix Rogers. The four flight commanders, under the leadership of Operations Officer

Close friends - Wally Emmer and Don Beerbower

Emmer, had the most influence in projecting the flying standards the squadron expected from its new pilots. They spent many hours with the replacements providing ground and aerial training. Bickel later said, "This must have been very nerve-racking for these brand new pilots."[2] But intense training was necessary in the development of a cohesive unit.

The key ingredient for the 353rd to continue doing its job well could only come from the commanding officer. Don needed to assume leadership. Ken Dahlberg, who had joined the squadron on D-day and in less than a month destroyed two enemy aircraft, long afterward made this observation about Don's leadership ability:

> We always felt like he was a good leader. . . . Now what made us feel like that? We probably intuitively or subliminally knew that he had planned the mission to maximize the results and minimize the loss. We probably subliminally understood that he was not interested in taking credit himself. He was always giving credit to the [other pilots], but not grandiosely. He just was a guy everybody believed in and you liked to follow. Some people you just like to follow because you have confidence [in them]. I think confidence, if you pick one word, in his ability to lead. And in combat, to lead you not into trouble but to lead you to success. . . .
>
> If I ask you the question, why one of your community leaders is a leader you might be hard pressed, he just is. It is a combination of things. It is confidence. It is respect. It is really maybe a form of admiration . . . and a feeling it is a good place to be, a comfortable place to be. It's a comfortable place to be with Don.[3]

On July 5 Don remained at A-2 while Rogers and Emmer led two uneventful eight-plane beach patrols. The squadron did not fly again until July 7, when an opportunity presented itself for the new officer cadre to show the replacements how to deal with the Luftwaffe. The 353rd had already flown three missions for the day, including a scramble and escorting P-47s and C-47s, when Don took three flights out for an evening fighter sweep. Bud Deeds flew on his wing in Red Flight. Koenig flew in the Red Three position. Bickel and Rogers led the other two flights.[4] Don and *Bonnie "B"* cleared the strip at the head of the well-armed fighters and then sped south past St. Lo to Laval, a distance of eighty-five miles. At Laval the Mustangs banked east and followed the main highway that ran between Brest, a German U-boat base on the Atlantic, and Paris. As the squadron cruised toward the French capital one hundred twenty miles away, they passed between a layer of strata cumulus clouds that topped out at twelve thousand feet, and a light, wispy cirrus layer at eighteen thousand feet. The three flights flew over Le Mans and Chartres before turning north-northwest at Rambouillet. Don held the Fighting Cobras on this course staying well clear of Paris as they approached the Seine River Valley. Over Perdreauville, south of the Seine, a large gaggle of thirty-plus Focke-Wulfs appeared in the distance at fourteen thousand feet on a two-hundred-ninety-degree heading. Though outnumbered three to one, Don didn't hesitate to attack the black-crossed FW-190s. The enemy pilots turned into the Mustangs when they realized they were being tapped, but after only a brief engagement, the Jerries dove away.[5] In the melee, Don caught a '190 moving into position to bounce a flight. With Deeds providing cover, Red One pushed *Bonnie "B"* to the max to stop the German pilot before he could fire at the four Americans.[6]

Don Beerbower: "A Focke-Wulf 190 in his last dive. This is an enlarged frame from a strip of my combat film. The next frame just a mass of flame and smoke, no 190."

The hasty retreat of the enemy revalidated much of Don's experience with the Luftwaffe. He and Jack Bradley had adopted an aggressive philosophy of engagement months earlier because of the Germans' reticence. Rarely had it failed them. In an interview many years later, Bradley explained their simple principle:

> When we got over there the RAF had all the experience in fighter tactics through the Battle of Britain, and they were very conservative, with good reason. And when we first started flying, they sent some of them down to fly with us and they kept telling us, "You shouldn't go over unless you have at least two groups or three groups because they'll out number you so bad you won't have a chance." After a few missions, Don and I talked about it, we said, "Oh bullshit." Our modus operandi after that was that if you see an enemy airplane, go shoot it down no matter whether he's above you, below you, ahead of you, behind you. And we used those tactics to pretty good advantage and I think the Germans thought we were crazy, but it worked. So we didn't fool around trying to see who was up in the sun or have excess altitude or excess speed. We tried to do those things whenever it was convenient but we didn't always follow those, really. When we'd see an enemy airplane, we'd go after them, wherever they were.[7]

The lack of experience of the German pilots showed in the squadron's first kills of the month. Beerbower, Bickel, and Koenig destroyed a Focke-Wulf apiece, while Rogers scored a double. Robert Reynolds and Woodfin Sullivan damaged two others. The Jackknife pilots suffered no losses.[8] One of the flight leaders came close to becoming a statistic, however, when he got a little careless in his bid to get credit for a victory. Carl Bickel had tagged onto one of the FW-190s as it dove away from the attacking P-51s. After scoring several hits along the fuselage, Bickel noticed the '190 beginning to smoke. He was quite anxious to get film footage of the aircraft going down, so he pulled up within fifteen plane lengths and gave the Jerry a solid burst. Suddenly, there was a tremendous explosion. He tried to jockey the stick back to climb away from the danger, but it was too late. In an instant, oil and burning fuel covered the front of his canopy. He felt intense heat as his Mustang passed through the fireball. Bickel's greatest fear was colliding with debris from the other aircraft. Though he came through unscathed, he wasn't out of danger yet. He had descended to two thousand feet in his pursuit of the German pilot, and now he was taking small arms fire from troops stationed along the strategic Seine River. Because Bickel could only see out the sides of the canopy, he immediately began a twisting, evasive climb away from the light flak. This exposed him to the heavy machine guns and twenty-millimeter cannon stationed in the area. It looked to Bickel as if the "whole valley was aflame with tracers and black puffs."

Seconds seemed like an eternity, but he finally pulled himself away from the threat. When he arrived back at A-2, the crew chief couldn't find any flak damage on the aircraft. Later, when the men viewed the gun film footage of Bickel's dramatic dogfight, everyone ducked when the enemy fighter exploded.[9]

Carl G. Bickel

Bickel's kill marked his third confirmed victory. He also had credit for two classified as probably destroyed and one listed as damaged. His plane, FT-Z, *Z-Hub*, was not flyable on July 7, so he had commandeered one of the new P-51Ds. Bickel would turn twenty-five in several days. The Nebraska-born, University of Northern Colorado and University of California Los Angeles-educated pilot had been drafted in 1941. He eventually joined the Army Air Corps, and later the 353rd Fighter Squadron when it was based in Oregon.[10] There he met North Dakota native Doris Froholm, who worked in Portland. They had been corresponding during his seven months in combat, and now she was stealing his heart.[11] Squadron Historical Officer Albert Feigen described Bickel as someone every officer and enlisted man considered a "right guy, quiet and unassuming, a most competent combat pilot and one of those men completely convinced that this is the finest fighter squadron in the world." Feigen continued, "Captain Bickel is a cheery good natured Officer; you usually see a bright smile about his distinctive mouth and almost never hear a harsh word. But with his good humor and admissions of constant hunger, 'for who is hungry is none other than I,' Captain Bickel has been found not only serious and pensive, but downright sentimental (which, for a fighter pilot, seems unusual)."[12]

Bickel's tent mate, Charles Koenig, improved his record to three-and-a-half victories on July 7. The two friends were the same age, but Koenig had more pilot time. The Californian had earned his wings at Luke Field, where he graduated on September 29, 1942, with Don, Wally Emmer, and Willie Y. Anderson.[13] He joined the squadron at Tonopah in January 1943. Somewhere along the line, the twenty-four-year-old Koenig had decided to christen his Mustang *Little Horse*, and soon it became his nickname, although his buddy Bickel addressed him as "One Small Horse." When the squadron arrived in France, Koenig changed the name of his steed, and thus his own, to *Le Petite Cheval* (The Little Horse). Because most of his initial combat flying was in a supporting role, his victory total had not yet allowed him to achieve ace status. This would soon change. Several weeks later, Feigen wrote about the gutsy example Koenig set when he faced a much larger enemy force: "Of all his distinguished performances, possibly the most noteworthy was . . . when he led eight of our aircraft in a fearless attack upon sixty ME 109's, destroying three and damaging a fourth . . . and showing us once again the stuff of which he is made."[14]

Charles W. Koenig

The fighter sweep turned out to be the crowning mission for Felix Rogers. With his two Focke-Wulf victories, the twenty-three-year-old Massachusetts native became an ace. Rogers had accomplished all of his kills and damaged aircraft to date in FT-O, *Beantown Banshee*. On the fateful July 7 sweep, he was flying *Arson's Reward*, which belonged to Operations Officer Wally Emmer.[15] Feigen portrayed Rogers as a one-of-a-kind member of the squadron: "That pilot of the shiny leather boots and double-barreled moustache . . . will not part with his nose garden (and, in fact, spends a good deal of time waxing and braiding it) although his oxygen mask mangles it unmercifully on every mission. A colorful figure with blond hair, and an occasional pipe, either on the volleyball court or in the cockpit of the Beantown Banshee, Captain Rogers' score of . . . German aircraft knocked down proves him a fighter as well as a character."[16]

Felix Michael Rogers

The only flight leader absent from the July 7 operation was twenty-three-year-old Willie Y. Anderson. The Swedish-born, Illinois-raised fighter pilot had four victories to his credit, the last two being the Me-410s he shot down over Germany in June when flying Bickel's *Z-Hub*.[17] Anderson showed his commitment to duty one day when he went out on a "test hop." While Anderson was putting his Mustang through its paces, he picked up a radio transmission from the squadron that Red Two, Hayden Holton, was aborting a mission. Anderson advised Red One that he would gladly replace Holton as Red Two. He soon joined the Red Flight Leader, sliding into position as his wingman. Feigen recognized both the humorous and the serious sides of Anderson when he wrote,

> The master of "Swede's Steed" is another "permanent party man" in the squadron, having become a part of the unit at Tonopah. Captain Anderson, something of a story book version of a fighter pilot, is a happy-go-lucky sort, usually laughing and talking about Captain Anderson. There is only one city in the world, Chicago; to look at the clippings from the Chicago papers, one would imagine there was only one Chicagoan in the war, Captain Anderson. But Captain Anderson is more than a funny-man; his Distinguished Flying Cross with Oak Leaf Cluster and his Silver Star attest to that fact.[18]

Willie Y. Anderson and General Brereton

Don Beerbower had been exceptionally busy in late June and early July, preparing for the change in his responsibilities and coordinating the squadron's agenda to maintain its momentum and cohesiveness. Despite his tremendous workload, he still found time to correspond with family and friends. Boyhood chum Bill Johnston was one of the people Don wrote to often. After Johnston had completed a tour of duty flying PBY Catalina patrol planes in the Pacific, he returned to America to assume duties as a Navy B-24 instructor-pilot in landlocked Kansas. In a letter Johnston sent to *Hill City News* editor Gay Huntley, he mentioned receiving correspondence from " 'Ace' D. B. which I will answer this afternoon. He's really doing good." In his letter, Johnston expressed a growing sense of optimism about the war when he said, "The Fritzies and the Nippies are in for a bad time–yes mighty bad." Johnston's correspondence, an article about Don receiving the Silver Star, Kenneth Boleman's death announcement, and letters from other servicemen appeared in the newspaper during the first week of July. Huntley really made an effort to use the *News* as a way to help the community keep its far-flung military personnel connected to home and each other. Johnston very likely spoke for all of those in distant places when he wrote, "[I] want to say that the paper has been reaching me regularly and again thanks to all you people who send it."[19]

On July 8 and 9 the Fighting Cobras flew three missions each day without any contact with enemy aircraft, but David O'Hara and Wally Emmer did lead successful Air-Sea-Rescue efforts, one in the English Channel and the other off the west coast of the Cotentin Peninsula. Four uneventful beach patrols followed on July 10 and 11.[20] But after a day of rest, action picked up when Don led Red Flight and O'Hara White Flight on a dive-bombing mission to the area around Angers on the Loire River. Replacement pilot Loyd Overfield in Willie Y. Anderson's *Swede's Steed* took Don's wing.[21] The eight Mustangs, each carrying two two-hundred-and-fifty-pound bombs, departed A-2 on a southerly heading in mid-afternoon. As they crossed the front lines near St. Lo, they enjoyed good visibility with two-tenths cumulus clouds. Don's orders authorized him to investigate German activity at several airdromes near Angers before deciding which one to hit. As the two flights approached the target area, the cumulus cloud cover increased to eight-tenths with a base at thirty-five hundred feet and tops at five thousand feet. They found no enemy activity at Seiches-sur-le-loir, Corne, or Varades. It was also quiet when they flew over Tierce at 1532. Although they discovered no planes to destroy, Don decided to expend the general-purpose bombs on the airstrip. The Mustangs began their bomb run in trail at twenty-five hundred feet and at an attack angle of twenty to thirty degrees. At the release point of five hundred feet they abruptly pulled up, their bombs falling toward the runway and adjacent gun positions. The "meager, inaccurate and light" flak didn't pose much of a risk, so the eight P-51s swung around and came screaming down low on the field, hitting the remaining functional gun emplacements. The pilots killed at least four German soldiers in the eighteen-minute bombing and strafing attack.[22] When the ships returned to A-2, Don peeled off in the normal manner followed by Overfield and the other two ships in Red Flight. As Overfield lowered the landing gear on *Swede's Steed*, he noticed a red warning light for the left wheel. After a go-around he cycled the system up and then down again. This time the light glowed green and the landing gear locked into place. Overfield came in on final approach to the south with the wind at six miles per hour from two hundred degrees. As he touched down, the ship still crabbed slightly into the wind instead of pointing straight down the runway. Overfield described what followed: "Upon contact with the mat the ship yawed violently forty-five degrees to the left. I applied full right rudder and brake and gave it a blast of the throttle. The ship righted itself for about ten yards then suddenly yawed to the right very violently. I applied full left brake and rudder with a blast of throttle but was unable to right the ship which performed a ground loop. The tail wheel and left tire were flat upon completion of the above maneuver."

The engine and propeller came through the accident fine, but the plane sustained major damage to the left landing gear and left wing. Staff Sergeant John Dimm, crew chief of the P-51B, had his work cut out for him repairing the fighter. Overfield, who had only clocked seventeen hours in a Mustang in three hundred eighty-one hours of total military flying time, was given fifty percent of the responsibility for the mishap by the investigation committee. The investigators attributed the remaining fifty percent on the runway, which "was in poor condition, with soft spots, at the time of the accident."

They recommended that all pilots be reminded to "go around again" if the approach didn't proceed correctly.[23]

The 353rd flew five patrols on July 14 and 15. The two missions on July 16 involved escorting medium bombers. All ended uneventfully[24] This changed on July 17 when John Montijo in Red Flight and David O'Hara in White Flight left A-2 in the early afternoon intent on defending the American beach area. George Hawkins was on Montijo's wing. Harvey Chapman led the second element with Jack Miller flying in the tail-end Charlie position.[25] The patrol proceeded routinely until Sweepstakes vectored Red Flight to St. Lo to investigate several bogies. The foursome was cruising seven miles northwest of the battered city at fourteen thousand feet above a three-tenths cumulus cloud cover when they spotted six bandits approaching from the southeast. The enemy saw Red Flight at the same time, turned to engage, and then broke for the cloud cover below, "executing violent evasive action." In one dogfight Montijo destroyed a Focke-Wulf while, in another, Chapman and Miller shared a victory, a first for both of them. Chapman, however, became separated from Red Flight during the melee. He ended up below the ten-thousand-foot cloud base, ten miles north of Vire. When he looked around he saw a gaggle of forty-plus FW-190s and Me-109s on a southeasterly heading. Giving little thought to his own safety, Chapman broke into the enemy formation "firing and [then] split-essed for the deck as they returned his fire." He and the other seven aircraft on the patrol returned home unscathed.[26]

The squadron flew two additional missions on July 17 which did not involve any contacts with the Luftwaffe. Of the two fighter sweeps on July 18, the second one included the destruction of an Me-109 by Woodfin Sullivan and Clifford Dean, capping Dean's first scrape with the enemy.[27] Deputy Group Commander Charles Teschner, who flew in the Red Flight Leader position, led the formation on this mission. Montijo and Beerbower anchored White and Blue Flights.[28] In the first group effort in several weeks, each squadron put up twelve ships for the sweep west and north of Paris. At Tille, the pilots spotted an aircraft parked along an airstrip. The 353rd won the job of strafing the parked Me-109. The "meager" antiaircraft fire proved accurate enough to rip holes in one of the squadron's planes. Sullivan and Dean made short order of the static Messerschmitt, and all ships returned to altitude and completed the fighter sweep. The only other victory went to the 355th when two of its pilots knocked down a Focke-Wulf near Amiens.[29]

The attack at Tille marked the third time in five weeks that Don had been involved in strafing an airfield. The Eighth and Ninth Air Forces had begun this activity during the winter, when the battle for aerial dominance over the Luftwaffe expanded from bombing aircraft manufacturing sites to assaulting enemy airdromes. The word "strafe" came from the German verb "to punish." Strafing described a method of aerial warfare developed by the Germans during World War I, when their pilots made low-level attacks against ground troops. French and British pilots quickly adopted the technique and the German name for it. American pilots in 1944 were not fond of strafing aircraft parked on camouflaged airstrips hidden in wooded areas or at established airdromes, because the pilots ran a greater risk of being shot down doing this than when engaging the enemy in the air. Unless the attacking Lightnings, Mustangs, and Thunderbolts achieved complete surprise, German gunners on the ground and in flak towers could easily bring their machine guns and twenty-millimeter cannons to bear on the fighters as they skimmed in low across the field. Many of the Eighth and Ninth Air Forces' top aces were lost strafing airfields, including Francis S. Gabreski, whose thirty-one aerial victories led all American pilots in the European theater.[30] Felix Rogers questioned how much the Allies really gained by strafing. He once reflected, "I really, even at this remove, question strafing airfields anyway because chances are you will lose one of yours and somebody has to ship an airplane from California and train a new pilot and put him in. And [it] is very questionable whether you did any damage to them. So I never believed in that. I would not lead someone down on an airfield. . . . I didn't see the exchange rate as being economical."[31]

Ken Dahlberg thought using bombers to hit the airfields from high altitude would have been much safer than low-level attacks using single-engine aircraft: "We had many discussions about it being an inefficient use of resources to use fighter planes to strafe. Now, it is true, [we] really destroyed a lot of German airplanes and the infrastructure, you know, the hangers and fuel tanks. So from that point, if you're going to go all out, I guess you do it. But it was hard on fighter pilots I'll tell you."[32]

The major threat to P-38 and P-51 pilots when strafing was damage to the engine's liquid-cooling system. A half-inch hole in a water line caused a rapid loss of the antifreeze blend from the radiator. A smaller hole allowed the aircraft to fly longer, but the odds of the pilot getting home were significantly reduced. The P-47 with its big, air-cooled radial engine did not suffer from this problem. The best way to avoid flak damage was to fly into and out of the danger zone before the defenders could train their guns on the attacking planes. The Eighth Air Force had established a special unit in March 1944 to experiment with strafing tactics. The recommendations from this group included:

- Knowing the lay of the land and installations around the target.
- Beginning the descent twenty miles out.
- Flying low and fast by the time they were five miles from the field.

- Approaching in line-abreast formation.
- Remaining low when flying away from the airdrome to limit exposure to enemy gunfire.
- Restricting the attack to one pass to avoid losses.[33]

Many years after the war, Jack Bradley summed up the method used by the 353rd Fighter Squadron:

> We would attack the thing by surprise if we could. [It] wasn't easy, of course, but we had pretty good tactics. We would come in low and make one pass. We'd go over maybe 10,000 or 12,000 feet and try to locate where the airplanes were parked. They were usually in the woods, camouflaged. [We'd] try to figure out where the antiaircraft guns were, and we'd make one pass at full speed about 8 feet off the ground. On occasion when we found a lucrative target and the antiaircraft wasn't too heavy, we'd make a second, but by then you had alerted every [German] in 10 miles. That was not a very good idea, so we normally didn't do that, but we did it occasionally.[34]

A pilot cruising at altitude does not have a sense of how fast he is going because of his distance from the objects thousands of feet below, but drop that same pilot to treetop level and he immediately senses the tremendous speed at which he is flying. High in the sky the terrain looks level, but once down low the pilot has to accommodate the gentle swell of the land and avoid trees, towers, buildings, power lines, or even the sudden appearance of birds. The time over the target is extremely brief when a ship is moving at three hundred fifty to four hundred miles per hour. In a split second the pilot has to choose between gun emplacements and parked or moving aircraft, all the while maintaining a peripheral awareness of his position in relation to the other members of his attacking force. Strafing can be both a fearsome and an exhilarating experience.

Because the risk to the pilot was greater when strafing than dogfighting, the Eighth Air Force, unlike the Ninth Air Force, included ground victories in the overall total of victories claimed by a pilot. Thus, John C. Meyer's thirty-seven victory credits tallied the most in the Eighth Air Force. Francis Gabreski, the aerial leader, ranked fourth with thirty-three-and-a-half.[35]

Between July 19 and July 22 the weather forced a reduction in aerial combat over northern France. The squadron flew only one mission during this period.

On July 20, Lieutenant Colonel Teschner led a four-plane fighter sweep across the Cotentin Peninsula to the Channel Islands and then south to the Gulf of St. Malo before returning home by way of Vire. Bud Deeds watched Teschner's wing. Don captained *Bonnie "B"* in the Red Three position with Edwin Pinkerton off to his side.[36] For all practical purposes, this mission seemed routine, and yet it was not. After Teschner broke ground, he turned west and climbed through a ten-tenths cumulus cloud layer that began at fifteen hundred feet and topped out at three thousand feet. Seven times Sweepstakes vectored the flight to investigate bogies and seven times the pilots' adrenalin began to pump as they scanned the empty sky.[37] Bud Deeds found this business frustrating.

> We'd go on these fighter sweeps daring the Germans to come up, and they were pretty smart. They had radar as good as we did. They would send some planes up and at a point our radar would pick them up and vector us on to them. You fly then for a while and those would disappear and off someplace else they'd come up on radar. And so they would vector us the other way. You never even got in sight of them and they'd go down off the radar. They just kept you flying around up there . . . until you used up enough gas you had to go home.

The pilots eventually dealt with the vectoring problem by going down to lower elevations, "and then we would find planes."[38]

The squadron flew one mission on July 23 when eleven Mustangs escorted a formation of B-26s to the Brest Peninsula. Wally Emmer led Red Flight with Jack Miller as his second element leader in the Red Three position. Both were flying P-51Ds.[39] Weather conditions were far from ideal when the three flights left A-2 late in the morning for the rendezvous point off the westernmost tip of the Cotentin Peninsula. At four thousand feet Emmer entered a soft, gray overcast that eventually turned to a haze which extended to eight thousand feet. Continuing on a northwesterly heading, Emmer leveled out at thirteen thousand feet and began searching the sky for the inbound twin-engine bombers. When the formation came into view, he slipped the three flights into position to cover the Marauders. The link-up took place over the Channel, eight miles north of Cape de la Hague.[40] The blended formation continued southwest without interference from the enemy until it reached the target area where the intruders were greeted with heavy flak bursts from the solid cloud layer below. The B-26s responded by unloading their ordnance and then abruptly turned northeast toward Normandy. As the fighters changed course with the bombers, Jack Miller noticed a drop in the oil pressure on his new ship. He continued on course but monitored his gauges closely as the formation proceeded to cross the base of the Cotentin Peninsula. Soon, he couldn't maintain altitude, and his engine temperature dropped near the red line. Miller broadcast his distress, "I called in my May Day and they told me I was still over enemy territory." Miller also learned that the cloud base was at a mere fifteen hundred feet. The controller directed him to stay on course until he crossed the Allied bridgehead. The tall, handsome Wisconsinite now faced the choice of ditching in the sea or hopefully setting down somewhere in friendly territory. His blood pressure rose as he continued losing altitude. The controller then radioed Miller that he had crossed the coastline, which disconcerted Red Three because he wanted to come down over land. He later explained, "Ditching a '51 was not a good idea and I didn't want to jump into the Channel." As Miller rolled his dying Mustang around toward the beach, he began descending through the cloud layer. He was approaching the fifteen-hundred-foot ceiling when the Norman countryside came into view: "I popped the canopy and by that time I was scared silly, and I jumped out the wrong side." Under tremendous stress, Miller had bailed out over the left side.

> Because of the engine torque we were instructed to bail out the right side. The fear of jumping is what made me do everything wrong. . . . The first time I tried to bail out the wind knocked me back in my seat. On the second try my foot caught on the edge of the cockpit and threw me across the fuselage. When I finally wiggled it loose, I was hurled against the tail of the ship. It knocked me out, fortunately only for a matter of seconds or I wouldn't be here telling about it. I came to folded over the horizontal stabilizer like a sack of meal. [I] managed to . . . push away from the plane. The ground was whirling up awful fast when I pulled the rip cord and passed out again. When I came to I was floating down and landed in the middle of a French farmer's tomato patch. Three kids were running about shouting, "*Boche! Boche!*" The thing that worried me most was landing right in the middle of a mine field. That would have been tough.

Alert American troops picked up Miller and took him to an aid station near Ste-Mere-Eglise, where doctors determined he had contusions of the abdomen and chest. After an uncomfortable but welcome ride back to the airstrip, Doc Snydman examined Miller at A-2. "He didn't have any x-ray equipment so he checked me into what he called a hospital overnight," Miller recalled. Because of his injuries, Miller knew he wouldn't be able to fly for a few days. Snydman encouraged Miller to take some time off in London to rest and heal. This he did. While in London, Miller found himself in so much pain that he admitted himself into a hospital. X-rays showed his collision with the P-51's horizontal stabilizer had broken some of his ribs and cracked his sternum. He did not return to combat flying until early August.[41]

Omer W. Culbertson, Kenneth H. Dahlberg, and John S. "Jack" Miller

With Emmer leading the squadron, Don had remained at A-2. After Emmer returned to the base, he reported what happened to Miller. Four hours later, as Don sat down at a field desk in his newly redecorated office, he mulled over Miller's brush with death. Don had a few minutes of free time before the evening meal and so composed a letter to Darrel and Arlene. A thin wall of canvas separated him from the rest of the tactical fighter squadron, just as a thin wall of time separated him from his next combat, death or his return home.

July 23, 1944
1710–

Dear Sis & Bro

Just got your letter of July 9, Arlene–I'm down at my new office in the Orderly Room. –Just got it redec'd.–really it's only a corner of a double tent which is the orderly room. My corner is closed off so I can eat people out in privacy. –Bet you can just see me doing that!–Well–I do–and [a] pretty thorough job of it at times. I'm in the midst of a revamp job on the armament section and whenever a pilot comes down with guns that have jammed, I have a personal interview with the armorer on the ship. It's a lot of work but I'm getting some results, I think. Darrel, you probably know something of the poor gun arrangement on a 51B and we have lots of stops due to failure to feed–We have about half 51D's now and they're much better and those armorers don't get much sympathy from me when they have a stoppage. I've lost too many chances myself by having guns jam. I'm sure I could have 25 victories now if they never had. I've gotten 2 with only one gun firing as is. I still keep my old 51-B as I have the guns in pretty good shape now and a good armorer and 4 guns are enough if they all fire okay. –My old ship is the oldest in the group now but still as good as any and faster than most if not all. –I have the Crew Chief set the Manifold Pressure Regulator up so I can get 78" mercury if I need it instead of only 67" as Technical O. calls for. It really isn't dangerous if I watch it. I've only used it all, once, and it felt good to have it. I may not have gotten to my last F.W.-190 soon enough to keep him from firing at another flight if I hadn't had it. All I did was tell Sgt. Panter I'd used that much and he changed all the plugs & checked it all over. –He's the best–!!!

I sure am glad Arlene can be so close and have a good job and all–you've been pretty lucky so far, haven't you? Gosh I hope we can get home together. I hoped to make it by my birthday but I'm not sure anymore. Still may just make it. More likely to get there in the first part of September though or around the middle. If you could get yours to start around the 10th we should hit okay I think. –I hope!!

I must go to chow now or I'll get left out. Write lots–both of you. Hoping to be seeing you before tooooo long.

Don

Don could not be certain when Jack Bradley would return from his thirty day furlough. He had left France for the States on June 30. Travel arrangements for crossing the Atlantic by ship were unpredictable. By Don's calculation, he expected Bradley to return within the next four to six weeks. Thus, he asked Darrel to try to arrange his leave in September.

31

THE CHURCH OF ST. ANNE

First Lieutenant Edwin H. Pinkerton . . . had been an instructor and a squadron operations officer at Luke Field, Arizona from January 1942 until March 1944 when he volunteered for overseas duty. When Pink joined us he had more than 2,000 hours to his credit, and it wasn't long before he had gained the esteem of every Officer and Enlisted Man in the squadron. Pink was a "pilot's pilot," destroying his first Jerry, an ME 109, soon after the move to France. . . .

Albert J. Feigen, squadron historian/intelligence officer
353rd Fighter Squadron Unit History

    Victory was in the wind on several major Allied fronts by late July 1944. In the Pacific, air, sea, and ground forces had finally secured the northern coast of New Guinea and the islands of Guam, Saipan, and Tinian in the Marianas. Allied leaders were planning the invasion of Luzon in the Philippines. In Eastern Europe, the Soviets were advancing along an eight-hundred-mile front that ran from Leningrad to the Carpathian Mountains. This massive attack, which began on June 23, had already resulted in the recapture of the Ukraine and eastern Poland. The campaign in Italy moved northward slowly but steadily. Only in northwest France did there appear to be a stalemate. The Allied lines extended to about where the military planners expected them to be on D-day Plus Five. Although the British had recently captured Caen and the Americans St. Lo, the victories occurred weeks after the preinvasion dates set for the capture of these key cities.
    The Battle of Normandy was now seven weeks old. Pressure increased on Allied Supreme Commander Dwight D. Eisenhower to break out of the German-infested *bocage* country, a region covered with small fields and meadows bordered by hedgerows. For centuries the Normans had used these hedges to define property lines and to contain grazing stock. Over time, raised banks developed that by 1944 were several feet above the surrounding ground. These natural defensive positions sometimes occurred in double rows, thus creating shallow trenches that remained well camouflaged from the air. Swamps,

streams, and canals created additional obstacles for infantry and armored units. And while the GIs and Tommies fought numerous small battles in an effort to capture limited objectives, Londoners agonized under heavy rocket attacks from the Germans. The British and American press criticized the military's inability to stop the terrifying V-1 bombings and the impasse in the *bocage*.[1] Eisenhower's answer to the gridlock came on July 19, when an immense Allied air force dropped its bombs on a specific sector of the enemy lines near Caen. The British Second Army followed up the attack with a six-mile advance before mud and the Germans stopped it. A similar aerial and ground offensive known as Operation Cobra was also planned for an area west of Caen near St. Lo, but inclement weather delayed its implementation until July 24; then the Allies quickly aborted the operation after the attackers dropped bombs among friendly troops. The mishap occurred because clouds partially obscured the American lines. Operation Cobra was postponed for one day.[2]

The 353rd Fighter Squadron participated in three missions on July 24. During the last operation of the day, Squadron Commander Don Beerbower, Edwin Pinkerton, and Carl Bickel led Red, White, and Blue Flights on a fighter sweep south of St. Lo.[3] The twelve ships from the 353rd and an equal number from the 355th climbed into the evening sky bound for Granville on the southwest coast of the Cotentin Peninsula. Once there, the two squadrons turned east and patrolled to Argentan in heavy haze before being vectored to intercept bogies north of their position in the vicinity of St. Lo. Finding nothing but "heavy, inaccurate flak bursts," the Mustangs returned to A-2.[4]

On July 25 the weather cooperated and the squadron flew three missions in support of Operation Cobra. Wally Emmer led the first and third patrols of the day. Don took responsibility for the late morning mission.[5]

The 354th Fighter Group was one of two groups assigned the critical task of protecting Operation Cobra's southern flank from interference by the Luftwaffe. The Allies focused the massive aerial bombardment on a thirty-two-square-mile area of German-fortified positions near St. Lo. Nine groups of P-38 and P-47 fighter-bombers hit the area first. Next came fifteen hundred eighty B-17s and B-24s. They were followed by more fighter-bombers. Finally, three hundred ninety-eight medium bombers released their ordnance into the smoke and dust of the obscured checkerboard landscape. In total, thirty-three hundred ninety tons of incendiaries, Napalm, and general-purpose high explosive and fragmentation bombs fell on the hedgerows, farm fields, and villages concealing the German ground forces in the target zone.[6] At his location near Criqueville-en-Bessin, Group Historical Officer Frederic Burkhardt described "a great surge of feeling" as aircraft flew overhead: "Every member of this Group who stood with his head bent way back watching that great air armada creep towards its target will always remember the excitement and depth of his emotions on that occasion. It was then, I believe, for most of us that we knew the war was won and it would be just a matter of time before Jerry would be crushed."[7]

Don joined heavy air traffic between 1011 and 1215 on his patrol, flying at nine thousand feet along a line from Granville, southwest of St. Lo, to Falaise, and on to Bernay and Beuzeville, east of Caen. With visibility at six miles, haze, and an eight-tenths stratus ceiling at fourteen thousand feet, three thousand Allied aircraft moved across Normandy as hectic radar operators tried to monitor everything and everyone. The squadron kept busy complying with requests from its controller to investigate numerous bogies. Although they turned out to be friendly aircraft, pilots discovered an "apparently serviceable" airfield northwest of Passais. A nearby partially camouflaged farmhouse appeared to be the control tower. They also spotted a triangular-shaped military installation with several large structures outside Messei. These appeared to be temporary enclosures, possibly covered with canvas. German gunners quickly responded to the circling fighters with intense and accurate antiaircraft fire. Flak remained heavy in a belt running from Flers to Les Tourailles to Briouze. One of the Mustangs sustained significant damage but returned safely to A-2 with the rest of the squadron.[8] No enemy aircraft tried to stop this mission, but later in the day Felix Rogers bounced a single Messerschmitt that was "making passes" at a P-38. When the Luftwaffe pilot glimpsed a P-51 on his tail, he broke for the clouds. Rogers pursued the '109 as it skipped in and out of the overcast to Vire, where he shot it down.[9]

The German Seventh Army suffered significant losses from the aerial bombardment. Regrettably, some aircrews released bombs on American soldiers and tankers who had been withdrawn to safety zones fifteen hundred yards north of the St. Lo-Periers road.[10] Friendly fire killed one hundred two men and wounded another three hundred eighty.[11] One of the individuals who lost his life was Lieutenant General Lesley J. McNair, who'd been visiting the 30th Infantry Division to observe the bombing attack. McNair had an excellent reputation among the U.S. Army's highest ranking officers. Eisenhower later said, "His death cast a gloom over all who had known this most able and devoted officer." He had recently replaced George S. Patton as the commander of a mythical U.S. Army Group in England. The Allies had successfully deceived the Germans into thinking this force would attack across the Strait of Dover at Calais. Patton awaited his impending activation along with the Third Army in Normandy. McNair, the former commander of the U.S. Army Ground Forces, had been responsible for the training of the soldiers now fighting overseas.¹² He and Don Beerbower were fellow Minnesotans, and his hometown of Verndale in Wadena County was a village about the same size as Hill City.¹³

Allied ground forces made little forward progress on July 25, even though the shell-shocked enemy troops the blast area floundered in total disarray. However, on July 26, the First Army began to advance southwest toward Coutances and Avranches.¹⁴ The 354th Fighter Group had an extremely busy day, flying eleven missions, three of which were assigned to the Fighting Cobras. The only pilots to engage the enemy on July 26 were those who went out with Wally Emmer at 1330. Of the four flights, only his and Carl Bickel's saw action.¹⁵ David O'Hara and Felix Rogers led the other two flights.¹⁶ The controller routed the patrol to Granville and then northeast to St. Lo. Emmer noted excellent visibility with two-tenths cumulus clouds between three thousand and four thousand feet, and a thin layer of cirrus at twenty thousand feet. Near St. Lo, the controller directed Emmer to turn to a heading of one hundred ninety degrees and investigate a "gaggle of bogies" heading northwest. Emmer and Bickel in Red and White Flights were cruising together at ten thousand feet. O'Hara and Rogers in Blue and Green Flights stayed below the cumulus clouds. At 1430 over the St. Sever Forest, Emmer intercepted forty Me-109s. Although outnumbered five to one, he attacked the German formation, knocking down two enemy aircraft and sharing another with Bickel. Six other Messerschmitts fell to the guns of Bickel, Harvey Chapman, Loyd Overfield, and Robert Reynolds. Clifford Dean had two kills. The rest of the Jerries had scattered by the time O'Hara and Rogers arrived with their flights. Enemy ground forces peppered the squadron with flak on the way home, but this did not interfere with everyone arriving back at A-2 by 1518.¹⁷ Squadron Historical Officer Albert Feigen later reported that Blue and Green Flights "were unspeakably angry to have missed out on the party; their laments could be heard for several hours after all the ships were safely down."¹⁸

O'Hara and Rogers had barely gotten over their frustration when a call came in for them to go out with Beerbower and Koenig to help lead an evening patrol. Russell Brown, flying FT-M, *Me Too, Evie*, took Rogers' wing.¹⁹ Harlow Eldred normally flew this ship.²⁰ The squadron patrolled for nearly three hours but sighted no enemy aircraft, although over Rennes at nine thousand feet they did receive "moderate accurate heavy" flak.²¹ The only serious problem on this mission occurred when the planes returned to A-2. As Brown banked onto final approach, he notified the tower of his low fuel and need to land immediately. Cleared by the tower operator, Brown made a three-point landing, but at the moment of touchdown he realized his right brake was locked and the wheel wasn't turning. He later told investigators, "I couldn't hold the plane on [the] runway and had all I could do to keep it from spinning to the right."

Brown cut the fuel mixture and switches as *Me Too, Evie* slid off the runway and hit a ditch, collapsing the left wheel assembly. The engine stopped abruptly when the prop hit the ground. Luckily, he had not been hurt. The investigators concluded the accident to be predominately Brown's fault when they wrote, "Abuse of the right brake while taxiing out or during takeoff is clearly indicated, causing the brake to freeze after takeoff. The committee attributes the accident to 75 [percent] pilot error inasmuch the pilot demonstrated poor technique while taxiing out into position or during takeoff. Extenuating circumstances were present in that the mission flown was scheduled on very short notice and required rapid ground assembly and takeoff." Brown had ninety-nine hours in Mustangs and five hundred thirty-two hours of military flying time. The committee recommended that "all squadrons emphasize to their pilots the dangers of brake abuse."[22]

Taxiing an aircraft at A-2 involved different procedure than at English bases, where a pilot typically had the option of having his crew chief ride on the wing to be his eyes, or he could zigzag the plane, navigating from the hardstand to the runway on his own. At A-2, trees and hedgerows created a problem. A pilot needed his crew chief on hand to get to and from the runway. As Jack Miller recalled, "You had to have the crew chiefs at the end of the runway because the taxi strip was through woods to the point where you couldn't zigzag your plane. With a '51 you can't see straight ahead. They would ride on the wing and give direction through this so-called maze of woods."[23]

Over the next five days, the 353rd flew twelve patrols, fighter sweeps, and escort missions. On July 28, Edwin Pinkerton led the squadron for the first time when he and Charles Koenig took eight aircraft out on a two-hour patrol. Pinkerton, with over two thousand hours of flying time and seven weeks with the squadron, appreciated this opportunity to develop his leadership skills in a combat situation, but the mission turned out to be uneventful. This wasn't the case on July 31, when Felix Rogers led eight Mustangs on the squadron's first patrol of the day.[24] Rogers and his wingman Harlow Eldred started the day's events late in the morning. Visibility was not very good because of haze up to ten thousand feet. In addition, a four-tenths cloud layer lingered between two thousand feet and six thousand feet, and a thin, broken layer of clouds floated at twenty thousand feet and thirty-one thousand feet. As Rogers proceeded across the Cotentin Peninsula, he was vectored by the controller to investigate bogies along the Gulf of St. Malo. In the vicinity of Granville, southwest of Coutances, Rogers found ten skittish Jerries. The Mustangs began a futile pursuit that took them in and out of clouds south across the Brest Peninsula to Vannes on the Bay of Biscay. The last they saw of the bandits were their contrails at thirty-three thousand feet. Rogers gave up the chase and turned his ship for home.[25] The mission would have ended without incident had it not been for a mishap involving Eldred. Everything seemed normal as he turned on final approach to A-2. The landing appeared to be normal, as well, until Eldred had rolled about two hundred yards down the runway. Suddenly, the right wheel assembly on the shiny, unpainted P-51B collapsed, causing the aircraft to swerve to the right and go off the strip. The plane suffered "major damage to the right wing, propeller and power plant." Eldred, who had almost one hundred forty hours in Mustangs, walked away unhurt. The investigating committee determined the cause of the accident was fifty percent pilot error. Even though Eldred had a green light in the cockpit indicating the landing gear was properly extended, the committee concluded the pilot "failed to take every possible precaution to ascertain the wheels were down and locked. . . . It is recommended that pilots flying the P-51 type aircraft, when feasible, rock the wings in the landing pattern as an additional safety measure to insure the landing gear [is] down and locked."[26]

The group continued putting up squadrons throughout the day on July 31, each one scheduled to overlap the one before it and the one after it. For example, the 356th flew from 1435 to 1705, the 353rd from 1625 to 1836, and the 355th from 1750 to 1947. Beerbower led the Fighting Cobras. They didn't encounter any enemy aircraft, but nonetheless the sweep turned out to be dangerous for the fifteen pilots. Lieutenant General Omar Bradley's forces had moved south of Granville toward Avranches, and were on the verge of a major breakout. Southeast of the fighting on a road located at T-6438, the pilots spotted a number of enemy Tiger tanks heading south. Further along this road, a column of German Red Cross vehicles crawled away from the fighting with their gruesome burden. The pilots were not carrying bombs that could destroy tanks, so Don reported the sighting and proceeded with the sweep. The Mustangs cruised below a twenty-five-hundred-foot five-tenths cumulus cloud base as they approached Vire, twenty miles northeast of Avranches, until hit by intense, accurate, "light and heavy" caliber antiaircraft fire. Jinxing away from the area, the squadron proceeded to Jersey Island, west of the Cotentin Peninsula. Over Pointe la Moye, light and inaccurate flak again threatened them. All told, four ships had sustained damage from the enemy fire. Fortunately, none of the strikes found a pilot.[27]

Damaged aircraft created an additional burden for ground crews that were already quite busy providing the normal maintenance necessary to keep the ships airborne. Men rose before sunrise for early morning missions and worked late into the evening when the schedule demanded it. Crew chiefs had to talk with returning pilots to assess damage to the aircraft, then expedite repair. George Chassey, crew chief of *Little Horse*, recalled, "If there were any problems we had to mark the plane out of commission and correct whatever needed to be corrected and then check it out again." Sometimes the repair required the ship to have a test flight before it was cleared for combat operations.[28]

July ended with a new record for the squadron. For the first time in eight months of combat flying, the 353rd had not lost a pilot because of enemy aircraft fire, flak, or mechanical failure. The closest call had been Jack Miller's collision with the tail assembly of his P-51. Soon he would be back from a recuperation furlough in London. The Fighting Cobras completed fifty-six missions in the month of July.[29]

The pilots may have felt some comfort with the improving odds of their survival until they confronted a scene south of the airstrip. For several days they had wondered about a flurry of activity in a field off the end of the runway. Now, when a pilot glanced down as he turned on final approach or lifted off A-2, he saw a grim reminder of the nearness of death laid out on the ground in an orderly fashion, multiple rows of dead soldiers, victims of the recent fighting south and west of airstrip.[30]

A major change in ground and air operations in Normandy took place on August 1 with the activation of the Third U.S. Army and the XIX Tactical Air Command, led by Lieutenant General George S. Patton and Brigadier General Otto P. Weyland, respectively. The Third Army and the XIX TAC had been training and planning together in England since early spring in an effort to develop into a "closely integrated team." Before this could be fully realized, Weyland needed to retrieve the fighter groups, such as the 354th, that were already in France under the temporary control of the IX TAC's Pete Quesada.[31]

Patton's forces joined the First U.S. Army at Avranches, a town located on the Gulf of St. Malo, where the Cotentin and Brest Peninsulas come together. Here, infantry and armor divisions were pushing south through a narrow corridor running along the coast. The Third Army planned to turn west with part of its force and capture the old French province of Brittany, while simultaneously covering the right flank of the Allied thrust as it wheeled east toward Paris. Patton, a former cavalry officer who believed in action and fast movements, had little interest in fighting the type of warfare that had been practiced in Normandy during June and July. He took full advantage of the Allied senior commanders' access to secret German radio transmissions, code named ULTRA, to keep tremendous pressure on the enemy.[32]

Patton's first order to Weyland seemed unorthodox. He did not want the XIX TAC to destroy the bridges in the area controlled by the Germans. Patton's concern was not in blocking the movement of the enemy to or from the battlefield. Instead, he wanted the Third Army to make quick thrusts over intact bridges without being impeded by waterways. For Weyland's part, his primary mission as a tactical air commander had three focuses:

- To gain, and then maintain, air superiority.
- To isolate the battlefield.
- To provide close air support to the combat forces.

Working in tandem with the Third Army, Weyland's aerial patrols would be dive-bombing, escorting aircraft involved in tactical bombing, and conducting armed reconnaissance over specific enemy-controlled areas. Within a week of XIX TAC's arrival in France, it had seven P-47 fighter groups and two P-51 fighter groups in place. The Thunderbolt, with its heavier armament and air-cooled engine, primarily took care of close ground support and dive-bombing, while the more vulnerable but more fuel-efficient Mustang drew the patrols, escort work, and long-range armed reconnaissance missions.[33]

P-47 RICK O' SHAY

As the Third Army threw its weight into the effort at Avranches, the Allies stood two weeks away from implementing Operation Dragoon, the invasion of southern France. The battleship *Texas* and other capital ships had been in the Mediterranean for a month, preparing to support this effort. Eisenhower planned to capture the major port of Marseilles and then send Lieutenant General Alexander M. Patch and the Seventh U.S. Army north through the Rhone River Valley to join Patton coming from the west.[34]

The month of August began on a good note for the 353rd Fighter Squadron. The single mission on August 1 was led by veterans Felix Rogers, Carl Bickel, and Willie Y. Anderson, who flew in the Red, White, and Blue Flight Leader positions in the twelve-ship squadron. Blue Flight included Anderson, his wingman Loyd Overfield, and Second Element Leader Edwin Pinkerton, with Harvey Chapman beside him.[35] Shortly after the squadron began escorting B-26s to a target along the Loire River, four Messerschmitts attempted to interfere with the raid. Blue Flight promptly responded to the challenge, knocking down three of the four '109s. Anderson, Overfield, and Pinkerton each earned credit for a kill.[36]

Also on August 1, James Keane left the unit for a thirty-day furlough in the States. Other pilots were in the pipeline to return home as well, but most would have to "await the return of the others before departing." Information arrived on this date from XIX TAC headquarters that several of the squadron's missing pilots were prisoners of war, including Ralph A. Brown, Ridley Donnell, Buford Eaves, Dennis Johns, Richard Klein, John Mattie, and Edward Parnell. Albert Feigen noted in his monthly report that the pilots owed a debt of gratitude to the "parachute man," George Sisk. The staff sergeant had packed the 'chutes that saved the lives of the pilots when they bailed out over enemy territory.[37]

Another American on the list of POWs was Colonel Kenneth Martin. The fact that he was alive came as "big news" to those who had served with him from November 1942 to February 1944.[38] The group's other past commander, James Howard, continued to make occasional contact with his old comrades in the unit. He was currently in France serving as the director of combat operations for the Ninth Air Force. Howard coordinated the fighters' and bombers' logistical needs for the Twelfth Army Group. Howard thought a lot of Martin and gave him the credit for the success of the Pioneer Mustang Group.[39]

The first mission of the day on August 2 turned out to be a dud when the Fighting Cobras received a recall message while escorting Thunderbolts seeking targets of opportunity. The skies cleared in the afternoon, allowing four flights to escort Marauders to Caudebec, France, fifty miles east of the British sector.[40]

The break in the weather created an opportunity for the Germans to fly an afternoon mission, as well. Unbeknown to the men at A-2, the reeling Luftwaffe made history high above their airstrip on August 2. *Oberleutnant* Erich Sommer, piloting an advanced twin-engine Arado Ar-234, sped over Normandy at 11,000 meters (36,089 feet) in the first jet aircraft to be used for aerial reconnaissance. At 1630 Sommer snapped a shot of landing strips A-1, A-2, A-3, and A-4 in his virtually untouchable Arado. The photograph revealed not only airfields and supply depots, but also the D-day battleship shelling around Pointe du Hoc northeast of A-2.[41]

Erich Sommer's aerial photograph of A-2 (center) at 1630 on August 2, 1944. Starting clockwise in upper right-hand corner, the other airstrips are: A-1, A-4, and A-3. Note shelling around Pointe du Hoc top center.

The world's last remaining Arado Ar-234 — SMITHSONIAN AIR AND SPACE MUSEUM, PHOTO BY SUMMER S. JOHNSON

The weather continued to interfere with aerial operations between August 3 and August 5. One mission resulted in a recall and another required the aircraft to land at alternate airstrips when A-2 was socked in. The other two missions involved escorting Marauders. The squadron met no enemy resistance, but Franklin Rose did have a close call on August 3 when he and his ship came to rest behind the control tower at A-2.[42] Rose had just returned from the B-26 escort mission to Chartres when the accident occurred. The junior pilot had been Red Four in Carl Bickel's lead flight. Rose had borrowed Emmer's FT-G, *Arson's Reward*, for the mission[43] The weather conditions and the fact that he only had three hours of flying time in P-51Ds, contributed to the mishap. Rose, landing to the north with a prevailing ninety-degree crosswind from the right, approached A-2 cautiously. As tail-end Charlie in his flight, he planned to land short on the runway behind the first three aircraft. He glided across the edge of the steel matting with his flaps set at forty degrees. Just before the wheels touched down, his left wing suddenly tipped toward the rising ground. Rose tried to level *Arson's Reward* by using his right rudder and aileron and a little throttle. This did not correct the aircraft's attitude so he immediately applied more power.

> When I used more throttle the plane was lifted slightly off the ground. The wind being very gusty, kept blowing me to the left side of the mat. The plane was not over two feet off the ground when it was blown entirely off the mat and the extended wheels struck a dirt ridge that is four feet higher than the runway. I knew then that I was going to crash and immediately cut the throttle. Both wheels were knocked off when they struck the dirt ridge. The plane skidded along on its belly and came to rest against an uprooted tree stump after having skidded around ninety degrees to the left. I unbuckled the safety belt and got out of the cockpit as fast as I could.

Rose escaped with only a "slight bump on the head." The control tower operator, sitting in a Plexiglas enclosure atop a truck that served as its foundation, was saved from serious injury by the uprooted stump. The crash landing completely demolished the new Mustang. The investigators concluded the "pilot exercised poor judgment and technique." They expected a pilot with four hundred twenty-one hours of military flying experience to have the know-how to adjust to the conditions. The committee concluded Rose failed to "give the aircraft throttle and go around thus avoiding a dangerous landing." The investigators recommended that newer pilots receive instruction in cross-wind landing procedures by "experienced pilots, such as flight leaders."[44]

Of the four accidents in recent weeks, Rose's was the only ship that could not be salvaged. The maintenance personnel possessed notable skill in repairing aircraft that were not severely damaged. In one instance, Sergeants Campbell, Free, Meadows, and Miller, and Private First Class Bush, established a squadron record by replacing an engine in less than six hours. When a ground crew first attempted this at Boxted, it had taken them a day-and-a-half and required an extra man. Experiences like this helped maintain good morale in the squadron, but the enlisted men had also developed the same cockiness about their outfit as the officers; and sometimes it got them in trouble. Albert Feigen recorded an incident in August that exemplified the pride people felt about being members of the Fighting Cobras: "[Two] of our enlisted men returning from town in a truck belonging to one of the other squadrons voiced their admiration for the 353rd and were promptly thrown out of the moving vehicle by its other occupants, sustaining serious injuries. This unfortunate incident brought about a meeting for enlisted men, two days later, in which new items of squadron policy were set forth. When among officers or men of the other two squadrons we were not to boast of, point up or describe the superior merits of the 353rd."[45]

Don Beerbower received welcome news on August 5 when he learned he had been promoted to major, effective July 25. The next day, when Don wore a gold leaf on his shirt collar, he received "sincerely hearty congratulations from all sides."[46]

By August 6 the Third Army had made good headway as it thrust west into Brittany, east in the direction of Paris, and south toward the Loire River. The German Seventh Army defensive line ran from Vire past Mortain to Mayenne and St. Suzanne. Throughout the day, Patton's officer in charge of secret ULTRA intercepts, Major Melvin C. Helfers, received messages indicating the Germans intended to counterattack on August 7 at Mortain. One of the messages requested night fighters for that evening and day fighters for the following morning to support armor and infantry units. The Allies suspected the Germans would try to sever the Allied supply line running through Avranches, twenty miles away, and then destroy the isolated Third Army. Fortunately for the Allies, the intelligence from ULTRA afforded Patton and Weyland a brief window of time to prepare for the anticipated early morning attack.[47]

The 353rd flew two missions on August 6. Don Beerbower, with Franklin Rose on his wing, took eight Mustangs up in the afternoon. Rose had not participated in an operation since his landing accident three days earlier. John Montijo led the other flight. A well-rested Jack Miller flew in combat for the first time since his collision with the horizontal stabilizer on his Mustang in July; he covered Montijo. Felix Rogers led a second two-flight mission later in the day.[48] Nothing unusual happened during either mission to suggest that something was afoot with the enemy's forces. Don left A-2 at mid-afternoon and flew southwest to Coutances. Then the two flights turned south, covering the Third Army's rear as they continued along the coast past the bottleneck at Avranches. Near St. Aubin, the controller vectored them northeast to St. Lo to check out some bogies showing up on radar. After finding nothing, Don returned home. Rogers took off at 1945 and was promptly vectored to St. Lo and then south to the Loire River. The only hint of anything brewing came in the form of ack-ack fired at the eight ships as they plied along between ten thousand and twelve thousand feet. Two aircraft sustained flak damage, but both pilots returned to A-2 with the other six ships at 2146.[49]

On August 6 Patton received approval from Omar Bradley, the new commanding officer of the Twelfth Army Group, to use three of his divisions to block the anticipated German counterattack the next day. Patton received further authorization to continue moving men and supplies of the Third Army

George S. Patton, Jr. and Omar N. Bradley conferring onboard a C-47

through the narrow corridor at Avranches and to continue striking east "around the Allied right flank." TAC Commanders Weyland and Quesada coordinated their air resources for the next day's fighting. Intelligence staff monitored the situation late into the night. When the assault began at Mortain in the early morning fog and darkness of August 7, some enemy units advanced several miles, but when the sky over the battlefield cleared, numerous American fighter-bombers began pouncing on the exposed elements of the German Seventh Army. The Luftwaffe attempted to support the attack, but it was outnumbered and outmanned. By mid-day the counteroffensive had petered out.[50]

Coincidentally, on August 7 four fighter groups, including the 354th, were reassigned back to the XIX TAC. Weyland now had nine fighter groups under his command. The timing of this reassignment resulted in the XIX TAC setting a record of six hundred one sorties for the day. The P-47 groups in particular stayed busy hitting motor transports, horse-drawn wagons, tanks, armored vehicles, a bridge, two locomotives, numerous freight cars, and a marshaling yard. In addition, the groups destroyed a combined total of thirty-three enemy aircraft, fourteen in the air and nineteen on the ground. But these victories cost the lives of ten pilots and their planes.[51]

The 353rd Fighter Squadron flew two missions of three flights each on August 7. Wally Emmer led both in a new *Arson's Reward*. This was the first time FT-G had been on the mission board since Rose demolished Emmer's first P-51D. In each of the day's operations, the Fighting Cobras penetrated the German rear area, centered on a line running through Argentan, Alencon, and Laval. Here, they lurked in a good position to intercept incoming enemy aircraft from the east and south. Emmer had Charles Koenig and Edwin Pinkerton as White and Blue Flight Leaders on the first mission. Harvey Chapman flew on Pinkerton's wing as Blue Two. The second element leader, Willie Y. Anderson, took a backseat to Pinkerton. Loyd Overfield held the Blue Four position.[52] Once airborne, the twelve Mustangs streamed south as they climbed for altitude. On this pleasant summer day with two- to five-tenths cumulus clouds beginning at three thousand feet and topping out at ten thousand feet, conditions favored German pilots trying to approach the battle area unseen. All remained quiet until the squadron reached Alencon. There, controller Ripsaw One directed Emmer southwest to Mayenne to investigate a sighting of bogies. The squadron had just passed the town when twelve Messerschmitts materialized at six thousand feet. The '109s were spread out and flying as solos and in pairs. When the enemy pilots realized their peril, many "adopted hide and seek tactics" to avoid engagement.[53] Chapman described the action taken by Pinkerton after Ripsaw One vectored the squadron to Mayenne:

When we arrived there at about 11,000 feet, we saw some P-47s and some Spits milling around below. Blue Flight, led by 1st Lt. Edwin H. Pinkerton, went down in a gentle, but fast, diving left turn to look things over. Suddenly Blue One rolled on his back and started down. I did likewise and when I got on my back I saw he was going after an Me-109 about 2,000 feet below us in a level turn from our left to our right. As I started down Blue One flicked his ship around in a direction away from me. I followed suit but the maneuver placed the whole flight with lines of flight widely spaced. In the dive I built up such high speed that my line of flight could not be quickly tucked in tighter to that of Blue One. We then dove through the cumulus clouds. Lt. Pinkerton . . . went through or under one, and I went through another large one. When I got to the bottom, I looked in the direction where Blue One should have come out. I couldn't find him anywhere. I saw two other P-51s near me, and joined with them, thinking they were Blue Three and Four. After seeing they were from another flight, I started a fruitless search for Blue One. Then I saw two Me-109s being chased in and out of a big cloud by a few P-51s. I joined in this scrap and looked over all P-51s I came in contact with to see if Blue One was one of them. I never found him or heard him on the radio, which was very congested throughout the encounter.

Edwin H. Pinkerton

Loyd J. Overfield

Pinkerton and his P-51D had disappeared south of Mayenne.[54]

Loyd Overfield, flying in the tail-end Charlie position in Blue Flight, found himself in trouble in the same area as Pinkerton. He had lost contact with

Willie Y. Anderson during the general melee involving the two groups of combatants. Overfield had successfully finished off a Jerry in a dogfight when Charles Koenig slid in beside him. Koenig later reported:

> While leading White flight, 353rd Fighter Squadron, on a controlled patrol, I observed 2nd Lt. Loyd Overfield shoot down a Me-109 in the vicinity of Mayenne. At the time I was circling above Lt. Overfield's ship at about 1,500 feet. I circled down to pick him up and he rejoined me in a turn to the south. As Lt. Overfield assumed a mutual support position, he rocked his plane violently and made a 180 degree turn north. I tried to contact him on the RT but couldn't. At this time I noticed he was streaming white smoke and rapidly losing altitude. I followed Lt. Overfield, continuing to observe him, and saw him land wheels-up in a field three or four miles south of Mayenne. After the dust cleared I observed him running to the west, away from his ship.

Overfield made the forced landing in an older P-51C.[55] To avoid capture, he left the area at once. After jogging a mile and a half, he came across a farm house where he sought shelter. The farmer and his family hid and fed Overfield before connecting him to the French underground. With the underground's assistance, he and two other pilots, one British and the other Australian, were able to work their way through the lines to safety. When Overfield appeared at A-2 four days later, his colleagues mistook him for a Frenchman, "clad in blue denims, a navy blue coat over a light blue shirt, with a blue tam on his head. . . ." Overfield brought with him details that confirmed Pinkerton's death. A Catholic priest had hidden the body and then secretly buried it on August 8 "in the cemetery of a quiet little French church, the Church of St. Anne, about five miles north-east of Mayenne." Pinkerton, who had volunteered for overseas duty, was survived by his wife, Helen, and an infant son.[56]

Overfield also reported he had shot down three '109s on the mission. After being confirmed, these kills brought the 353rd's total to seven for the day. Of the other four victories, two were credited to Anderson and one apiece to Emmer and Koenig.[57]

Another squadron in the group chalked up numerous victories on August 7, but at a heavy cost. At 1615, two minutes after Emmer's remaining ten aircraft completed landing at A-2, the 356th Fighter Squadron began their operation. Major Richard Turner took twelve Mustangs on the group's fourth mission of the day. The controller vectored him to an area east of Chartres where someone noticed a Messerschmitt crash-landing in the middle of a field.

As the pilots examined the scene more closely, they discovered a series of protective aircraft enclosures or revetments concealed in the woods. Turner decided to strafe the airfield. The squadron made several passes and destroyed twelve Me-109s and one Ju-88, but in the process they lost three pilots—Harber, Miller, and Simonson. In addition, four of their aircraft sustained flak damage, some of which had come from the church steeple in the village of Sours, south of the camouflaged strip. When Turner returned to A-2 at 1820, Emmer and the 353rd had already been back in the air for forty-five minutes. They saw no enemy aircraft but at 1915, from a height of four hundred feet, the pilots observed "American armored columns . . . racing towards Le Mans on all roads leading to that city."[58] Patton was flanking the German Seventh Army.

32

OH, MY GOODNESS

There were four of us, and we managed to surround a lone Me 109 at about a thousand to fifteen hundred feet over a beautiful pastoral scene with horses grazing in the pasture below. The poor guy in the Me 109 knew he was trapped, so he pulled back his canopy and bailed out. As we circled, we could see that his chute wasn't going to open. His body hit the pasture and bounced until it came to rest near the grazing horses. They looked up curiously for a moment, and then went back to eating. . . . It struck me how war seems to strip all our notions bare. It robs life of any value and makes death only a momentary interruption in the struggle for the one thing it leaves standing–self-preservation.

Carl G. Bickel, flight leader
Before the Contrails Fade Away

Major Don Beerbower did not participate in either of the 353rd Fighter Squadron's missions on August 7. Crew Chief Leon Panter had replaced the propeller on *Bonnie "B"* the previous evening, and now their ship needed a test flight before it would be deemed airworthy. Morning fog kept Don grounded, so he used the free time to answer correspondence from Darrel and Arlene. In the first paragraph of the letter Don obliquely referred to his recent promotion to major.

Aug 7, 1944

Dear Sis and Bro–
    Got the pics and a letter from each of you since I last wrote so guess I'd better get busy. There was no change in our APO when we came over here to France. Have a pleasant change to make now though if you'll note.
    No I didn't have to have a new wing on the Bonnie "B" that time– New tip and a new section on the leading edge for about 3 feet inside the tip. The locomotive on the side is for one destroyed–I've blown up two but never got around to painting them both on.

As for answering your question about the flak holes–the Bonnie "B" has about 3 times (no kidding) as many holes–patches–from flak as any other ship. Brought home 3 little holes the other day from 20 millimeter stuff behind the line–all in the tail. I don't know just how many holes there have been but I do know that twice now, new holes have been made in old patches!

They built up the dorsal fin on my ship as an experiment. Supposed to make it more stable and more easily trimmed. It helps some–especially on instruments. Also have a reverse automatic tab on the rudder which makes it harder and a little more positive on a fast turn or reversement. They are putting both on the new P-51D's now.

Our food now is "B" rations–not too bad, first month over here was "C"–out of cans!

My crew chief is SSgt. Leon Panter–he's about 35. All the men call him "Pappy." As far as just being a soldier he's as big a gold brick as anyone–but a smart one! But as a crew chief–He's the best we've got. He not only knows his business as well or better than all the others but he has imagination and ingenuity that makes the Bonnie "B" the most "personalized" ship on the whole base!–as well as the oldest! He had to put a new prop on her last nite though so I have a test hop soon as the fog lifts. . . .

[Two lines censured]

We're considered the second best fighter group in the eighth and ninth air forces which is a lot. The 56th group in the 8th is supposed to be the hottest, but they've been in combat about twice as long as us and only have less than 100 victories more than us. We'll hit the 500 mark well before 10 months which is way shorter than it's been done before by the other two groups who have done it over here. Our group has more victories than the rest of the 9th air force combined. (For about 3 months, I had more victories myself than any other group in the ninth!)

Guess I'd better wind up before the morning is gone.

Love
Don

Should be home about the 15th or 20th of Sept.

Don's world revolved around *Bonnie "B"*, Leon Panter, command duties, and combat. He had decided against moving from a P-51B to a P-51D. As the squadron commander, he could easily have arranged to fly a new Mustang. Certainly he had flown the D model in practice flights. But as Don indicated to Darrel and Arlene, *Bonnie "B"* was very likely the fastest ship in the squadron, and the gun-jamming problem had become less of an issue. The Malcolm hood gave the fighter a comfortable cockpit, and the dorsal fin extension and reverse-automatic tab improved her handling. An unbreakable bond existed between Don and his ship. It had been forged while outmaneuvering opponents in dogfights, leading formations through thick cloud banks, and returning safely from long missions. Don knew he could depend on *Bonnie "B"* and the sweet, steady throb of her engine.

Everything suggests Don planned to fly *Bonnie "B"* until he left for the States. The oldest fighter in the squadron would remain with Don until he went home.

The trust that existed between Don and Leon Panter had its beginning in November 1943, when the Fighting Cobras were preparing for combat operations at Boxted. Their mutual respect developed during the weeks they spent together prepping their original airplane. Don's confidence in Panter soon extended to the other members of the crew, James Downes and Donald Langran. In early August, Squadron Historical Officer Albert Feigen described the special relationship between these four men:

> The "Bonnie B" has been on 100 missions, returning only six times because of mechanical trouble. Her last 25 missions have been accomplished without turning back, a record which reflects the ability of her crew chief, Staff Sergeant Leon H. Panter, and his assistant, Sergeant James Downes. "Pappy" and Jim, teaming up with Corporal Donald E. Langran (who finds that caring for the armament of the Ninth Air Force's leading ace is a position fraught with danger) are a smoothly functioning team, enjoying Major Beerbower's faith and personal friendship.[1]

Langran's wife, Naomi, monitored the activities of the squadron through news dispatches about pilots like fellow Texan Jack Bradley. And Langran wrote home to her almost daily. In his letters he mentioned how well the crew got along together and how "proud he was of his pilot, Major Beerbower." Langran proved to be a skillful artist as well as a skilled armorer. He and a friend, Sergeant Hugh A. Bourbon, won a fifty dollar prize in 1945 for their design of a unit patch for the 354th Fighter Group.[2]

Armorer Donald E. Langran

Elayne Beerbower also received correspondence from her husband, revealing his satisfaction with his job situation, despite its dangerous nature. In a letter Don sent Elayne during the summer, he mentioned his interest in staying in the service after the war ended. He cautioned her, "Don't tell Dad." Don knew his father expected him to return to Hill City to help run the family creamery, and he didn't want his dad to hear second-hand about his inclination to do otherwise. He also mentioned in the letter, "I've got something to tell you." Whatever Don had in mind, he would never get the chance to discuss it with Elayne.³

Don's anticipated return to Minnesota in mid-September for a thirty-day leave coincided with the beginning of ruffed grouse hunting. Duck season opened a couple of weeks later. Don must also have looked forward to fall fishing for big pike on Hill Lake, and a round of golf with his father on the inviting course at Pokegama Lake near Grand Rapids. September and October would be a perfect time to be back in Minnesota with his wife and daughter and to enjoy some of his favorite outdoor activities.

The men were given a day of rest on August 8.⁴ The 354th Fighter Group as a whole had lost five ships and a number of others were damaged from the previous day's action. The ground crews needed time to make repairs.

Axis plans did not allow the German Seventh Army a respite from fighting. ULTRA intercepts on August 8 called for its 47th Panzer Corps to continue the attack toward Avranches. Chancellor Adolf Hitler insisted on achieving this objective. He seemed unaware of the potential danger on his left flank. Twelfth U.S. Army Group's Omar Bradley seized the opportunity to envelope the enemy force. After consulting with Third Army's George Patton and XIX Tactical Air Command's O. P. Weyland and others, he ordered the Third Army to link up with the British and Canadians advancing south from the Caen area. As the fighting intensified on August 8 around Mortain, Patton directed his XV Corps to move north on the axis Le Mans-Alencon-Sees and to "prepare for further action against [the] enemy flank and rear."[5]

Left to right: Omar N. Bradley, Otto P. Weyland, and George S. Patton, Jr. Seated: Patton's dog Willie

One of the problems Weyland faced after the XIX TAC became operational was stopping the harassing raids by German night fighters behind the Third Army lines. The Luftwaffe's best fighter-bomber, the Junkers Ju-88, had sophisticated radar, armament, and speed. It was successfully carrying out its primary mission to destroy the British heavy bomber force which operated at night.[6] Some of the Ju-88s were now being used to support the ground effort in and around Normandy. The experience of the 3rd Armored Division fighting near Mortain typifies how the Germans used the night fighter:

> The Thunderbolts ruled Normandy skies in daylight, but at dusk Hitler's Luftwaffe took over. Kraut bombers rode herd on division columns from sunset to dawn and, in isolated cases, inflicted casualties by strafing and bombing attacks. Service Company of the 32nd Armored Regiment suffered losses one evening when machine guns in an adjoining field opened up on a circling Ju-88 and disclosed the position. The German dropped a number of anti-personnel bombs, killing one man and wounding five.
>
> Frequently, for no sensible reason, the Kraut fliers seemed to keep division spearheads under surveillance without attempting to bomb or strafe. On the longer Normandy night drives it was not unusual to have a dozen or more enemy airplanes dropping flares at spaced intervals along the route.[7]

Junkers Ju-88 U.S.A.F. PHOTO

Weyland specifically did not want the raids to disrupt the movement of troops, equipment, and supplies over the bridges and roads in the narrow corridor at Avranches. Since the XIX TAC consisted only of day fighters, he asked for assistance from the IX Air Defense Command's P-61 Black Widow night fighters to deal with the enemy threat.[8]

As the German Seventh Army pressed the attack, Weyland sent fighters on armed reconnaissance missions north, east, and south of Paris in an effort to block the flow of German troops, equipment, and supplies by rail to the battlefield west of the French capital. This allowed Patton to continue slipping behind the Seventh Army without being threatened by other enemy forces. Weyland's new focal point began paying dividends. On August 8 fighter-bombers destroyed twenty-nine locomotives, and one hundred thirty-seven freight cars, and cut rail lines in seven places. In addition, aircraft operating closer to the battle lines destroyed or damaged numerous motor and horse-drawn vehicles, tanks, flak positions, and fuel dumps. Five enemy planes were shot down by Weyland's pilots. A record seven hundred seventeen sorties cost only eleven American ships.[9]

Weather conditions during the second week of August remained favorable for combat operations, thereby allowing Weyland to maximize XIX TAC support of the Third Army. Between August 6 and August 12, nine groups flew an average of six hundred sorties per day.[10]

With warm summer temperatures and minimal rainfall across northern France, smoke and dust drifted upward into the atmosphere creating haze that restricted visibility at lower altitudes. At A-2 dust had become an operational problem. As airplanes taxied to and from the squadron areas, the propeller wash stirred up all the loose particles of sand and dirt along the way. Crew chiefs had to don masks and goggles to protect themselves as they guided the pilots from the hardstands to the landing strip. The dust also interfered with the mechanics of the airplanes. Fine particles had a habit of finding their way into carburetors, making it difficult to keep the planes flying.[11] This added work for the ground crews and gave the pilots something else to worry about as they raced down the runway. No one wanted an engine to miss on takeoff.

A pilot could not feel safe in the air without a competent crew chief overseeing his ship's maintenance. The crew chief knew he held the pilot's life in his hands every time he prepared or repaired the plane for combat. In almost all instances, mutual respect existed between pilot and his crew chief. Both men needed to work in harmony for the operational mission to be successful.[12] Jack Miller described the special bond between him and Robert Reagan, crew chief of their Mustang *Dingus*:

> [I] went out to the flight line, did a preflight and talked a little bit with the crew chief. The last thing you did before you got in was to relieve yourself, then get in the plane, climb in. And the crew chief and the assistant crew chief were generally there to help strap you in and what not. I always remember my crew chief, a fellow by the name of Reagan; just as he was getting ready to climb down he'd give my shoulder a squeeze. Gives you an idea how close the pilots were to their crew chiefs.[13]

On August 9 the 354th Fighter Group completed five missions east of Paris in the area around Epernay and Reims. The 353rd Fighter Squadron handled two of these.[14] Don Beerbower had not flown in combat since August 6. With the new propeller on *Bonnie "B"* functioning properly, he decided to lead the squadron's first mission of the day. At the morning briefing he and others reviewed the information the pilots needed to know about the operation north of Epernay: weather conditions, flight altitude, route, target location, radio frequencies, the controller's call sign, an intelligence report, and press time. Press time was when all pilots started their engines. As the briefing ended, all pilots synchronized their "hack" watches.[15] Finally, everyone picked up a parachute and headed to their aircraft. At press time the pilots fired up the Packard Merlin engines, and along with their crew chiefs, taxied behind Don and Leon Panter from the squadron area along the perimeter track to the strip. In so doing, the procession passed a number of flight personnel, including Don Chisholm, *Le Petite Cheval's* armorer. "I was standing beside the track as *Bonnie "B"* went by. Major Beerbower looked down, smiled at me, and continued on."[16]

Before Don taxied onto the runway, Panter hopped down from the wing of *Bonnie "B"* and moved away from the old warhorse. With a thumb's up Panter signaled he was clear of the aircraft. Jackknife 31 acknowledged his crew chief with a parting glance, completed his run-up and instrument check, and requested clearance from the tower operator for departure.

Sixteen fighters prepared for takeoff on the armed reconnaissance mission. Don led the way in the Red One position, with wingman Bud Deeds beside him as they turned into the wind. Behind them waited Second Element Leader Bruce Carr and Charles Olmsted in the Red Three and Four positions. Felix Rogers followed as White One with Omer Culbertson, Russell S. Brown, and Andrew Ritchey trailing as White Two, Three, and Four, respectively. Farther

Red One Don M. Beerbower

Red Two Frederick B. Deeds

Red Three Bruce W. Carr

Red Four Charles A. Olmsted

back taxied Blue Flight Leader Carl Bickel and Blue Two, Three, and Four: Clifford Dean, Robert Reynolds, and Ira Bunting. Green Flight Leader John Montijo brought up the rear. Jack Miller would be flying next to him with Second Element Leader James Burke and his wingman Jerry Leach completing the foursome.[17]

At 1103 Don slid the Malcolm hood forward over the cockpit, signaled Deeds in *Joy*, and increased the throttle on *Bonnie "B"*. The ships, loaded down with full ammunition compartments and topped-off tanks of aviation gasoline, advanced along the strip at A-2. As the big four-bladed propellers bit into the oxygen-rich morning air, the Mustangs gained speed, then, *Bonnie "B"* and *Joy* gained lift from their wings and transitioned to flight. The 353rd had initiated the group's second mission of the day; the 356th having departed the airstrip twenty-three minutes ahead of the Fighting Cobras.[18] Both squadrons navigated toward Epernay, following orders which had come in from XIX TAC at 0125. Orders always designated parameters within which the group had to carry out its mission. On August 9, these ran from Paris northeast to Soissons, then southeast to Reims, Chalons-sur-Marne, and Vitry-le-Francois, before turning southwest to Troyes and Joigny, and then northwest through Melun to Paris. The boundary lines extended approximately a hundred miles west to east and a hundred miles north to south. Three possible targets fell within Weyland's parameters:

- A fifty-car train with ten to fifteen large guns and no engine at T-4450 east of Paris.
- An ammunition storage dump in the woods adjacent to a railroad spur south of Reims at T-2262.
- One hundred freight cars in the marshaling yards at S-6070.[19]

The 356th, with its earlier start, had orders to hit the fifty exposed rail cars southeast of Epernay. The 353rd planned to follow in its sister squadron's wake, but would be looking for the ammo dump located between Epernay and Reims. These cities were twenty miles apart.[20]

As Don made a climbing turn away from Cricqueville-en-Bessin, Carr and Olmsted slipped into position beside Red One and Red Two. White, Blue, and Green Flights soon formed up on Jackknife 31 and the other three aircraft in Red Flight. The Mustangs ascended through the thick haze that hung like a creamy veil over northern France. As they gained altitude, Don contacted Ripsaw One on "D" channel. Weyland's orders required each squadron to maintain contact with the controller throughout the mission.[21] *Bonnie "B"*, on an easterly heading with the other ships in a line-abreast formation, cleared the last of the haze at nine thousand feet. Except for three-tenths cirrus clouds at twenty thousand feet, visibility aloft was good. Don guided the four flights over the familiar terrain north of Paris. To his front he watched the Marne River meandering past Chateau Thierry, the site of a major American victory in World War I. Epernay, Don remembered, lay just twenty miles farther upriver. As the squadron descended to six thousand feet, he soon spotted the city on the south side of the Marne. The four flights banked north at around noon to begin searching the area toward Reims, where a railroad spur would lead them to the German ammo dump.[22]

At 1200 the 356th located fifty oil and freight cars along the river between Epernay and Chalons-sur-Marne. The twelve fighters strafed the train; fires erupted from the tank cars, incinerating forty percent of the rolling stock. Guiding down the tracks, the three flights soon discovered thirty camouflaged flak cars. After making one pass, the 356th turned for home. The twenty-millimeter antiaircraft fire became too intense for the pilots to press the attack.[23]

While the 356th was assailing the rail cars, the 353rd began circling in the vicinity of T-2262. After fifteen minutes of futile searching, Don decided to move north toward Reims to seek out other targets of opportunity.[24] Reims, the ancient capital of the old French province of Champagne, had witnessed invading armies since the days of the Roman Legions and Attila the Hun. It soon came into focus through the summer haze. Don had been to Reims in May, when the squadron escorted B-26s to a target there, and he had flown over or near the area on other occasions. He recognized the major highways, rail lines, and airfields. As the fighters cruised at six thousand feet north past the city, the silky-smooth penetrating hum of their inline V-12 engines turned the heads of any civilians or military personnel within earshot. Then the former French aerodrome, *Base aerienne 112*, came into Don's view three miles beyond Reims. This extensive facility, renamed by the Germans as *Flugplatz A213*, lay adjacent to the villages of St. Thierry and Courcy. It had been an important Luftwaffe air

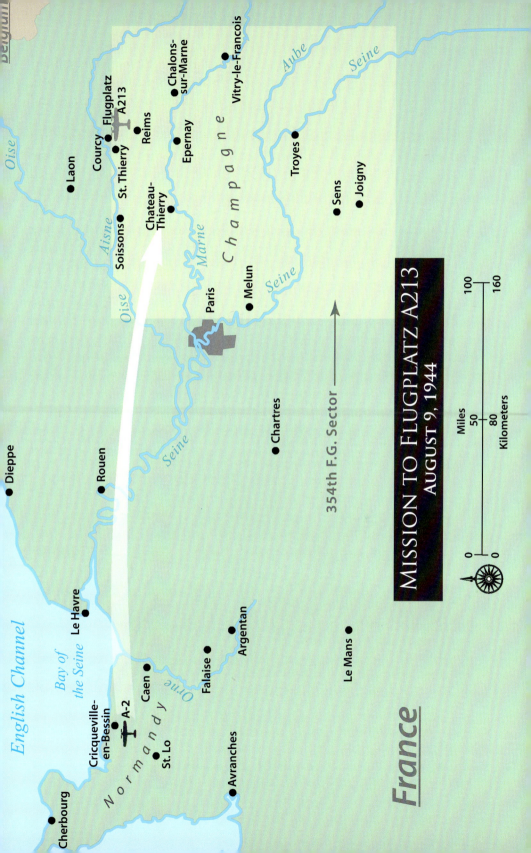

base and maintenance depot since 1940.[25] From his vantage point in the rapidly advancing *Bonnie "B"*, Don could see approximately thirty twin-engine aircraft parked in revetments.[26] White Flight Leader Felix Rogers worried that this unscheduled target could be a trap; "There were sixteen of us and we couldn't find what we were looking for in the air, but we went over the airfield at Reims, in France, and it was loaded with what looked like airplanes from high altitude. You never could be sure that they were or were not dummies."[27]

Nonetheless, the squadron commander had already made the decision to attack. Don radioed his instructions to Blue and Green Flights to remain at six thousand feet. Don instructed Section Leader Bickel to steer Red and White Flights as they dropped down to approach the target at ground level. Sixteen Mustangs proceeded north past the German airdrome. When Don thought they'd gone far enough beyond the enemy installation to safely descend, he and the seven ships with him lowered their noses and turned toward the target.

Red and White Flights maintained a "fairly dense" line-abreast formation as they raced across the rolling wheat fields and vineyards to the airdrome. In the shrinking distance ahead, Don could see transmission towers. The electric power lines between them "dipped way down, seemingly to the ground so that there [was] a big loop from tower to tower." The lines hung too low to go

FT-B Strafing a German hangar, Focke-Wulf 190 and Junkers Ju-88 in background. Staff Sergeant Nathan Glick: "I was bitter when the Big Bomber Boys had the 354th go to strafing and dive-bombing. We lost Beerbower ... and others that way."

under, so the only choice was to pop up over them and then drop back down to the deck and shoot. Rogers described what happened as they cleared the obstruction: "[The] German twenty-millimeter was bursting right along the top of the line. So they were fooled about as much as no one. And most of us in that first pass got hits of no real consequence. . . . [They] had flak towers so they could shoot down as we went across the field. All you could do was fire at what was in front of you. There was no room to maneuver because you had aircraft on both sides of you. And I fired at what I thought was a Ju-88 but looked suspiciously like a dummy to me. I fired into a hangar and then pulled off to the other side."[28]

Attacking the field from north to south, Red Flight bore down on the target, and Don singled out a Ju-88 and opened fire with *Bonnie "B"*'s four fifty-caliber machine guns. The enemy fighter-bomber exploded in its revetment. The American ships rapidly cleared the airdrome and its dangerous flak batteries, and Don and Bud Deeds banked to the right, followed by Carr and Olmsted, and Rogers' White Flight. As Don led these ships away, he called Bickel and told him Red and White Flights would make a second pass from east to west concentrating on the gun emplacements.[29] Finding the airfield from low level was no longer a problem because smoke raged skyward from the burning aircraft and hangars. Carr had destroyed a Ju-88 and damaged another. His wingman, Olmsted, had also damaged an enemy ship. In Rogers' flight, Culbertson claimed a victory while Brown and Ritchey shared one together.[30]

Bickel began his descent for a north-to-south attack, maintaining radio contact with Don. To achieve maximum success against this lucrative target, Blue and Green Flights needed to strike the remaining Ju-88s moments after Red and White Flights hit the main antiaircraft positions.[31] While Bickel was descending, Rogers was wrestling with the words Don had spoken to Red and White Flights as they roared west away from *Flugplatz A213*—"We're going to do it again." Years later Rogers reflected, "Believe me in the great big pass we made, since they knew we were coming the first time, they were out in force the second time. . . . I was not a big willing participant, but I was right beside him when we went back."[32]

Don maintained contact with Bickel as he led the two flights north and then circled around until again positioned to attack. From the flak towers the enemy gunners drew a bead on Red and White Flights approaching from the east. As the eight Mustangs closed on the airdrome, French civilians watched the drama play out. Bud Deeds, just off Don's wing, described the twenty-millimeter cannon crews' response to the attack: "As we came in range, in line-abreast formation, the guns opened fire on us and we returned fire." *Bonnie "B"*'s Brownings sent a deadly stream of rounds racing ahead of the ship. Bruce

Carr watched Don demolish the gun emplacement but also take "several hits" in the process. He watched as Red One "swung over to knock out another emplacement [but] . . . it got several hits on him." Deeds quickly glanced from his front to check the status of his commanding officer, and he could see that one wing on *Bonnie "B"* was damaged and the canopy was missing. The wingman later reported, "The plane was climbing and it appeared that the Major was hit." Don had pulled back on the stick, straining to gain altitude. His ship climbed to a thousand feet and then "partially stalled, half rolled" and began to fall toward the earth. As Carr watched, "Major Beerbower fell out of the side of the airplane, struck the left side and draped over the left tail-plane. At about 400-500 feet he came loose and did not attempt to pull his rip-cord." Deeds had to divide his attention between flying *Joy* and observing Red One's fate. He saw *Bonnie "B"* nose "straight down in a dive, exploding when it hit the ground." He did not see Don hit the tail of the ship but he confirmed, "The pilot fell free while it was in the vertical dive, but no apparent attempt was made to open his 'chute."[33] Rogers was close to Red Flight and saw the enemy fire hit his former flight leader. He did not see Don fall from the aircraft or see a parachute.[34] As Red and White Flights crossed the airdrome, Blue and Green Flights initiated their strafing attack. Bickel was listening to Don through his headset; "He was talking to us over the radio when his radio suddenly went silent." Bickel looked around and saw *Bonnie "B"* crash.[35]

Jack Miller in Green Flight watched Don exit the cockpit and then fall to his death; "You don't forget something like that. He fell free and his parachute was streaming back behind him but it didn't blossom out. I saw him hit the ground."[36]

French farmer Mancel Lemaire observed the antiaircraft fire strike *Bonnie "B"* as well. He watched the ship climb three hundred meters, turn upside down, and then the pilot "became separated from the plane; his parachute did not open." Lemaire and his workmen ran to the crash scene near the edge of

Mancel Lemaire

his vineyard, *Clos du Mont d'Hor*, several hundred meters south of the small village of St. Thierry. He later gave an eyewitness account to a French investigating officer, First Lieutenant Ladurantie: "The plane has been crushed at several meters distance from the place where the pilot had fallen. The latter was killed when falling. . . . [The] pilot seemed to be 20 or 25 years old, had fair-colored hair, and pretty long, he was of a middle size, had long yellow shoes [flying boots], and wore at the left hand a ring."[37]

It had all happened so suddenly.

The attack had begun at 1220. When it ended a few minutes after Don's death, two more Ju-88s had been destroyed in the pass made by Blue and Green Flights. Bickel shot-up one of the aircraft while Reynolds and Bunting received credit for the other night fighter. The return trip to Cricqueville-en-Bessin was solemn and without incident. The pilots passed a black cloud billowing up from a burning oil barge south of Andelys on the Seine River. The formation returned to A-2 at 1340.[38]

German officials at *Flugplatz A213* reported to higher authority that one of their gun crews had shot down a P-51 Mustang at 1230. The search party located the aircraft and the deceased pilot five hundred meters south of St. Thierry. The body lay next to the wreckage. It was identified by the name found on a "strip of leather." After cross-referencing this with information on the

12th Century Mont d'Hor monastery overlooks Lemaire's vineyard   LE CLOS DU MONT D'HOR PHOTO

plane, the Germans concluded the pilot was the squadron commander of the force that had attacked the airdrome.[39]

Mancel Lemaire waited until the officials left his property before cutting away a piece of metal from the side of *Bonnie "B"*. It included the pilot's name, Major Don M. Beerbower, and "15 or 17 little painted '*croix gammees*'." First Lieutenant Ladurantie later determined this meant the number of German aircraft shot down by the pilot.[40]

A final farewell.

After Jack Miller rolled to a stop at A-2, he waived his crew chief over to climb up on the wing of his ship. Miller recalled seeing Leon Panter waiting expectantly for Don and *Bonnie "B"*: "I waved him over to get on my wing. He knew right away Don went down."[41]

When Bickel and the other pilots described to Wally Emmer what had happened to Don, Emmer became "livid with anger." He wanted to return to the German airdrome and avenge his friend's death: "I'll get the bastards!" Bickel tried to dissuade him from doing this.[42] Miller also witnessed Emmer's reaction:

"Emmer and Beerbower were part of the original group and they were extremely close friends. You get upset when you lose a close friend. . . . Emmer was walking around a little bit out of his mind."[43]

Group Historical Officer Frederic Burkhardt described a scene in which Don's companions "choked back manly tears" as they recounted the last moments of the mission.[44] The veteran pilots had developed a way to handle the loss of those they flew with in the squadron. They intentionally avoided getting to know the replacements and worked hard at not developing an intimate friendship with the other senior pilots. They had learned it was easier to accept death this way. Willie Y. Anderson tented with Bickel, Koenig, and Montijo, but they never became "buddy, buddy" until after the war when he and Bickel developed a close and lasting friendship. Anderson had not been on the mission. He learned about it as soon as the squadron returned to the airstrip. Anderson commented over a half-century later:

> Well, you have to understand that at the time Don was killed, it was not an untoward incident. They would come back from a mission and somebody was killed. It happened. When the flight came back they said, "Don was killed." Another friend gone. "Oh, my goodness." You become inured to that and you don't like to see it happen. And by that time most of us ceased having close buddies because every time you got a close buddy, he was killed. You just shied away from getting close to anybody and so, when Don was killed and they came back, "Any reason he could have survived?" "No, he bailed out and his 'chute didn't open." That's what I remember. "Oh, shit." We felt bad but we'd felt bad so many times before when we'd lost so many good friends that it was one of those things that happens during war. Everybody is innocent. "Well, that's a shame."[45]

Ken Dahlberg had gained great respect and admiration for his commanding officer in the two months he had been with the Fighting Cobras. He appreciated Don's quiet leadership style and his achievements as a fighter pilot. Dahlberg had learned in flight training and in combat the value of protecting himself from the loss of a colleague, but this death was unlike the others: "You had a certain armor around you that you couldn't let the loss of a buddy be too emotional. It had to be unemotional from a pure military point. It had to be '*C'est la guerre* [such is war].' Yet, this situation was different, Don pierced that armor. . . ."[46]

Emotions went beyond the pilots. Albert Feigen had worked closely with Don for months. Feigen did not try to conceal his feelings. He wrote in his

Albert J. Feigen

monthly report, "When fifteen ships returned, the entire group was stunned. How could a man who had destroyed nearly twenty enemy aircraft while flying 134 sorties, with more than 250 combat hours to his credit, be shot down by some worthless lie-fed puppet."[47]

In the late afternoon, another armed reconnaissance mission visited the Reims area. The group, under the command of Captain Verlin B. Chambers from the 356th, included all three squadrons staggered a few minutes apart.[48] Chambers left A-2 with the 356th at 1630, followed by the 355th at 1650, followed by the 353rd at 1658.[49] Emmer, now "unofficially" the squadron commander, led the twelve ships provided by the Fighting Cobras. Feigen had been observing Emmer during the three hours between the squadron's two missions. He later wrote, "Since [early afternoon] Captain Emmer had said almost nothing. Feeling Major Beerbower's loss more deeply than any man knows, it seemed obvious that his single purpose was to return to that field north of Reims and shoot every living thing out of it."[50]

Four of the pilots who had flown on the first mission went up again with Emmer: Clifford Dean, Bud Deeds, Jack Miller, and Robert Reynolds. Miller took Emmer's wing. The acting C.O. piloted the new *Arson's Reward*.[51] The three flights bore through haze until they reached a spectacular, billowing formation of six-tenths cumulus clouds at six thousand feet. The twelve pilots kept ascending until they left the opaque condensation behind at ten thousand feet. High overhead a thin canopy of cirro stratus clouds capped the atmosphere. Leveling out, the squadron flew with deadly determination east in the direction of Reims. Emmer maintained communications with Chambers and Ripsaw One.[52] As he flew north of the Marne Valley toward Reims, the controller directed him to investigate targets away from the scene of the Fighting Cobra's earlier mission.[53] Emmer found nothing to attack. The hunting was poor for the other two squadrons as well; neither found targets to strafe or enemy ships to bounce. At 1815, however, Lt. Robert M. Parkins' Mustang developed engine trouble. He was forced to bail out at fifteen hundred feet near Laon. As the 355th Squadron Commander Maurice G. Long watched, Parkins fell away toward the French countryside. His parachute did not open. Long could not tell if Parkins had struck "some part" of his P-51.[54]

Fifteen minutes later, Emmer tipped his ship to the west away from the Reims area and the remains of his longtime friend.[55] At 1855 the squadron approached the Seine River five miles north of Rouen at an altitude of eleven thousand feet on a heading of two hundred and seventy-five degrees. The haze had crept up to nine thousand feet and the visibility had dropped to three miles. Theodore Sedvert, flying in the Blue Two position, remembered how the somber flight home was shattered by shell fire. He later reported, "Red One, Captain Wallace N. Emmer, suddenly burst into flames after an explosion in the center of his fuselage which, by all appearances, was caused by a direct hit from an enemy 88 mm antiaircraft shell. The fuselage paneling on the side over the fuselage tank came off and several other large pieces fell off. The ship flew level for a few moments and then began to spin violently." Sedvert looked away to check his position on Blue One, Robert Reynolds. When he glanced back again he saw a pilot in a parachute harness at about ten thousand five hundred feet. Jinxing to avoid the flak, he adjusted his position on Reynolds and immediately scanned the area below his ship for the descending 'chute; but it had vanished.[56]

Red Two Jack Miller had briefly lost visual contact with Emmer. When Miller recovered it, he immediately followed the spiraling, burning *Arson's Reward* downward until the ship melted into the clouds and haze. He was convinced Emmer was either dead or trapped alive in the aircraft.[57] The pilots returned to A-2 unsure of Emmer's fate. He had been seen huddled over in the cockpit of his burning ship moments before bailing out. No one knew the extent of his injuries or whether he had survived and become a prisoner of the Germans. Like Don, Emmer's time with the squadron went back to Tonopah. Members of the squadron regarded Emmer with respect, as a skilled pilot and a "swell fellow." He had an aggressive streak that fit in well with the philosophy of the Fighting Cobras. Albert Feigen described Emmer, as a "savage combat flyer, anxious to attack the enemy against any odds, [who] fought with the grim purpose of destroying as many of the enemy as possible."[58]

Colonel George Bickell moved quickly to fill the void at the top of the 353rd Fighter Squadron. That evening Felix Rogers signed Squadron Order Number 15. It read, "The undersigned hereby assumes command during the temporary absence of Major Jack T. Bradley, vice Major Don M. Beerbower relieved this date." Carl Bickel replaced Emmer as the operations officer. David O'Hara and Robert Reynolds were bumped up into the flight leader vacancies caused by the promotions of Rogers and Bickel.[59]

Wally Emmer

Each man in the squadron reacted to the loss of Beerbower and Emmer in his own way. Carl Bickel felt unsettled. He commented to Jack Miller, "Well, I wonder who is next to go?" Miller was fighting his own battle with the grim scenes he had witnessed within a span of several hours. After determining he was not scheduled to fly the next day, Miller did something out of character for him during his time in combat—"It's the only night I can ever remember getting drunk," he declared.[60] Jack Bradley was on leave in Brownwood, Texas, when David O'Hara "somehow got a call through to me.... I was horrified! I didn't want to come home on leave anyway." Bradley immediately attempted to go through channels to expedite returning to France. He told transportation personnel, "I've got to get back to my squadron!" But they only laughed at him. He was told he would have to go back the "routine way." His orders routed him through Atlantic City, New Jersey, where he was delayed a couple of weeks before being sent by ship to England.[61]

Leon Panter was grappling with his own demons. He had been the crew chief for the leading ace in the Ninth Air Force and for his squadron's commanding officer. Now the younger man he deeply cared for was dead. The Mustang he fondly maintained was destroyed. Its letter designation, FT-E, and name, *Bonnie "B"*, no longer appeared on the status board at operations. Panter thought hard about all these things. He wanted to find a way to honor Don's memory. Several days later he went to see Carl Bickel.[62] Albert Feigen recorded their meeting:

> Sergeant Panter approached First Lieutenant Carl G. Bickel, newly appointed operations officer, requesting permission to crew his new ship, FT-U. The request was granted, the new Mustang relettered "E"—Sergeants Panter and Downes and Corporal Langran teamed up to crew "*Bonnie B III*" for the Operations Officer. There could have been no more sincere tribute to Don M. Beerbower.[63]

Bonnie B III *bombed up and ready for action.*

Carl Bickel

33

In Humble Gratitude

I shall not attempt to describe the sincere respect and admiration felt for him by all those who knew him here. As long as any one of us remains, the name and the character and the heroism of Don Beerbower will be remembered.

Albert J. Feigen, squadron historian/intelligence officer
(letter to Clarence E. Beerbower)

The sudden change in the leadership of the 353rd Fighter Squadron did not prevent Colonel George Bickell, commanding officer of the 354th Fighter Group, from assigning the Fighting Cobras three missions to the Brest Peninsula on August 10, 1944. Captain Felix Rogers confronted the challenge of overseeing squadron operations, while at the same time preparing the unit for imminent transfer to new airstrip A-31 south of Gael in Brittany,[1] not to mention psychologically moving the unit beyond the recent tragic events.

Rogers had been a protégé of Don Beerbower, having come up through Don's flight at Portland. Rogers described Don's impact on him as significant.

> I arrived from flying school in the second group of pilots assigned to meet my flight commander, First Lieutenant Don Beerbower. There followed more than 300 hours of operational training and more than five months of disciplined leadership that molded us into [a] tautly ready unit; ready, that is, to face the Luftwaffe with confidence and élan. In a great unit, we were the best flight! We were that great because of the natural leadership skills of Lieutenant Beerbower in the air and on the ground. All of us respected him and learned to obey him instinctively. After the training period was over, we followed him in combat in an easy transition. After thirty seven years of service and three wars and having arisen to four star rank, I attribute a large measure of my success to my initial service under Major Beerbower.[2]

Bickell's policy of providing pilots with ever-increasing levels of responsibility, inherited from Kenneth Martin and James Howard, also helped prepare Rogers for his new job. He had advanced from wingman to element leader to flight leader, and now squadron commander. With the help of the new officer cadre, Rogers shifted the attention of the men away from the loss of Beerbower and Emmer and back to the daily routine of fulfilling their mission. Jack Miller summed up how well everyone adjusted to the change in leadership when he said, "We just continued on as we were, that's all."[3]

The squadron did carry on under the able leadership of Rogers and Jack Bradley when he returned in early October, and finally, Glenn Eagleston.[4] Looking back, Rogers could proudly assert, "[The] unit . . . ended World War II as the highest scoring squadron in the history of United States Military Aviation."[5]

Allied personnel killed in the sector that included *Flugplatz A213* were interred at the "*cimetiere de l'ouest-rue de Bezanne*" [West Cemetery, Bezanne Street] in Reims.[6] On August 10, a German *unterfeldwebel* [sergeant] by the name of Mane and an "undertaking" detail transported Don's body to this location. His remains had been stripped of all personal effects. He was buried in his flying suit in Row 3, Grave 25.[7]

The Luftwaffe personnel at *A213* sent the specifics about Don's death to a number of reporting stations, including the prisoner-of-war concentration point at Brussels, Belgium, and the POW Transit Camp for Air at Oberursel, Germany. The only evidence they possessed that identified the downed flyer was the strip of leather from his flight suit and the name Mancel Lemaire had observed on the fuselage of *Bonnie "B"*.[8] The process of officially confirming Don's death had begun. It would take time for the information to move through Axis channels to the Allies in London and Washington, and finally to the family in Hill City, Minnesota.

Bonnie Beerbower was nearly 15 months old when her father died in France in the summer of 1944. The little girl and her mother had enjoyed living with Bill and Anna Kutcher on the family farm in Spang Township, five miles northwest of Hill City. Judging from all appearances, the area seemed unaffected by the war; but life had indeed changed, because most of the young men were missing. The exceptions tended to be farmers whose work was essential, those who failed their draft physicals, or service personnel home on leave. Two such servicemen who happened to be in town visiting their families in early August included Don's friends, Sergeant Paul Boleman and Captain Morley Christensen. The day Boleman arrived in Hill City, a fierce storm of "cyclonic style" ripped through the village and the surrounding townships.[9] At the Kutcher farm, the women had spent the day processing chickens. The Kutchers took the dressed poultry into Grand Rapids, where they sold some to grocery stores; others were taken to the locker plant for freezing. By the time the family returned home, ominous black clouds thundered and spit lightening a mile west of the outbuildings. Racing into the farmyard, Bill dropped the women off near the house before parking the car in the garage. Anna hurried to the kitchen with the groceries while Elayne struggled with the wash boiler they'd used to transport the chickens to town. Just before she got to the steps, a tremendous gust of wind caught the empty container, sending it and Elayne tumbling across the grass to the edge of the field fifty feet away. A moment later, her mother came to the door and shouted above the fury, "Everyone in the basement!" When Anna saw her twenty-three-year-old daughter sprawled on the ground, she yelled in astonishment: "What are you doing over there!"[10]

Editor Gay Huntley described the tempest as the worst to hit the area in anyone's memory. The high winds knocked down trees, small buildings, and chimneys. It took Frank Dichtel and his crew four days to repair the damaged telephone lines.[11]

The devastating storm and Don's overseas duty undoubtedly dominated discussion when Elayne, Bonnie, and the Kutchers were guests at the home of Mr. and Mrs. Ed Skinner on Sunday, August 13.[12] The Skinners lived near the dance hall on the east side of Hill Lake. Ed liked hearing directly from Elayne about Don's service in France.[13] Two days later, Darrel and Arlene arrived home from Pampa, Texas, for a short furlough. On Saturday, August 19, Lavaun and Marshall Hankerson, and their children, Jo Nett and George, came from southern Minnesota to visit for a few days.[14] Marshall was conveniently stationed at Wold-Chamberlain Field near Minneapolis, not far from his former teaching post at Medford.[15] Clarence and Josie Beerbower now had all their family around them, with the exception of Don.

Marshall returned to his naval duty station on Monday, August 21, while Lavaun and the children stayed on with her parents. Before he departed for the Twin Cities, word of Don's recent promotion arrived.[16] The *Hill City News* carried a front-page story about it on August 24. The brief article and Don's photograph ran under the headline, "Hill City's Ace Now 'Major Beerbower.' " It was another proud moment for the family. Don had accomplished so much in his short military career.

Don's August 26 birthday celebration was postponed until his anticipated return from France in mid-September. On August 27 Clarence drove Darrel and Arlene to Minneapolis to catch a train to Texas, while Lavaun and the children returned to Medford.[17]

The tranquility of summer was almost over.

Elayne normally received letters from her husband several times a week. When they quit arriving at the farm she thought it unusual. Then, recent letters to Don were returned, one after the other. Bill Kutcher expressed the concern growing in everyone's mind when he said, "What's going on here? This doesn't look good."[18]

On Friday, September 1, a relaxing Labor Day weekend was about to begin in Hill City. It had been a routine day at the Northland Telephone Exchange office until a Casualty Message Telegram came across the wire from the War Department. It said Don was missing in action. Frank Dichtel promptly took the dreaded news over to the Beerbowers. Don's parents chose not to phone

Frank Dichtel

Elayne but instead drove immediately out to the Kutcher farm. When they arrived, Josie rushed across the yard to Elayne and Anna. Clarence gave the two women a hurried wave as he headed to the barn to see Bill.[19] Huntley wrote an article about the telegram's contents on September 7. The headline read, "Maj. Don Beerbower Reported Missing."

> When this word went about town last week expressions of regret and hope that Hill City's ace pilot would soon turn up were heard on every hand.

On Friday Don's parents, Mr. and Mrs. C. W. Beerbower and his young wife received the wire that carried [the] message: "Missing since August 9th." It was rather a discouraging message you will have to admit, but hopes are held that our Don is all right and will be putting in an appearance one of these days. . . .

Don was expected home on leave this month and his family and all of his friends were looking forward to that happy event.

On September 15 the *Duluth News Tribune* carried an *Associated Press* dispatch from the Ninth Air Force in France describing Don's last mission. Huntley picked up the story and ran it on September 21: "Major Don Beerbower's plane was struck by antiaircraft fire as he was buzzing a German gun position attempting to draw fire away from other pilots. . . . Capt. Wallace Emmer of St. Louis was also reported as missing the same day, Aug. 9. Together he and Don had destroyed 32½ Nazi planes."

The article ended with a quote from Carl Bickel in which he stated he lost radio contact with his squadron commander and then saw *Bonnie "B"* explode as it hit the ground. No mention was made about anyone seeing a parachute. These additional details put a damper on everyone's hopes for Don's survival.

The Allies swept across France in August and September 1944. At the forefront of this historic campaign was the larger-than-life Lieutenant General George Patton. On August 29 the Third Army's 90th Infantry Division, short of fuel and supplies, halted at Reims. Several days later one of its units, the 315th Engineer Combat Battalion, stopped at *Flugplatz A213* to prepare the damaged facility for use by the Ninth Air Force.[20] In the wake of the Third Army came the Graves Registration Service (GRS). The men of this organization collected, identified, and buried the remains of deceased American personnel in temporary cemeteries. On September 28 a detail led by Sergeant William R. Wilkinson disinterred "16 fighters of the Allied Forces" buried at the West Cemetery in Reims, including Don. Sergeant Wilkinson signed a handwritten statement prepared by a French civil official which concluded, "I relieve the cemetery keeper of his liability about the removal of the bodies."[21] Wilkinson delivered the remains to a temporary American military cemetery at Champigneul, ten miles west of Chalons-sur-Marne. The GRS reburied Don at 1600 that afternoon in Plot B, Row 2, Grave 38. They laid Sergeant Mercer of the 80th Infantry Division on his right and the body of a soldier named Wolf, of unknown rank and organization, on his left.[22]

On September 30 the German authorities in Saalfeld sent information to the Allies through the International Committee of the Red Cross in Geneva, Switzerland, stating that the remains of Major Don M. Beerbower had been interred on August 10, 1944, at the West Cemetery in Reims.²³ Casualty information moved out of Germany slowly because of the tremendous strain on its military infrastructure.

In early October Elayne received a letter from the War Department informing her that Don had been flying alone when his plane went down near Reims at 12:20 on August 9.²⁴ Except for this correspondence and the *Associated Press* news release in September, no other information was forthcoming. The Kutchers and the Beerbowers tried to maintain daily contact by telephone. Clarence and Josie told Elayne, "If we hear anything, we'll come."²⁵

In the meantime, Don's family and many others prayed, waited for news, and went about their normal routine. On Friday, October 6, Josie and her mother-in-law, Lula, and Mrs. W. B. Russell and her mother, took "a load of finished surgical dressings and Red Cross materials" to the county seat at Aitkin. Two days later Clarence, Josie, Lula, and a friend, Glen Saylor, attended a dinner party at the Russells' home.²⁶ Elayne tried to stay busy helping her father and his hired man with the fall crop. By mid-month the harvest had ended. Most of the leaves had fallen and, with them, much of the rich color of autumn had vanished as well. On October 18 Elayne and Bonnie left by bus for Medford to visit Lavaun and her family.²⁷ They remained at the Hankerson home through the weekend, returning to Hill City on Monday, October 23. Once back, Elayne and her parents participated in the United War Relief drive, another of the many ways citizens were helping on the home front.²⁸

The waiting came to an end on October 27 when a telegram arrived from the War Department notifying Elayne that her husband was dead.²⁹ Gay Huntley reflected the mood in Hill City when he wrote in the *News*: " 'Killed in action August 9' was the brief telegram received from the War Department Friday evening by the Beerbower family concerning their son Major Don M. Beerbower, who was previously reported as missing. The entire community was saddened by the news and expressions of sympathy were sent from everyone to Mr. and Mrs. Beerbower and to the young wife. No details were given in the wire."³⁰

The Beerbower children returned home as soon as possible. Lavaun and her family arrived the next day; Darrel was granted an emergency leave from his duties at Pampa, Texas. On November 1, Clarence and Josie met their surviving son and Arlene in Minneapolis. The heartbroken parents had no additional information about Don to discuss as they strained to make conversation during their drive north through the bland, pre-winter landscape along U.S. Highway 169 to Hill City.³¹

Elayne struggled with overwhelming grief. She had suddenly been thrust into the position of Don's high school classmate, Grace Christensen Boleman, and other young mothers from the squadron such as Helen Pinkerton and Elizabeth Seaman. Navy Lieutenant Bill Johnston visited Elayne during the week of November 5.[32] Home on leave for a few days from his B-24 training base at Hutchinson, Kansas, Johnston drove out to the Kutcher farm with his parents to offer condolences. He had been Don's best friend. As boys they had enjoyed participating together in church, school, scouting, sports, and social activities. Billy J. and Don had no clue of what lay ahead of them when they left high school at the end of the 1930s. Both later satisfied their interest in flying and their desire to protect the freedom they cherished by serving in the skies over the Central Pacific and Western Europe. They had sustained their friendship through a chance visit in California in 1943, regular correspondence during the war, and an appreciation of the inherent risk each took every time they flew in combat. Now Don was gone. His family and wife were filled with anguish. When Johnston left Hill City after a week at home, he wondered if Elayne would have the strength to cope with the death of her husband.[33]

Elayne Beerbower's smile betrays her sadness as she stands beside Bill Johnston in front of Dave's Grocery, Grand Rapids, Minnesota

Elayne felt fortunate to be residing with her parents and to be surrounded by their love and the home she had known all her life. Like other war widows, she had to find a way to live with her anguish, and farm chores that kept her mind on short-term objectives each day offered the solution. It would be twelve months before she received any income from the military to compensate for Don's loss. Elayne later admitted, "I don't know how Bonnie and I would have made it without my parents' help."[34]

On November 9 Gay Huntley reported that Mr. and Mrs. Frank Bishop, parents of an area soldier, received a telegram during the week saying their son John had been killed in France. Huntley eulogized, "Bishop did his full duty as a citizen and a soldier and he made the supreme sacrifice." His family held a memorial service for him a few days later. Huntley added "John J. Bishop" to the Roll of Honor on the front page of the *Hill City News*, listing it with those who had fallen before him: Glenn Foust, George R. Ill, George K. Boleman, and Don M. Beerbower.[35]

There had not been a memorial service for Don because Clarence continued to hope that his son still lived. He refused to accept Don's death without evidence from the military.[36] A letter that arrived from the War Department early in the month provided no additional information. Clarence's frustration came to a head on November 11, Armistice Day. He wrote to the Adjutant General of the Army at the War Department:

> On October 30th the War Department wrote us that an official message had been received stating that Major Don M. Beerbower, 0-730341, Air Corps, who was previously reported as missing, was killed in action on August 9th. Please inform us what the facts are that lead to this conclusion. As it stands now we are just as much in the dark as we were when he was reported missing. We would much rather have all the facts even though they hurt, than have all this suspense. Was it because of a lapse of time that he was reported killed? Was his grave found? Was his plane found?[37]

Beerbower wanted something concrete to confirm the loss of his son. Brigadier General Edward F. Witsell responded promptly to the distraught father. On November 27 he wrote in part:

> Your desire for details regarding the death of your son, which would offer you some comfort in your sorrow, is most understandable and I regret that no information is available in the War Department, other than that contained in the official casualty message received from the Commanding General, European Theater of Op-

erations, that Major Beerbower was killed in action in France on 9 August 1944. I hope you will understand that in order to fulfill the vital responsibility of reporting casualty information in the most expeditious manner, our overseas commanders have been obliged to limit their reports to include the fact, place, cause and date of death.

Since matters pertaining to burial of our army personnel come within the jurisdiction of the Quartermaster General, Washington, D.C., a copy of your letter has been referred to that official for reply regarding the location of your son's grave.

I realize how futile any words of mine may be to assuage your grief, but I trust that the knowledge of your son's heroic sacrifice in action may always be a source of sustaining comfort.

My deepest sympathy is with you in your bereavement.[38]

The family would have been surprised to learn that Don's remains were now in the possession of the Army. Regrettably, the complex logistics required in fighting a war on many fronts had delayed this information from arriving in Washington in a timely manner.

Gay Huntley knew Hill City as well as anyone living in the area. He had observed and listened to its people for thirty-four years. He was a deeply religious man who opposed war and the human tragedy that followed in its wake. And yet, he ultimately put his full support behind the Beerbowers, Bolemans, Christensens, Dichtels, Hankersons, Johnstons, Sailers, and the many other young men and women, including his own sons, who were fighting and dying to protect the American way of life he so profoundly respected. On the eve of Thanksgiving, Huntley wrote about the sacrifice many had made for their country, their community, and their family:

> Thanksgiving is with us once more and it is fitting, nay, necessary, more than ever this year to give reverent thanks to the Almighty for the manifold blessings we have received and are receiving.
>
> Did you say you have nothing for which to be thankful? Your sons, brothers, husband or sweetheart are with the armed forces and facing untold dangers, perhaps injury or even death. . . . None of us like war, we didn't want war with any other nation or people. But war came to us and we can be exceedingly grateful that our men are willing to face the danger because of their love for our country. They don't like the job nor did they ask for it but they are doing the work [in] a manner that brings tears to our eyes as our hearts overflow in

humble gratitude. Let us kneel and give devout thanks to the Almighty for this great blessing."[39]

The 353rd Fighter Squadron's success in destroying German planes continued throughout the bloody winter of 1944-1945. More of Don's friends died or became prisoners of war. By spring, the Allies were closing in on the remnants of Hitler's Third Reich. On April 29, 1945, at *Stalag Luft VIIA* near Moosburg an der Isar, Bavaria, Ed Regis, Jim Cannon, and other members of the 353rd Fighter Squadron found themselves caught between the advancing elements of Patton's Third Army and the retreating German Wehrmacht. Artillery rounds from both sides whistled over the POW camp. Regis maintained an optimistic attitude about being liberated until an officer who seemed to know something about artillery said, "There's a good possibility of getting a short shell on those things. It might hit the camp." About mid-morning a flight of P-51 Mustangs from one of the squadrons from the 354th Fighter Group made a pass over the compound in support of the 14th Armored Division. Regis burst with excitement when he recognized the ships' familiar markings; "They buzzed the compound. I mean they buzzed it about 50 feet as they came across!"[40]

Two days after Patton's forces liberated them, Lieutenant Colonel Jack Bradley and Lieutenant Colonel Glenn Eagleston,[41] who had recently surpassed Don as the leading ace in the Ninth Air Force, arrived at Moosburg "in search of people." Regis, who had been Eagleston's wingman, returned with them to the group's new base at Ansbach, Bavaria. Although the ride back was slow and tiring, he was elated to be free and safe. They arrived at squadron headquarters at 0100. A sergeant opened the mess hall at once and served steak and eggs to Regis and the other ex-POWs. The meal tasted so very good, but after months of prison camp food, it made them all sick.[42]

When the Japanese attacked Pearl Harbor in 1941, Regis had felt surprise, disbelief, and anger; he had experienced a tremendous uneasiness when he pondered how the war would affect him and his family. Now, after five months of combat flying and a year in captivity, he was heading home. The war had changed him forever. He had developed the ability to handle real fear and hunger, and to maintain his self-control under very trying circumstances. He had also learned to hate the Nazis, "especially the SS and Gestapo." Years later Regis pondered what life would have been like had Hitler's forces won the war. "The world today," he said, "would be something I can't even imagine."[43]

Young men in sleek Mustangs no longer fly sorties in the skies over Western Europe. The sight and sound of massive formations of heavy bombers and their fighter escorts carrying out deadly missions will not be seen or heard again. The pilots of the 353rd Fighter Squadron fought bravely in harrowing dogfights and daring strafing attacks against an enemy whose objective was the domination and oppression of others. The unique blend of American design, British horsepower, and youthful courage that came together in their P-51s challenged, and then defeated, the airmen of Nazi Germany. Victory exacted a terrible price, however. It came, in part, as a result of pilots willing to risk imprisonment, injury, and their lives. It also came at great personal loss to their families.

On October 8, 1948, the body of Major Don M. Beerbower was permanently interred in Plot A, Row 30, Grave 42 at the United States Military Cemetery, Epinal, France.[44]

Lavaun and Marshall Hankerson visiting Don's resting place - July 1989

Afterword

Beerbower was one of the finest. He was quiet, athletic, and absolutely fearless. . . . We were deeply saddened by [his] loss. . . . I considered him the greatest fighter pilot in the European theater. I'm sure that if it hadn't been for his untimely death, he would have gone on to be America's top ace.

James H. Howard, Brigadier General
Roar of the Tiger

He died as he lived setting a thrusting example for the rest of us. I've carried that example with me always.

Felix Michael Rogers, General
(letter to the Minnesota Aviation Hall of Fame)

On September 5, 1944, the 359th Bombardment Squadron, 303rd Bombardment Group dispatched ten B-17s from its base at Molesworth, England, to the 1st Bombardment Division for an attack on a chemical plant operated by the I. G. Farbin Industry at Ludwigshaven, Germany. It was the squadron's third attempt in five days to destroy the facility. The bombers received excellent protection from their fighter escort. No enemy aircraft challenged the 359th's heavies, although they were dogged by "moderate to intense and fairly accurate" antiaircraft fire in the Dormstadt-Frankfurt area.[1] First Lieutenant John W. Parker was flying aircraft #42-31483, a workhorse with ninety-three missions to her credit. On the return trip across Germany, the ship lost the propeller on the right inboard engine. As the whirling prop detached, it left behind a frightening tear below the cockpit. Then a second engine also choked out. The big aircraft lost altitude and fell behind the formation. Fortunately for the crew, the straggler did not attract the attention of prowling enemy fighters. When Parker entered Allied-controlled territory in France, he decided to make an emergency landing at a former German airdrome near Reims, *Flugplatz A213*. The recently captured airfield now went by the American designation A-62. Parker landed the crippled bomber without incident, taxied off the runway, and shut down the durable, olive drab B-17G for the last time. The crew soon returned to Molesworth.[2] The Flying Fortress remained at A-62 until it was condemned by the Eighth Air Force and later salvaged due to battle damage on November 14, 1944.[3]

The 353rd Fighter Squadron's air echelon arrived from Brittany at its new base, A-66, on September 16, 1944. The strip, near Orconte, France, was only sixty miles southeast of A-62, the airdrome where Major Don Beerbower had been killed.[4] Several days later, Operations Officer Carl Bickel drove a Jeep to A-62. He hoped to locate the wreckage of *Bonnie "B"* and the grave of his friend. He couldn't gather any information from the temporary staff at the base; units were constantly coming and going. Nor could Bickel find a grave or anyone who had any knowledge of a burial recorded at A-62. He drove over to a patch of woods where he believed Beerbower's plane had crashed, but he found nothing. When Bickel returned to the airfield, he stopped to look at a lone B-17 parked nearby. Her tail number was #42-31483.[5] The name on the nose of the aircraft caught his attention–it was Bonnie-"B".[6]

B-17 #42-31483 at A-62

MAYNARD PITCHER PHOTO

Acknowledgements

My research into the life of Major Don M. Beerbower began in 1998. Since then, there has been no person more important to the writing of *The Oranges are Sweet* than Don's wife, Elayne. We had numerous interviews and exchanged many letters before her death in 2010. Elayne's decision to allow me to use portions of her husband's diary for this book provided valuable historical information about him and his colleagues in the 353rd Fighter Squadron.

Many other people helped me along the way. My parents, Archie and Jean Sailer, uncle and aunt, Chet and Vi Sailer, Marshall Hankerson, and Darrel and Arlene Beerbower all provided interviews, memoirs, photographs, and correspondence that greatly aided me in this effort. Arlene's willingness to allow me to use Don's letters to Darrel and herself was a very important contribution of primary source documents. Others familiar with the Hill City community provided useful information. These included Bill and Esther Lange, Helen Averill, Clark Rice, and Don Kitzrow, a friend who generously helped me on many occasions.

I am very grateful for the interviews, photographs, and correspondence from 354th Fighter Group members Willie Y. Anderson, Jack Bradley, Lowell Brueland, James Cannon, George Chassey, Don Chisholm, Ken Dahlberg, Bud Deeds, Elmer Fechtner, Fred Fehsenfeld, Nathan Glick, Clayton Kelly Gross, John Mattie, Jack Miller, Ed Regis, F. Michael Rogers, Richard Springer, Chuck Tighe, and Michael Triventi. Jim Cannon's detailed answers to my never-ending questions made it easier for me to understand the finer points of aerial combat. I will always cherish his friendship.

Doris Bickel, Dorothy Cannon, and Naomi Langran were also most helpful to me. Doris and her son, Peter, graciously allowed me to use Carl Bickel's fine memoir as a resource for this book. In addition, Raymond Panter provided background information about Leon Panter, and Tripp Alyn furnished important details and images about Wallace Emmer.

Clarence E. "Bud" Anderson gave me timely assistance whenever I needed it, and Bradford Shwedo provided data about Allied intercepts of German radio transmissions in 1944. William C. Healy helped me understand the aerial logistics involved in the strategic bombing of Germany. I want to thank Elizabeth Sosin for arranging my in-depth interview with him.

History cannot be written without access to archival records. The following individuals provided me critical and timely support: Archie Difante, Dr. Daniel

Haulman, Anne O'Connor, and Patsy Robertson at the Air Force Historical Research Agency; Shirley Davies with the Aitkin County Historical Society; Bob Zosel from the Wadena County Historical Society, and Robin Cooksin and Timothy Nenniger at the National Archives and Records Administration. I cannot adequately express my gratitude for the many hours Anne O'Connor committed to this project while I was writing the initial draft of the manuscript between 2007 and 2009, and to Archie Difante in 2010 and 2011. Becky Jordan at Parks Library, Iowa State University, never failed to locate information, find key photographs, and answer my numerous questions.

I am indebted to Daniel Lemaire for arranging the assistance I received from Lieutenant Peron at Base aerienne 112, Reims, France, and Chantal Lemaire for information about her father-in-law, Mancel Lemaire. The translation of French correspondence by Danielle Sailer and Gail Stevens aided me greatly. I very much appreciate the photographic contributions from Linda Kirk, Summer Johnson, Jeff, and Joe Sailer, drawings by Jay and John Sailer, reference research by Tony Sailer, and computer support from Michael Huerbin.

I want to thank Ethelyn Pearson for never wavering in her belief I should write *The Oranges are Sweet*, and Darrel Janson for his passion about aviation history and for loaning me many of his books.

Bonnie Beerbower Hansen, Norley Hansen, Melanie Olson, Dawn Monrean, George Hankerson, Linda Beerbower, and Cathryn Day provided important photographs and images from their family collections. Albert "Ben" Beerbower sent me photographs, letters, genealogy records, and memories. I very much appreciate his assistance and friendship. The steady support of the Beerbower family encouraged me more than they realize. Without it, I could not have written this book.

The publication management, map creation, and book design of Chip Borkenhagen, production artistry by Jean Borkenhagen, editing of Jon Eastman, indexing of Jeff Evans, artwork of Ron Finger, website development by David Huerbin, proofreading by Tenlee Lund, and the skilled work of many people at Bang Printing, provided critical professional support to me. Chip Borkenhagen and I have "soldiered" together for the past two very busy years. The book's quality is a reflection of the dedication of this fine artist, craftsman, and friend.

David Anderson's detailed model of *Bonnie "B"* contributed significantly to the book's cover.

I would be remiss if I did not acknowledge my history professors at Moorhead State College in Moorhead, Minnesota, who between 1965 and 1969 taught me how to research, document, interpret, and write about the past. I am also indebted to the many instructor pilots and command pilots I flew with as a U.S. Army aviator. What I learned from them helped me relate to, and express, Don Beerbower's experiences in flying school and in combat. I especially want to cite the example of courage and craftsmanship set for me by Aircraft Commander James Ellsworth on a mission to Dam Doi, South Vietnam, on September 15, 1970, when we spent nine hours in the air, offered assistance to downed U.S. Navy helicopter gunship pilots, and flew through heavy nighttime monsoon rains to return to our base at Bien Hoa.

Thank you to the many unnamed individuals who assisted with this endeavor, and finally, for the quiet support and patience of my wife, Lois, which provided the tonic I needed to complete *The Oranges are Sweet*.

Notes

Abbreviations:

AFHRA	Air Force Historical Research Agency
AR	Accident Report
CMS	Combat Mission Schedule
DMB	Don Merrill Beerbower
ER	Encounter Report
IARC	Individual Aircraft Record Card
IDPF	Individual Deceased Personnel File
ISU	Iowa State University
MACR	Missing Air Crew Report
MF	Microfilm
NARA	National Archives and Records Administration
NPRC	National Personnel Records Center
OR	Operations Report
RG	Record Group
WWII AAF	World War II Army Air Force(s)

For additional abbreviations, see page 442.

Part One
page 1

1. 354th Fighter Group Staff, "Operations Report A, No. 340," (Microfilm B0312, Air Force Historical Research Agency).
2. 353rd Fighter Squadron Staff, "Unit History," (MF A0782-A, AFHRA), 196, 197, and World War II Army Air Forces, "354th FG, 353rd FS Staff, Combat Mission Schedule, No. 192," (Record Group 18, National Archives and Records Administration).

Chapter 1
pages 2-8

1. Esther and William Lange, ed., *The Hill City Saga*, (Self-published articles from the *Hill City News*, 1989), 16, and *Hill City News*, October 27, 1955.
2. Ibid., 16, and October 26, 1939.
3. Ibid., 57.
4. Robert N. Lemen III, *The Rabey Line – Being an Account of the Life and Death of a Short-Line Railroad in the Minnesota Northwoods*, (Self-published, 1970), 15.
5. Lange, *The Hill City Saga*, 10A.
6. Ibid., 46-47.
7. Marshall R. Hankerson, *Marshall Hankerson - Reflections: The Beerbowers, Hanker-*

sons and Sailers of Hill City, transcript of a video tape interview with the author, April 7, 2000.
8. Lange, The *Hill City Saga*, 90A-94, 116.
9. William F. Kucera [Kutcher], "World War I Military Service Record," (Minnesota Historical Society).
10. Stan Watson, *Precious Moments – The History of Spang Community*, (Self-published, 1993), 103 and Elayne A. Beerbower, letter to the author, January 20, 2007.
11. Albert B. Beerbower, "Beerbower Genealogy Records," (Personal Collection).
12. Don M. Beerbower, "Birth Certificate No. 14923, 1921," (Saskatchewan Department of Health).
13. Robert C. Zosel, interview with the author, February 28, 2000 (Wadena County Historical Society), and Darrel W. Beerbower, letters to the author, January 15 and May 14, 1999.

CHAPTER 2
pages 9-16

1. Chester T. Sailer, *Sergeant Chet Sailer – Reflections: A Third Army Soldier in W.W. II from "The Bulge" to Czechoslovakia*, transcript of an audio tape interview with the author, January 27, 1995, and Archie G. Sailer, *This is My Life*, (Personal Memoir, 1990).
2. Lemen, *The Rabey Line*, 29.
3. Samuel Eliot Morison and Henry Steele Commager, *The Growth of the American Republic*, Vol. 2, (New York: Oxford University Press, 1962), 646.
4. Sailer, *This is My Life*.
5. Morison and Commager, *The Growth of the American Republic*, 642.
6. *Hill City News*, May 19, 1932.
7. Hankerson, interview, April 7, 2000.
8. Lemen, *The Rabey Line*, 30.
9. Hankerson, interview, February 6, 2007.
10. Ibid., interviews, April 7, 2000 and February 6, 2007.
11. Ibid.
12. Elayne Beerbower, interview with the author, September 20, 2006.
13. Hankerson, letter to the author, November 23, 2006.
14. Hankerson, interview, April 7, 2000.
15. *Hill City News*, July 1, 1931.
16. Ibid., October 27, 1955.
17. Darrel Beerbower, (Personal Memoir, 1996).
18. *Hill City News*, July 7, 1932.
19. Ibid., August 11, 1932 and *Minnesota Legionnaire*, August 3, August 10, and August 17, 1932.
20. Darrel Beerbower, (Personal Memoir).
21. *Hill City News*, June, 9, 1932.
22. Hankerson, letter, January 14, 2007.
23. Ibid., interview, April 7, 2000.
24. Sailer, *This is my Life*.
25. Frank Dichtel, *Memories at Age 94*, (Personal Memoir, 1986) and Viola Dichtel

Sailer, interview with the author, September 28, 2009.

Chapter 3
pages 17-22

1. Lemen, *The Rabey Line*, 30.
2. Hankerson, letter, January 14, 2007.
3. Ibid., interview, April 7, 2000.
4. Ibid.
5. DMB, "Membership Roll – 1933," (United Methodist Church), and Helen Averill, letter to the author, February 18, 1999.
6. Lange, *The Hill City Saga*, 16A, 17A.
7. Hankerson, letter, November 23, 2006.
8. *Hill City News*, June 18, 1942.
9. Ibid., January 28 and November 18, 1937, March 3, June 2, June 9, and November 24, 1938.
10. Ibid., February 2, 1939.
11. Ted S. Pettit, ed., *Handbook For Boys*, (New Brunswick, NJ: Boys Scouts of America, 1955), 19.
12. *Hill City News*, March 2 and May 25, 1939.
13. Ibid., March 23, 1939.
14. DMB, "School Records," (Hill City High School), and Bonnie Harcey, letter to the author, January 27, 1999.
15. *Hill City News*, May 25, 1939.
16. Ibid., June 8, 1939.
17. Elayne Beerbower, letter, January 12, 2007.
18. Darrel Beerbower, (Personal Memoir).

Chapter 4
pages 23-34

1. *Hill City News*, October 19, 1939.
2. Ibid., October 26, 1939.
3. Ibid., May 30, July 11, September 19 and November 14, 1940.
4. Ibid., May 8, 1941.
5. Hankerson, letters, January 14 and February 1, 2007.
6. Elayne Beerbower, letter, January 12, 2007.
7. Ibid., January 20, 2007.
8. *Hill City News*, January 25, April 4 and June 20, 1940.
9. Darrel Beerbower, letter, November 29, 1998; Hankerson, letter, March 27, 2007; Clark Rice, letter to the author, August 23, 2007.
10. *Hill City News*, September 19, 1940.
11. Arlene M. Beerbower, letter to the author, October 1, 2006.
12. Elayne Beerbower, interviews, June 2, 1999 and September 20, 2006.
13. Ibid., letters, January 12 and January 20, 2007.
14. DMB, "Academic Records," (Iowa State University), and Becky S. Jordan, letter to

the author, April 19, 2007.
15. Albert B. Beerbower, electronic correspondence to the author, February 28, 2007.
16. Darrel Beerbower, (Personal Memoir).
17. Morison and Commager, *The Growth of the American Republic*, 768.
18. *Hill City News*, October 10, 1940.
19. Jordan, letter, April 19, 2007.
20. DMB, "Academic Records," (ISU).
21. Elayne Beerbower, interview, September 20, 2006 and letter, February 5, 2007.
22. *Hill City News*, March 27, 1941.
23. DMB, letter to Darrel and Arlene Beerbower, June 18 and July 6, 1942.
24. *Hill City News*, June 19, July 10 and September 4, 1941.
25. Hankerson, interview, April 7, 2000.
26. *Hill City News*, June 13, 1940, October 23, 1941 and April 23, 1942.
27. Elayne Beerbower, interview, September 20, 2006.
28. Darrel Beerbower, (Personal Memoir).
29. DMB, "Academic Records," (ISU).
30. Ibid., "Military Service Record: Physical Examination for Flying, October 21, 1941," (National Personnel Records Center); Rice, letter, August 23, 2007.
31. *Hill City News*, November 20, 1941.
32. Ibid., December 11, 1941 and April 23, 1942.
33. DMB, "Academic Records," (ISU).
34. Ibid., letter, September 25, 1943.
35. *Hill City News*, January 8, 1942.

Chapter 5
pages 35-39

1. Morison and Commager, *The Growth of the American Republic*, 790.
2. Ibid., 785.
3. DMB and Glenn J. McKean, "Academic Records," (ISU).
4. Memorial Union, "About Memorial Union," (ISU). www.mu.iastate.edu/about.php.
5. Sweeting, C. G., *Combat Flying Clothing: Army Air Forces Clothing during World War II*, (Washington, D.C.: Smithsonian Institution Press, 1984), 21, 22.
6. DMB, "Military Service Records," (NPRC), 1.
7. Ibid., 2.
8. Ibid., "Military Service Records," (NPRC), 2, 6.
9. *Hill City News*, January 29 and February 5, 1942.
10. DMB, "Military Service Records," (NPRC), 16.
11. Williams Field, www.azdeq.gov/environ/waste/sps/download/phoenix/wafb.pdf.
12. DMB, Diary, August 22, 1942.
13. Ibid., "Military Service Records," and "Physical Examination for Flying, February 11, 1942," (NPRC), 17.
14. Santa Ana Army Air Base, "History of the SAAAB," (Costa Mesa Historical Society). www.costamesahistory.org/saaab.htm.
15. DMB, Diary, August 22, 1942.

16. Josie F. Beerbower, letter to Wayne and Elizabeth Beerbower, October 15, 1942.
17. DMB, "Military Service Records," (NPRC), 18.

Chapter 6
pages 40-48

1. Thunderbird Field, "The Road to Modern Glendale," (City of Glendale). www.glendaleaz.com./kidzone/glendalehistory.cfm.
2. Josie Beerbower, letter to Wayne and Elizabeth Beerbower, October 15, 1942.
3. Ibid., October 15, 1942.
4. David Donald, ed., *American Warplanes of World War II – Combat Aircraft of the United States Army Air Force, US Navy, US Marines, 1941-1945*, (New York: Barnes & Noble Books, 2000), 34, 35.
5. Sandra D. Merril, *Donald's Story – Captain Donald R. Emerson: A 4th Fighter Group Pilot Remembered*, (Berlin, MD: Tebidine Publishing, 1996), 90, 93.
6. DMB, Diary – Introduction: My Buddies and John T. Opsvig, Arthur W. Owen, William J. Purvis, eds., *LUKE FIELD*, Vol. Two, No. Four, (Phoenix: Published by the Aviation Cadets of Class 42-I, 1942, AFHRA).
7. DMB, Diary, August 22, 1942.

Chapter 7
pages 49-56

1. Minter Field, "Historic California Posts: Minter Field," (California State Military Museum). www.militarymuseum.org/MinterField.html.
2. Donald, *American Warplanes of World War II*, 251, 252.
3. DMB, Diary – Introduction: My Buddies, Officers.
4. WWII AAF, USAF Flight Safety Records, "Accident Report 42-6-9-4," (IRIS No. 00877046, AFHRA).
5. Elayne Beerbower, interviews, September 20, 2006 and May 25, 2007.
6. DMB, Diary, August 22, 1942.
7. Lou Thole, *Forgotten Fields of America*, Vol. 4, (Missoula, MT: Pictorial History Publishing Company, 2007), vii.
8. Josie Beerbower, letter, October 15, 1942.
9. DMB, Diary, August 22, 1942.
10. Josie Beerbower, letter, October 15, 1942.

Chapter 8
pages 57-68

1. Robin Higham, ed., *Flying American Combat Aircraft in WWII : 1939-45*, (Mechanicsburg, PA: Stackpole Books, 2004), 226, 228.
2. DMB, Diary, August 22, 1942.
3. Luke Field, "U.S. Air Force Fact Sheet – Luke AFB History," (Luke AFB). www.luke.af.mil/factsheets/factsheet.print.asp?fsID=5049&page=1.
4. Opsvig, Owen, Purvis, *LUKE FIELD*.

5. DMB, Diary – Introduction: Officers.
6. James Cannon, letter to the author, October 21, 2005.
7. Clarence E. Anderson and Joseph P. Hamelin, *To Fly and Fight – Memoirs of a Triple Ace*, (Pacifica, CA: Pacifica Military History, 1990), 45.
8. DMB, Diary, August 28, 1942.
9. Ibid., August 31 and September 1-6, 1942.
10. Ibid., August 31 and September 3, 1942.
11. Ibid., September 11, 1942.
12. Ibid., September 15 and September 22, 1942.
13. Opsvig, Owen, Purvis, *Luke Field*.
14. DMB, Diary, September 23 and 24, 1942.
15. Higham, *Flying American Combat Aircraft in WWII*, 231.
16. Clarence W. Beerbower, letter to Wayne Beerbower, October 13, 1942.
17. Elayne Beerbower, interviews, June 2, 1999 and September 20, 2006.
18. William Y. Anderson, *Captain Willie Y. Anderson – Reflections: P-51 Mustang Fighter Ace 1941 – 1945*, transcript of an audio tape interview with the author, January 6, 2000.
19. DMB, letter, October 13, 1942.
20. Ibid., October 15, 1942.
21. *Hill City News*, October 8, 1942.
22. DMB, Diary, September 29, 1942.

Chapter 9
pages 69-74

1. Josie Beerbower, letter, October 15, 1942.
2. DMB, Diary, October 1, 2, 1942.
3. Ibid., October 2, 1942.
4. Ibid., October 3, 1942.
5. Ibid., October 4, 1942.
6. Hamilton Field, "Historic California Posts, Camps, Stations and Airfields: Hamilton Air Force Base," (California State Military Museum). www.militarymuseum.org/HamiltonAFB.html.
7. DMB, Diary, October 5, 1942.
8. Mauer Mauer, ed., *Air Combat Units of World War II*, (Washington D.C.: U.S. Government Printing Office, 1983), 209.
9. Bill Gunston, *The Anatomy of Aircraft*, (Stamford, CT: Longmeadow Press, 1988), 64-67.
10. Anderson and Hamelin, *To Fly and Fight*, 42, 46.
11. DMB, Diary, October 13, 1942.
12. Anderson and Hamelin, *To Fly and To Fight*, 48, 49.
13. 354th FG Staff, "Unit Historical Data Sheet: 15 November 1942 to 30 September 1943," (MF B0312).
14. William A. Ong, *Target Luftwaffe – The Tragedy and the Triumph of the World War II Air Victory*, (Kansas City, KS: Lowell Press, 1981), 93.
15. Ibid., 142, 144, 145.

16. IV Fighter Command Staff, "Biographical Questionnaire for Officers of IV Fighter Command: Owen Seaman," (MF B0311, AFHRA).
17. Ong, *Target Luftwaffe*, 142-144.
18. 354th FG Staff, "Unit Historical Data Sheet," (MF B0312).
19. James Cannon, *Lieutenant Colonel James Cannon – World War II P-51 Mustang Fighter Pilot: The 353rd Fighter Squadron*, transcript of an audio tape interview with the author, June 23, 2003.

Chapter 10
pages 75-82

1. DMB, Diary, January 16-18, 1943.
2. Anderson and Hamelin, *To Fly and Fight*, 54-55.
3. Jack T. Bradley, *Colonel Jack Bradley – Reflections: World War II P-51 Mustang Fighter Ace*, transcript of an audio tape interview with the author, January 9, 2000.
4. Cannon, interview, June 23, 2003.
5. IV FC Staff, "Biographical Questionnaire: Seaman."
6. Cannon, interview, June 23, 2003.
7. DMB, Diary, January 20, 1943.
8. 354th FG Staff, "Unit Historical Data Sheet," (MF B0312).
9. 353rd FS Staff, "Unit History," 63.
10. DMB, Diary, Introduction: My Buddies.
11. 353rd FS Staff, "Unit History," 63.
12. WWII AAF, Safety Records, "AR 43-2-5-6," (IRIS No. 00877114, AFHRA).
13. 353rd FS Staff, "Unit History," 64.
14. Ong, *Target Luftwaffe*, 155, 156.
15. Cannon, letter, March 14, 2006.
16. Anderson, interview, January 6, 2000.
17. IV FC Staff, "Biographical Questionnaire: Kenneth R. Martin."
18. Cannon, interview, June 23, 2003.
19. Bradley, interview, January 9, 2000.
20. John D. Mattie, *Lieutenant Colonel John Mattie – World War II P-51 Mustang Fighter Pilot: Tonopah, Nevada to Barth, Germany*, transcript of an audio tape interview with the author, July 15, 2003.
21. DMB, Diary, February 16, 1943.
22. Ibid., February 26 and March 1, 1943.

Chapter 11
pages 83-90

1. DMB, Diary, March 4 and 7, 1943.
2. Cannon, letter, May 1, 2006.
3. Anderson and Hamelin, *To Fly and Fight*, 60.
4. WWII AAF, Safety Records, "AR 43-3-20-4," (IRIS No. 00877128, AFHRA).
5. 353rd FS Staff, "Unit History," 67.
6. Ibid.

7. *Hill City News*, June 3, 1943.
8. WWII AAF, Safety Records, "AR 43-4-16-32," (IRIS No. 00877138, AFHRA).
9. Richard R. Springer, letter to the author, July 20, 2006.
10. Cannon, interview, June 23, 2003.
11. WWII AAF, Safety Records, "AR 43-4-16-32," (IRIS No. 00877138, AFHRA).
12. Mattie, interview, July 15, 2003.
13. Cannon, letter, June 5, 2003.
14. 353rd FS Staff, "Unit History," 68.
15. DMB, Diary, May 7 and May 9, 1943.

Chapter 12
pages 91-95

1. DMB, Diary, June 25, 1943.
2. Ibid.
3. Hankerson, letters, November 23, 2006 and February 1, 2007.
4. DMB, Diary, June 25, 1943.
5. Elayne Beerbower, interview, September 20, 2006.
6. DMB, Diary, June 25, 1943.
7. *Hill City News*, May 27, 1943.
8. DMB, Diary, June 25, 1943.
9. Ibid.
10. *Hill City News*, May 27, June 3 and June 10, 1943.
11. James M. Landis, Director, Office of Civilian Defense, "Get Ready To Be Bombed," *The American Magazine*, June 1943.
12. *Hill City News*, July 30, 1942.
13. Ibid, January 21, July 1, 1943 and November 16, 1944.
14. James H. Howard, *Roar of the Tiger*, (New York: Pocket Books, 1993), 5-39, 58-87, 150-189.
15. 356th FS Staff, "Unit History," (MF A0783, AFHRA) 9, 13.
16. *Hill City News*, June 10, June 17 and July 15, 1943.
17. DMB, Diary, June 25, 1943.
18. Ibid., June 25, 1943.
19. 353rd FS Staff, "Unit History," 11, 12.

Chapter 13
pages 96-106

1. DMB, Diary, July 1, 1943.
2. Elayne Beerbower, letter, September 1, 2005 and interview, September 20, 2006.
3. WWII AAF, Safety Records, "AR 44-7-4-14," (IRIS No. 00877169, AFHRA).
4. 353rd FS Staff, "Unit History," 14.
5. DMB, Diary, Introduction: My Buddies, July 5 and August 15, 1943.
6. Mattie, letter, May 8, 2003 and interview, July 15, 2003.
7. 353rd FS Staff, "Unit History," 12.
8. Carl G. Bickel, *Before the Contrails Fade Away*, (Personal Memoir, 2005), 125, 126.

9. DMB, Diary, August 15, 1943.
10. Elayne Beerbower, interviews, May 7 and June 2, 1999 and September 20, 2006.
11. DMB, Diary, August 15 and August 18, 1943.
12. *Hill City News*, August 19, 1943.
13. Bickel, *Before the Contrails Fade Away*, 126.
14. Edward R. Regis, *Lieutenant Colonel Edward Regis – World War II Fighter Pilot: The 353rd Fighter Squadron*, transcript of an audio tape interview with the author, June 30, 2003.
15. Bickel, *Before the Contrails Fade Away*, 123.
16. DMB, Diary, September 10, 1943.
17. J. Ward Boyce, ed., *American Fighter Aces Album*, (Mesa, AZ: The American Fighter Aces Association, 1996), 176.
18. Regis, interview, June 30, 2003.
19. Anderson, interview, January 6, 2000.
20. Opsvig, Owen, Purvis, *LUKE FIELD*.
21. Cannon, letter, May 30, 2006.
22. DMB, letter to Darrel and Arlene Beerbower, September 25, 1943.
23. *Hill City News*, September 23, 1943.
24. Hankerson, letter, November 23, 2006.
25. DMB, Diary, September 25, 1943.
26. Ibid., letter, September 25, 1943.
27. Elayne Beerbower, letters, July 11, 2007 and February 11, 2008.
28. DMB, letter, September 25, 1943.
29. Ibid., Diary, September 25, 1943.
30. Ibid., letter, September 25, 1943.
31. Ibid.
32. Mattie, interview, July 15, 2003.

Part Two
page 107

1. 354th FG Staff, "OR A, Nos. 339 and 340," (MF B0312), XIX Tactical Air Command Staff, "354th FG, Operations Order No. 9, Mission X51-1 and Mission X51-1: Summary," (IRIS No. 23856, AFHRA).
2. Felix Michael Rogers, *General F. Michael Rogers – World War II P-51 Mustang Fighter Ace: The 353rd Fighter Squadron Mission Near Reims, France, August 9, 1944*, transcript of an audio tape interview with the author, June 23, 1999.
3. 354th FG Staff, "OR A, No. 340," (MF B0312), and WWII AAF, "354th FG, 353rd FS Staff, CMS No. 192," (RG 18, NARA).
4. Ibid., "OR A, No. 339," (MF B0312).

Chapter 14
pages 108-119

1. 356th FS Staff, "Unit History." 27.
2. Clayton Kelly Gross, *Live Bait – WWII Memoirs of an Undefeated Fighter Ace*,

(Portland, OR: Inkwater Press, 2006), 94.
3. DMB, Diary, October 6-8, 1943.
4. Camp Kilmer, "Information Office Fact Sheet – 1958," (Rutgers University). www2.scc.rutgers.edu/njh/WW2/ww2women/kilmer.htm.
5. Sailer, *This is my Life*.
6. DMB, Diary, October 11, 13 and 15, 1943.
7. John E. Johnson, *Full Circle – The Tactics of Air Fighting: 1914 -1964*, (New York: Ballantine Books, 1964), 221-226.
8. Samuel Eliot Morison, *The History of the United States Naval Operations in World War II – The Invasion of France and Germany: 1944 – 1945*, Vol. XI, (Edison, NJ: Castle Books, 2001), 19.
9. *United States Naval Administration in World War II – History of Convoy and Routing: 1939-1945*, (Washington D.C.: Commander in Chief, United States Fleet, Navy Department Library, 1945), 44, 45.
10. Samuel Eliot Morison, *The History of the United States Naval Operations in World War II – The Atlantic Battle Won: May 1943 – May 1945*, Vol. X, (Edison, NJ: Castle Books, 2001), 244-248, 365.
11. Samuel Eliot Morison, *The History of the United States Naval Operations in World War II – The Battle of the Atlantic: 1939 – 1943*, Vol. I, (Edison, NJ: Castle Books, 2001), 334.
12. Arthur F. Brown, ed., *History in the Sky: 354th Pioneer Mustang Fighter Group*, (San Angelo, TX: Newsfoto Publishing Co., 1946).
13. Athlone Castle, "*Athlone Castle 1936*," (The Ocean Liner Virtual Museum). www.oceanlinermuseum.co.uk/Athlone%20Castle.html.
14. DMB, Diary, October 22, 1943.
15. U.S. Tenth Fleet Staff, "Records of the Tenth Fleet, Convoy Report: UT-4," (RG 38, NARA).
16. Morison, *The Atlantic Battle Won: May 1943 – May 1945*, 133, 134, 230.
17. U.S. Tenth Fleet Staff, "Convoy Report: UT-4."
18. USS Texas, "Battleship Texas Historic Site," (Texas Parks and Wildlife Department). www.tpwd.state.tx.us/spdest/findadest/parks/battleship.
19. U.S. Tenth Fleet Staff, "Convoy Report: UT-4."
20. Howard, *Roar of the Tiger*, 195-196.
21. Bickel, *Before the Contrails Fade Away*, 127.
22. WWII AAF, "Individual Deceased Personnel File: Wah Kau Kong," (United States Army Human Resources Command).
23. Rogers, interview, June 23, 1999.
24. U.S. Tenth Fleet Staff, "Convoy Report: UT-4."
25. Richard E. Turner, *Big Friend, Little Friend – Memoirs of a World War II Fighter Pilot*, (Garden City, NY: Doubleday, 1969), 17.
26. Regis, interview, June 30, 2003.
27. Morison, *The Atlantic Battle Won: May 1943 – May 1945*, 162, 188, 371.
28. Turner, *Big Friend, Little Friend*, 16.
29. U.S. Tenth Fleet Staff, "Convoy Report: UT-4."
30. Bickel, *Before the Contrails Fade Away*, 129.
31. Turner, *Big Friend, Little Friend*, 17.

32. U.S. Tenth Fleet Staff, "Convoy Report: UT-4."
33. 353rd FS Staff, "Unit History," 82.
34. Turner, *Big Friend, Little Friend*, 18, 19.
35. Regis, interview, June 30, 2003.
36. Turner, *Big Friend, Little Friend*, 18, 19.

Chapter 15
pages 120-130

1. War and Navy Departments, *A Short Guide to Great Britain*, (Washington D.C.: U.S. Government Printing Office, 1943), 1-22.
2. Anderson, interview, January 31, 2000.
3. Lewis H. Brereton, *The Brereton Diaries – The War in the Air in the Pacific, Middle East and Europe: 3 October 1941 – 8 May 1945*, (New York: William Morrow and Company, 1946), 217, 218, 221.
4. Bradley, interview, January 9, 2000.
5. Bill Gunston, *The Anatomy of Aircraft*, 80-83.
6. Francis H. Dean, *America's Hundred Thousand – The U.S. Production Fighter Aircraft of World War II*, (Atglen, PA: Schiffer Publishing, Ltd., 1997), 323-326, 330, 331.
7. DMB, Diary, November 12, 1943.
8. Elayne Beerbower, "27th ATG Form 025," (Personal Collection).
9. Leon H. Panter, "World War II Army Enlistment Records," (RG 64, NARA).
10. DMB, letter, August 7, 1944.
11. Cannon, letter, August 4, 2003.
12. Roger A. Freeman, *The Ninth Air Force in Colour: UK and the Continent – World War Two*, (New York: Sterling Publishing Co., 1995), 61.
13. WWII AAF, "Individual Aircraft Record Card: P-51B #43-12457," (MF ACR #82, AFHRA).
14. Donald, *American Warplanes of World War II*, 208-210.
15. Bradley, interview, June 27, 1999.
16. Howard, *Roar of the Tiger*, 198.
17. Ibid., 197, 198.
18. 353rd FS Staff, "Unit History," 79.
19. Cannon, letter, December 7, 2005.
20. DMB, Diary, November 29 and 30, 1943.
21. Boyce, *American Fighter Aces Album*, 92.
22. Turner, *Big Friend, Little Friend*, 20-22.
23. DMB, Diary, November 29, 1943.
24. WWII AAF, "354th FG, 353rd FS Staff, CMS No. 1," (RG 18, NARA).
25. Cannon, interview, June 23, 2003.
26. Turner, *Big Friend, Little Friend*, 22, 23.
27. 354th FG Staff, "MR, December 1, 1943," (MF B0312).
28. 353rd FS Staff, "Unit History," 83.
29. Turner, *Big Friends, Little Friends*, 25.
30. Cannon, letter, November 16, 2005.
31. Brown, *History in the Sky*.

32. WWII AAF, "CMS No. 1" (RG 18, NARA).

Chapter 16
pages 131-141

1. WWII AAF, "CMS No. 2," (RG 18, NARA).
2. DMB, Diary, December 5, 1943.
3. Ibid., November 29 and December 8, 1943.
4. WWII AAF, "CMS No. 3," (RG 18, NARA).
5. Harry E. Slater, *Lingering Contrails of THE BIG SQUARE A: A History of the 94th Bomb Group (H) 1942-1945*, (Nashville, TN: Carley Publishing, 1980), 23, 140, 141.
6. William C. Healy, *Lieutenant Colonel William C. Healy – Reflections: B-17 Flying Fortress Pilot 1941-1945*, transcript of a video tape interview with the author, August 5, 2001.
7. WWII AAF, "CMS No. 4," (RG 18, NARA).
8. 354th FG Staff, "MR, December 13, 1943," (MF B0312).
9. WWII AAF, "Missing Air Crew Report–1464," (RG 92, NARA).
10. 354th FG Staff, "Encounter Reports: Glenn T. Eagleston and Wallace N. Emmer, December 13, 1943," (MF B0312).
11. Boyce, *American Fighter Aces Album*, 170.
12. Cannon, interview, June 23, 2003.
13. 354th FG Staff, "ER: Eagleston, December 13, 1943," (MF B0312).
14. 353rd FS Staff, "ER: Eagleston, December 13, 1943."
15. Cannon, interview, June 23, 2003.
16. Bill Gunston, *The Anatomy of Aircraft*, 56-63.
17. 353rd FS Staff, "Unit History," 80.
18. WWII AAF, "CMS, No. 5," (RG 18, NARA).
19. 354th FG Staff, "MR, December 16, 1943," (MF B0312).

Chapter 17
pages 142-151

1. WWII AAF, CMS No. 6," (RG 18, NARA).
2. Roger A. Freeman, *The Mighty Eighth: A History of the Units, Men and Machines of the US 8th Air Force*, (New York: Sterling Publishing Co., 2001), 246.
3. 96th BG (H) Staff, "Bremen Mission, December 20, 1943," (MF B0191, AFHRA).
4. 338th FS Staff, "Mission Summary Report, December 20, 1943," (MF A0776, AFHRA).
5. 354th FG Staff, "MR, December 20, 1943," (MF B0312).
6. 96th BG (H) Staff, "Bremen Mission, December 20, 1943."
7. 338th FS Staff, "Mission Summary Report, December 20, 1943."
8. 354th FG Staff, "MR, December 20, 1943" (MF B0312).
9. Ibid., "ER: Jack T. Bradley, James J. Parsons and Thomas S. Varney, December 20, 1943," (MF B0312).
10. Marshall Stelzriede, *Marshall Stelzriede's Wartime Story: The Experiences of a B-17*

Navigator during World War II, www.stelzriede.com.
11. WWII AAF, "IARC: B-17F #42-3288," (MF ACR #41, AFHRA).
12. Ibid., "MACR–1704," (RG 92, NARA).
13. 354th FG Staff, "ER: Varney, December 20, 1943," (MF B0312).
14. Ibid., "ER: Parsons, December 20, 1943."
15. WWII AAF, "MACR–1704," (RG 92, NARA).
16. 338th FS Staff, "Mission Summary Report, December 20, 1943."
17. WWII AAF, "IDPF: James W. Kerley," (USAHRC).
18. Ibid.
19. Ibid., "MACR–1704," (RG 92, NARA).
20. Mattie, interview, July 15, 2003.
21. WWII AAF, "IDPF: Owen M. Seaman," (USAHRC).
22. Cannon, letter, October 21, 2005.
23. WWII AAF, "IDPF: Seaman," (USAHRC).
24. Ibid., "CMS No. 6," (RG 18, NARA).
25. 96th BG (H) Staff, "Bremen Mission, December 20, 1943."
26. 354th FG Staff, "MR, December 20, 1943," (MF B0312).
27. WWII AAF, "CMS No. 7," (RG 18, NARA).
28. 353rd FS Staff, "Unit History," 96.
29. WWII AAF, "IDPF: Melvin M. Brunner and Kerley," (USAHRC) and "MACR–1704," (RG 92, NARA).
30. Ibid., "IDPF: Seaman," (USAHRC).

Chapter 18
pages 152-160

1. 354th FG Staff, "MR, December 24, 1943," (MF B0312).
2. Cannon, interview, June 23, 2003.
3. Brereton, *The Brereton Diaries,* 227, 228.
4. WWII AAF, CMS No. 8," (RG 18, NARA).
5. 354th FG Staff, "MR, December 24, 1943," (MF B0312).
6. 353rd FS Staff, "Unit History," 84.
7. *Hill City News,* December 23 and December 30, 1943.
8. Elayne Beerbower, letter, March 24, 2008; Arlene Beerbower, letter, March 26, 2008; Hankerson, letter, March 27, 2008.
9. *Hill City News,* January 13, 1944.
10. 353rd FS Staff, "Unit History," 97.
11. Cannon, interview, June 23, 2003.
12. 353rd FS Staff, "Unit History," 84.
13. 354th FG Staff, "MR, December 30, 1943," (MF B0312).
14. Ibid., "ER: Don M. Beerbower, December 30, 1943," (MF B0312).
15. Ibid., "ER: Carl A. Lind, December 30, 1943," (MF B0312).
16. Cannon, interview, June 23, 2003.
17. Ibid.
18. David Donald, ed., *Warplanes of the Luftwaffe,* (Westport, CT: AIRtime Publishing Inc., 1999), 38-41.

19. Brereton, *The Brereton Diaries*, 231, 232.
20. Ibid., 232.
21. Jonna Doolittle Hoppes, *Calculated Risk: The Extraordinary Life of Jimmy Doolittle – Aviation Pioneer and World War II Hero*, (Santa Monica, CA: Santa Monica Press LLC, 2005), 323-324.
22. WWII AAF, "CMS No. 10," (RG 18, NARA).
23. 354th FG Staff, "MR, December 31, 1943," (MF B0312).
24. WWII AAF, "CMS No. 1-10," (RG 18, NARA).
25. DMB, Diary, January 3, 1944.

Chapter 19
pages 161-175

1. Adolf Galland, *The First and the Last: The Rise and Fall of the German Fighter Forces, 1938-1945*, (New York: Ballantine Books, 1960), 158, 159.
2. WWII AAF, "CMS No. 11," (RG 18, NARA).
3. 354th FG Staff, "MR, January 4, 1944," (MF B0312).
4. 353rd FS Staff, "Unit History," 104.
5. 354th FG Staff, "MR, January 5, 1944," (MF B0312).
6. WWII AAF, "CMS No. 13," (RG 18, NARA).
7. 354th FG Staff, "MR, January 4, 5 and 7, 1944," (MF B0312).
8. WWII AAF, "CMS No. 14," (RG 18, NARA).
9. Brereton, *The Brereton Diaries*, 234.
10. 354th FG Staff, "MR, January 11, 1944," (MF B0312).
11. 353rd FS Staff, "ER: Bradley, January 11, 1944."
12. Donald, *Warplanes of the Luftwaffe*, 71-79, 196-207.
13. 353rd FS Staff, "Unit History," 82.
14. Brereton, *The Brereton Diaries*, 234.
15. 354th FG Staff, "MR, January 11, 1944," (MF B0312).
16. Howard, *Roar of the Tiger*, 232, 289.
17. 353rd FS Staff, "Unit History," 96.
18. Howard, *Roar of the Tiger*, 234.
19. Rogers, interview, June 23, 1999.
20. 353rd FS Staff, "Unit History," 196.
21. Donald J. Chisholm, letter to the author, May 25, 2003.
22. Freeman, *The Mighty Eighth*, 79.
23. WWII AAF, "MACR–1810" (RG 92, NARA).
24. 353rd FS Staff, "Unit History," 96.
25. Ibid., 98, 100, 102.
26. Ibid., 96.
27. Mattie, interview, July 15, 2003.
28. Nathan Glick, letter to the author, May 7, 2008.
29. WWII AAF, "IARC: P-51B #43-12375," (MF ACR #82, AFHRA).
30. Dean, *America's Hundred Thousand*, 323.
31. 353rd FS Staff, "Unit History," 98.
32. Ibid., 97.

33. Freeman, *The Mighty Eighth*, 120.
34. WWII AAF, "MACR–2046," (RG 92, NARA).
35. 353rd FS Staff, "Unit History," 97.

Chapter 20
pages 176-190

1. 353rd FS Staff, "Unit History," 97, 105.
2. IV FC Staff, "Biographical Questionnaire: Jack T. Bradley."
3. Cannon, interview, June 23, 2003.
4. Mattie, interview, July 15, 2003.
5. Rogers, interview, June 23, 1999.
6. Bradley, interview, January 9, 2000.
7. 353rd FS Staff, "Unit History," 105.
8. DMB, Diary, January 29, 1944.
9. 354th FG Staff, "MR, January 29, 1944," (MF B0312).
10. Ibid., "ER: Beerbower, January 29, 1944," (MF B0312).
11. Ibid., "ER: Robert L. Meserve, January 29, 1944," (MF B0312).
12. Ibid., "MR, January 29, 1944," (MF B0312).
13. 353rd FS Staff, "Unit History," 97.
14. 354th FG Staff, "ER: Wah Kau Kong, January 30, 1944," (MF B0312).
15. Donald, *Warplanes of the Luftwaffe*, 250.
16. 353rd FS Staff, "Unit History," 111, 113.
17. 354th FG Staff, "Unit History." (MF B0311), 1784-1785.
18. DMB, Diary, February 6, 1944.
19. 354th FG Staff, "Unit History," (MF B0311), 1785.
20. Freeman, *The Mighty Eighth*, 99, 119, 121.
21. 354th FG Staff, "Unit History," (MF B0311), 1783, 1785.
22. WWII AAF, "CMS No. 23," (RG 18, NARA).
23. Opsvig, Owen, Purvis, *LUKE FIELD*.
24. WWII AAF, "CMS No. 23," (RG 18, NARA).
25. 354th FG Staff, "MR, February 8, 1944," (MF B0312).
26. 353rd FS Staff, "Unit History," 27.
27. DMB, Diary, February 8, 1944.
28. 354th FG Staff, "MR, February 8, 1944," (MF B0312).
29. Anderson and Hamelin, *To Fly and Fight*, 56, 83.
30. 354th FG Staff, "Unit History," (MF B0311), 1785, 1786.
31. Ibid., "MR, February 10, 1944," (MF B0312).
32. Ibid., "Unit History," (MF B0311), 1786.
33. WWII AAF, Safety Records, "AR 44-2-10-509," (IRIS No. 00877269, AFHRA).
34. Ibid., "CMS No. 25," (RG 18, NARA).
35. 354th FG Staff, "MR, February 11, 1944," (MF B0312).
36. WWII AAF, "MACR–2166," (RG 92, NARA).
37. Brereton, *The Brereton Diaries*, 239.
38. 354th FG Staff, "Unit History," (MF B0311), 1786, 1787.
39. Ibid., 1828.

CHAPTER 21
pages 191-206

1. 354th FG Staff, "Unit History," (MF B0311), 1788.
2. Freeman, *The Mighty Eighth*, 107, 112.
3. Ibid., 108, 354th FG, "Unit History," (MF B0311), 1788, and Slater, *Lingering Contrails of THE BIG SQUARE A*, 141, 148, 149.
4. 354th FG Staff, "MR, February 20, 1944," (MF B0312).
5. WWII AAF, "CMS No. 26," (RG 18, NARA).
6. Ibid., "ER: Beerbower, February 20, 1944," (MF B0312).
7. Ibid.
8. 354th FG Staff, "MR, February 20, 1944," (MF B0312), and WWII AAF, "CMS No. 26," (RG 18, NARA).
9. Frank Olynyk, *Stars & Bars: A Tribute to the American Fighter Ace 1920 – 1973*, (London: Grub Street, 1995), 140, 159, 348, 600, 601.
10. WWII AAF, "CMS No. 26," (RG 18, NARA).
11. Olynyk, *Stars & Bars*, 3, 4.
12. Bradley, interview, June 27, 1999.
13. Walter J. Boyne, *Aces in Command: Fighter Pilots as Combat Leaders*, (Dulles, VA: Brassey's, Inc., 2001), vii-viii, 1.
14. 354th FG, "Unit History," (MF B0311), 1802.
15. Ibid., "MR, February 21, 1944," (MF B0312).
16. WWII AAF, "CMS No. 27," (RG 18, NARA).
17. Cannon, interview, June 23, 2003, and letters, August 4, 2003 and June 14, 2004.
18. WWII AAF, "MACR–2329," (RG 92, NARA).
19. Mattie, interview, July 15, 2003.
20. WWII AAF, "MACR–2329," (RG 92, NARA).
21. Mattie, interview, July 15, 2003.
22. Ibid.
23. 354th FG Staff, "ER: Beerbower, February 21, 1944," (MF B0312).
24. WWII AAF, "MACR–2328," (RG 92, NARA).
25. 354th FG Staff, "ER: Beerbower, February 21, 1944," (MF B0312).
26. Ibid., "ER: Don McDowell," (MF B0312).
27. Ibid., "ER: Eagleston," (MF B0312).
28. Ibid., "ER: Beerbower," (MF B0312).
29. Ibid., "ER: McDowell," (MF B0312).
30. 353rd FS Staff, "Unit History," 115, 126.
31. Ibid., 116.
32. WWII AAF, "MACR–2327," (RG 92, NARA).
33. Ibid., "IDPF: Kong," (USAHRC).
34. 353rd FS Staff, "Unit History," 115 and 354th FG Staff, "Unit History," (MF B0311), 1789.
35. 353rd FS Staff, "Unit History," 116.
36. Galland, *The First and the Last*, 167, 168, 195, 199, 237.

Chapter 22
pages 207-220

1. 354th FG Staff, "MR, February 29, 1944," (MF B0312).
2. DMB, Diary, February 29, 1944.
3. Johnson, *Full Circle*, 227-229.
4. DMB, Diary, March 2, 1944.
5. 353rd FS Staff, "Unit History," 116, 124.
6. Freeman, *The Mighty Eighth*, 113.
7. Slater, *Lingering Contrails of THE BIG SQUARE A*, 154.
8. 354th FG Staff, "MR, March 3, 1944," (MF B0312).
9. DMB, Diary, March 3, 1944.
10. WWII AAF, "CMS No. 34," (RG 18, NARA).
11. Ibid., "MACR–2804," (RG 92, NARA).
12. Ibid., "MACR–2805," (RG 92, NARA).
13. 354th FG Staff, "MR, March 4, 1944," (MF B0312).
14. Freeman, *The Mighty Eighth*, 113.
15. *Hill City News*, March 23, 1944.
16. Sailer, *This is my Life*.
17. WWII AAF, "CMS No. 35," (RG 18, NARA).
18. 354th FG Staff, "MR, March 6, 1944," (MF B0312).
19. WWII AAF, "MACR–2803," (RG 92, NARA).
20. 353rd FS Staff, "Unit History," 126.
21. Anderson, interview, January 6, 2000.
22. 353rd FS Staff, "Unit History," 124.
23. Regis, interview, June 30, 2003.
24. Anderson, interview, January 31, 2000.
25. 353rd FS Staff, "Unit History," 123.
26. WWII AAF, "CMS No. 37," (RG 18, NARA).
27. 353rd FS Staff, "Unit History," 110.
28. Regis, interview, June 30, 2003.
29. 353rd FS Staff, "Unit History," 110.
30. Mattie, interview, July 15, 2003.
31. 353rd FS Staff, "Unit History," 124, 125.
32. Mattie, interview, July 15, 2003.
33. Anderson, interview, January 31, 2000.
34. 354th FG Staff, "MR, March 18, 1944," (MF B0312).
35. WWII AAF, "MACR–3152," (RG 92, NARA).
36. 354th FG Staff, "MR, March 18, 1944," (MF B0312).
37. WWII AAF, "CMS Nos. 6, 15, 39, 40," (RG 18, NARA).
38. Ibid., Safety Records, "AR 44-3-19-516," (IRIS No. 00877288, AFHRA).
39. Ibid., "IDPF: James J. Parsons," (USAHRC).
40. Ibid., Safety Records, "AR 44-3-19-516," (IRIS No. 00877288, AFHRA).
41. Anderson, interview, January 6, 2000.

CHAPTER 23
pages 221-238

1. WWII AAF, "CMS Nos. 40-43," (RG 18, NARA).
2. Ibid., "MACR–3277," (RG 92, NARA).
3. 353rd FS Staff, "Unit History," 124.
4. Galland, *The First and the Last*, 205-207.
5. Ken Delve, *D-DAY The Air Battle*, (Ramsbury, UK: The Crowood Press Ltd., 2004), 63-65.
6. WWII AAF, "CMS No. 44," (RG 18, NARA).
7. 353rd FS Staff, "Unit History," 125.
8. Brown, *History in the Sky*.
9. XIX TAC Staff, "History of the XIX Tactical Air Command," (MF B5898), 3, 4.
10. Brereton, *The Brereton Diaries*, 237.
11. 353rd FS Staff, "Unit History," 125, 135.
12. Ibid., 134.
13. Ibid., 41, 122, 139.
14. Freeman, *The Mighty Eighth*, 129-130.
15. 354th FG Staff, "MR, April 8, 1944," (MF B0312).
16. Regis, interview, June 30, 2003.
17. WWII AAF, "MACR–3560," (RG 92, NARA).
18. Gordon Gammack, "I.S.C. Ace's Score: 13½," (*Des Moines Register*, May 23, 1944).
19. Regis, interview, June 30, 2003.
20. Gammack, "I.S.C. Ace's Score."
21. Ibid.
22. Cannon, interview, June 23, 2003.
23. 354th FG Staff, "MR, April 8, 1944," (MF B0312).
25. Brereton, *The Brereton Diaries*, 257.
24. Cannon, interview, June 23, 2003.
25. IX Fighter Command Staff, "354th FG, MR, April 8, 1944," (File No. 535.332, AFHRA).
26. Donald, *Warplanes of the Luftwaffe*, 80-83.
27. Dean, *America's Hundred Thousand*, 334.
28. WWII AAF, "CMS No. 49," (RG 18, NARA).
29. 353rd FS Staff, "Unit History," 136.
30. WWII AAF, "CMS No. 50," (RG 18, NARA).
31. 353rd FS Staff, "Unit History," 136.
32. Donald, *American Warplanes of World War II*, 177-181.
33. WWII AAF, "CMS No. 52," (RG 18, NARA).
34. Ibid., "MACR–3635," (RG 92, NARA).
35. Bickel, *Before the Contrails Fade Away*, 151.
36. WWII AAF, "MACR–3636," (RG 92, NARA).
37. IX FC Staff, "ER: James Cannon, April 11, 1944," (MF B5721).
38. 354th FG Staff, "MR, April 11, 1944," (MF B0312).
39. IX FC Staff, "ER: Beerbower, April 11, 1944."

40. 354th FG Staff, "MR, April 11, 1944," (MF B0312).
41. Ibid., "Unit History," (MF B0311), 1876.
42. 353rd FS Staff, "Unit History," 136.
43. Freeman, *The Mighty Eighth*, 129-134.
44. 354th FG Staff, "MR, April 13, 1944," (MF B0312).
45. IX FC Staff, "ER: Carl G. Bickel, Eagleston, and Clayton Kelly Gross, April 13, 1944."
46. Ibid., "ER: Beerbower."
47. 354th FG Staff, "MR, April 13, 1944," (MF B0312).
48. WWII AAF, "MACRs–4028 and 4107," (RG 92, NARA).

Chapter 24
pages 239-254

1. IV FC Staff, "Biographical Questionnaire: George R. Bickell," and 354th FG Staff, "Unit History," (MF B0311), 1874, 1878.
2. 353rd FS Staff, "Unit History," 134.
3. DMB, letter, April 10, 1944.
4. 354th FG Staff, "MR, April 18, 19 and 23, 1944," (MF B0312).
5. W WII AAF, "CMS Nos. 58 and 59," (RG 18, NARA).
6. 354th FG Staff, "MR, April 23, 1944," (MF B0312).
7. *Hill City News*, May 11, 1944.
8. 353rd FS Staff, "Unit History," 137; and 354th FG Staff, "MR, April 23, 1944."
9. Galland, *The First and the Last*, 260-262.
10. Gammack, "I.S.C. Ace's Score."
11. Albert Beerbower, "From Land O'Lakes to Luftwaffe," by Major Donald W. Dresden, IX FC publication, April 1944, (Personal Collection).
12. 353rd FS Staff, "Unit History," 137, 138.
13. Regis, interview, June 30, 2003.
14. WWII AAF, "MACR–4233," (RG 92, NARA).
15. Regis, interview, June 30, 2003.
16. 354th FG Staff, "MR, Nos. 63 and 64, April 27, 1944," (MF B0312).
17. *Hill City New*, May 11, 1944.
18. 353rd FS Staff, "Unit History," 148.
19. Cannon, interview, June 23, 2003.
20. Clayton Kelly Gross, *Captain Clayton Kelly Gross – Reflections: P-51 Mustang Fighter Ace 1941-1945*, transcript of an audio tape interview with the author, April 5, 2000.
21. Bradley, interview, June 27, 1999.
22. Albert Beerbower, "From Land O'Lakes to Luftwaffe."
23. IX FC Staff, "Operations Order 192, April 29, 1944," (File No. 535.332).
24. WWII AAF, "CMS No. 65," (RG 18, NARA).
25. 354th FG Staff, "MR, April 29, 1944," (MF B0312).
26. WWII AAF, "MACR–4422," (RG 92, NARA).
27. Cannon, interview, June 23, 2003.
28. WWII AAF, "MACR–4422," (RG 92, NARA).

29. IX FC Staff, "Field Order 192, April 29, 1944."
30. 354th FG Staff, "MR, April 29, 1944," (MF B0312).
31. Cannon, interview, June 23, 2003.
32. 353rd FS, Staff "Unit History," 138.
33. WWII AAF, "CMS No. 68," (RG 18, NARA).
34. 354th FG Staff, "MR, May 1, 1944," (MF B0312).
35. 353rd FS Staff, "Unit History," 145.

Chapter 25
pages 255-272

1. Brereton, *The Brereton Diaries*, 261-269.
2. DMB, letter, May 5, 1944.
3. 354th FG Staff, "MR, May 7 and 8, 1944," (MF B0312).
4. WWII AAF, "MACR–4678," (RG 92, NARA).
5. 354th FG Staff, "MR, May 8, 1944," (MF B0312).
6. Ibid., "MR, May 9, 1944," (MF B0312).
7. Ibid., "MR, May 10, 1944," (MF B0312).
8. WWII AAF, "MACR–4680," (RG 92, NARA).
9. Ibid., "MACR–4681," (RG 92, NARA).
10. 353rd FS Staff, "Unit History," 146.
11. IX FC Staff, "Operations Order 250, May 12, 1944," (File No. 535.332).
12. WWII AAF, "CMS No. 77," (RG 18, NARA).
13. 354th FG Staff, "Unit History," (MF B0312), 9.
14. WWII AAF, Safety Records, "AR 44-5-12-510," (IRIS No. 00877315, AFHRA).
15. 354th FG Staff, "Unit History," (MF B0312), 9.
16. Ibid., "MR, May 12, 1944," (MF B0312).
17. WWII AAF, "MACR–4753," (RG 92, NARA).
18. 354th FG Staff, "MR, May 12, 1944," (MF B0312).
19. Anderson, interview, January 31, 2000.
20. Rogers, interview, June 23, 1999.
21. Bradley, interview, January 9, 2000.
22. XIX TAC Staff, "Ordnance – Armament Handbook for Tactical Air Liaison Officers," (MF 5900), 384.
23. Chisholm, letter, July 22, 2003.
24. WWII AAF, "CMS No. 78," (RG 18, NARA).
25. 353rd FS Staff, "Unit History," 146.
26. IX FC Staff, "Operations Order 266, May 19, 1944," (File No. 535.332).
27. 354th FG Staff, "Unit History," (MF B0312), 11.
28. WWII AAF, "CMS No. 79," (RG 18, NARA).
29. 354th FG Staff, "MR, May 19, 1944," (MF B0312).
30. WWII AAF, Safety Records, "AR 44-5-19-519," (IRIS No. 00877319, AFHRA).
31. Ibid., "CMS No.80," (RG 18, NARA).
32. 354th FG Staff, "Unit History," (MF B0312), 11, 12.
33. *Hill City News*, May 11, May 18, May 25 and July 20, 1944.
34. WWII AAF, "CMS Nos. 81-83," (RG 18, NARA).

35. 353rd FS Staff, "Unit History," 42.
36. 354th FG Staff, "MR, May 24, 1944," (MF B0312).
37. WWII AAF, "CMS No. 84," (RG 18, NARA).
38. Ibid., "MACR–5121," (RG 92, NARA).
39. 353rd FS Staff, "Unit History," 31, 32, 44.
40. WWII AAF, "CMS Nos. 85-87," (RG 18, NARA).
41. 354th FG Staff, "MR, May 25, 1944," (MF B0312).
42. Ibid., "Unit History," (MF B0312), 12.
43. Dwight D. Eisenhower, *Crusade in Europe*, (Garden City, NY: Doubleday & Company, Inc., 1949), 223, 231 and 289.
44. 353rd FS Staff, "Unit History," 41.
45. Bickel, *Before the Contrails Fade Away*, 156, 157.
46. WWII AAF, "CMS No. 88," (RG 18, NARA).
47. Ibid., "MACR–5133," (RG 92, NARA).
48. 354th FG Staff, "MR, May 28, 1944," (MF B0312).
49. WWII AAF, "MACR–5137," (RG 92, NARA).
50. Cannon, interview, June 23, 2003.
51. 354th FG Staff, "MR, May 28 and June 2, 1944," (MF B0312).
52. John S. Miller, *First Lieutenant John S. Miller, World War II P-51 Fighter Pilot: The 353rd Fighter Squadron – 1944*, transcript of an audio tape interview with the author, June 18, 2003.
53. Anderson, interview, January 6, 2000.
54. WWII AAF, "IDPF: Don McDowell," (USAHRC).

Chapter 26
pages 273-288

1. 354th FG Staff, "Unit History," (MF B0312), 12.
2. Slater, *Lingering Contrails of THE BIG SQUARE A*, 188, 363.
3. Healy, interview, August 5, 2001.
4. Eighth Air Force Staff, "Mission No. 379" and VIII FC Staff, "Intelligence Summary No. 197," (File No. 520.332, AFHRA).
5. WWII AAF, 94th BG (H) Staff, "MR, May 29, 1944," (RG 18, NARA).
6. Healy, interview, August 5, 2001.
7. WWII AAF, 94th BG (H) Staff, "MR, May 29, 1944," (RG 18, NARA).
8. Healy, interview, August 5, 2001.
9. Eighth Air Force Staff, "Mission No. 379" and VIII FC Staff, "Intelligence Summary No. 197."
10. Ibid.
11. Healy, interview, August 5, 2001.
12. WWII AAF, 94th BG (H) Staff, "MR, May 29, 1944," (RG 18, NARA).
13. 354th FG Staff, "MR, May 29, 1944," (MF B0312).
14. WWII AAF, 94th BG (H) Staff, "MR, May 29, 1944," (RG 18, NARA).
15. Healy, interview, August 5, 2001.
16. WWII AAF, 94th BG (H) Staff, "MR, May 29, 1944," (RG 18, NARA).
17. 354th FG Staff, "MR, May 29, 1944," (MF B0312).

18. WWII AAF, "CMS Nos. 90-192," (RG 18, NARA).
19. Ibid., 94th BG (H) Staff, "MR, May 29, 1944," (RG 18, NARA).
20. VIII FC, "Intelligence Summary No. 197."
21. Healy, interview, August 5, 2001.
22. 354th FG Staff, "Unit History," (MF B0312), 12.
23. WWII AAF, "CMS No. 90," (RG 18, NARA).
24. Warren Mack and Al Zdon, *One Step Forward: The Life of Ken Dahlberg*, (Minneapolis, MN: I Was There Press, 2008), 51.
25. 354th FG Staff, "MR, May 30 and May 31, 1944" (MF B0312).
26. 353rd FS Staff, "Unit History," 144, 147.
27. Ibid., 155, 159.
28. WWII AAF, "CMS Nos. 91-92," (RG 18, NARA).
29. 354th FG Staff, "MR, June 3, 1944," (MF B0312).
30. WWII AAF, "MACR–5541," (RG 92, NARA).
31. 353rd FS Staff, "Unit History," 155, 177.
32. William Y. Anderson, letters, February 14 and March 6, 2000.
33. DMB, letters, June 13 and August 7, 1944.
34. Miller, interview, June 18, 2003.
35. 353rd FS Staff, "Unit History," 179.
36. 354th FG Staff, "Unit History," (MF B0312), 18.
37. 353rd FS Staff, "Unit History," 148.
38. Ibid.

Part Three
page 289

1. Frederic Lafarge, Administrateur du Musee de la Base aerienne 112, *Un siècle d'aviation a Reims* [A century of aviation at Reims], Base aerienne 112, Reims, France.
2. XIX TAC Staff, "354th FG, Mission X51-1: Summary," (IRIS No. 23856).

Chapter 27
pages 290-301

1. Morison, *The Invasion of France and Germany 1944 – 1945*, 56, 86-89, 118-126, 132, 335, 336.
2. Ibid., 107-108.
3. 354th FG Staff, "Unit History," (MF B0312), 20, 21.
4. 353rd FS Staff, "Unit History," 159.
5. *Hill City News*, June 15, 1944.
6. 354th FG Staff, "Unit History," (MF B0312), 21.
7. WWII AAF, "CMS Nos. 93-95," (RG 18, NARA).
8. 354th FG Staff, "MR, No. 94," (MF B0312).
9. Bickel, *Before the Contrails Fade Away*, 158, 159.
10. Turner, *Big Friend, Little Friend*, 94-96.
11. WWII AAF, Safety Records, "AR 44-6-6-533," (IRIS No. 00877327, AFHRA).
12. Anderson, interview, January 31, 2000.

13. 354th FG Staff, "Unit History," (MF B0312), 21, 22.
14. WWII AAF, "CMS No. 94," (RG 18, NARA) and 353rd FS Staff, "Unit History," 174, 196, 197.
15. 354th FG Staff, "MR, No. 95," (MF B0312).
16. Bickel, *Before the Contrails Fade Away*, 159.
17. 354th FG Staff, "MR, No. 95," (MF B0312).
18. WWII AAF, "CMS No. 95," (RG 18, NARA).
19. *U.S. Army in World War II Atlas: The European Theater*, (Minnetonka, MN, The National Historical Society, 1996) 6, 7, 12, 13, 24.
20. Miller, interview, June 19, 2003.
21. 354th FG Staff, "MR, No. 96," (MF B0312).
22. *Hill City News*, June 15, 1944.
23. 354th FG Staff, "MR, No. 96," (MF B0312).
24. WWII AAF, "MACR–5695," (RG 92, NARA).
25. Ibid., "CMS No. 95," (RG 18, NARA).
26. Bickel, *Before the Contrails Fade Away*, 160.
27. 354th FG Staff, "MR, No. 96," (MF B0312).
28. Frederick B. Deeds, transcript of an audio tape interview with the author, March 7, 2011, and letters to the author, March 17 and March 30, 2011.

CHAPTER 28
pages 302-315

1. Ken Delve, *D-Day The Air Battle*, 123-125, 131.
2. Bradley, interview, June 27, 1999.
3. Mack and Zdon, *One Step Forward*, 13, 21-25.
4. Dahlberg, interview, August 26, 1999.
5. Cannon, interview, June 23, 2003.
6. Clayton Kelly Gross, electronic correspondence to the author, April 13, 2000.
7. Turner, *Big Friend Little Friend*, 99-101.
8. 353rd FS Staff, "Unit History," 156.
9. 354th FG Staff, "Unit History," (MF B0312), 23.
10. WWII AAF, "CMS Nos. 98, 99," (RG 18, NARA).
11. 354th FG Staff, "MR, No. 102," (MF B0312).
12. 354th FG Staff, "Unit History," (MF B0312), 33.
13. Brereton, *The Brereton Diaries*, 280, 281, 286.
14. 354th FG Staff, "Unit History," (MF B0312), 24.
15. Ibid., "MR, Nos. 103, 104," (B0312).
16. WWII AAF, "CMS Nos. 100-102," (RG 18, NARA).
17. 354th FG Staff, "MR, No. 105," (MF B0312).
18. DMB, letter to Darrel and Arlene Beerbower, June 17, 1944.
19. 354th FG Staff, "Unit History," (MF B0312), 24-26.
20. Donald, *Warplanes of the Luftwaffe*, 54.
21. Brereton, *The Brereton Diaries*, 288.
22. WWII AAF, "CMS Nos. 103, 104," (RG 18, NARA).
23. 353rd FS Staff, "Unit History," 157.

24. WWII AAF, "MACR–6289," (RG 92, NARA).
25. Bickel, *Before the Contrails Fade Away*, 166.
26. WWII AAF, "CMS No. 105," (RG 18, NARA).
27. Anderson, interview, January 6, 2000.
28. 353rd FS Staff, "Unit History," 157.
29. Ibid., 167, 196.
30. Michael Triventi, transcript of an audio tape interview with the author, February 7, 2009.
31. Brereton, *The Brereton Diaries*, 288.
32. 353rd FS Staff, "Unit History," 157.
33. WWII AAF, "CMS Nos. 106-108," (RG 18, NARA).
34. 354th FG Staff, "MR, No. 112,"(MF B0312).
35. Morison, *The Invasion of France and Germany: 1944 – 1945*, 176-178, 181, 195.
36. 353rd FS Staff, "Unit History," 158.
37. Freeman, *The Mighty Eighth*, 168.
38. Brereton, *The Brereton Diaries*, 289, 290.
39. 354th FG Staff, "MR, No. 115," (MF B0312).
40. Mack and Zdon, *One Step Forward*, 47.
41. WWII AAF, "CMS Nos. 109-111," (RG 18, NARA).
42. 353rd FS Staff, "Unit History," 152, 158, 159.

Chapter 29
pages 316-332

1. Brereton, *The Brereton Diaries*, 213, 291.
2. 353rd FS Staff, "Unit History," 158.
3. Brereton, *The Brereton Diaries*, 291.
4. WWII AAF, "CMS No. 112," (RG 18, NARA).
5. Bradley, interview, January 9, 2000.
6. Dean, *America's Hundred Thousand*, 325-329, 334, 605, 606.
7. Bickel, *Before the Contrails Fade Away*, 161, 162.
8. Anderson, interview, January 6, 2000.
9. Triventi, interview, February 7, 2009.
10. Bickel, *Before the Contrails Fade Away*, 161, 166, 169.
11. 353rd FS Staff, "Unit History," 152, 183.
12. George Chassey, transcript of an audio tape interview with the author, February 7, 2009.
13. WWII AAF, "CMS Nos. 113, 114," (RG 18, NARA).
14. 353rd FS Staff, "Unit History," 158.
15. WWII AAF, "CMS Nos. 115-117," (RG 18, NARA).
16. 354th FG Staff, "OR A, Nos. 114, 117," (MF B0312).
17. 353rd FS Staff, "Unit History," 158.
18. Ibid., 152, 159, 167.
19. Turner, *Big Friend, Little Friend*, 136, 137.
20. WWII AAF, "CMS Nos. 119-124," (RG 18, NARA).
21. 354th FG Staff, "OR A, No. 123," (MF B0312).

22. WWII AAF, "CMS No. 121," (RG 18, NARA).
23. Ibid., Safety Records, "AR 44-6-28-532," (IRIS No. 00877337, AFHRA).
24. Ibid., "CMS Nos. 122-125," (RG 18, NARA).
25. 354th FG Staff, "OR A, No. 124," (MF B0312).
26. Mack and Zdon, *One Stop Forward*, 55, 56.
27. Olynyk, *Stars & Bars*, 140, 159, 160, 248, 280, 281, 351.
28. 353rd FS Staff, "Unit History," 159, 176, 177.
29. Morison, *The Invasion of France and Germany: 1944 – 1945*, 198, 215.
30. Brereton, *The Brereton Diaries*, 298, 300, 301.
31. World War II Army Air Forces, "Ninth Air Force Motion Picture Film," (Control No.: NWDNM (m) – 18-CS-1803, NARA).
32. 354th FG Staff, "Unit History," (MF B0312), 37, 38.
33. Ibid.
34. Turner, *Big Friend, Little Friend*, 119-123.
35. Bickel, *Before the Contrails Fade Away*, 177, 178.
36. *Hill City News*, July 20, 1944.
37. 354th FG Staff, "Unit History," (MF B0312), 44.
38. Triventi, interview, February 7, 2009.
39. WWII AAF, "CMS Nos. 125-127," (RG 18, NARA).
40. 353rd FS Staff, "Unit History," 169, 170.
41. *Hill City News*, July 6 and July 13, 1944.
42. Elayne Beerbower, letter, March 27, 2009.
43. *Hill City News*, July 13, 1944.

Chapter 30
pages 333-348

1. 353rd FS Staff, "Unit History," 175.
2. Bickel, *Before the Contrails Fade Away*, 178.
3. Dahlberg, interview, August 26, 1999.
4. WWII AAF, "CMS Nos. 128-133," (RG 18, NARA).
5. Ibid., "CMS No. 158," (RG 18, NARA).
6. DMB, letter, July 23, 1944.
7. Bradley, interview, January 9, 2000.
8. 353rd FS Staff, "Unit History," 170.
9. Bickel, *Before the Contrails Fade Away*, 169, 170.
10. Olynyk, *Stars & Bars*, 144.
11. Bickel, *Before the Contrails Fade Away*, 177.
12. 353rd FS Staff, "Unit History," 203.
13. Olynyk, *Stars and Bars*, 385.
14. 353rd FS Staff, "Unit History," 204.
15. Olynyk, *Stars and Bars*, 528-529.
16. 353rd FS Staff, "Unit History," 175, 197.
17. Olynyk, *Stars and Bars*, 117.
18. 353rd FS Staff, "Unit History," 189, 204.
19. *Hill City News*, July 6, 1944.

20. 353rd FS Staff, "Unit History," 170.
21. WWII AAF, "CMS No. 144," (RG 18, NARA).
22. 354th FG Staff, "OR A, No. 191," (MF B0312).
23. WWII AAF, Safety Records, "AR 45-7-13-523," (IRIS No. 00877343, AFHRA).
24. 353rd FS Staff, "Unit History," 170, 171.
25. WWII AAF, "CMS No. 152," (RG 18, NARA).
26. 354th FG Staff, "OR A, No. 215," (MF B0312).
27. 353rd Fighter Squadron Staff, "Unit History," 171.
28. WWII AAF, "CMS No. 155," (RG 18, NARA).
29. 354th FG Staff, "OR A, No. 225," (MF B0312).
30. Gene Gurney, *Five Down and Glory*, (New York: Ballantine Books, Inc., 1958), 150, 169.
31. Rogers, interview, June 23, 1999.
32. Dahlberg, interview, August 26, 1999.
33. Freeman, *The Mighty Eighth*, 126, 127.
34. Bradley, interview, January 9, 2000.
35. Gurney, *Five Down and Glory*, 4, 5, 169.
36. WWII AAF, "CMS No. 157," (RG 18, NARA).
37. 354th FG Staff, "OR A, No. 229," (MF B0312).
38. Deeds, interview, March 7, 2011.
39. WWII AAF, "CMS No. 158," (RG 18, NARA).
40. 354th FG Staff, "OR A, No. 234," (MF B0312).
41. Miller, interview, June 18, 2003.

Chapter 31
pages 349-366

1. Eisenhower, *Crusade in Europe*, 258-260, 267, 268, 292.
2. Brereton, *The Brereton Diaries*, 310-314.
3. WWII AAF, "CMS Nos. 159-161," (RG 18, NARA).
4. 354th FG Staff, "OR A, No. 240," (MF B0312).
5. WWII AAF, "CMS Nos. 162-164," (RG 18, NARA).
6. Brereton, *The Brereton Diaries*, 315.
7. 354th FG Staff, "Unit History," (MF B0312), 69, 70.
8. Ibid., "OR A, No. 245," (MF B0312).
9. 353rd FS Staff, "Unit History," 171.
10. Brereton, *The Brereton Diaries*, 312, 313.
11. Freeman, *The Mighty Eighth*, 164.
12. Eisenhower, *Crusade in Europe*, 8, 9, 11, 12, 231, 272, 288.
13. Larry and Dorothy Lehner, *McNair, Verndale to St. Lo*, (Verndale, MN: Verndale Historical Society, 1976), 9.
14. Eisenhower, *Crusade in Europe*, 272, 273.
15. 354th FG Staff, "OR A, No. 256 and Fighter Sweeps H," (MF B0312).
16. WWII AAF, "CMS No. 166," (RG 18, NARA).
17. 354th FG Staff, "OR A, No. 256 and Fighter Sweeps H," (MF B0312).
18. 353rd FS Staff, "Unit History," 171.

19. WWII AAF, "CMS Nos. 165 and 167," (RG 18, NARA).
20. 353rd FS Staff, "Unit History, 196."
21. 354th FG Staff, "OR A, No. 259," (MF B0312).
22. WWII AAF, Safety Records, "AR 45-7-26-526," (IRIS No. 00877349, AFHRA).
23. Miller, interview, June 18, 2003.
24. WWII AAF, "CMS Nos. 168-180," (RG 18, NARA).
25. 354th FG Staff, "OR A, No. 293," (MF B0312).
26. WWII AAF, Safety Records, "AR 45-7-31-532," (IRIS No. 00877351, AFHRA).
27. 354th FG Staff, "OR A, Nos. 295-297," (MF B0312).
28. Chassey, interview, February 7, 2009.
29. 353rd FS Staff, "Unit History," 169.
30. Turner, *Big Friend, Little Friend*, 125.
31. XIX TAC Staff, "Unit History," (MF B5849), 245, 246.
32. Bradford J. Shwedo, *XIX Tactical Air Command and ULTRA: Patton's Force Enhancers in the 1944 Campaign in France*, (Maxwell Air Force Base, AL: Air University Press, 2001), 1-5, 20, 21.
33. XIX TAC Staff, "Unit History," (MF B5849), 660, 738, 893, 894, 904, and "Unit History," (MF B5899), 1531-1535.
34. Morison, *The Invasion of France and Germany: 1944 – 1945*, 236, 238, 248, 265.
35. WWII AAF, "CMS No. 118," (RG 18, NARA).
36. 353rd FS Staff, "Unit History," 186.
37. Ibid., 169, 170, 175.
38. 354th FG Staff, "Unit History," (MF B0312), 74.
39. Howard, *Roar of the Tiger*, 274, 283, 292, 293.
40. 353rd FS Staff, "Unit History," 186.
41. WWII AAF, "Luftwaffe Aerial Photo, DT/SP-1, Box #1-Print 89," (RG 373, NARA) and "Arado Ar 234 B-2 Blitz (Lightning) – Summary," (Smithsonian National Air and Space Museum), www.nasm.si.edu./collections/artifact.cfm?id.
42. 353rd FS Staff, "Unit History," 187.
43. WWII AAF, "CMS No. 185," (RG 18, NARA) and 353rd FS Staff, "Unit History," 197.
44. WWII AAF, Safety Records, "AR 45-8-3-525," (IRIS No. 00877353, AFHRA).
45. 353rd FS Staff, "Unit History," 186.
46. Ibid., 174.
47. Shwedo, *XIX Tactical Air Command and Ultra*, 15, 16, 30, 45-50.
48. WWII AAF, "CMS Nos. 159-188," (RG 18, NARA).
49. 354th FG Staff, "OR A, Nos. 327, 331," (MF B0312).
50. Shwedo, *XIX Tactical Air Command and Ultra*, 46-52, 57, 58.
51. XIX TAC Staff, "Unit History," (MF B5899), 1346-1354.
52. WWII AAF, "CMS No. 190," (RG 18, NARA).
53. 354th FG Staff, "OR A, No. 333," (MF B0312).
54. WWII AAF, "MACR–8226," (RG 92, NARA).
55. 354th FG Staff, "Unit History," (MF B0312), 1196, 1198.
56. 353rd FS Staff, "Unit History," 187, 188.
57. Ibid., 187.
58. 354th FG Staff, "OR A, Nos. 333-336," (MF B0312).

Chapter 32
pages 367-387

1. 353rd FS Staff, "Unit History," 174, 189.
2. Naomi Langran, letter to the author, July 6, 2000.
3. Elayne Beerbower, interview, June 2, 1999.
4. 353rd FS Staff, "Unit History," 188.
5. Shwedo, *XIX Tactical Air Command and ULTRA*, 58-62.
6. Donald, *Warplanes of the Luftwaffe*, 173, 178, 179.
7. *Spearhead in the West, 1941-1945: The Third Armored Division*, (Frankfurt am Main, Germany: Kunst und Webedruck, 1945), 72, 74.
8. *Air-Ground Teamwork on the Western Front: The Role of the XIX Tactical Air Command during August 1944 – An Interim Report*, (Washington, D.C.: Reprinted by the Center for Air Force History, 1992), 12, 28.
9. Ibid., 17, 30.
10. Ibid., 12.
11. Chassey and Triventi, interviews, February 7, 2009.
12. Chassey, interview, February 7, 2009.
13. Miller, interview, June 19, 2003.
14. 354th FG Staff, "OR A, Nos. 339-344," (MF B0312).
15. Miller, interview, June 19, 2003.
16. Donald J. Chisholm, interview with the author, April 30, 2011.
17. WWII AAF, "CMS No. 192," (RG 18, NARA).
18. 354th FG Staff, "OR A, Nos. 339, 340," (MF B0312).
19. XIX TAC Staff, "OR No. 9, Mission X51-1," (IRIS No. 23856).
20. Bickel, *Before the Contrails Fade Away*, 178.
21. XIX TAC Staff, "OR No. 9, Mission X51-1," (IRIS No. 23856).
22. 354th FG Staff, "OR A, Nos. 339, 340," (MF B0312).
23. Ibid., "No. 339," (MF B0312).
24. Ibid., "No. 340," (MF B0312) and Rogers, interview, June 23, 1999.
25. Lafarge, *Un siecle d'aviation a Reims*.
26. 354th FG Staff, "OR A, No. 340," (MF B0312).
27. Rogers, interview, June 23, 1999.
28. Ibid.
29. WWII AAF, "MACR–8150," (RG 92, NARA).
30. 354th FG Staff, "OR A, No. 340," (MF B0312).
31. 353rd FS Staff "Unit History," 188.
32. Rogers, interview, June 23, 1999.
33. WWII AAF, "MACR–8150," (RG 92, NARA).
34. Rogers, interview, June 23, 1999.
35. *Hill City News*, September 21, 1944.
36. Miller, interview, December 13, 2003.
37. DMB, "Military Service Records," and "Correspondence: Major General Edward F. Witsell, letter, with a report from First Lieutenant Ladurantie, to Elayne Beerbower, August 21, 1945," (NPRC).
38. 354th FG Staff, "OR A, No. 340," (MF B0312).

39. WWII AAF, "MACR–1850," (RG 92, NARA).
40. DMB, "Witsell, letter to Elayne Beerbower, August 21, 1945," (NPRC).
41. Miller, interview, June 17, 2003.
42. Bickel, *Before the Contrails Fade Away*, 179 and Chisholm, interview, April 30, 2011.
43. Miller, interview, June 17 and June 18, 2003.
44. 354th FG Staff, "Unit History," (MF B0312), 63, 64.
45. Anderson, interview, January 31, 2000.
46. Dahlberg, interview, August 26, 1999.
47. 353rd FS Staff, "Unit History," 188.
48. 354th FG Staff, "Unit History," (MF B0312), 64.
49. Ibid., "OR A, Nos. 342-344," (MF B0312).
50. 353rd FS Staff, "Unit History," 189.
51. WWII AAF, "CMS No. 193," (RG 18, NARA).
52. 354th FG Staff, "OR A, No. 343," (MF B0312).
53. 353rd FS Staff, "Unit History, 189."
54. 354th FG Staff, "OR A, Nos. 342-344," (MF B0312).
55. Ibid., "OR A, No. 343," (MF B0312).
56. WWII AAF, "MACR–8149," (RG 92, NARA).
57. Miller, interview, June 17 and June 18, 2003.
58. 353rd FS Staff, "Unit History," 189.
59. Ibid., 194-195.
60. Miller, interview, June 17, 2003.
61. Bradley, interview, January 9, 2000.
62. Bickel, *Before the Contrails Fade Away*, 181.
63. 353rd FS Staff, "Unit History," 189.

Chapter 33
pages 388-398

1. 353rd FS Staff, "Unit History," 183, 189.
2. Felix Michael Rogers, letter to Minnesota Aviation Hall of Fame, Inc., June 28, 1999.
3. Miller, interview, June 18, 2003.
4. 353rd FS Staff, "Unit History," 243, 327.
5. Rogers, letter, June 28, 1999.
6. Lieutenant Peron, Adjoint O.S.A., Base aerienne 112, letter to the author, November 29, 2004.
7. WWII AAF, "IDPF: Don M. Beerbower," (USAHRC).
8. Ibid., "MACR–8150," (RG 92, NARA).
9. *Hill City News*, August 10 and August 24, 1944.
10. Elayne Beerbower, interview, July 3, 2009.
11. *Hill City News*, August 10 and August 17, 1944.
12. Ibid., August 17, 1944.
13. Elayne Beerbower, interview, July 3, 2009.
14. *Hill City News*, August 24, 1944.

15. Hankerson, letter, July 11, 2009.
16. *Hill City News*, August 24, 1944.
17. Ibid., August 31, 1944.
18. Elayne Beerbower, interview, July 3, 2009.
19. Ibid..
20. Hugh M. Cole, *The Lorraine Campaign*, (Washington, D.C.: U.S. Government Printing Office, 1993), 20, 117, 120.
21. Peron, letter, November 29, 2004.
22. WWII AAF, "IDPF: Beerbower," (USAHRC).
23. Ibid.
24. DMB, "Military Service Records: War Department letter to Elayne Beerbower, September 30, 1944," (NPRC).
25. Elayne Beerbower, interview, July 3, 2009.
26. *Hill City News*, October 12, 1944.
27. Elayne Beerbower, interview, July 3, 2009.
28. *Hill City News*, October 19 and October 26, 1944.
29. DMB, "Military Service Records: Casualty Message Telegram to Elayne Beerbower, October 27, 1944," (NPRC).
30. *Hill City News*, November 2, 1944.
31. Ibid.
32. Ibid., June 1, 1939, November 9 and November 16, 1944.
33. Elayne Beerbower, interview, July 3, 2009.
34. Ibid.
35. *Hill City News*, November 9 and November 16, 1944.
36. Elayne Beerbower, interview, July 3, 2009.
37. WWII AAF, "IDPF: Beerbower," (USAHRC).
38. Ibid.
39. *Hill City News*, November 23, 1944.
40. Regis, interview, June 30, 2003.
41. 353rd FS Staff, "Unit History," 327.
42. Regis, interview, June 30, 2003.
43. Ibid.
44. WWII AAF, "IDPF: Beerbower," (USAHRC).

Afterword
pages 399-400

1. 359th BS (H) Staff, "MR, September 1, September 3, and September 5, 1944." (MF A0587, AFHRA).
2. 303rd BG (H) Staff, "Mission No. 236," (303rd Bomb Group Association), 1-3, www.303rdbg.com.
3. WW II AAF, "IARC: B-17G #42-31483," (MF ACR #52, AFHRA).
4. 353rd FS Staff, "Unit History," 201, 202.
5. Ibid., 203.
6. *Bonnie-"B"*, (303rd Bomb Group Association), Nose Art, www.303rdbg.com.

Appendix I

Ninth Air Force Aces: Ten or more Aerial Victories

Name	Squadron	Dates	Victories
Eagleston, Glenn T.	353rd	Jan 1944– Mar 1945	18.5*
Beerbower, Don M.	353rd	Jan 1944– July 1944	15.5
Bradley, Jack T.	353rd	Dec 1943– Mar 1945	15
Dahlberg, Kenneth H.	353rd	June 1944–Dec 1944	15**
Carr, Bruce W.	353rd	Mar 1944–Apr 1945	14
Emmer, Wallace N.	353rd	Feb 1944– Aug 1944	14
Stephens, Robert W.	355th	Dec 1944–Aug 1944	13
Brueland, Lowell K.	355th	Feb 1944– Mar 1945	12.5
East, Clyde B.	15th	June 1944–Apr 1945	12
Frantz, Carl M.	353rd	Jan 1944– May 1944	11
Turner, Richard E.	356th	Jan 1944– July 1944	11
O'Connor, Frank Q.	356th	Jan 1944– May 1944	10.75

Top Five American Fighter Groups in World War II: Aerial Victories

Group	Theater	Victories
49th Fighter Group	PTO	671
56th Fighter Group	ETO	667
354th Fighter Group	ETO	605.25***
357th Fighter Group	ETO	595.5
31st Fighter Group	MTO	569.5

Top Five American Fighter Squadrons in World War II: Aerial Victories

Squadron	Group	Theater	Victories
353rd Fighter Squadron	354th FG	ETO	290.5
9th Fighter Squadron	49th FG	PTO	258
487th Fighter Squadron	352nd FG	ETO	235.5
61st Fighter Squadron	56th FG	ETO	233
62nd Fighter Squadron	56th FG	ETO	220

Source: Haulman, Daniel L., ed. *USAF Wartime Aerial Victory Credits.* Air Force Historical Research Agency (AFHRA), Maxwell AFB, AL, 2000. Website version: www.au.af.mil/au/afhra/avc.asp. 2009.
*Eagleston had two additional aerial victories in Korea.

**Dahlberg's 15th aerial victory credit was confirmed by AFHRA on May 16, 2007.
***The 354th Fighter Group victory total would be higher but the XIX Tactical Air Command's Victory Credit Board Reports, Numbers 71, 79, 80 and 81, are missing. Source: Haulman, *USAF Wartime Aerial Victory Credits*, "Introduction." AFHRA.

APPENDIX II

354TH FIGHTER GROUP: COMMANDING OFFICERS

Name	Dates
Martin, Kenneth R.	Nov 1942– Feb 1944
Howard, James H.	Feb 1944– Apr 1944
Bickell, George R.	Apr 1944– May 1945

353RD FIGHTER SQUADRON: COMMANDING OFFICERS*

Name	Dates
Seaman, Owen M.	Nov 1942– Dec 1943
Priser, Robert L.	Dec 1943– Jan 1944
Bradley, Jack T.	Jan 1944– June 1944
Beerbower, Don M.	June 1944–Aug 1944
Rogers, Felix M.	Aug 1944– Oct 1944
Bradley, Jack T.	Oct 1944– Oct 1944
Eagleston, Glenn T.	Oct 1944– May 1945

Sources: 354th Fighter Group Staff. "Unit History." Microfilms B0311 and B0312, AFHRA. 353rd Fighter Squadron Staff. "Unit History." Microfilm A0782-A, AFHRA.

*Wallace N. Emmer was unofficially squadron commander on August 9, 1944.

APPENDIX III

MAJOR DON M. BEERBOWER: AERIAL AND GROUND VICTORIES

Date	A/C Type	Result		Aerial/Ground
1943				
Dec 30	Dornier 217	Probably Destroyed	.5	Aerial
1944				
Jan 5	Messerschmitt 110	Destroyed	1	Aerial
Jan 11	Messerschmitt 110	Destroyed	1	Aerial
	Messerschmitt 110	Damaged	2	Aerial
Jan 29	Messerschmitt 109	Destroyed	1	Aerial

	Focke-Wulf 190	Damaged	1	Aerial
Feb 11	Messerschmitt 110	Destroyed	1	Aerial
	Messerschmitt 110	Damaged	1.33	Aerial
Feb 20	Messerschmitt 109	Destroyed	1	Aerial
	Messerschmitt 110	Destroyed	1	Aerial
	Messerschmitt 109	Damaged	1	Aerial
Feb 21	Messerschmitt 110	Destroyed	1	Aerial
	Focke-Wulf 190	Damaged	1	Aerial
	Messerschmitt 109	Damaged	1	Aerial
Mar 16	Messerschmitt 109	Destroyed	1	Aerial
Mar 18	Messerschmitt 109	Destroyed	1	Aerial
Apr 8	Focke-Wulf 190	Destroyed	2	Aerial
	Messerschmitt 109	Destroyed	1	Aerial
	Focke-Wulf 190	Damaged	2	Aerial
Apr 11	Messerschmitt 109	Damaged	1	Aerial
Apr 13	Focke-Wulf 190	Damaged	1	Aerial
Apr 29	Messerschmitt 109	Destroyed	1	Aerial
May 12	Messerschmitt 109	Unconfirmed Destroyed	*	Aerial
May 19	Focke-Wulf 190	Destroyed	1	Ground
June 12	Messerschmitt 109	Destroyed	1	Ground
June 14	Messerschmitt 109	Destroyed	1.5	Aerial
July 7	Focke-Wulf 190	Destroyed	1	Aerial
Aug 9	Junkers 88	Destroyed	1	Ground
Totals:		Destroyed	15.5	Aerial
		Destroyed	3	Ground
		Unconfirmed Destroyed	1	Aerial
		Probably Destroyed	.5	Aerial
		Damaged	11.33	Aerial**

Sources: <u>Aerial Victories</u>. Haulman, Daniel L., ed. *USAF Wartime Aerial Victory Credits*. AFHRA, 2000. Olynyk, Frank. *Stars & Bars: A Tribute to the American Fighter Ace 1920–1973*. London: Grub Street, 1995. <u>Ground Victories</u>. 353rd Fighter Squadron Staff. "Unit History." Microfilm A0782-A, AFHRA.

*Unconfirmed Destroyed–a victory category used by the Ninth Air Force but not recognized by AFHRA.

**On March 12, 1945 Squadron Intelligence Officer Albert J. Feigen sent a letter to Clarence Beerbower stating: "All the claims for Major Beerbower's enemy aircraft destroyed, probably destroyed and damaged have been confirmed." The squadron statistics compiled by Feigen are consistent with the 15.5 aerial victories, 1 unconfirmed destroyed aerial victory, 3 ground victories and .5 probably destroyed aircraft found in Appendix III. The only difference is in the totals for damaged aircraft, 11.33 by Olynyk versus 14 by Feigen. A complete text of Feigen's letter can be found in Appendix IV.

APPENDIX IV

Letter to Clarence Beerbower

353rd Fighter Squadron
354th Fighter Group
APO 141, c/o Postmaster
New York, N. Y.
<u>12 March 1945</u>

Dear Mr. Beerbower,

In answer to your letter of 21 February 1945, I am forwarding herewith as much information as security regulations permit, in hopes that you will in some measure become further acquainted with the superior record your son established in this organization.

Major Beerbower has been officially reported killed in action on 9 August 1944, at Reims, France. There is no official record, however, of the place of burial.

The flying Form #5 has been submitted to the War Department in Washington, D. C., where it must remain on file. I am sending you extract copies of all orders awarding Major Beerbower decorations (precisely the same information which constitutes one half of the Form #5). Omitted is an order for the 20th oak leaf cluster to the Air Medal; no order was ever delivered to this unit. Orders for later clusters, however, are sufficient proof of the awarding of twenty-five bronze oak leaf clusters (or five Silver Oak Leaf Clusters). <u>Omitted too is the order for the first cluster to the Silver Star</u>; the decoration has not appeared on orders at this writing, but will be forwarded to you as soon as it has been delivered here. <u>Orders for the Distinguished Service Cross have already been forwarded to Mrs. Elayne Beerbower.</u>

Since the Form #5 cannot be sent to you, I am sending, in addition to the extract copies of decorations orders, the following information contained in it. Major Beerbower's total combat flying time was Two Hundred and Fifty-five Hours and Twenty Minutes (255:20). His total flying time (since primary training) was just under One Thousand Hours. I regret that detailed description of individual missions flown cannot be sent at this time.

All the claims for Major Beerbower's enemy aircraft destroyed, probably destroyed and damaged have been confirmed. A collected list of these follows:

DESTROYED: (totaling nineteen and one half)

Five ME-110's
Five FW-190's
One JU-88
Eight and One Half ME-109's (one shared with another pilot)

PROBABLY DESTROYED: (totaling one half)

One Half DO-217 (shared with another pilot)
DAMAGED: (totaling fourteen)

Five ME-110's
Four ME-109's
Five FW-190's

Major Beerbower's personal effects are now stored at the following address:

Army Effects Bureau
601 Hardesty Avenue
Kansas City, 1, Missouri

I suggest that you contact the Bureau, requesting that the property be forwarded to you. I am sure that you will be shown every courtesy and consideration.

I understand that our Public Relations Officer has forwarded to Mrs. Elayne Beerbower any number of pictures, both negatives and positive prints, of Major Beerbower, his airplane and the officers and men with whom he lived. During the entire career of the 354th Fighter Group no Officer has established a more distinctive combat record than your son. I shall not attempt to describe the sincere respect and admiration felt for him by all those who knew him here. As long as any one of us remains, the name and the character and the heroism of Don Beerbower will be remembered.

Albert J. Feigen
1st Lt., Air Corps
Intelligence Officer

4 Incls:
    Incl 1- Extract orders, Air Medal and clusters to the Air Medal from 1 to 19 (incl) in nine orders.
    Incl 2- Extract orders, Air Medal clusters from 21 to 25 (incl) in three orders.
    Incl 3- Extract orders, Distinguished Flying Cross and two Oak Leaf clusters thereto, in three orders.
    Incl 4- Extract order, Silver Star Medal.

Source: Darrel and Arlene Beerbower, Personal Collection. Letter from Albert J. Feigen to Clarence Beerbower, March 12, 1945.

Appendix V

Distinguished Service Cross Citation*

11 December 1944

CITATION: "For extraordinary heroism in action against the enemy, 9 August 1944, while leading his squadron on an armed reconnaissance mission. On that date, he located an enemy airfield on which many aircraft were parked. Major Beerbower, in order to test the ground defenses, made an experimental pass at the field destroying an enemy plane and a gun emplacement. Then, while his squadron swept over the field from one direction, he fearlessly attacked from another quarter, boldly exposing himself to concentrated fire from all sides of the field and effectively screening his comrades from the intense ground fire. Major Beerbower's airplane was struck repeatedly and crashed into the ground. The outstanding heroism and devotion to duty displayed by Major Beerbower on this occasion reflect highest credit upon himself and the Armed Forces of the United States."

Other decorations and awards include:
Silver Star**
Distinguished Flying Cross with two Oak Leaf Clusters
Air Medal with 25 Oak Leaf Clusters
Purple Heart
American Campaign Medal
European-African-Middle Easter Campaign Medal with three Bronze Service Stars (for participation in the Air Offensive Europe, Normandy, and Northern France)
World War II Victory Medal
Distinguished Unit Citation Emblem

Foreign Decorations:
British Distinguished Flying Cross

Sources: Don M. Beerbower. Military Service Records, National Personnel Records Center, St. Louis, MO and AIR 2/9006, The National Archives, Kew, UK.

*The Distinguished Service Cross is second only to the Congressional Medal of Honor.
**The Feigen letter in Appendix IV refers to a Silver Medal with one oak leaf cluster. Two Silver Stars exist in the Elayne Beerbower Collection.

Appendix

Distinguished Service Cross

Silver Star

Distinguished Flying Cross
with two Oak Leaf Clusters

British Distinguished Flying Cross

Purple Heart

Appendix VI

Comparative American Officer Ranks of World War II

Army
General
Lieutenant General
Major General
Brigadier General
Colonel
Lieutenant Colonel
Major
Captain
First Lieutenant
Second Lieutenant

Navy
Admiral
Vice Admiral
Rear Admiral
Commodore
Captain
Commander
Lieutenant Commander
Lieutenant
Lieutenant Junior Grade
Ensign

Abbreviations

A.........................Advanced Landing Ground or Strip (e.g. A-2)
A-.........................Attack (e.g. A-20 Boston)
A/A ....Antiaircraft
AAF ....Army Air Field or Army Air Force(s)
AC ....Air Corps
A/C or a/c............Aircraft
A/D ....Airdrome
AT- ....Advanced Trainer
Ar- ....Arado
B- ....Bomber
BT- ....Basic Trainer
BG ....Bomb or Bombardment Group
BS ....Bomb or Bombardment Squadron
C- ....Cargo
CO ....Commanding Officer
DC- ....Douglas Commercial
Do- ....Dornier
E/A or e/a ....Enemy Aircraft
ETO ....European Theater of Operations
F- ....Fighter
FC ....Fighter Command
FG ....Fighter Group
Fi- ....Fieseler
FS ....Fighter Squadron
FT-E ....353rd FS letter code (FT) and a/c letter code (E) for *Bonnie "B"*
FW ....Fighter Wing

FW- ....Focke-Wulf
Gp ....Group
(H) ....Heavy
He- ....Heinkel
IP ....Initial Point
Ju- ....Junkers
KIA.....................Killed in Action
L/F ....Landfall
M/E or m/e..........Multi-engine
Me- ....Messerschmitt
MTO ....Mediterranean Theater of Operations
MIA ....Missing in Action
OH- ....Observation Helicopter
OPS or Ops ....Operations Office
P- ....Pursuit
PBY- ....Patrol, Bomber, Consolidated Aircraft Corporation
PT- ....Primary Trainer
POW ....Prisoner of War
PTO ....Pacific Theater of Operations
RAF ....Royal Air Force
R/T.....................Radio Transmitter
R/V.....................Rendezvous
S/E or s/e ....Single-Engine
SOP ....Standard Operating Procedure
Sqdn ....Squadron
TAC ....Tactical Air Command
T/D ....Touchdown
T/E or t/e ....Twin-Engine
T/G ....Target
TOT ....Time Over Target
T/U ....Time Up
U- ....*Untersee boot* (Undersea boat)
UH- ....Utility Helicopter
USAAF ....United States Army Air Force(s)
USO ....United Service Organizations
UT-.....................Troops to United Kingdom
V- ....*Vergeltungswaffe* (Vengeance Weapon)

GLOSSARY

Abort ....Returning from a mission before reaching the target
Ace ....A fighter pilot with five or more aerial victories
Ack-Ack ....Antiaircraft fire or flak
Attitude ....The position of an aircraft in relation to the horizon

Bandits	Enemy aircraft
Base aerienne	French Air base
Barrel Roll	The combination of a loop and a roll
Big Friends	Multi-engine Allied bombers
Bogies	Potentially dangerous unidentified aircraft
Bounce	To attack or be attacked by an aircraft
Chandelle	Reversing course via a steep, climbing turn with power
Contrails	Condensation or vapor trails from high-flying aircraft
Deflection Shot	A side-angle shot
Element	A formation of two fighters
Flak	Antiaircraft fire or ack-ack
Flight	Two elements of fighters
Flugplatz	German flying place/airdrome
Gaggle	A cluster or group of loosely organized enemy aircraft
Group	Three or four squadrons of fighters
Hardstand/spot	A hard surface area used to park aircraft
Immelmann	A half-loop followed by a half-roll
Inverted Split-S	A half-roll followed by a half outside loop
Jinxing	Sudden action to avoid flak
Little Friends	Allied fighters
Loop	A complete vertical circle
Lufberry	Fighters circling in a tight turn
Mayday	Distress call
Operations	The office(r) responsible for the daily assignment of pilots and aircraft
Outside Loop	A loop with the pilot on the outside of the vertical circle
Revetment	Protected enclosure for an aircraft
Roll	A complete revolution along the aircraft's longitudinal axis while maitaining level flight
Section	Two flights of fighters or half a squadron
Slow Roll	A complete revolution along the aircraft's longitudinal axis while maintaining level flight at reduced speed
Snap Roll	A fast, complete revolution along the aircraft's longitudinal axis while maintaining level flight
Sortie	A mission flown by one aircraft
Spin	A steep, spiraling dive
Split-S	A half-roll followed by a half-loop
Squadron	Three or four flights of fighters
Stall	The loss of lift caused by insufficient airspeed
"S" Turns	A slow, banking turn to the right, left and right while maintaining level flight
Trim	Adjusting the control tabs to maintain proper flying attitude

BIBLIOGRAPHY

ARTICLES, BOOKS, GUIDES, NEWSPAPERS, REPORTS, AND WEBSITES:

Air-Ground Teamwork on the Western Front: The Role of the XIX Tactical Air Command during August 1944 – An Interim Report. Washington, D.C.: Reprinted by the Center for Air Force History, 1992.

Anderson, Clarence E. and Joseph P. Hamelin. *To Fly and Fight – Memoir of a Triple Ace.* Pacifica, CA: Pacifica Military History, 1990. Available from www.cebudanderson.com.

Arado Ar 234 B-2 Blitz – Summary. Smithsonian National Air and Space Museum, Washington, D.C. www.nasm.si.edu/collections/artifact.cfm?id.

Athlone Castle. "Athlone Castle 1936." The Ocean Liner Virtual Museum. www.oceanlinermuseum.co.uk/Athlone%20Castle.html.

Boyce, J. Ward, ed. *American Fighter Aces Album.* Mesa, AZ: The American Fighter Aces Association, 1996.

Boyne, Walter J. *ACES In Command: Fighter Pilots as Combat Leaders.* Dulles, VA: Brassey's, Inc., 2001.

Brereton, Lewis H. *The Brereton Diaries – The War in the Air in the Pacific, Middle East and Europe: 3 October 1941 - 8 May 1945.* New York: William Morrow and Company, 1946.

Brown, Arthur F., ed. *History in the Sky: 354th Pioneer Mustang Fighter Group.* San Angelo, TX: Newsfoto Publishing Co., 1946.

Camp Kilmer, NJ. "Information Office Fact Sheet – 1958." Rutgers University. www2.scc.rutgers.edu/njh/WW2/ww2women/kilmer.htm.

Cole, Hugh M. *United States in World War II – The European Theater of Operations: The Lorraine Campaign.* Washington, D.C.: U.S. Government Printing Office, 1993.

Dean, Francis H. *America's Hundred Thousand – The U.S. Production Fighter Aircraft of World War II.* Atglen, PA: Schiffer Publishing, Ltd., 1997

Delve, Ken. *D-DAY The Air Battle.* Rambury, UK: The Crowood Press Ltd., 2004

Donald, David, ed. *American Warplanes of World War II – Combat Aircraft of the United States Army Air Force, US Navy, US Marines, 1941 – 1945.* New York: Barnes & Noble Books, 2000.

_____. *Warplanes of the Luftwaffe.* Westport, CT: AIRtime Publishing Inc., 1999.

Eisenhower, Dwight D. *Crusade in Europe.* Garden City, NY: Doubleday & Company, Inc., 1949.

Freeman, Roger A. *The Mighty Eighth: A History of the Units, Men and Machines of the US Eighth Air Force.* New York: Sterling Publishing Co., 2001.

The Ninth Air Force in Colour: UK and the Continent – World War Two. New York: Sterling Publishing Co., 1995.

Galland, Adolf. *The First and the Last: The Rise and Fall of the German Fighter Forces, 1939-1945.* New York: Ballantine Books, Inc., 1960.

Gammack, Gordon. "I.S.C. Aces's Score: 13½." *Des Moines Register,* May 23, 1944.

Gross, Clayton Kelly. *Live Bait – WWII Memoirs of an Undefeated Fighter Ace.* Portland,

OR: Inkwater Press, 2006.
Gunston, Bill. *The Anatomy of Aircraft*. Stamford, CT: Longmeadow Press, 1988.
Gurney, Gene. *Five Down and Glory*. New York: Ballantine Books, Inc., 1958.
Hamilton Field, CA. "Historic California Posts, Camps, Stations and Airfields: Hamilton Air Force Base." California State Military Museum. www.militarymuseum.org/HamiltonAFB.html.
Haulman, Daniel L., ed. *USAF Wartime Aerial Victory Credits*. AFHRA, 2000. *USAF Wartime Aerial Victory Credits*. AFHRA, 2000. Website version: www.au.af.mil/au/afhra/avc.asp. 2009.
Higham, Robin, ed. *Flying American Combat Aircraft in WWII: 1939-45*. Mechanicsburg, PA: Stackpole Books, 2004.
Hill City News. Publications. "Years 1910-1955." Minnesota Historical Society (MHS), St. Paul, MN.
Holcomb, Michael. *Hill City – Created by Dreams Built by People*. Self-published, 2003.
Hoppes, Jonna Doolittle. *Calculated Risk: The Extraordinary Life of Jimmy Doolittle – Aviation Pioneer and World War II Hero*. Santa Monica, CA: Santa Monica Press LLC, 2005.
Howard, James H. *Roar of the Tiger*. New York: Pocket Books, 1993.
Johnson, John E. *Full Circle – The Tactics of Air Fighting: 1914 – 1964*. New York: Ballantine Books, Inc., 1964.
Lafarge, Frederic. Paper. *"Un siecle d'aviation a Reims."* Administrateur du Musee de la Base aerienne 112, Reims, France.
Landis, James M. "Get Ready To Be Bombed." *The American Magazine*, June 1943.
Lange, William and Esther, eds. *The Hill City Saga*. Self-published articles from the *Hill City News*, 1989.
Lehner, Larry and Dorothy. *McNair, Verndale to St. Lo*. Verndale, MN: Verndale Historical Society, 1976.
Lemen III, Robert N. *The Rabey Line – Being an Account of the Life and Death of a Short-Line Railroad in the Minnesota Northwoods*. Self-published, 1970.
Luke Field, AZ. "U.S. Air Force Fact Sheet-Luke AFB History." Luke AFB. www.luke.af.mil/factsheets/factsheet_print.asp?fsID=5049&page=1.
Mack, Warren and Al Zdon. *One Step Forward: The Life of Ken Dahlberg*. Minneapolis, MN: I Was There Press, 2008.
Mauer, Mauer, ed. *Air Combat Units of World War II*. Washington D.C.: U.S. Government Printing Office, 1983.
Memorial Union. "About Memorial Union." Iowa State University. www.mu.iastate.edu/about.php.
Merril, Sandra D. *Donald's Story – Captain Donald R. Emerson: A 4th Fighter Group Pilot Remembered*. Berlin, MD: Tebidine Publishing, 1996.
Minnesota Legionnaire. Publications: "July-August 1932." The American Legion, Minnesota Veterans Service Building, St. Paul, MN.
Minter Field, CA. "Historic California Posts: Minter Field." California State Military Museum. www.militarymuseum.org/MinterField.html.
Morison, Samuel Eliot and Henry Steele Commager. *The Growth of the American Republic (Volume 2)*. New York: Oxford University Press, 1962.
Morison, Samuel Eliot. *The History of the United States Naval Operations in World War II*

The Battle of the Atlantic: 1939-1943 (Volume I). Edison, NJ: Castle Books, 2001.

_____. *The History of the United States Naval Operations in World War II – The Atlantic Battle Won: May 1943- May 1945 (Volume X)*. Edison, NJ: Castle Books, 2001.

_____. *The History of the United States Naval Operations in World War II – The Invasion of France and Germany: 1944-1945 (Volume XI)*. Edison, NJ: Castle Books, 2001.

Olynyk, Frank. *Stars & Bars: A Tribute to the American Fighter Ace 1920 – 1973*. London: Grub Street, 1995.

Ong, William A. *Target Luftwaffe – The Tragedy and the Triumph of the World War II Air Victory*. Kansas City, KS: The Lowell Press, 1981.

Opsvig, John T., Arthur W. Owen, and William J. Purvis, eds. *LUKE FIELD*, Vol. Two, No. Four. Phoenix, AZ: Published by Aviation Cadets of Class 42-I, 1942. AFHRA.

Pettit, Ted S., ed. *Handbook for Boys*. New Brunswick, NJ: Boy Scouts of America, 1955.

Pitts, Jesse Richard. *Return to Base: Memoirs of a B-17 Copilot, Kimbolton, England, 1943-1944*, Charlottesville, VA: Howell Press, Inc., 2004.

Santa Ana Army Air Base, CA. "History of the SAAAB." Costa Mesa Historical Society. www.costamesahistory.org/saaab.htm.

Short Guide to Great Britain, A. War and Navy Departments, Washington, D.C.: U.S. Government Printing Office, 1943.

Shwedo, Bradford J. *XIX Tactical Air Command and ULTRA: Patton's Force Enhancers in the 1944 Campaign in France*. Maxwell AFB, AL: Air University Press, 2001.

Sims, Edward H. *American Aces in Great Fighter Battles of World War II*. New York: Ballantine Books, Inc., 1958.

Slater, Harry E. *Lingering Contrails of THE BIG SQUARE A: A History of the 94th Bomb Group (H) 1942-1945*. Nashville, TN: Carley Publishing, 1980.

Spearhead in the West, 1941-1945: The Third Armored Division. Frankfurt am Main, Germany: Kunst und Webedruck, 1945.

Stelzriede, Marshall. *Marshal Stelzriede's Wartime Story: The Experiences of a B-17 Navigator during World War II*. www.stelzriede.com.

Sweeting, C. G. *Combat Flying Clothing: Army Air Forces Clothing during World War II*. Washington, D.C.: Smithsonian Institution Press, 1984.

_____. *Combat Flying Equipment: U.S. Army Aviator's Personal Equipment, 1917-1945*. Washington, D.C.: Smithsonian Institution Press, 1989.

Thole, Lou. *Forgotten Fields of America (Volume IV)*. Missoula, MT: Pictorial History Publishing Company, 2007.

Thunderbird Field, AZ. *"The Road to Modern Glendale."* City of Glendale (AZ). www.glendaleaz.com./kidzone/glendalehistory.cfm.

Turner, Richard E. *Big Friend, Little Friend – Memoirs of a World War II Fighter Pilot*. Garden City, NY: Doubleday, 1969.

U.S. Army in World War II Atlas: The European Theater. Minnetonka, MN: The National Historical Society, 1996.

USS *Texas*. "Battleship *Texas* Historic Site." Texas Parks and Wildlife Department. www.tpwd.state.tx.us/spdest/findadest/parks/battleship.

Watson, Stan. *Precious Moments – The History of Spang Community*. Self-published, 1993.

Williams Field, AZ. "Site History: 1941-1948." Arizona Department of Environmental Quality. www.azdeq.gov/environ/waste/sps/download/phoenix/wafb.pdf.

Author Interviews, Collections, Correspondence, Documents, and Memoirs:

Beerbower, Albert B. Personal Collection. "Beerbower Genealogy Records."
_____. "Letters from Clarence W. and Josie F. Beerbower to Wayne P. and Elizabeth Beerbower."
_____. "From Land O'Lakes to Luftwaffe" by Major Donald W. Dresden, April 1944. IX Fighter Command publication.
Beerbower, Darrel W. and Arlene M. Personal Collection. "Darrel W. Beerbower, Personal Memoir." 1996.
_____. "Letters from Don M. Beerbower to Darrel W. and Arlene M. Beerbower."
_____. "Letter from 1st Lt. Albert J. Feigen to Clarence W. Beerbower." March 12, 1945.
Beerbower, Don M. Records. "Academic Records." Parks Library and Office of the Registrar, Iowa State University, Ames, IA.
_____. "Birth Certificate." Saskatchewan Department of Health, Regina, SK.
_____. "Membership Roll: 1933." United Methodist Church, Hill City, MN.
_____. "Military Service Records and Correspondence." National Personnel Records Center (NPRC), St. Louis, MO.
_____. "School Records." Hill City High School, Hill City, MN.
Beerbower, Elayne A. Personal Collection. "Don M. Beerbower, Diary: 1942-1944."
_____. "27th ATG Form 025."
Bickel, Carl G. *Before the Contrails Fade Away*. Personal Memoir, 2005.
Dichtel, Frank. *Memories at Age 94*. Personal Memoir, 1986.
Kutcher [Kucera], William F. Records. "World War I Military Service Record." MHS.
McKean, Glenn J. Records. "Academic Records." Office of the Registrar, Iowa State University, Ames, IA.
Panter, Leon H. Records. "World War II Army Enlistment Records." Record Group 64, NARA.
_____. "Military Service Records." NPRC.
Rogers, Felix Michael. "Letter to Minnesota Aviation Hall of Fame." Minnesota Aviation Hall of Fame, Plymouth, MN.
Sailer, Archie G. *This is my Life*. Personal Memoir, 1990.
Sailer, Paul M. Personal Interviews. Anderson, William Y. *Captain Willie Y. Anderson – Reflections: P-51 Mustang Fighter Ace 1941-1945*. 2000.
_____. Beerbower, Elayne A. Interviews. 1999-2009.
_____. Bradley, Jack T. *Colonel Jack Bradley – Reflections: World War II P-51 Mustang Fighter Ace*. 1999-2000.
_____. Cannon, James. *Lieutenant Colonel James Cannon – World War II P-51 Mustang Fighter Pilot: The 353rd Fighter Squadron*. 2003.
_____. Chassey, George. Interview. 2009.
_____. Chisholm, Donald J. Interview. 2011.
_____. Dahlberg, Kenneth H. *Major Kenneth Dahlberg – World War II P-51 Mustang*

_____. *Ace: The 353rd Fighter Squadron – Summer 1944.* 1999.
_____. Deeds, Frederick B. Interview. 2011.
_____. Gross, Clayton Kelly. *Captain Clayton Kelly Gross – Reflections: P-51 Mustang Fighter Ace 1941-1945.* 2000.
_____. Hankerson, Marshall R. *Marshall Hankerson – Reflections: The Beerbowers, Hankersons and Sailers of Hill City.* 2000.
_____. Healy, William C. *Lieutenant Colonel William C. Healy, Reflections: B-17 Flying Fortress Pilot, 1941-1945.* 2001.
_____. Mattie, John D. *Lieutenant Colonel John Mattie – World War II P-51 Mustang Fighter Pilot: Tonopah, Nevada to Barth, Germany.* 2003.
_____. Miller, John S. *First Lieutenant John S. Miller, World War II P-51 Fighter Pilot: The 353rd Fighter Squadron – 1944.* 2003-2004.
_____. Regis, Edward R. *Lieutenant Colonel Edward Regis – World War II Fighter Pilot: The 353rd Fighter Squadron.* 2003.
_____. Rogers, Felix Michael. *General F. Michael Rogers – World War II P-51 Mustang Fighter Ace: The 353rd Fighter Squadron Mission Near Reims, France, August 9, 1944.* 1999.
_____. Sailer, Chester T. *Sergeant Chet Sailer – Reflections: A Third Army Soldier in W.W. II from "The Bulge" to Czechoslovakia.* 1995.
_____. Sailer, Viola Dichtel. Interviews. 1998-2011.
_____. Springer, Richard, R. Interview, 2011.
_____. Triventi, Michael. Interview. 2009.
_____. Zosel, Robert C. Interview. 2000. Wadena County Historical Society, Wadena, MN.
Sailer, Paul M. Personal Correspondence: Clarence E. Anderson, William Y. Anderson, Arlene Beerbower, Albert B. Beerbower, Darrel W. Beerbower, Elayne A. Beerbower, Lowell Brueland, James Cannon, Donald J. Chisholm, Frederick B. Deeds, Archie Difante, Nathan Glick, Clayton Kelly Gross, Marshall R. Hankerson, Bonnie Beerbower Hansen, Daniel L. Haulman, Becky S. Jordan, Naomi Langran, Chantal Lemaire, John D. Mattie, Ronald L. Morton, Tim Nenninger, Anne O'Connor, Lieutenant Peron, Edward R. Regis, Clark Rice, Patsy Robertson, Bradford J. Shwedo, Richard R. Springer, and Michael Triventi.

MILITARY SOURCES:

IV Fighter Command Staff. "Biographical Questionnaire for Officers of IV Fighter Command: Bickell, George R., Bradley, Jack T., Martin, Kenneth R. and Seaman, Owen M." Microfilm B0311, Air Force Historical Research Agency (AFHRA), Maxwell AFB, AL.
VIII Fighter Command Staff. "Intelligence Summary No. 197." File Number 520.332, AFHRA.
IX Fighter Command Staff. "Encounter Reports." Microfilm 5721, AFHRA.
_____. "354th Fighter Group Mission Reports, Field and Operations Orders." File Number 535.332, AFHRA.
XIX Tactical Air Command Staff. "Operations Order No. 9, Mission X51-1 and Mission X51-1: Summary." IRIS No. 23856, AFHRA.
_____. "Ordnance – Armament Handbook for Tactical Air Liaison Officers." Micro-

film 5900, AFHRA.

_____. "Unit History." Microfilms 5849, 5898, and 5899, AFHRA.

94th Bomb Group (H) Staff. "Mission Report, May 29, 1944." Record Group 18, National Archives and Records Administration (NARA), Washington, D.C.

96th Bomb Group (H) Staff. "Report of Bremen Mission, December 20, 1943." Microfilm B0191, AFHRA.

303rd Bombardment Group (H). "Mission No. 236." 303rd Bomb Group Association. www.303rdbg.com.

338th Fighter Squadron Staff. "Mission Summary, December 20, 1943." Microfilm A0776, AFHRA.

353rd Fighter Squadron Staff. "Encounter Reports and Unit History." Microfilm A0782-A, AFHRA.

_____. "Combat Mission Schedules." Record Group 18, NARA.

354th Fighter Group Staff. "Encounter, Mission, Operations Reports and Unit Historical Data Sheet: 15 November 1942 to 30 September 1943." Microfilm B0312, AFHRA.

_____. "Unit History." Microfilms B0311 and B3012, AFHRA.

356th Fighter Squadron Staff. "Unit History." Microfilm A0783, AFHRA.

359th Bombardment Squadron (H) Staff. "Mission Reports." Microfilm A0587, AFHRA.

Eighth Air Force Staff. "Mission No. 379." File Number 520.332, AFHRA.

United States Naval Administration in World War II – History of Convoy and Routing: 1939-1945. Washington, D.C.: Commander in Chief, United States Fleet, Navy Department Library, 1945.

U.S. Tenth Fleet Staff. "Records of the Tenth Fleet, Convoy Report: UT-4." Record Group 38, NARA, College Park, NJ.

World War II Army Air Forces. USAF Flight Safety Records. "Accident Reports: 42-6-9-4, 43-2-5-6, 43-3-20-4, 43-4-16-32, 44-2-10-509, 44-3-19-516, 44-5-12-510, 44-5-19-519, 44-6-6-533, 44-6-28-532, 44-7-4-14, 45-7-13-523, 45-7-26-526, 45-7-31-532, 45-8-3-525." IRIS Nos. 00877046 through 00877353, AFHRA.

_____. "Individual Aircraft Record Cards: B-17F #42-3288." Microfilm ACR #41. "B-17G #42-31483." Microfilm ACR #52. "P-51B #43-12375 and P-51B #43-12457." Microfilm ACR #82, AFHRA.

_____. "Individual Deceased Personnel Files: Beerbower, Don M., Brunner, Melvin M., Kerley, James W., Kong, Wah Kau, McDowell, Don, Parsons, James J., Seaman, Owen M." U.S. Army Human Resources Command, Alexandria, VA.

_____. "Luftwaffe Aerial Photo – DT/SP, Box #1–Print 89," Record Group 373, NARA.

_____. "Missing Air Crew Reports: 1464, 1704, 1750, 1810, 2046, 2166, 2327, 2328, 2329, 2803, 2804, 2805, 3152, 3277, 3560, 3635, 3636, 4028, 4107, 4233, 4422, 4678, 4680, 4681, 4753, 5121, 5133, 5137, 5541, 5695, 6289, 8149, 8150, 8226." Record Group 92, NARA.

_____. "Ninth Air Force Motion Picture Film." Control Number MWDNM (m) – 18-CS-1803, NARA.

INDEX

Page numbers in *italics* are photographs or images

A

A-1 Advanced Landing Strip (ALS), France, 306, 357, *358*
A-2 ALS, France, 1, 107, 307, 312, 316–317, *318*, 319–320, 322–326, *329*, 329–331, *330*, 334, 337, 341–342, 345–347, 350, 352–355, 357–359, *358*, 361, 364, 366, 373, 375, 381–382, 384–385
A-3 ALS, France, 357, *358*
A-4 ALS, France, 323, 357, *358*
A-31 ALS, France, 388
A-62 ALS, France, 400, *400*
A-66 ALS, France, 400
Air-Sea-Rescue, 150, 272, 310, 340
Ajo Army Airfield, Arizona, 65, 67
Alford, W. Frank, 95, *100*
Allen, Lieutenant, 263
Allen, Mrs., 11
Allin, F. W., 14
American Volunteer Group (AVG), 94
Anderson, Clarence E. "Andy, Bud," 49–50, 59, *59*, 72–73, 183, *184*, 186
Anderson, John, 77, 84–85, 89
Anderson, William Y. "Willie Y.", 45, 50, 80, 96, *100*, 102, 121, 132, 138, 212–215, 219–220, 236–237, 244, 255, 258, 261, 264, 270, 272, 284, 287, 296, 307, 311, 314, 318, *318*, 322, 324, 331, 333, 338–340, *340*, 357, 362, 364, 383
Angell, T., 113–114
Angel's Playmate (P-51), 1
Ar-234 (tech data/photo), 357, *359*
Arkansas (battleship), 290, 292, 326
Arnold, Henry H. "Hap," 182, 214, 244, 255
Arnold, John H., 174, 260, 284–285, 300
Arson's Reward (P-51), 1, 338, 359, 362, 384–385
Associated Press, 392
AT-6 Texan (tech data/photo), 57, *58*
Athies Airdrome, England, 284
Athlone Castle (merchant troop transport), *112*, 113–115, 118, 120, 330

B

B-17 Flying Fortress (tech data/photos), 133, *133-134*, *144*, *277*, *279*
B-24 Liberator (tech data/photos), 133, *134*, *241*
B-25 Mitchell (tech data/photo), *36*, 122
B-26 Marauder (tech data/photo), 232, *233*
Baer, Harry R., 140, 164, 174
Baird, J.J., *100*
Bakalar, John E., 294, 313, 320
Barris, Lieutenant, 94
Bartholdi (Huntley), Emily, 3
Bartow Army Air Base, Florida, 285
Base aerienne 112, France, 289, 376
Bauer, Malena H., 21
Beantown Banshee (P-51), 1, 249, 323–324, 338–339
Beck, Bill, 72
Bedehop, Ben, 106
Beerbower, Albert B. "Ben," *18*, 29
Beerbower, Albert E., 6
Beerbower (Ziegenhagen), Arlene M., *22*, 31, 40, 42–44, 47, 50, 52–55, 59–63, 86, 92, 103, 109, 154, 253, 256, 305, 308, 313, 327, 347–348, 367, 369, 390, 393
Beerbower, Bonita Lea "Bonnie, Bonnie Lea," 1, 92–93, 95, 97, 102–104, 124–125, 154, 240, 264–266, u*265*, 331, 389–390, 393, *394*, 395
Beerbower, Clarence W. "C.W.", 5–6, *6*, 8, *10*, 10–11, 16–17, 22, 38, 44, 62–64, 66–67, *68*, 69, 91, *92*, 93, 103, 105, 108, 154, *265*, 266, 327, 331, 388, 390–393, 395–396, 438–439
Beerbower, Darrel W., 6, 14–15, *17–18*, 18, 22, *22*, 26–27, 29, 31, *32*, 34, 40, 42–44, 47, 50, 52–55, 59–62, 86, 92, *92*, 103, 109, 154, 231, *232*, 240, 253, 256, 305, 308, 313, 327–328, 347–348, 367, 369, 390, 393
Beerbower, David G., *18*, 29
Beerbower, Dawn Marie, 92
Beerbower, Don Merrill, *xvi*, 1, 8, 11, 14–16, *17–18*, 18–22, *20–21*, 23, 26–32, *30*, *32*, 34, 35–48, *41–42*, 50–68, *58*, 68, 69–82, *70*, 77, 83–90, *87*, 91–95, *92*, 97–106, *98*, *100*, *104–105*, 107, 108–111, 113–115, 118, 120, 123–124, *126*, 126–129, 131–132, 134–135, 140–141, 143, 148–150, 152–160,

162–164, 167–172, *168,* 174, 178–180, *180,* 182–184, 186–190, *188,* 192–198, *195,* 200, 202–208, *205,* 210–218, *218–219,* 221, 223–224, *226,* 228–232, 234, 237, 240–244, *242,* 246–249, *248,* 252–253, 255–256, 258–267, 269, 272–278, 280–282, *283,* 284–285, 289, 294, 296, 298–303, 305–310, 313, 315, 320–321, 323–324, *326–327,* 327–331, *329, 333,* 333–336, 338, 340–342, 345, 347–348, 350–352, 354, 360–361, 367–370, *374,* 374–376, *378,* 378–398, *398,* 399–400, 436–438

Beerbower (Kutcher), Elayne A., 69–70, *70,* 72–75, 79, 82, 84, 86, 91–99, *98,* 103–106, *104–105,* 108, 124, 132, 154, 189–190, 240, 265–266, 331–332, 370, 389–391, 393–395, *394*

Beerbower, Elizabeth, 29, 57

Beerbower (Carson), Josephine F. "Josie," *6,* 8, *10,* 10–11, *17,* 28–29, 32, 34, 38, 44, 57, 67, 69, 74, *92,* 93, 103, *104,* 105, 154, *265,* 266, 327, 331, 390–393, 396

Beerbower, (Hankerson) Lavaun, 38, 92, *92,* 103, *104,* 154, 390, 393, *398*

Beerbower, Lula D., 6, 29, 38, 266, 393

Beerbower, Wayne P., 29, 57, 67, 69

Bela, Joe, *13*

Bellona (light cruiser), 290

Benes, Anna,

Bennett, Edgar "Ed," 58, 63, 67, 72

Berry, Virginia, 9

Betzer, Frank, 99

Betzer, Lizzie, 99

Bevier, Harvey J. "Frenchy," 45, 50

Bickel, Carl G., 95, 107, 108, 114, 132, 135, 233–234, 236–237, 260, 264, 269, 272, 287, 295, 297–298, 300, 311, 314, 317–320, *318,* 323–324, 329, 331, 333–334, 336–337, *337,* 339, 350, 352, 357, 359, 367, 375, 378–383, 386–387, *387,* 392, 400

Bickell, George R., 73, 99, 100, *101,* 149, *151,* 155, *155,* 164, 185, 188, 192, 208, 211, 215–216, 232, 235, 239, *239,* 244, 246, 262, 268, 273, 282, 294–296, 305, 307, 320–321, 324, *326,* 385, 388–389

Bierbauer, Philip, 6

Bisher, Harry E. "Bish," 45, 50

Bishop, Frank (Mr. and Mrs.), 395

Bishop, John J., 395

Blakeslee, Donald J. M. "Don," *127,* 127–129, 131–132, 135, 140–141, 142, 149, 189, 207, 276, 314

Block Island (escort carrier), 115

Boleman (Christensen), Grace L., 332, 394, 396

Boleman, George K. "Kenneth," 331–332, *332,* 340, 395

Boleman, LeeRoy, 332, 396

Boleman, Paul, *xvi,* 11, 16, 27, 332, 389

Bonnie-"B" (B-17), 400, *400*

Bonnie "B", Bonnie "B" II, (P-51), 1, 107, 124–125, 132, 159–160, 163, *168,* 170, *170,* 174, 194, *195,* 202, 226, 237, 242, *242,* 244, 253, 259, 269, 278, 282, 285, *286,* 289, 296, 300, 305, 307, 310, 323, 327, 331, 334–335, 345, 367–369, 374–376, 378–380, 382, *382,* 386, 389, 392, 400

Bonnie "B" III (P-51), 387, *387*

Bosch, George, 58–59, 64

Bourbon, Hugh A., 369

Bowman, Harold W., 168

Boxted Airdrome, England, 59, 126, 129, 134, 139–140, 142–143, 148, 152–153, 158–159, 162–164, 169, 172, 174–175, 178–179, 181–184, 186–187, 188–190, 191–194, 197–198, 201, 203, 206, 208, 211, 213–214, 217, 220–222, 225, 227–229, 234–236, 238–240, *248,* 272, 360, 369

Bradley, Jack T., 76, 78–79, 81, 85, 94, 98–99, *100,* 106, 125–126, 128, 141, 143–145, 149, 152, 157–158, 162–164, 167, 172, 176–180, *177,* 186–189, 194, 196, 204, 207, 213, 216, 219, 224–225, 227, 230, 232, 236, 238, 241, 244–245, 247, 258–264, 266, 269–270, 272, 282, *283,* 287, 289, 295, 298, 301–307, 310–312, 315, 316–317, 320–321, *321,* 324, 328, 335–336, 344, 348, 369, 385–386, 389, 397

Bradley, Margie, 177

Bradley, Omar N., 306, 354, 361, *361,* 370, *371,* 387

Brereton, Lewis H., *121,* 121–122, 158, 169, 172, 174, 186, 189, 191, 225, 230, 232, 255, 287, 306–307, 316, 326, *326,* 327, *340*

Bridges, D. R. "Red," 58–59, 64

Bronston, Billy B., 181, 200–201, *201,* 203

Brown, Ralph A., 213, 234–235, 357
Brown, Richard H., 294, 312, 314
Brown, Russell S., 284, 352–353, 374, 379
Brueland, Lowell K., *283*
Bruhn, Elmer, xv
Brunner, Melvin M., 145, 147
Bryant, Carleton F., 290
BT-13 Valiant (tech data/photo), 49, *50*
Budleski, Stanley, P, 145–147
Buer, Glendon, 188
Buford, Lieutenant, 152
Bullock, Lieutenant, 89
Bunting, Ira J., 294, 314, 375, 381
Burke, James G., *180,* 181, 211, 234, 270, 282, 314, 322, 375
Burkhardt, Frederic, 188, 282, 309, 316, 328, 330, 350, 383
Bush, Private First Class, 360

C

C-47 Skytrain (tech data/photo), 297 *297*
Cambridge American Cemetery, England, 218
Camp Kilmer, New Jersey, 108, 110, 113, 301, 330
Campbell, Lieutenant, 90
Campbell, Sergeant, 360
Cannon Ball (P-51), 198, 231, 249
Cannon, James "Jim," 59, *59,* 76, 80–81, 83–85, 89, 94, *100,* 102, 126, 128–129, 135, 138–141, 143, 147, 152, 157, 162, 172, 174, 176, 178, 180, 187, 196, *197,* 197–198, 204, 211, 229–231, *230,* 234–235, 237, 244, 247, 249–252, 263, 271, 303, 397
Capetown Castle (merchant troop transport), 118
Carlson, Carl, *100*
Carr, Bruce W., 1, 267, 282, 305, 308, 312, 320, 374, *375,* 376, 379–380
Carson, (Beerbower), Josephine F., 6
Carter, Leslie, 20, 27
Carter, Mrs. W., 32
Casey, William M., 89
Cassen, Harms, 148
Chamberlain, Franklin D., 294
Chambers, Verlin B., 384
Champigneul American Cemetery, France, 392
Chapman, Gordon W., 78–79, *80*
Chapman, Harvey H., 284, 322–323, 342, 352, 357, 362
Chassey, George I., 319, *319,* 355
Chatfield, Stanley E., 78, 89
Chennault, Claire, 94
Chinaman's Chance/No tickee-No washee (P-51), 205
Chisholm, Donald J., 169, 262, *262,* 374

Christensen, Morley, 19, 31, 389
Christensen, Roy, 20
Churchill, Winston S., 1, 111
City of Bismarck (DC-3), *96*
Class 42-H, 38, 43, 59, 62, 76, 176
Class 42-I, 43, 45, 48, 53, 55–56, 62–64, 67, 72, 76–77, 79, 98, 138, 183, 212, 217
Class 43-F, 301
Coffey, Richard M., 79, 89
Cohen, Philip D., 213, 244, 259–260, 267, 305
Collins, J. Lawton "Lightning Joe," 314, 326
Coningham, Arthur, 326
Convoy UT-1, 111
Convoy UT-4, 111, 113, 115, *116–117*
Cooke, H. D., 113
Coolum, Marco J., 145, 147–148
Coyle, John P., 145, 147
Culbertson, Omer W., 140, 174, 333, *347,* 374, 379
Culbritson, Robert A., 37

D

Dahlberg, Kenneth H. "Ken," 1, 294, 303, 305, 310, 314–315, 323–324, 334, 343, *347,* 383
Dailey, James, xvi
Dalglish, James B., 149
Day's Pay (B-17), *273*
DC-3 airliner (tech data/photo), 96, *96*
Dean, Clifford H., 294, 342, 352, 375, 384
Debden Airdrome, England, 186
Debonair Duke (C-47), 326
Deeds, Frederick B. "Bud," 1, *301,* 301–302, 307–309, 334–335, 345, 374, *374,* 379–380, 384
Deenethorpe Airdrome, England, 168
Dehon, William B., Jr., 213, 224, 242, 249, 257–258, *258*
Des Moines Register, 228, 243
DH-98 Mosquito (tech data), 309
Dichtel, Frank, 15, *15,* 33, 390–391, *391,* 396
Dimm, John, 341
Ding Hao! (P-51), *169,* 210
Dingus (P-51), 373
Do-217 (tech data), 157–158
Doenitz, Karl, 292
Donnell, Ridley, E., 77–78, 84, 95, *100,* 101, 132, 140, 159, 164, 178, *180,* 187, 196, 204, 211–212, *212,* 218, 226, 357
Donohoo, Thomas L., 140, 198, 311, *311,* 312
Doolittle, James H. "Jimmy," 31, 35, 158, 168, 182
Dorchester (troop transport), 111

Downes, James, 285, 369, 387
Dresden, Donald, 244, 247–248
Drinkwater, John, 36
Duluth News Tribune, 392
Duncan, Cecil, 94, 106
Durham, Bernard F., 126
Dutton, Al, 73

E

Eagleston, Glenn T. "Eaggie, Eagle," 78, 99, *101,* 132, 135, 138, *138,* 159, 161–164, 172, 179, 180, *180,* 186, 198, 202, 204, 212, 214, 216–217, 219, 221, 225, 236–237, 244, 249, 252, 255–256, 262–264, 269–270, *283,* 284, 287, 296, 298, 300, 307, 314, 320–321, 324, 389, 397
Eaker, Ira, 158
Earhart, Amelia, 31
Earls Colne Airdrome, England, 152
East, Clyde B., 435
Eaves, Buford M. "Bu, Hardrock," 78, 94, *100,* 128, 135, 138–139, 141, 214, 240, 357
Edgewood Arsenal, Maryland, 93
Edmund B. Alexander (troop transport), 110
Eichorn, H. C., 20
Eisenhower, Dwight D. "Ike," *223,* 223–224, 268, 313, 326, 329–330, 349–351, 356
Eldred, Harlow R., 267, 352–354
Ellington Field, Texas, 98
Elliot, Edward P., 129
Elrod, William T., 213, 224, 244, 259, 267, 300
Emmer, Wallace N. "Bud, Wally," 77–78, 84, 94, 99, *101,* 101–102, 128, 138, 140–141, 143, 149, 153, 159, 172, 178, 180, *180,* 183, 185, *188,* 193–194, 196, *197,* 198, 208, 212, 214, 219, 224, 237, 241, 244, 249, 256, 262–263, 266–267, 269–270, 282, *283,* 298, 300, 305, 307–308, 320, 322–324, 328, *333,* 333–334, 338, 340, 345, 347, 350, 352, 359, 362, 364, 366, 382–386, *386,* 389, 392
Empress of Australia (ocean liner troop transport), 118
Enoree (tanker), 115
Enterprise (aircraft carrier), 93
Epinal American Cemetery, France, 398

F

Fair Isle (cargo transport), 115
Feeble Eagle (P-51), 296, 307
Feigen, Albert J., 227, 268, 283, 285, 288–289, 337–339, 349, 352, 357, 360, 369, 383–385, *384,* 387, 388
Five Grand (B-17), 275–276, 279, 281
Fixmer, Doraldine T., 21
Flugplatz A213, France, 289, 376, *377,* 379–381, 389, 392, 400
Flying Tigers, 94
Forrest, James B., 267, 300
Fort Des Moines, Iowa, 37, 240
Foust, Glenn, 93, 395
Fox, Edward F., 126, 188, *209,* 209–210, 218, 226
Frantz, Carl M., 78, *100,* 135, 141, 143, 169, 183, 185, 186, 209, 211, 229, 231, 237, 241–242, 252, 257–258, 262–263, 267–270, 282, *283,* 284, 296, 298, 300–301, *301,* 311, 313, 320–321, 324
Free, Sergeant, 360
Froholm (Bickel), Doris, 337
FW-190 (tech data/photos), 165, *166, 335*
FW-190 "Dora-9" (tech data), 230

G

Gabreski, Francis S., 343–344
Gammack, Gordon, 226, 243–244, 294
Georges Leygues (light cruiser), 290
Giltner, Joe, 174–175
Glasgow (light cruiser), 290
Glick, Nathan H., 172, *173,* 224, 378
Golden Eagle (cargo transport), 113–114
Goodall, Lieutenant, 209, 229
Goodnight, Robert, *283*
Goxhill Airdrome, England, 287
Graham, Don, 182
Great Lakes Naval Station, Illinois, 154
Green Fury, Green Fury II (B-17), 145–148, 150
Greenham Common Airdrome, England, 118, 121–123, 196
Gross, Clayton Kelly, 207, 247, 304, *304*
Gross, Norman C., 77, 89
Grumbles, "Grump," 50
Gumm, Charles F., Jr., 141
Guzak, Steven V., 38

H

Haas, Tom, xv
Hall, Max, 97
Hamilton Field, California, 69, 71–73, 77, 82–83, 183, 226, 301
Hankerson, Betty, 4
Hankerson, George, 4, 10–11, 15, 17, 93
Hankerson, George "Hank," 390
Hankerson, JoNett, 38, 92, 103, 390

Hankerson (Beerbower), Lavaun "La Vonne," 6, 11, 14, 18
Hankerson, Marshall R. "Marsh," *xvi,* 4, 11–12, *13,* 18, 27, 38, 92, 103, *104,* 154, 396, *398*
Hankerson, Robert "Bob," 15, 93
Hanson, Ralph M., 140, 174
Harber, Lieutenant, 366
Hart, Vincent J., 213, 222–223, 226
Hartman, Elsie, 15, 18–19, 21
Hawkins, George W., 333, 342
Healy, William C. "Bill," 35, 133, 273–282, *274*
Helfers, Melvin C., 360
Henley, David W., 213, 221, 230, 244, 256
Herrick, Lois E., 21
Hewlitt, E. W., 71
Higley Field, Arizona, 38
Hill City News, 2, 4, 9, 12, 14, 20, 23–27, 31–33, 67, 85, 154, 210, 242, 265, 290, 331, 340, 390, 393, 395
Hitler, Adolf, 23, 26, 35, 122, 152, 206, 208, 255, 265, 290, 294, 309, 314, 370, 397
Hoenoff, Reverend, 92
Holton, Hayden H., 267, 282, 339
Hoover, Herbert, 10, 16
Hornet (aircraft carrier), 35, *36,* 158
Horsa gliders, *299*
Howard, James H. "Big Jim," 93–94, *94,* 99, 125, 149, *151,* 155, 164–165, 168–169, *169,* 183, 190, *190,* 194, 197–198, 208, 210, 216, 222, 225, 227, 230, 239, 247, 268, 285, 287, 324, 357, 389, 399
Howell, Lieutenant, 85
Hubbard, Lloyd, 183, 185–186
Hubbard, W. E., 58–59, 64–65
Huffman, Leon A. C., 267, 300
Hunt, Edward E., 95, *100,* 132, 163, 192, 194, 206, 211–212, 214, 225, 230, 232, 242, 244–246, 257, 269–270, *283,* 298, 300, 320, 324
Huntley, Billy, *25*
Huntley, (Bartholdi) Emily, *25*
Huntley, Gay C., 2–4, 11, 14, 19, 23–27, *25,* 30–33, 67, 85, 93, 154, 210, 265, 290, 332, 340, 390–393, 395–396
Huntley, Marjorie, *25*
Huntley, Philip, *xvi,* 11, *13, 25,* 93
Huntley, Robert, *25*
Huntley, Ruth, *25*

I

Ill, George R., 395

J

Jackson, Bernard C. "Bernie," 145, 147
James, Jimmy, 69
James, Myrtle, 69
James, Norma, 69
Janssen, Johann, 150
Jersig, Frederick W., 213
Johns, Dennis L., 174, 226, 230, 357
Johnson, Charles C., 73, 80
Johnson, Flying Instructor, 40, 45
Johnson, John E., 40, 45
Johnson, R. S., *198*
Johnston, William J. "Bill, Billy J.", 19, *20,* 27, 31, 85, 340, 394, *394*
Joy (P-51), 1, 229, *230,* 296, 301, 380
Ju-88 (tech data/photos), 139, *140, 372*

K

Karsnia, Frank, xv
Kaslow, Floyd, *xvi,* 12, *13,* 21, 247
Keane James P., 140, 171, 198, 215–216, 263, 267, 298, 308, 312, 320, 322, 330, *331,* 357
Kegebein, Robert R., 213, 237–238, *238,* 252
Kelly Field, Texas, 76, 81
Kepner, William E., 182–183
Kerley, James W., 78, *100,* 128, 131, 135, 147–148, *148,* 150, *151,* 152, 159, 240, 264
Kesselring, Albert, 292
Kilpatrick, Paul H., 51
King Peter of Yugoslavia, 266
Klein, Richard M. "Dick", 95, *100,* 143, 181, *182,* 213, 357
Koenig, Charles W. "Little Horse," 78, *100,* 140, 169, 204, 219, 256, 262, 264, 272, 314, *318,* 319, 324, 331, 333–334, 336–338, 352–353, 362, 364
Kong, Wah Kau, 95, 99, *100,* 101–103, 114, *114,* 140, 143, 148–149, 159, 162, 164, 180, 184–186, 188, *188, 204,* 204–205, *206,* 213, 218, 240, 246
Kutcher (Benes), Anna, *5,* 6, 11, 21, 26, 34, *265,* 266, 332, 389–391, 393
Kutcher (Kucera), William F. "Bill," 5, *5,* 6, 11, 21, 26, 28, 34, 62, 64, 66–67, *68, 265,* 266, 331–332, 389–391, 393
Kutcher, Adeline, 106, 331
Kutcher, (Beerbower) Elayne, 6, 11, *12,* 19, *20–21,* 21–22, 26, 28, *28,* 30, 34, 37–38, 44, 47, 51, 54, 61–64, 66–68, *68*

L

LaBarge, Lieutenant, 89
Ladurantie, Lieutenant, 381–382
Lamb, Billy J., 213, 216–217, 237–238
Lamb, Lieutenant, 94
Lane, James, 152
Lang (Sailer), Helen G. "Ella," 4
Lang, J. G., 2
Langran, Donald E., 285, 369, *370,* 387
Langran, Naomi, 369
Lashenden Field, England, 225–226, 238–241, 249, 251–253, 259, 260, 264, 267–269, 272, 274, 278, 281–282, 284–285, *286,* 287, 294–298, 300, 305–309, 311, 313–315, 317, 329
Lasko, Captain, 260
Lawrence, C. E., 217
Leach, Jerry D., 126, 152, 171, 198, 214, 375
Leigh-Mallory, Trafford, 191
Lemaire, Mancel, *380–381,* 380–382, 389
Leydens, Mrs. Paul A., 84
Leydens, Paul A., 77, 84–85, *85*
Lind, Carl, 95, *100,* 132, 156, 167, 222–223, 226, 246
Lindbergh, Charles, 24, 31
Lindquist, Thelma M., 21
Lipscy, Margie M., 21
Little Horse "Le Petite Cheval" (P-51), 169, 262, 264, 319, 338, 355, 374
Logan, N. Grant, 95, *100,* 140, *171,* 171–172, 246
Long, Maurice G., 235, 385
Ludwig, Alfred J., 37
Luke Field, Arizona, 47, 54, 56, 57, 59, 61, 64–67, 69, 79, 86, 98, 102, 212, 301, 338, 349
Luke, Frank, Jr., 57
Lutzow (heavy cruiser), 113

M

Mace, Wallace, 73
MacGregor, Aviation Cadet, 51
Magee, John Gillespie, Jr., 65
Mane, Sergeant, 389
Mantz, Paul, 21
Margie Maru (P-51), 177, *224,* 224–225, 244, 282, 284, 317
Martin, Kenneth R., 73, 75, 79–81, *81,* 89, 99, 114, 122, 126–127, 135, 139, 142, *142,* 150, 152, 155–157, 164, 172, 175–176, 181–183, 188–190, *189,* 239–240, 252, 268, 324, 357, 389
Martindale, Vadis D., 21
Mattie, John D., 75, 77–78, 82, 95, 97–99, *100,* 106, 132, 135, 138, 143, 148–149, 152, 171–172, *173,* 177, 183, 185, 191, 194, 198–199, *199,* 203, 205, 212, 214–215, 218, 240, 357
Maxwell Field, Alabama, 38
McCauley, James W., 187, 190, 219, *326*
McCloud, Dr., 92, 97, 99
McDonald, Joseph J., 142, 145, 147
McDowell, Clara, 272
McDowell, Don "Doc," 95, 97, *101,* 132, 197, 202–203, 216–217, *218,* 219–220, 234–235, 241, 246, 252, 259–260, 264, 269, 272, *272,* 300
McGlade, Bob, *13*
McKean, Glenn J. "Mac," *30,* 30–31, 34, 35, 38–39, 45–48, 50–52, 74
McKinney, Aviation Cadet, 51
McNair, Leslie J., 351
Me Too, Evie (P-51), 352–353
Me-109 (tech data/photos), 165, *166, 170*
Me-110 (tech data/photo), 139, *140*
Me-262 (tech data/photo), 242, *243*
Me-410 (tech data/image), 181, *181*
Meadows, Sergeant, 360
Medford Army Airfield, Oregon, 90
Membury Airdrome, England, 123
Meserve, Robert L. "Bob," 126, 132, 164, 179, 196–197, *197,* 200–201, 211, 224, 235, 244, 262–263, 269, 295, 300, 311–312, 315, 320, 324
Meyer, John C., 344
Miller, John S. "Jack," 267, 272, 285, 287, 298, 300, 342, 345–347, *347,* 353, 355, 360–361, 366, 373, 375, 380, 382, 384–386, 389
Mills, Aviation Cadet, 51
Minter Field, California, 47–50, *49,* 52, 55–56, 58, 69
Modansky, Judah H., 276, 278–279
Monarch of Bermuda (ocean liner troop transport), 118
Moneta, William, 85, 172, 183, 185, 203, 205, 226–227
Montcalm (light cruiser), 290
Montgomery, Bernard L., 326
Montijo, John G., 76, 85, 90, 107, 223, 264, 282, 284, 298, 331, 342, 361, 375, 383
Moore, William, 32
Moran, Lieutenant, 235, 263
Morris, Edward M., 89
Morrison, James G., *142*

Morton, Ronald L., 17
Munger, Donald J., 140, 179, 184–187, *187*
My Buddy (P-51), 172, *173,* 203
Mykkanen, Johnny, 69
Mykkanen, Lee, *xvi, 13,* 27, 69, 85

N

Nall, John B., 140, 150, 161–162, *162*
Napier Field, Alabama, 285
Neil, Jerry, 295
Nelson (Sailer), Jean E., 93
Nevada (battleship), 326
Northern Pacific troop train, *109*

O

O'Connor, Frank Q., *283*
O'Hara, David B., 95, *100,* 143, 150, 185, 188, 209, 224, 230, 246, 252, 320, 340, 342, 352, 386
Olmsted, Charles A., 1, *317,* 333, 374, *375,* 376, 379
Olson, Stanley F., 38–39
Operation Argument (Big Week), 192
Operation Cobra, 350
Operation Crossbow, 152, 171, 309
Operation Dragoon, 356
Operation Overlord, 223, 225, 268, 300
Operation Torch, 64
Overfield, Loyd J., 315, 340–341, 352, 357, 362–364, *363*
Owen, Arthur W., 78, 84, *100,* 132, 161–162, 178, 196, 221

P

P-36 Hawk (tech data/photo), 64, *65*
P-38 Lightning (tech data/photo), 111, *153*
P-39 Airacobra (tech data/photo), 71, *71*
P-47 Thunderbolt (tech data/photos), *153, 225, 356*
P-51A/Mustang Mark I (tech data/photo), 122-123, *123*
P-51B/C Mustang (tech data/photos), 125, *160, 170,* 185, *261*
P-51D Mustang (tech data/photos), 317, *317, 387*
Pahkar, Gaylord, *xvi*
Paine Field, Washington, 77
Panter, Leon H. "Pappy," 124–125, *125,* 159, 244, 285, 296, 348, 367–369, 374, 382, 386–387
Parker, John W., 399–400
Parkins, Robert M., 385
Parnell, Edward V., Jr., 213, 217, 233–235, 252, 357
Parsons, James J. "Snapper," 78, *100,* 132, 138, 144–146, 164, 178, *180,* 186, 196, *197,* 217–220, *218,* 240, 263, 272
Parsons, Jeanette, 218
Patch, Alexander M., 356
Patton, George S., Jr. "Old Blood and Guts," 268–269, *269,* 351, 355–356, 360–361, *361,* 366, *371,* 371–372, 392, 397
PBY-5A Catalina (tech data/photo), 85, *86*
Pearl Harbor, Hawaii, 33, 40, 85, 274, 397
Perkins, Bill, 270–271
Pfaff, Roy, 113, 115
Phillips, William J., 213, 217, 267
Pinkerton, Edwin H. "Pink," 294, 345, 349–350, 353, 357, 362–364, *363*
Pinkerton, Helen, 364, 394
Pipes, Glenn H., 126, 164, 167, 184, 186, 244, 258, 263, 269–272, *271,* 300
Poddington Airdrome, England, 170, *170*
Pomeroy, Staff Sergeant., 97
Portland Army Air Base, Oregon, 97, 106
Post, Wiley, 31
POW Transit Camp for Air, Belgium, 389, 397
Pretty Baby (P-51), 1
Priser, Robert L., 155, *155,* 158–159, 162, 164, 174–175, 176, 196, 216
PT-17 Stearman (tech data/photo), 41, *42,* 43

Q

Queen Elizabeth (ocean liner troop transport), 301
Queen Mary (ocean liner troop transport), 275
Quesada, Elwood R. "Pete," *121,* 121–122, 124, 126–127, 172, 182–183, 186, 190–191, 306, 329, 355, 362

R

Rabey, Ardis, 69
Rabey, Del, 69
Randolph Field, Texas, 38
Rawlings, Orrin D., 294, 312
Read, Charles, F., 140, 174
Reagan, Robert D., 217, 373
Regis, Edward R. "Ed," 95, 99, *101,* 102, 115, 118, 120, 132, 135, 161–162, 186, 193, 198, 213, 221, 227–228, 230, 244–246, *245,* 252, 271, 397
Regis, Mary, 213
Reid, Lieutenant, 274
Reynolds, Robert, 213, 230, 244, 257, 264, 267, 312, 323, 336, 352, 375, 381, 384–386
Ricci, Albert J., 126, 164, 213, 215, *216,* 218, 226
Rice, Clark, 27
Richardson, Ben C., 187
Rick O' Shay (P-47), 356

Rickenbacker, Eddy, 31
Rigor Mortis (P-51), 1, 245, 296
Ritchey, Andrew J., 315, 374, 379
Robak, Ben, *13*
Robedeau, Ralph A., 51
Rody, John, 140, 174, 244, 263, 295–296, 310, *310,* 312
Rogers, Felix Michael, 95, 99, *100,* 106, 107, 114, 132, 135, 152–153, 159, 162, 167, 169, 177, 186, 188, 193, 223, 239, 241, 246, 249–252, 256, 261, 269–270, 284, 320, 323–324, 331, 333–334, 336, 338–339, *339,* 343, 351–354, 357, 361, 374, 378–380, 385–386, 388–389, 399
Roosevelt, Franklin D., 16, 24–25, 33, 111, 287
Rose, Franklin, Jr., 315, 359–362
Rougham Field, England, 274–275, 281
Russell, Mrs. W. B., 393

S

Sailer (Dichtel), Viola, 391
Sailer, Archie G., *xvi, 13,* 27, *27,* 91, 93, 110, 211
Sailer, Chester T. "Chet," 9, 12, *13,* 27, *27,* 91, 93
Sailer, Joe, 4, 9, 11–12, *16,* 20, *27,* 33, 93, 154, 396
Salem Army Airfield, Oregon, 94
Santa Ana Army Air Base, California, 38, 43
Santa Rosa Army Air Base, California, 83–84, 90, 95, 98, 102, 223
Sawday, James "Jim", *xvi, 13,* 32
Saylor, Glen, 393
Scampy (P-51), 179
Scharnhorst (battleship), 113
Schoen, Charles, *xvi*
Schultz, Donald M. "Don," 77, 94–95
Scott, Orville L., 213
Seaman, Elizabeth, 151, 394
Seaman, Owen M., 73, 76–77, 79, 83–84, 86, 89, 91, 96, 99, *100,* 103, 106, 126, 128, 135, 139, 141, 143, 147–152, *151,* 155, 159, 175–176, 178, 189, 216, 240, 308
Sedvert, Theodore W., 294, 385
Service, Robert W., 63
Sharp, Clayton, 20
Sheets, Millar, 41
Silva, Robert G., 95, *100,* 143, 157, 194, *209,* 209–210, 218, 226, 246
Simonson, Lieutenant, 366
Sisk, George, 357
Skenyon, Leo F., 140, 174
Skibbereen (P-51), 1, 312, 330, *330*

Skinner, Ed, 26, 390
Skinner, Mrs. Ed, 390
Slinger (escort carrier), 113, 115
Smith, G. S., 275–276, 279–280
Smith, Gordon E., 142, 145–147, 148
Snyder, Marie, 29
Snydman, Leonard "Doc," 300, 346
Sommer, Erich, 357, *358*
Sorensen, Herbert, 21
South Plains Army Airfield, Texas, 231
Spangle, M. E., 279–280
Spanier, Donald G., 145, 147, 150
Spillman, Kenneth, 217
Springer, Richard R., 88, *88*
Stalag Luft III, Germany, 246, 252, 271
Stalag Luft VIIA, Germany, 397
The Stars Look Down (P-51), 330
Stephens, Robert W., 239, *283*
Stewart, W. C., 50
Stoney Cross Airdrome, England, 295–296
Stretz, Donald, *100*
Strom, Chuck, 69
Sullivan, Woodfin M., 213, 259–260, 267, 296, 322, 336, 342
Surprise (merchant troop transport), 118
Swede's Steed (P-51), 264, 307, 340–341

T

Tennant, John H., 97
Teschner, Charles G., 259, 342, 345
Texas (battleship), 113, 115, 290, *291,* 292, 298, 319, 326, 356
Thompson, James M., 145–147
Thunderbird Field, Arizona, *36,* 41–43, 45, 48
Tonopah Army Airfield, Nevada, 75, *77,* 80–83, 95, 98–99, 102, 138, 162, 189, 196, 203, 212, 218, 223, 301, 338–339
Totz, Donald F., 145, 147, 150
Triventi, Michael F., 312, *312,* 330
Trumpeter (escort carrier), 113, 115
Turner, Richard E., 115, *173,* 190, 194, *283,* 295, 304, 320–321, *321,* 329, 364, 366

U

U-220 (submarine), 115
Uhlenberg, Charlie, *100*
ULTRA, 355, 360–361, 370
Urquhart, Edwin D., 213, 267, 298, 322
U.S. Army Ground Forces, 78, 269, 351
U.S. Military Cemetery, England, 272

V

V-1/Fieseler Fi-103 (tech data/photo), 309, *310*
Varney, Thomas S., 95, *100,* 140, 144–146, 164, 188, 233, 246, 258, 260
Vashaw, Bud, *xvi,* 85
Vashaw, Roland, 12, *13,* 33
Visser, Johann, 150

W

Walker, Harold, 9, 12, 14
Wallace, F. J., 20
Walsh, Jerome T., 37
Weber, Frank E., 213, 231, 244, 257
Weller, Marvin, *13,* 27
Weller, Selma, 22
West Cemetery, Reims, France, 389, 392–393
West Malling Airdrome, England, 264
West, William R., 322
Weyland, Otto P., 225, 355–356, 361–362, *371,* 371–373, 375–376
Wheeler Field, Hawaii, 76
Wilkinson, William R., 392
Williams Field, Arizona, 38, 56
Willkie, Wendell, 25
Wilson, Don, 19
Wilson, Durward, 15
Wilson, June J., 21
Wilson, Woodrow, 24
Witsell, Edward F., 395
Wold-Chamberlain Field, Minnesota, 91–92, 94, 106, 390
Wright Field, Ohio, 169

Y

Yaeger, Bernard W., 21

Z

Zemke, Hub, 276
Z-Hub (P-51), 337, 339
Ziegenhagen (Beerbower), Arlene M. 22

Military Units

1st Air Task Force, 178, 258, 263, 276, 281
1st Bombardment Division, 234, 399
1st Infantry Division, 292
2nd Air Task Force, 143–144, 147, 180, 258, 275–276, 278
2nd Bombardment Division, 249
3rd Air Task Force, 234, 249, 258, 276
3rd Armored Division, 372
3rd Bombardment Division, 275–276
4th Air Defense Wing, 90
4th Combat Camera Unit, 294
4th Combat Wing, 276, 279
4th Fighter Command, 89
4th Fighter Group, 127, 186, 207, 276, 314
9th Fighter Squadron, 435
13th Combat Wing, 276, 279–281
14th Armored Division, 397
27th Air Transport Group, 124
29th Infantry Division, 292
30th Infantry Division, 351
31st Fighter Group, 435
32nd Armored Regiment, 372
45th B Combat Wing, 275–276, 278
45th Combat Wing, 143, 279
47th Panzer Corps, 370
49th Fighter Group, 435
56th Fighter Group, 276
61st Fighter Squadron, 435
62nd Fighter Squadron, 435
67th Tactical Reconnaissance Group, 122, 126
70th Fighter Wing, 187, 219, 226, 320
78th Fighter Group, 183
78th Fighter Squadron, 73
80th Infantry Division, 392
82nd Airborne Division, 292, 295
90th Infantry Division, 392
92nd Bomb Group (H), 170
92nd Combat Wing, 276
94th Bomb Group (H), 133, 274–281
95th Bomb Group (H), 210
96th Bomb Group (H), 143, 145, 149
100th Bomb Group (H), 210
100th Fighter Wing, 225
101st Airborne Division, 292, 295, 298
133 Squadron, 127
136 Station Hospital, 217
303rd Bombardment Group, 399
315th Engineer Combat Battalion, 392
326th Fighter Squadron, 71

328th Fighter Group, 71–73
329th Fighter Squadron, 73
335th Fighter Squadron, 127
338th Fighter Squadron, 143, 147
353rd Fighter Squadron (Fighting Cobras), 73, 76, 82, 83, 90, 97, *100,* 102, *102,* 107, 110, 114, 124, 126, 128–129, 131–132, 135, 138, 140, 143–144, 146–148, 150, 152, 155, 157–158, 162–163, 169, 175–178, 180–181, 185, 187, 191–192, 194, 197–198, 204, 206–208, 211–216, 221–222, 224–227, 230–232, 234–235, 237, 240–241, 244, 246, 248–249, 252, 256–260, 263, 265–267, 270, 272, 307–308, 311–315, 316–317, 319, 324, 331, 333–335, 337, 340, 342, 344, 350, 352–355, 357, 360–362, 364, 366, 367, 369, 374–376, 383–385, 388, 397–399
353rd Fighter-Bomber Squadron, 273, 282–284, 288, 294–298, 302–304, 306
354th Fighter Group (Pioneer Mustang Group), 73, 75–76, 78, 82–83, 93–94, 103, 108, 110, 113, 118, 120–122, 127, 129, 131, 135, 142, 149, 155, 158, 172, 174, 183, 190, 192, 207–208, 221, 224–225, 230, 239, 249, 255, 258, 263, 265, 268, 316, 328–329, 350, 352, 355, 357, 362, 369–370, *378,* 388, 397
354th Fighter-Bomber Group, 273, 275–276, 278, 280–281, 287, 294, 296, 303, 305, 307, 314–315
355th Fighter Squadron, 73, 106, 110, 135, 141, 153, 155, 163, 178, 186, 192, 208, 215, 225, 235, 247, 252, 260, 263, 298, 303–304, 308, 322, 342, 350, 354, 384–385
356th Fighter Squadron, 73, 80, 90, 93, 94, 107, 115, 125, 135, 152–153, 155, 163, 178, 190, 194, 208, 223, 225, 231, 257, 270, 288, 303–304, 308, 320, 329, 354, 364, 375–376, 384
356th Fighter-Bomber Squadron, 295
357th Fighter Group, 174, 182–183, 192
358th Fighter Group, 225
359th Bombardment Squadron, 399
362nd Fighter Group, 225
363rd Fighter Squadron, 174–175, 225
364th Fighter Group, 435
401st Bomb Group (H), 168

487th Fighter Squadron, 435
501st Parachute Regiment, 298
506th Parachute Regiment, 298
1576th Quartermaster Battalion, 211
VIII Bomber Command, 208, 210, 235, 248, 281
VIII Fighter Command, 174, 182, 263, 275–276, 281
IX Air Defense Command, 372
IX Fighter Command, 121, 182, 239, 263, 275–276, 281
IX Tactical Air Command, 306, 329, 355
IX Troop Carrier Command, 297
XIX Tactical Air Command, 225, 355–357, 362, 371–373, 375
XV Corps, 371
Eighth Air Force, 110, 122, 127, 131–132, 158, 161, 164, 167, 174, 182, 208, 225, 253, 255, 274, 314, 342–344, 368, 400
Eighth Air Force Service Command, 208
First U.S. Army, 298, 302, 306, 352, 355
Force "O," 290, 292
Fourth Air Force, 71
German Seventh Army, 1, 351, 360, 362, 366, 370, 372–373
German 6th Parachute Regiment, 298
Graves Registration Service, 392
Ninth Air Force, *121,* 121–122, 125, 127, 158, 161, 172, 174, 182, 194, 225, 230, 232, 244, 247, 255, 260, 265, 287, 290, 296–297, 301–302, 306–307, 313, 315–317, 321, 326, 330, 342–344, 357, 368–369, 386, 392, 397
Panzer Group West, 365
Portland Air Defense Wing, Oregon, 90
Royal Air Force, 29, 31, 90, 122, 150, 155, 161, 191, 208, 210, 231, 249, 264, 336
San Diego Air Defense Wing, California, 73
Second British Army, 302, 350
Seventh U.S. Army, 356
Squadron VF-6, 93
Task Force 69, 113
Tenth Air Force, 94
Third U.S. Army, 351, 355–356, 360–361, 371, 373, 392, 397
Twelfth Army Group, 357, 361, 370
U.S. Army Ground Forces, 351